Badiou in Jamaica

Anamnesis

Anamnesis means remembrance or reminiscence, the collection and re-collection of what has been lost, forgotten, or effaced. It is therefore a matter of the very old, of what has made us who we are. But *anamnesis* is also a work that transforms its subject, always producing something new. To recollect the old, to produce the new: that is the task of *Anamnesis*.

a re.press series

Badiou in Jamaica
The Politics of Conflict

Colin Wright

re.press Melbourne 2013

re.press

PO Box 40, Prahran, 3181, Melbourne, Australia
http://www.re-press.org

National Library of Australia Cataloguing-in-Publication Data

Wright, Colin, author.
Badiou in Jamaica : the politics of conflict / Colin Wright.

9780987268266 (paperback)
9780987268273 (ebook)

Series:Anamnesis.
Includes bibliographical references.

Subjects: Badiou, Alain—Philosophy.
          Political science—Philosophy.
          Conflicts—Political aspects.
          Change—Political aspects.
          Jamaica—Politics and government.

320.01

Designed and Typeset by *A&R*
Typeset in *Baskerville*

Printed on-demand in Australia, the United Kingdom and the United States. This book is produced sustainably using plantation timber, and printed in the destination market on demand reducing wastage and excess transport.

To my father, in my name

Contents

Acknowledgements   9

Abbreviations   11

Introduction: Change, Novelty, Conflict   17

PART I: THE SCHEMA OF CONFLICT

1.   Early Maoism: Escaping the Dialectic?   27

2.   Organising Radical Novelty   69

3.   The Conflict of Names   113

4.   Active and Reactive Subjects   147

5.   Towards an Evental Historiography   187

PART II: THE JAMAICAN SITUATION

6.   The Morant Bay Revolt: Event or Exception?   227

7.   Rastafarian Fidelities: Towards an Evental Culture   269

8.   The Problem of Violence   305

Conclusion: A Polemology of Novelty   339

Bibliography   347

Acknowledgements

The seed of this book was probably planted during my involvement in the establishment of the *Centre for the Study of Post-Conflict Culture* at The University of Nottingham, so I should certainly thank those who have been central to its activities, but particularly Bernard McGuirk and Cristina Demaria. That seed was nourished further by the members of the *Centre for Critical Theory*, also at The University of Nottingham. David Fraser deserves a mention for forwarding me material on the juridical debates around martial law and the state of exception. For convincing me that it was an idea worth pursuing, I must acknowledge the kindness, patience and good humour of Peter Hallward. Bruno Bosteels was also generous enough to enter into correspondence with me early on, and his take on Badiou has certainly shaped my own. Alberto Toscano's work has always pre-empted the kinds of questions I have wanted to ask, and often answered them to boot. My colleagues and friends Neal Curtis and Tracey Potts have offered open ears and sometimes comfy shoulders. I would also like to thank my PhD students, Adity Singh and Luca Bosetti, who have made me think about Badiou and Lacan in ways I would not have done alone. I am grateful to the editors of *Theory & Event*, *Subjectivity* and *Culture, Theory and Critique* who gave me permission to reproduce elements of arguments already published with them, and also to the reviewers of those articles whose feedback certainly helped me to clarify my argument. At the Jamaican end of things, I'm grateful for the support and hospitality of the late Barry Chevannes, of Carolyn Cooper, of Donna Hope, of Sonjah Stanley Niaah and of Herbie Miller, all at the Mona Campus of the University of the West Indies. A special mention should also go my spiritual sistren, Mamma G. I thank my children, Solomon and Matilda, for being so scrupulous in forcing on me the distractions I need without always realising it. I thank Abi for being their mother, for doing her very best to keep those distractions to a minimum, and for being my lifelong soul-mate, no matter what.

Abbreviations

Works by Badiou have been abbreviated as follows:

BE   *Being and Event*, trans. Oliver Feltham, London: Continuum, 2005.

BOE   *Briefings on Existence: A Short Treatise on Transitory Ontology*, trans. Norman Madarasz, New York: SUNY Press, 2006.

C   *The Century*, trans. Alberto Toscano, Cambridge: Polity, 2007.

D   *Deleuze: The Clamour of Being*, trans. Louise Birchill, London: University of Minnesota Press, 2000.

DI   *De l'Idéologie*, Paris: Maspero, 1976.

E   *Ethics: An Essay on the Understanding of Evil*, trans. Peter Hallward, London: Verso, 2002.

EA   *Éloge de l'Amour*, Paris: Flammarion, 2009.

HC   *L'Hypothèse Communiste*, Clamecy: Lignes, 2009.

HI   *Handbook of Inaesthetics*, trans. Alberto Toscano, California: Stanford University Press, 2005.

IT   *Infinite Thought: Truth and the Return of Philosophy*, trans. Oliver Feltham and Justin Clemens, London: Continuum, 2004.

LW   *Logics of Worlds*, trans. Alberto Toscano, London: Continuum, 2009.

M   *Metapolitics*, trans. Jason Barker, London: Verso, 2005.

MP	*Manifesto for Philosophy*, trans. Norman Madaraz, New York: SUNY Press, 1999.
MS	*The Meaning of Sarkozy*, trans. David Fernbach, London: Verso, 2008.
NN	*Number and Numbers*, trans. Robin Mackay, Cambridge: Polity Press, 2008.
NR	*Le noyau rationnel de la dialectique hégèlienne*, Paris: Maspero, 1978.
OB	*On Beckett*, Manchester: Clinamen Press, 2003.
P	*Polemics*, trans. Steve Corcoran, London: Verso, 2006.
PP	*Peut-on penser la politique?*, Paris: Éditions du Seuil, 1985.
SM	*Seconde manifeste pour la philosophie*, Paris: Fayard, 2009.
SP	*Saint Paul: The Foundations of Universalism*, trans. Ray Brassier, California: Stanford University Press, 2003.
TC	*Théorie de la contradiction*, Paris: Maspero, 1975.
TS	*Theory of the Subject*, trans. Bruno Bosteels, London: Continuum, 2009.

Works by Lacan have been abbreviated as follows:

SX	*Le Séminaire de Jacques Lacan. Livre X. L'angoisse*, Paris: Éditions du Seuil, 2004.
SXI	*The Seminar of Jacques Lacan. Book XI. The Four Fundamental Concepts of Psychoanalysis*, trans. Alan Sheridan, London: W. W. Norton & Company, 1998.
SVII	*The Seminar of Jacques Lacan. Book VII. The Ethics of Psychoanalysis*, trans. Dennis Porter, London: Routledge, 2008.
SXVII	*The Seminar of Jacques Lacan. Book XVII. The Other Side of Psychoanalysis*, trans, Russell Grigg, London: W. W. Norton & Company, 2007.
SXX	*The Seminar of Jacques Lacan, Book XX. On Feminine Sexuality, The Limits of Love and Knowledge*, trans. Bruce Fink, London: W. W. Norton & Company, 1999.
SXXII	*Le Séminaire de Jacques Lacan. Livre XXII. Le Sinthome*, Paris: Éditions du Seuil, 2005.

introduction

Introduction

Change, Novelty, Conflict

How does genuine novelty enter the world? How is it distinct from mundane change? And how can it be made to endure? These seem to be the three key questions animating Alain Badiou's philosophy of the event. One possible answer to all three—albeit one that Badiou himself does not explicitly spell out—is *conflict*. After all, genuine novelty is profoundly disruptive per definition, and thus anathema to the most powerful stakeholders in things-as-they-are. Some conflicts, although by no means all, threaten the full-blown reinvention of a world, rather than its mere reform. And only through an ongoing conflict with the inertia of the old can the radically new persist into the alternative future it promises. If no event can irrupt or endure in its consequences without being accompanied by turmoil and contestation, it follows that conflict is a significant *potential* index of true transformation. What is needed, then, is some kind of conceptual schema for establishing the difference between clashing interests intrinsic to the world as it is, and conflicts in which entirely new worlds struggle to be born.

And yet these fairly intuitive assertions become extremely complex when set against the backdrop of the free-market, militarized, parliamentary 'democracies' that dominate our times. The neoliberal model of globalisation, for which these democracies are arguably little more than handmaidens, relies on the discursive control of both History and the putative legitimacy of the conflicts fought in the name of global 'peace and security'. On the one hand then, a post-historical, post-ideological, post-political narrative à la Francis Fukuyama (1992) eradicates the possibility or indeed desirability of novelty. We are said to have become Nietzsche's Last Man, apathetically satisfied in our risk-free consumer bubble. Within that bubble, where History appears to have been placed on pause, what little novelty exists is of the vacuously cyclical kind stemming from the in-built obsolescence of commodities, and the ceaseless reinvention of ersatz and ephemeral desires. Politics, on this model, becomes the responsible administration of a continuity that can accommodate the flux only of consumer appetites.

On the other hand, the macro-scale military interventions that late capital requires (predicated as it still arguably is on the violence of primitive accumulation) are presented not as antagonistic clashes with uncertain outcomes and therefore real stakes, but as acts of *policing* necessary to protect the global status quo. Conflict, on this model, becomes the containment of something like 'civil unrest' on a trans-national scale, while change becomes meticulously planned 'regime change'—in other words, change that protects and extends the conditions in which capital can be intensified. In this way, both Gulf Wars, former Yugoslavia, Rwanda, Iraq, Afghanistan and more recently Egypt, Libya, the Yemen and Syria are all so many links in the signifying chain that legitimises both the need for, and the supposedly benign democratising effects of, a global police force defending the principles of liberalism and free-market economics. Neoliberal globalisation therefore both nullifies novelty by putting an apparent end to History, and absorbs the conflicts it itself generates in a diffuse security operation seemingly devoid of stakes (is this not what Jean Baudrillard meant, long ago, when he baffled the world by asserting that the Gulf War never happened?).

Against this backdrop, a more elusive problem than Badiou's three interlinked core questions therefore demands to be posed: *how can political subjects in a neoliberal world invent a new time at the end of times?* How can novelty disrupt the smothering effects of what Alan Liu has called the "gigantic now" of capitalist modernity (Liu: 2004, p.3)? How can the conflicts that attend novelty evade the ubiquity of liberal reformism as, for many, the only political game in town? And how can one distinguish between the 'structural' conflicts internal to capital's violent dissolution of traditional communal bonds on the one hand, and non- or trans-structural conflicts that carry at least the promise of permanent transformation on the other?

Particularly since 9/11, these seem to me to be the pressing problems of our era, Alain Badiou the contemporary thinker best placed to address them. After all, the only preoccupation that can rival the primacy of mathematics across his oeuvre is the equally consistent focus on political sequences defined by conflict. Time and again, he distils a logic of change from rigorous analyses of remarkable sequences of conflict such as the French and Haitian Revolutions, the Paris Commune, the Bolshevik revolution of October 1917, Nazism, Stalinism, the Chinese Cultural Revolution and—seminally for him personally—the events of May '68. His ostensibly polemical rather than philosophical writings (with Badiou, I would argue that such a distinction is inherently dubious) also tackle more recent international conflicts such as the war in Kosovo, Le Pen's success in the French elections of 2001, the Israeli-Palestinian conflict, 9/11, the occupation of Iraq, and the divisive effects of Sarkozy as a latter-day Pétain (see *P* and *MS*). *Badiou in Jamaica: The Politics of Conflict* aims to extrapolate from the centrality of this theme of conflict within Badiou's work a theory of radical novelty suitable to our putatively post-historical yet conflict-riven era.

However, the dominant reception of Badiou in the Anglophone world, centring on a certain reading of *Being and Event* in particular, constitutes a serious obstacle to this project. *Being and Event* is of course a monumental achievement, one genuinely deserving of the comparisons invited by its grandiose title (Heidegger's *Being and Time*, Sartre's *Being and Nothingness* etc.). Indeed, I will be arguing that the key concept of the titular 'event' is a vital contribution to the theorisation of conflict and change. But this magnum opus status also makes *Being and Event* very difficult to escape—for Badiou as much as for his readers. Despite its many innovations, *Logics of Worlds* arguably remains a sequel burdened by the philosophical equivalent of 'second album syndrome'. One of the important lessons of Badiou's philosophy of the event, however, is that the causality of 'first' and 'second' can be tied into a torsional knot that has recursive effects. Thus, as Bruno Bosteels has argued (see his translator's preface to *TS*) it may be fruitful to read the prequel through the lens of the sequel rather than the other way round, precisely to displace the reading of *Being and Event* that occludes the problematics of conflict. There are five, interlinked elements of this dominant reading:

1. *The absolute singularity of evental rupture*: as Peter Hallward has pointed out (Hallward: 2003, 284), the abstract other-worldliness of the event conceived in this way negates the value of any investigation into the hierarchical constitution of the social, including Marxist analyses of class composition and/or Leninist examinations of the weak links in imperial formations etc.. This prohibits an analytics of pre-evental conflict, that is, of the 'counter-hegemonic' movements that resist the status quo without being conditioned by an event, but potentially pave the way for one.

2. *The strict separation between 'individual' and 'subject'*: this denies the importance of a militant or combative political, even utopian imaginary (of the kind theorised by Castoriadis and Bloch for example) that can resist and contest oppression even in the absence of an event, and therefore of subjects. This threatens to endorse a quietist anticipation of the grace-like event, and also fails to theorise the proximity between resistant individuals engaged in pre-evental conflicts and the emergence of subjects proper.

3. *The exclusive focus on the faithful subject*: this downplays the necessarily contested nature of the truths unleashed by events and the tremendous resources at the disposal of the 'state of the situation' by means of which events are suppressed. This encourages exclusively voluntarist readings of the subject, such that only 'betrayal' threatens a truth-procedure rather than, much more pragmatically, Statist denial, erasure, co-optation, or raw repressive violence.

4. *The starkly ahistorical nature of the event*: in the name of a sublation of the historical dialectic itself, this leads to an aggressive denial of the historical determination of worldly situations, including both the historical reproduction of conflictual relations, and the vital deployment of historical discourse within conflicts where change is genuinely at stake. The image of the event as a punctual moment essentially outside of time is unhelpful in the task of inventing what I have termed 'a new time at the end of times'.

5. *The relegation of 'culture' to a synonym for the given*: this not only prohibits any notion of 'cultural politics' but also of 'political culture', thereby underestimating the value of affirmative cultural production in the maintenance of fidelity. This reductive perspective on culture also sanctions a certain blindness with regard to cultural practices as a form of the 'subject-language' required to put a truth to transformative work.

As with familiar debates regarding fundamentalist interpretations of religious texts, it is important to acknowledge that there is plenty in *Being and Event* to support this reading. Badiou has at times read himself in just this way. But it is just as important to acknowledge that there are abundant resources within *Being and Event* that can be marshalled to contest the interpretation of the event as utterly punctual, radically singular, and therefore 'other-worldly'. It is in order to challenge or stretch some of these hermeneutic tendencies in Badiou scholarship, specifically to underline the value of the concept of the event for theorising conflict, that this book is organised into two unequal halves. The first, entitled 'The Schema of Conflict', is primarily a critical close reading of Badiou's wider oeuvre, before and after *Being and Event*, intended to both foreground the theme of conflict and prevent either the event or the faithful subject being abstracted from the inescapably worldly dimensions of conflict.

Chapter 1 therefore explores Badiou's complex relation with that other, long-dominant theory of conflict, the Marxist dialectic. By tracking Badiou's break with Althusser's notions of contradiction and overdetermination (*TC*); his 'scissional' account of dialectical materialism (*NR*); and his creative combination of Lacanian psychoanalysis and Maoism to arrive at a novel conceptualization of destruction (*TS*), his work from the 1970s can be characterised as a critique of the inability of economist, determinist, and structuralist notions of dialectical contradiction to engage with the problem of *radical* novelty. While acknowledging *Being and Event* as a decisive break with any dialectical conception of historical change, I also try to sketch some important dialectical continuities in the later work.

Chapter 2 focuses on Badiou's abiding concern with the thorny issue of political organisation. I argue that his analyses of sequences of conflict—the French Revolution, October 1917, Stalinism, National Socialism, the Chinese Cultural Revolution and May '68—both separate themselves from orthodox Marxist historiography and maintain the Marxist concern with an adequate *form* of revolutionary discipline. Badiou's interpretation of these conflicts, however, describes a growing anti-state but also anti-party tendency, culminating in the activism of the *Organisation politique*. This avowedly post-Leninist and even post-Maoist group which Badiou helped to found has developed a form of political innovation distanced from what might be called 'constitutive contradictions', in order to concentrate divisive ones.

Chapter 3 explores a key dimension of conflict surrounding the naming of an event. While *Being and Event* makes it clear that the event requires an interventional nomination on the part of a faithful subject, I stress in this chapter the capacity of the State for bullish 'counter-nomination', i.e., its capacity to draw on an existing battery of signifiers in order to reduce the novelty of the event to the relations and interests constitutive of the status quo. Badiou's controversial treatment of the name 'Jew' is assessed, but the chapter closes by attempting to separate Badiou's event from Carl Schmitt's 'exception', before then exploring this distinction in the strengths and weakness of the Not in Our Name movement as an attempted response to the war in Iraq.

Chapter 4 builds on the tension between evental nomination and sovereign counter-nomination by mapping the active and reactive modes of subjectivity to which the event can give rise. This reading of Badiou is specifically intended to off-set his former focus in *Being and Event* on the singular, non-relational subject of fidelity as, apparently, the only type of genuine subject. By *Logics of Worlds*, we are confronted by a much more complex, inter-subjective and therefore increasingly conflictual field incorporating 'reactive' and 'obscure' subjects as well as faithful ones. In particular, this chapter intends to open up the question of the phenomenology of the transition from individual to subject that seems notable by its absence in Badiou's work, as well as exploring the capacity of psychoanalysis to bridge this gap.

Chapter 5 functions as an excursus linking the two sections of the book. It sets out to challenge the notion of the event as ahistorical by developing a specifically 'evental historiography'. It maps Badiou's changing relation to history, from his reconceptualization of historical materialism during his ostensibly Maoist phase, particularly the concept of 'periodization' developed in *Theory of the Subject*, through his apparent break with history in *Being and Event*, and on to the notion of 'evental resurrection' elaborated in Book 1 of *Logics of Worlds*. From this trajectory, a four-step methodology for the proposed evental historiography is outlined and linked to Badiou's recent advocacy of the Idea of Communism.

If the first half of the book is primarily exegetical, the second half pushes toward something still quite rare in Badiou scholarship, a sustained application of the philosophy of the event to a specific historical sequence. The schema of conflict extrapolated in the first half is therefore put to work in the second on the rich and instructive history of conflict in pre- and post-Independence Jamaica. Why Jamaica? There are a number of reasons. The first and least important is biographical: Jamaica happens to be my birthplace and the background to my formative years. But the specific status of Jamaica, as a former British colony and a textbook example of structural economic underdevelopment, opens up a series of important questions. Its troubled history certainly offers a panoply of modes of resistance and revolt through which to hone a differential typology of conflict. In its relations with Britain, it also allows an investigation into the connections between anti-colonial resistance and the metropolitan emergence of an ideology of imperialism, with liberalism playing a very specific, if ambivalent role. Moreover, the plight of Jamaica today encourages an engagement with neoliberal globalisation as a form of neo-imperialism, with similarly ambivalent consequences for emancipatory politics. Perhaps more importantly for the against-the-grain reading of Badiou I am trying to develop, the co-existence in Jamaica of an incredibly vibrant popular culture centring particularly on music on the one hand, and deep and persistent problems with urban violence and government-facilitated conflict on the other, demands precisely the kind of examination of 'cultural politics' that Badiou's philosophical framework brackets out. As such, a Badiouian intervention into Jamaican historical, political and cultural narratives, and vice versa, poses difficult, perhaps intractable, but certainly important theoretical questions. Is there a possible rapprochement between postcolonial theory and a theory of conflict animated by the notion of the event?

Can cultural studies be re-radicalised by an engagement with Badiou's work, and, conversely, can Badiou be brought closer to the relations between politics, even in his exalted sense, and culture, particularly cultural forms of resistance?

Chapter 6, therefore, builds on Chapter 5 by exploring the relationship between conflict and history. It enumerates the many uprisings and rebellions during Jamaica's slave era, and their complex role in the movement for abolition and then emancipation. This has the advantage of demonstrating both the importance of conflict in pushing even reformist change, and also the dangers of such changes presenting themselves as *simulations* of events. It is argued that, for all its undoubted significance, the abolition of the slave trade was not an event, but that it may have laid the foundations for one. This suggests a complex relation between reform and radical transformation deeply incompatible with Badiou's emphasis on out-of-the-blue rupture. The chapter focuses on a particular conflict which, it is claimed, inaugurated a different logic of conflict in Jamaica, namely, the Morant Bay Revolt of 1865. This dramatic and bloody revolt demonstrates two responses to a major conflict, one reformist, which in Jamaica culminated in independence modelled on the British Westminster system of parliamentary representation, the other insistently antagonistic and anti-representational, which in Jamaica took the form of a divisive, militant black consciousness pitted against the supposedly inclusive Jamaican nation.

Chapter 7 goes on to analyse the clearest form this divisive subjectivity has taken in Jamaica, but also beyond, in the enigmatic Rastafari movement: it therefore focuses on the relationships between conflict, subjectivity and culture. It is argued that Rastas are faithful not, as they would claim, to the coronation of Emperor Haile Selassie of Ethiopia in 1930, but precisely to the excrescent multiple of 'post-emancipation Jamaican slaves' exposed by the Morant Bay Revolt in 1865. It is further claimed that the millenarian dimensions of the movement and its idiosyncratic relation to Biblical history constitute not a 'pre-modern' irrationalism, as even admiring historians such as Eric Hobsbawm argue in relation to other 'archaic' social movements (Hobsbawm: 1965), but an embodied version of the evental historiography outlined in Chapter 5, one brilliantly adapted yet militantly opposed to its specific 'world'. Most importantly, however, this chapter also argues that the cultural dimensions of the Rastafari movement, particularly the influence it has had on the roots reggae tradition, suggest an 'evental culture' which can play a key role in organising militant fidelity without the need for anything resembling a central party. In order to distinguish evental culture from culture in the banal sense, a theory of the 'braiding' of truths in evental culture is sketched drawing on Lacanian topology.

Finally, Chapter 8 engages with the vexed but unavoidable question today of the relation between politics, conflict and violence. If neoliberal globalisation simultaneously distinguishes representational politics and supposedly fanatical violence as antonyms and justifies its own violent interventions on humanitarian grounds (war fought in the name of peace), and if the Leninist tradition perhaps came close to imagining politics and violence as synonyms (destruction as creation), it is argued that Badiou's *subtractive* notion of destruction offers a usefully different articulation. Through an analysis of Mahatma Gandhi's own religiously inspired anti-colonial activism in British India, an important limitation of the conceptualisation of the 'subject body' and undue faith in the law is identified. This is then contrasted to the Rastafari movement's more cautious appeal to the motif of religion, which manages to draw on the progressive aspects of millenarianism and a generic concept of 'love' without lapsing into ossified institutional forms. The Rasta discourse of 'love and unity', then, is presented as a response to the ongoing violence of Jamaican society, in a country with one of the highest per capita murder rates in the world.

The brief conclusion, 'Towards a Polemology', concentrates the theory of conflict extrapolated from Badiou's work, early and late, and tested through its application to a post-colonial context. It is argued that the concept of conflict can cleave together many of the useful ambiguities and tensions inherent to Badiou's paradoxical project (the *emergence* of absolute novelty, the decision on the undecideable, the organisation of the uncountable etc.), whilst providing a political orientation in our supposedly post-political, post-historical times. Overall then, *Badiou in Jamaica: The Politics of Conflict* brings out five emphases that counter or at least qualify the dominant reading of *Being and Event* identified above:

1. An emphasis on the *immanence* of the evental break (without lapsing into vitalist ontologies of becoming) which situates singularity *in* a world or situation, rather than outside it, coupled with an account of the survival of a version of the dialectic into Badiou's 'post-Maoism'[1] in the form of a materialist torsion of the universal *within* the particular (Chapters 1, 4 and 7)

2. A focus on the *pre-evental* resource of 'courage' as a disposition of openness to the event even in its apparently permanent absence, which thus acts as a bridging affect between resistant individuals and militant subjects (Chapters 4, 6 and 7)

3. A more rounded account of the necessarily violent confrontations between the subjective figures that deny and occult events, including the State's powers of 'counter-nomination', and the faithful subjects that affirm them (Chapters 2, 4 and 8)

4. The proposal of an 'evental historiography' that resurrects past truths from the very referents within official historical discourse intended to suppress them, and deploys them in current conflicts in order to invent a new time in which novelty can endure (Chapters 2, 5 and 7)

5. The proposal of an 'evental culture' that both sustains the consistency of a subject-body, thereby addressing Badiou's ongoing question regarding political *organisation*, and invents a novel language with which to force a truth, but, crucially, without lapsing into the 'disaster' that Badiou discerns when distinct truth-domains are conflated (Chapter 7)

Readers already familiar with Badiou will no doubt recognise him in what follows, but I hope the reading I offer, and the application I undertake, defamiliarises him enough to open his work up to new questions, and new conflicts.

---

1. The term 'post-Maoism' has been coined by Bruno Bosteels, for whom it indexes a complex continuity, rather than the simple chronological 'recovery' liberal readers might prefer. See Bosteels: 2005.

part 1: the schema of conflict

Early Maoism: Escaping the Dialectic?

The purpose of this opening chapter is twofold. Firstly, by focusing on Badiou's early and largely untranslated Maoist writings, whilst also signaling consistencies with his later thought, it suggests the global persistence across his oeuvre of what I claim is his key concern: conflict as the site of the emergence of political novelty. Secondly, this approach also demonstrates that Badiou's thought has been shaped, from the outset, by a critical dialogue with that long-dominant philosophy of conflict, Marxist dialectics.

The adjective 'long-dominant' implies a faded glory, and at least in the market place of academic ideas, this would be extremely hard to deny. The height of postmodern cynicism regarding Enlightenment grand narratives coincided with contempt for the dialectic. Concepts like 'contradiction', 'overdetermination' and the 'negation of the negation' quickly seemed pungent with the musk of archival dust. However, is it not in the nature of the dialectic never to simply fade away? After all, such fading can always be described dialectically. Indeed, since Marxist dialectics includes a theory of knowledge, the formalisation by that theory of the play of negation and sublation within the political economy of the market place of ideas extends to its own dwindling fortunes there. In this sense, the dialectic ultimately evades being consigned to the dustbin of History by the whims of intellectual fashion precisely because of its grasp of History as a movement of negation and affirmation. This is perhaps the source of its stubborn resilience as well as its incipient dogmatism. To paraphrase Derrida, one might say that the spirit of Marx continues to haunt us, despite repeated attempts at its exorcism (Derrida: 1994).

And in fact the new world (Dis)order unleashed by 9/11 and the financial crisis has led some to dust off the laws of the dialectic in order to conceptualise the latest conflicts of our globalised era. However, if we can agree with recent critics of the new Empire that "the time is over when the mere mention of such categories [as 'Capitalism' and 'primitive accumulation'] consigned one—in the hip academy, especially—irrevocably to the past" (Boal et al.: 2005), it does not follow that the ghostly return of capitalist violence (did it ever go away?) is best understood through unreconstructed Marxist categories. As, properly speaking, a logic of praxis rather than a rigid theoretical formalism, the 'laws' of any renewed contemporary dialectic could only be immanent to the conflicts they both describe and galvanise. If Marx's spectre eternally returns, the unity of theory and practice demands that it is always in new phantasmatic forms.

It is in (and with) this very spirit that Badiou's works dating from his Maoist period[1]—particularly *Theory of Contradiction* (1975), *The Rational Kernel of the Hegelian Dialectic* (1978) and *Theory of the Subject* (1982)—explicitly attempt to push Marxism beyond the various formalisms (economic, scientific, structuralist) to which it has been both historically and conceptually prone. But it is in this effort to strip the dialectic of its inherent tendency toward formalism by making it equal to the singularity of a given conjuncture that Badiou forces it also toward the question of the *radically new*. For revolutionary history tends to emphasise the 'out of the blue' character of the irruption of revolutionary fervour, or at least the incalculability of that 'tipping point' which articulates merely systemic conflict with truly fundamental upheaval. What Badiou asks in these early works is how the dialectic, as a logic of historical conflict, can account for this decisive excess that seems to come from nowhere. And it is ultimately the paradox of this problem of a *dialectical* account of radical newness, of the emergence of a transmundane novelty from within a determining relational structure, which leads Badiou to his starkest and most original statements in *Being and Event*. But while it is a relatively straightforward matter to unpack the interrogations of the dialectic within the early 'Maoist Badiou'—and I will be following Jason Barker (2002) and Oliver Feltham's (2008) lead in doing so here—a far more intractable question is the extent to which the notion of the 'event' represents neither an advance on, nor a modification of, the Marxist dialectic, but rather an absolute and irrevocable break with it. Does the concept of the event escape the dialectic? Or, is the dialectic always capable of transforming its attempted negation into the cunning of its own reason? Can we refer to Badiou's "relation to Maoism, which amounts to a form of post-Maoism" (Bosteels: 2005, p.576). In fact, in several interviews with Bruno Bosteels, Badiou has indicated his sympathy for a newly dialectical interpretation of his philosophy of the event. Thus, it is partly in response to Bosteels' question (and challenge) that I undertake this chapter:

> What are the consequences, for anyone intent not just on understanding but on working *with* this philosopher's thought, of a sustained confrontation with the history and theory of dialectical thinking? (Bosteels in Hallward: 2004, p.154).

THE 'YENAN' BEACON IN THE MAY '68 STORM

Badiou's most 'frontal' assault on formalist reductions of the Marxist dialectic is to be found in two short books, *Theory of Contradiction* (1975) and *The Rational Kernel of the Hegelian Dialectic* (1978). These formed part of the 'Yenan series' published by Maspero and co-edited with long-time collaborator, Sylvain Lazarus. Before look-

---

1. I am using this crude designator 'Maoist' simply to categorise certain texts. Obviously, my guiding question in this chapter undermines the notion of any delimitable periodisation of the influence of Maoism on Badiou's thought, irrespective of what Badiou himself might say about a perceived biographical break in his own allegiance to it.

ing at these two works, it is worth reflecting on the rationale behind the Yenan series, since it invokes the febrile context in which questions of the politics of conflict
and the fate of Marxism were sharply posed.

'Yenan' is a reference to the walled city in the Shenshi province of China
where Mao Zedong established a brief Communist republic in 1935, long before
the Chinese Communist Party's (CCP) final victory over the Kuomindang in 1948.
It was also the location at which, recovering from the legendary Long March, Mao
formulated his own version of Marxism, tailored to the specificities of the Chinese
context (particularly the massive predominance in China of the rural peasantry
over the industrialised proletariat). The signifier 'Yenan' therefore has several important resonances that immediately spell out Badiou's intention with this series.
Firstly, it is a declaration of a commitment to Maoism as well as the 'Maoist' nature of that commitment itself, i.e, its subjective militancy. Secondly, it invokes an
heroically isolated experiment in political novelty which ended when Mao abandoned the 'Red Capital' in 1937 under pressure from advancing Nationalist troops.
Thirdly, however, and most importantly, it stands for the Maoist displacement
rather than mere unreflexive application of Marxist theory to Chinese peculiarities in order to make Marxism live, breath and *work* in a new context. Slavoj Žižek
has insisted on this distinction between displacement and application in his preface
to a collection of Mao's writings:

> [I]t is too facile either to condemn his [Mao's] reinvention of Marxism as the-
> oretically 'inadequate', as a regression with regard to Marxism's standards [...],
> but it is no less inadequate to blur the violence of the cut and to accept Mao's re-
> invention as a logical continuation or 'application' of Marxism (Mao: 2007, p.2).

These defiant connotations, and this acknowledgement of the 'violence of
the cut', are explicitly mobilised by Badiou as an intervention into the post-May
'68 context in which he and his increasingly isolated Maoist collaborators in the
UCFML (*Union des communistes de France, Marxiste-Léniniste*) found themselves.[2] As
we shall see in the next chapter, May '68 has generally come to be seen as a
parting of the ways, whether partial or complete, with Marxism. Soviet Marxism
had already lost much of its romantic sheen with Khruschev's exposé of Stalinist
excesses, with his nonetheless Stalinesque crushing of the Hungarian uprising in
1956, and with Solzhenitsyn's literary indictment of the gulags. However, May '68
seemed to spell a crisis specifically for Western Marxism. It suggested that the exclusive emphasis on class struggle in Marxism rendered it blind to the sexual, racial and anti-colonial forms of radicalism catalysed by the student activism and
massive industrial unrest of those tumultuous weeks in France (and elsewhere).
Class, it seemed, was no longer the privileged locus of exploitation, nor the primary driving force behind the new social movements that coalesced in the New
Left. On top of this theoretical difficulty came the shocking betrayal of the striking worker's by the French Communist Party (PCF hereafter). This was an act of

---

2. The *Union des communistes de France, Marxiste-Léniniste* was a Maoist splinter organisation that
defined itself against rival French Maoist organisations of the 1970s such as the *Gauche Prolétari-
enne* and the *Parti Communiste Marxiste-Léniniste de France*. It existed from 1970 to 1985. For an account of its opposition to these other Maoist groups, see note 50 in Bosteels: 2005, pp. 575-634.

perfidy widely seen to condemn not only the Marxist analytic, but also its 'official' organisational party form.

Moreover, this condemnation took on a high-profile relentlessness with the rise to prominence, from the mid-1970s, of the *nouveaux philosophes*, thinkers who made whole careers out of publicly ridiculing the Left and its supposed hero-worship of Nietzschean nihilism. Their number included ex-Maoists like André Glucksmann (whose tarring of all Marxism with the brush of Stalinism found mawkish expression in a book, *Les Maîtres penseurs*, published in the same year as Badiou's *Theory of Contradiction*), as well as the currently almost ubiquitous media figure of Bernard-Henri Lévy.[3] As apostates not only from Marxism, but also from its Maoist variant, such *nouveaux philosophes* remain the target of Badiou's sharpest salvos to this day. So fundamental was this general shift against class-based orthodox Marxism that the term 'post' in the post-Marxism subsequently promulgated by the likes of Alain Touraine, Chantal Mouffe and Ernesto Lacalau can justifiably be considered a temporal as well as a theoretical designator invoking May '68 as, inescapably, a fork in the Marxist path.

Badiou's semiotic strategy, then, in the deployment of 'Yenan' as a kind of orienting sign at this fork or crossroads is transparent. Just as the actual city became, from 1935, "a beacon of hope for progressive-minded young Chinese and Western sympathisers alike" (Short: 1999, p.354), so Badiou and the UCFML were attempting, in the mid-1970s, to turn the 'Yenan' signifier into a Marxist beacon guiding would-be progressives away from the ruinous rocks of anti-Marxist reaction. Badiou certainly perceived May '68 as constituting a political sea-change: "I admit without any reticence that May '68 has been for me, in the order of philosophy, as in everything else, a veritable 'road to Damascus'" (*TC*, p.9). Despite this suggestive biblical metaphor, however, his conversion was not at all to some *new* religion—such as the politics of Deleuzian desire or the Lacanian insight into the post-revolutionary persistence of the master-signifier. Rather, the flash of insight that would illuminate the Yenan 'beacon' concerned the urgent necessity of renewing the truths of an old faith: May '68 demonstrated for Badiou not the redundancy of Marxism *tout court*, but the shortcomings of bad Marxism. In this sense, the renewed theory of revolt outlined in the Yenan series is itself a revolt against a counter-revolutionary sequence in the aftermath of May '68 characterised by both revisionist and reactionary tendencies. Already, Badiou is centrally concerned with the play of active and reactive elements within and without Marxist dialectics as a theory of conflict.

THEORY OF CONTRADICTION

It is from this perceived crisis in Marxism that *Theory of Contradiction* emerges to engage directly in the struggle between "Marxism-Leninism and modern revision-

---

3. Bernard-Henri Lévy has achieved such celebrity status in France that he has become an acronym, 'BHL'. His wife is an actress, his daughter a bestselling novelist. The book that perhaps typifies his contribution to the nouveaux philosophes' critique of Marxism is *La barbarie à visage humain* of 1977, in which the supposed internal corruption of Marxism is said to lead inexorably to the Soviet camps.

ism, between true and false Marxism" (*TC*, p.7). And yet the book concerns itself neither with transformations in class relations nor with new social movements such as feminism or black civil rights. Instead, *Theory of Contradiction* identifies and contests a damaging formalism within the theory of dialectical materialism.

This might seem an esoteric issue at such a moment. Yet at the heart of the anti-Marxist theoretical backlash was a perceived poverty within the Marxist vocabulary when it came to describing the universities, the streets and the factories of the May movement. One of the primary messages of *Theory of Contradiction*, then, is that dialectical materialism is not a system in the usual sense of speculative philosophy. It does not provide a static hermeneutic grid that comprehends the present and might even predict the future. Its value does not lie in its consistent application to phenomena that are as unchanged by that application as the application is by those phenomena. On the contrary, argues *Theory of Contradiction*, the real value of dialectical materialism lies in its fluid reaction to the concrete exigencies of the ideological struggle—including those resulting from May '68. This fundamental problem of the theoretical application of Marxism already contains the problem of conceptual adequacy to an unfolding novelty that will continue to exorcise Badiou long after his *ostensibly* Maoist phase.

No surprise, then, that the opening chapter of *Theory of Contradiction* deals with the dialectical theory of knowledge, since every theory of knowledge must confront this issue of the adequation between concept and object. And yet only a dialectical theory of knowledge can grasp the *dynamic* relation between knowledge, knower, and 'thing' known. A non or anti-dialectical theory of knowledge fixes, and thus subdues, this dynamism, weakening the dialectic's conceptual purchase on the present. Badiou's cue here is clearly Mao's *On Practice* (itself a polemic against subjectivist dogmatism) where, with typical practicality, Mao insists that:

> The dialectical-materialist theory of knowledge places practice in the primary position, holding that human knowledge can in no way be separated from practice and repudiating all the erroneous theories which deny the importance of practice or separate knowledge from practice (Mao: 2007, p. 54).

For Mao, "[k]nowledge begins with practice, and theoretical knowledge is acquired through practice, and must then return to practice" (*ibid.*, p.61).[4] Beyond the obvious pragmatism, this position suggests that, in opposition to the obfuscating function of bourgeois knowledge, Marxist knowledge is integrated into the social contradictions it reveals. Thanks to an immanent relation with conflict, it is itself an instrument in and of class struggle. Indeed, an unduly 'sociological' understanding of Marxism as merely articulating the laws of social formations threatens to divorce description from proscription, theory from practice: the "science of social formations only has interest for the masses insofar as it reflects and concentrates their real revolutionary movement" (*TC*, p.16). Properly Marxist statements are simultaneously objective assessments *and* subjective demands, descriptions *and* violent interventions into their objects, theories *and* weapons of social transforma-

---

4. This was a dialectical pattern Mao would condense in the aphorism 'unity-criticism-unity' by which contradictions among the people were to be resolved (see 'On the Correct Handling of Contradictions Among the People', pp.130-166 in Mao: 2007).

tion. Marxist truth "is, in itself, dictatorship, and, if necessary, terror" (*TC*, p.17). This Robespierrist sentiment echoes Mao's rather chilling declaration that 'communism is not love, [it] is a hammer, which we use to crush our enemies'.

While theory appears to oppose itself to practice by attempting to reveal truths (social contradictions) by penetrating appearances (ideology), such a unity of contraries is only mechanistically dialectical. That is, it remains at the level of *reciprocal constitution*: theory is theory insofar as it opposes practice, and vice versa. Such binarism is static and apolitical. The true lesson of Maoist dialectics is that both terms, theory and practice, are always already internally split, facing each other as non-identical, dynamic contradictions. This a priori internal splitting is what Badiou terms 'scission', the central concept in his early reconceptualisation of the dialectic. Thus, at a deeper level of Marxist theory, this very contradiction between theory and practice becomes the object of the dialectical theory of knowledge: "Otherwise said: the process of knowledge has for its internal nature the theory/practice contradiction" (*TC*, pp.17-18). If this contradiction ultimately finds its resolution in the realm of practice, as Mao insists, this is but a momentary stabilisation in a general movement characterised by flux and conflict. Theoretical knowledge cannot be set in permanent categories of abstraction, and yet in its dialectical interface with revolutionary practice it can become a subjective force in its own right.

Mao argues that knowledge can actually take on the role of the 'principal aspect' of a contradiction in certain circumstances, i.e., the role of that element which determines the way a fundamental contradiction is constrained to manifest itself in a given conjuncture. In Mao's own political life, the prime example of this shifting of contradictory aspects is surely the CCP's tense cooperation with Chiang Kai-Shek's Nationalist troops during the second Sino-Japanese war (1937-1945). Mao reasoned at this time that the fundamental bourgeois-proletariat contradiction of the class struggle had been temporarily superseded by the foreign imperialist-nationalist contradiction specific to the Chinese situation. One can understand this as an instance of wily *Realpolitik*, although it was really Stalin's rather than Mao's strategy, yet the claim that knowledge can take on such a 'principal aspect' is a surprisingly Gramscian argument which challenges the hoary old economism of superstructural determination by the base. In this way, Maoism ascribes a separate and elevated significance to the quasi-autonomous power of political subjectivity, as refined and conditioned by the dialectical process of revolutionary knowledge. Badiou will hold on to the first aspect of this lesson—the centrality of the political subject—right through the 'desert years' of the 80s and beyond. The second aspect, however, regarding even revolutionary knowledge, will undergo a radical transformation in *Being and Event* where truth will become incompatible with knowledge.

Nonetheless, in *Theory of Contradiction*, Badiou is willing to posit a kind of meta-statement of dialectical truth. He finds this in Mao's dictum, 'it is correct to revolt against the reactionaries'. Thanks in part to an ambiguity in the French phrase *on a raison* ('it is right', 'it is correct', but also 'one has reason' in the broadly Kantian sense of a cognitive faculty), Badiou distinguishes three overlapping meanings for this dictum which underline three dimensions of revolt: its necessity, its ultimate justice, and its immanent rationality.

Firstly, reason refers to the *necessity* of revolt, not as an imperative of the super-ego but as a law of historical inevitability. This law demonstrates that there *is* revolt and that it has a rationality, the cold, transindividual and objective proletarian rationality Marx analysed in *Capital*. Bourgeois knowledge is guilty of covering over this underlying dialectical necessity by providing, under headings such as 'history', detailed accounts of the supposedly contingent causes of specific revolts. Within bourgeois historiography it is as if, without the final trigger at the end of a long chain of interconnected phenomena, no revolt would have taken place, as if the history of class conflict were but a history of preventable mishaps. By *Being and Event*, Badiou will be assigning this epistemological domestication of the dialectic, or at least of the event, to the 'encyclopaedia of knowledge', and this is where the criticism of the discourse of History—as the assemblage of dissimulating 'facts' that blind us to the forces of true change—should be located. We will be addressing this in Chapter 5, but if the early Badiou of *Theory of Contradiction* believes that "the masses [...] make history, including the history of knowledge" (*TC*, p.9), he is already critical of the bourgeois positivism that claims to ensnare historical facticity in a net of causality.

Secondly, the word 'reason' in Mao's dictum can be read as a resource of militant courage insofar as it indicates that a revolt *will have* reason (again, this aprioristic temporality will come to govern the notion of 'truth' in Badiou's later work). The necessity or inevitability of revolt simultaneously offers a practical certainty of proletarian victory. This certainty is not of the order of a carrot-on-a-stick dangled before the proletariat for motivational purposes. Nor is it simply the pull, on the present, of a future already inscribed in it. Rather, it is the chiasmus of the two: "Reason is here the crossroads of revolutionary legitimacy and optimism" (*TC*, p.23). This Maoist conflation of subjective optimism with objective legitimacy already suggests the kind of aggressive singularity which will bring Badiou's political thought, at various points, close to a naked decisionism.

Thirdly, however, 'reason' can be read as the capacity for revolt to immanently create the consciousness of its own rationality, to develop a knowledge internal to the revolt and fully appropriate to it. As a *practice*, revolt theorises its own rules of reason and refines them in its unfolding contradictions. It concentrates into a cutting edge its rational quality, forging from it a weapon in the class struggle. It is therefore an eminently practical reason (though, again, hardly in Kant's sense). Still at this stage, Badiou seems to believe that the revolutionary party is the 'brain' that registers, tests and disseminates this reason among its agents, guiding the participants in the revolt toward properly Communist goals (*TC*, p.24). As we will see, this faith in the revolutionary party does not last across Badiou's work.

Being dialectical, the immanence of this rationality of revolt is always set *against* something. Indeed, to imagine a non-oppositional, freestanding reason is to lapse into metaphysical idealism. Equally, entertaining the possibility of an absence of reactionaries against whom one must revolt is political naïveté, since dialectical materialism instructs us that there will always be contradictions (one of Mao's crucial points was that this also applied to the post-revolutionary path towards communism). Revolutionary reason, therefore, emerges dialectically from its fight against reactionary reason and "this 'against the' is an internal condition of truth" (*TC*, p.25). By *Theory of the Subject*, this oppositional condition for the rationality of revolt will lead to an equivocation around the class struggle, with the proletariat emerging from the inner contradictions of the bourgeoisie itself. In *Theory of Contradiction*, however, the proof adduced is historical rather than 'structural': Badiou cites the forging of the theory of dialectical materialism itself within the furnace of Marx and Engel's polemics against petit-bourgeois idealism, against utopian socialism, against Proudhonian federalism, and against Bakunian anarchism. It was from this crossing of dialectical swords that the original Marxist truth emerged.

MAKING THE DIALECTIC DIALECTICAL

Having outlined a Maoist theory of dialectical knowledge and having provided its logical kernel through an analysis of the dictum 'it is correct to revolt against the reactionaries', Badiou proceeds to test, against this new measure, the various laws of the dialectic espoused during its long history.

Friedrich Engels, for Badiou, is already the source of a major misreading of dialectical materialism. Engels' zeal to establish a properly scientific theory of dialectics—uniting, in a global epistemo-ontology, the natural laws of competition described by Darwin on the one hand and the social laws of contradiction described by Marx on the other—has had, according to Badiou, the unfortunate consequence of displacing the theory of contradiction from its rightful place at the heart of dialectical materialism. Rather than being a science of splits and ruptures, Engels produced a science of connections and links. One might read Engels as appropriating the discourse of science, rather as Freud would with psychoanalysis, in order to lend an intrinsically controversial mode of thought a more acceptable gloss in an age of scientific obsession. Nonetheless, it is clear that Engels in fact views science in a fairly unreconstructed manner as a neutral tool for continuing Marx's task of cleansing Hegelianism of its idealism.

Badiou finds this damning absence of contradiction in each of the three laws of the dialectic proposed by Engels in the *Anti-Dühring* (Engels: 1935): 1) The law of the passage from quantity to quality, and vice versa; 2) The law of the interpenetration of contraries; 3) The law of the negation of the negation. In his critique of these laws, Badiou follows Mao practically to the letter. Mao held that the first law regarding the famous Hegelian passage from the in-itself to the for-itself, so crucial for the way early Marx in particular thinks the emergence of class consciousness, is but a specific case of the second law regarding the unity of contraries and does not deserve to be considered separately (see Mao: 2007, p.181). For Badiou, furthermore, "the dialectical essence of [the first law] is not the simple affirmation of the reversibility of the passage, but the notion of qualitative *rupture* subsequent upon a quantitative *accumulation*" (*TC*, p.32). The reversibility of terms suggests a closed, non-dynamic structure in which revolution could always be recouped into the pre-existing order. Badiou prefers to stress a permanent break. Thus, in Marx's own terms, capital accumulation ultimately creates the contradiction between the bourgeoisie and the proletariat who will break violently and *irreversibly* with them. Even Engels' second law is in danger of privileging identity over contradiction, for he conceives of each contrary term as possessing an inner unity. As we will see, Badiou believes a version of this mistake is also discernible within structuralist Marxism. Regarding the third law, Mao simply asserted that "[t]here is no such thing as the negation of the negation [...] in the development of things, every link in the chain of events is both affirmation and negation" (Mao: 2007, p.181). Engels' three dialectical laws echo a quasi-Darwinian vision of contradiction as the fight for survival between agonistic self-identical elements, yet "the restriction of 'polar opposites' to moments of crisis leaves only a narrow field to the thought of contradiction" (*TC*, p.36). That is, moments of visible, even spectacular, social conflict are but contingent manifestations of deep-seated contradictions that continuously shape the whole of society. Engels' analysis seems to stop at the level of mere epiphenomena.

Badiou claims that it is only by going back to Lenins' *Philosophical Notebooks* and his careful study of Hegel's *Logic* there that we can recover the proper centrality of contradiction within dialectical materialism. In contrast both to Engels' three dialectical laws and Stalin's subordination of the dialectic to the economy, Lenin's principal insight that 'one divides into two' gives proper primacy to scission and struggle. 'One divides into two' means firstly that every unity tends toward its self-dissolution because it merely holds together, temporarily, the internal contradictions that constitute it. This is why, according to Badiou, Lenin makes "struggle the sole and absolute principle of dialectical thought: the essence of the dialectic as rebellious philosophy" (*TC*, p.43). Secondly, 'one divides into two' also means that the one of any proclaimed unity is itself only ever achieved through a movement of division. No 'one' can claim the primordial purity characteristic of metaphysical thought and its pathos of origins. Both of these meanings, structural incompletion and the imaginary nature of unity, will come to play a crucial role in Badiou's later theory of sets, but we are still dealing here with politics *stricto sensu*. Thus, the opposite thesis, that two divides into one, has diametrically opposed political implications, as illustrated by the famous debate between these two positions in Mao's China from 1958 to 1963 (to which Badiou alludes several times throughout his work).[5] Yang Hsien-chen's apparently 'philosophical' but actually deeply political advocacy of the division of two into one suggests the fixed and stable unity of an irreproachable Party dictatorship, as well as a kind of utopian stasis in which all contradictions have been permanently resolved. Conversely, the properly Leninist insistence (which Mao cites in his intervention into this debate)[6] on the division of the one into two tends toward a 'permanent revolution' of just the kind unleashed *against* the Party itself in the Cultural Revolution. If Marx railed against that 'feudal socialism' which, in the early nineteenth century, yearned to return to a prelapsarian, pre-industrial plenitude, he never applied this critique to his own projection of an essentially apolitical communist future. With Lenin, however, we have the beginnings of an insight into the never-ending nature of political struggle.

---

5. See p.69 of *NR*, pp.89-102 of *C*,
6. See 'Talk on Questions of Philosophy', pp.169-185 in Mao: 2007.

But if Lenin underscores the ontological pre-eminence of scission, it is Mao who really pursues its practical consequences for dialectical materialism ('Mao-Zedong-thought', to recycle Lin Biao's sycophantic coinage, is, for Badiou, "[r]ebel thought *par excellence*, revolted thought of revolt: dialectical thought" (*TC*, p.51)). It is here, finally, that Badiou can positively articulate a version of Marxism alive to all the complexities proliferating in the wake of May '68. He does so through Mao's five dialectical theses:

1. All reality is process
2. All process remains, in the last resort, a system of contradictions
3. In a process, there is always a contradiction which is principal
4. All contradiction is asymmetrical: one term of a contradiction is always dominant over the collected movement of the contradiction itself (this is the theory of the principal aspect of a contradiction)
5. The principal distinction to make is between antagonistic and non-antagonistic contradictions.

These theses are taken from Mao's most philosophically oriented and arguably original contribution to Marxist theory, *On Contradiction*, written and delivered as a lecture during his period at Yenan. Badiou's notion of 'scission' radicalises Mao's first two points, splitting identity all the way down. The last three principles, however, are central for thinking Badiou's conceptualisation of conflict.

The intersection of the third thesis, that there is always an underlying fundamental contradiction, with the fourth, that this fundamental contradiction is constrained to manifest itself via a dominant aspect within a given configuration, leads to the absolutely crucial distinction made in the fifth thesis between qualitatively distinct modalities of contradiction. The notion of contradictions that can be non-antagonistic acknowledges the primacy of contradiction itself—that is, all systems are contradictory—without in any way conflating this with radical qualitative change. On the contrary, it recognises the *constitutive* nature of certain contradictions, and the *destructive* nature of others.

Perhaps it is easiest to understand this in terms of parliamentary democracy. Just because there are multiple parties with different views that seem to come into conflict with one another, it does not follow that such *agonistic* elements are enough to indicate radical or, for that matter, even reformist change. The 'contradiction' of the British Westminster system, for example, based as it is on the minimal two-party structure, is not dynamic at all. It is the reciprocal difference that founds the very stability of the parliamentary model. Antagonistic contradictions, by complete contrast, indicate those conflicts which must entail a wholesale transformation of the existing 'rules of the game', suggesting a magnitude of change so great that a new game, a new order of (social) being, will ensue.

In Badiou's hands, then, Mao's dialectical theses provide the basis for critical interventions into the most damaging elements in the post-May '68 context. Prominent among these are the revisionist 'rightism' of Althusserian structuralism on the one hand, and the reactionary 'ultra-leftism' of Deleuzian 'anarchism' on the other.

INTERVENING IN THE THEORETICAL CONJUNCTURE:
ALTHUSSER AND DELEUZE

The fundamental problem that contemporary Marxism faces, explained Badiou back in 1975, is not the metaphysical assertion of the transcendence of timeless truths and therefore the denial of change. Rather, philosophical revisionism's latest strategy involves embracing Mao's emphasis on scissional process, but with the proviso that process be thought only on the parliamentary model just invoked, as *a law of formal alteration within a given reality composed of self-identical elements*. For Badiou, this formalism is the latest avatar of a metaphysical invariant.

Unsurprisingly, one can discern this in a certain Hegel, in the Absolutisation of Knowledge whereby everything that seems destroyed is in fact preserved through the movement of sublation. Although Hegel's dialectic apparently confronts the profound negativity of death, its idealistic side tries to gather up and maintain all that dies in the living Whole of World Spirit. By contrast, the Maoist insistence on scission means that "[t]here are radical novelties because there are cadavers that no trumpet of Judgement will come to raise" (*TC*, p.86), i.e., there are ruptures which truly break with their situations. However, while one would expect such a metaphysical concept of change in Hegel's idealist system, Badiou cautions against a similar pattern in the thought of the most original and influential voice in French Marxism prior to May '68: Badiou's former teacher and new critical target, Louis Althusser.

Despite Althusser's strenuous efforts throughout the 1960s to purge Marxism of its Hegelian elements, to found a scientific Marxism on this *coupure* with Hegel, Badiou argues that he in fact repeats the Hegelian nullification of contradiction through his famous notion of a 'process without a subject'. In *For Marx*, Althusser offers his most Maoist essay on overdetermination,[7] and in *Lenin and Philosophy* he provides the famous analysis of 'Ideological State Apparatuses'.[8] The latter seems to make of subjects merely the interpellative correlates of a structural determination: hailed into being by power itself, subjects are but positions in a determined and determining socio-economic matrix. Perhaps because of his partial use of Lacan, Althusser at this stage views power as a necessary condition for the emergence of subjectivity. No critical social theory based on a political anthropology can get behind or before the socialised subject because there is nothing there.[9] The autonomous subject of rational intention is, according to Althusser, a chimera of bourgeois ideology. If the origin of political transformation is not to be found in the expression of the will of an oppressed section of humanity, from where does it come? In the former essay, Althusser argues that it is promised in the existence, even within 'structures in dominance', of overdeterminations in the sense used by Freud in *The Interpretation of Dreams*, i.e., palimpsests of codes whose dense layering

---

7. 'Contradiction and Overdetermination', pp. 87-128 in Althusser: 1969.

8. 'Ideological State Apparatuses: Notes Towards an Investigation', pp.127-188 in Althusser: 1971.

9. Badiou will go over this argument twenty three years later when, in the third chapter of his *Metapolitics*, he will focus on Althusser's process without a subject again, pointing out that "The subject, in Althusser's sense, is a function of the State. Thus, there will be no political subject, because revolutionary politics cannot be a function of the State" (*M*, p. 63).

leads to uncontainable polysemia. For Althusser, such overdeterminations always complexify and condition the fundamental contradiction between the forces and relations of production. This is the only way that one can understand, for example, the growth of the Russian Revolution from soil orthodox Marxism sees as revolutionarily barren (a predominantly agrarian rather than industrialised economy, an exiled revolutionary vanguard, and so on). To the extent that these overdeterminations outrun or exceed power's structuring capacities to create, somewhere in the capitalist system, a 'weak link', the 'subject' of History must now be understood as an attribute of structure, an unfolding process, rather than a contingently mobilised class identity.

Although Althusser shapes this anti-humanist notion of a process without subject through a reading of Lenin, Badiou argues that his old teacher only attributes to Lenin "his own dialectical myopia" (*TC*, p.56). Read closely, Lenin attacks not the general category of the subject as such, but rather the idealist predicates of the *bourgeois* subject. Rather than sweeping away the whole category, Lenin splits the one of the subject into two: either it is religious (recall that Althusser draws on Pascal to describe his constitutively faithful subject) or it is materialist. For Badiou, Lenin's dialectical materialism is actually a process very much *with* a subject. Althusser's objective formalism is, in contrast, a pre-eminent example of the new metaphysical invariant. It provides a protocol for thinking change, but simultaneously subordinates the explosively divisive power of the dialectic under a non-dialectical 'rule'.

> At bottom, the theory of the "process without subject that doesn't end" annuls the first principle [of process] through the objective fixity which it encloses [...] The first principle of the dialectic must then be doggedly defended against its revisionist corruption (to think process as objective structural identity) (*TC*, pp.60-61).

Against this static structuralism, one must therefore insist that "there is no identity other than a split one" (*ibid.*); that the struggle between terms does not end with the emergence of a victorious 'one', but rather with a new unity in which both terms of the previous contradiction have been divided; that "the dialectical concept of synthesis is the engendering of a new scission and nothing else" (*TC*, p.65). To ignore these Maoist principles by indulging a theory of change as a form of permutation—which Badiou playfully refers to here as "the law of exchange"—is to entertain "the impulse of every ideology of the structuralist type", and thus "the essential conservatism of all structural thought [which] risks at this point changing the dialectic into its opposite: metaphysics" (*TC*, p.71). Althusser gave in to this conservatism not only when he dismissed the May movement as 'infantile leftism', but also when he remained a member of the PCF even after its betrayal of the workers at the barricades.

However, if there was, post-May '68, a widespread recognition of structuralist Marxism's inability to theorise radical change, one of the forms this recognition took, which Badiou labels 'anarchism', turns out to be just as conservative in practice as its Althusserian counterpart. Of course, Bakunin's early anarchist critiques of Marxism at the First International highlighted its tendency toward dictatorship long before Stalin's systematic use of State terror. Anarchism has always recognised the problem of the 'changing of the guards' inherent in any emancipatory political theory that does not revise or reject the centrality of the apparatuses of State power (see Bakunin: 2002). In this tradition, then, Badiou situates both the libidinised Marxism outlined in Jean-François Lyotard's *L'Economie libidinale* and the schizo-analysis of desire put forward in Gilles Deleuze and Félix Guattari's two volumes of *Capitalism and Schizophrenia*. Both of these startlingly original projects can be said to contest the State through, on the one hand (and to use Deleuze and Guattari's vocabulary), a kind of Dionysian obliteration of the subject individuated by the 'molar' categories of the State, and through the immanent construction of transindividual 'haeccities' on the other. However, for Badiou, these wild philosophies of polymorphous political subjectivities demonstrate the merging of ultra-leftism with revisionism. Despite appearances, the post-May '68 politics of desire are revisionist to the extent that they still think change as combinatory permutation: "in truth, anarchism is the simple inverse of conservative structuralism" (*TC*, p.75).[10]

TENDENCY NOT STRUCTURE, FORCE NOT PLACE

Badiou proposes to evade such anarcho-structuralist deviations by adding to the notion of structure the crucial dimension of 'tendency'. This is a time-honoured category of Marxist economics, recently given fresh importance in Hardt and Negri's analysis of the emergence of immaterial labour and the information economies of global capitalism (see Hardt & Negri: 2005). It is used in *Theory of Contradiction*, however, to underscore Mao's insistence on contradictory processes within apparently stable unities. Tendency is the dialectical trajectory of change embodied in and disguised by a given 'structure in dominance', and thus the flux covertly active within a seemingly monolithic fixity. This cleaving together of structure and tendency is what allows dialectical materialism to chart the correct course between ultra-leftism and rightist revisionism. By contrast, "[t]aking into unilateral consideration [only] one of the two, causes a passage into metaphysics" (*TC*, p.81). If one ignores structure, one takes tendency as something already realised, given, an unfolding fact without need of subjective support (an accusation which might be levelled in fact at Hardt and Negri's arguably exorbitant belief in the 'tendency' of late capitalism to produce a resistant 'multitude'). Conversely, if one ignores tendency, one immediately absorbs novelty into the parameters of the old, thereby sustaining the established order.

To further refine the structure-tendency distinction, Badiou introduces another binary, one that will play a central role in both *The Rational Kernel* and *Theory of the Subject*: that between 'place' and 'force'. Structure maintains its dominance through a practice of *placing*. Structural elements are determined-determining places that are also pre-established roles conducive to the continuation of the existing

---

10. As Jason Barker rightly points out (Barker: 2002), this is an ungenerous reading of Deleuze to say the least (Barker: 2002, 115). Deleuze's *Repetition and Difference*, to cite only the most obvious text, is just as opposed to serial logics of combinatory difference as is the Badiou of *TC*, perhaps more so (Barker: 2002, p 37). Similar accusations would attend Badiou's book-length critique of Deleuze some twenty two years later.

structure. It is this dimension of placing that Althusser's structuralism struggles to get beyond. However, every element so placed is simultaneously the vector of a dialectical tendency that carries a force undermining both that placing and the overall structure imposing it. What is specific about dialectical materialism, therefore, as a thought of both identity and non-identity, is that it is simultaneously a logic of places that describes the structural determination of social elements, and a logic of forces that identifies the 'anti-structural' tendencies these same elements transmit. The dialectic therefore provides not only an explanatory logic of the mechanics of exploitation here and now (structure), but also an emancipatory logic of the potential for resistance with a view to an alternate future (tendency).

This diatribe against change conceived of as structural permutation is already a distancing from a simplistically State-centred conception of radical politics. It follows Mao's lead in the Chinese Cultural Revolution, which involved the recognition that even the Communist Party would necessarily divide into Right and Left deviations and harbour bourgeois tendencies within itself (again, that a Communist party could be vulnerable to this was suggested, for Badiou, by the example of the PCF). Lenin himself chastised those who imagined that the Bolshevik revolution was an opportunity to say, in a vengeful spirit, 'now it's our turn', pointing out that only another generation of bourgeoisie could result from such a niggardly politics of resentment (Lenin: 1992). In Badiou's language, such a permutation of fixed contraries would not be a qualitative rupture with the old structure at all. Another term would merely occupy the place of dominance without domination itself being challenged. 'Revolution' would remain stuck in its old astronomical sense of a turning that is ultimately a re-turning. The whole emphasis on scission as opposed to reciprocal contradiction is geared towards emphasising that, far from sharing a complimentarity, there is *nothing* in common between the bourgeoisie and the proletariat: the latter is the immanent voiding of the former, not its adversarial yet defining Other. By *Theory of the Subject*, it becomes clear that proletarian logic boils down to the displacement of the place of dominance itself—in other words, the Marxist, rather than the neo-liberal, 'withering away of the state'.

Already, Badiou's Maoism invites a rethinking not only of the theory but also of the practice of (revolutionary) conflict. For Maoist contradiction stresses scission, asymmetry and unformalisable difference in order to contest the Statist politics of ultimately compatible, symmetrical forces that I have been calling 'parliamentary' and which still, in our globalised era, dominates the discourse of conflict. Badiou's brief analysis of the Cold War illustrates the stakes in the opposition between reciprocal and scissional contradiction. The very existence, he claims, of the nuclear option transforms war into an equality of absolute destructive force. Beyond the degree zero capacity to destroy the earth itself, additional atom bombs mean nothing. Without a technological or numerical advantage, direct conflict becomes a pure battle of wills concentrated on the red launching button, and the decision to deploy or not to deploy (although indirect conflict can flourish in the form of proxy wars). Precisely through confrontations like the Cuban Missile crisis, which both intensify and justify the reciprocal, binary standoff, the respective superpowers can be complicit in extending their spheres of ideological and political influence, becoming united, therefore, in their shared interest in perpetuating the standoff. Yet, in this tense 'peace' that also resembles a permanent war, both superpowers clearly put men in the place of death in order to pursue their own inhuman agendas.[11]

If the bourgeois strategy of war revolves around this apparent equalisation of forces, turning inter-state violence into a sort of parliamentary theatre behind which real power-politics are at play, the proletarian strategy of war is quite different. It involves the neutralisation of the imperialist symmetry of forces through the mobilisation of all the modes of dissymmetrical force which escape Statist placement. As an arguably ill-judged apologia for Mao's own brutal pursuit of the atom bomb,[12] Badiou adds here that these qualitatively different means of revolutionary violence may, nonetheless, include the nuclear option! I will be turning to the question of violence in the final chapter. Nonetheless, Badiou's main point here is that the conflict between sovereign states generally takes place above the heads of the masses and is governed by different laws. As such, he echoes Georg Lukács' point that "to rebel against law *qua law*, to prefer certain actions *because* they are illegal, implies for anyone who so acts that the law has retained its binding validity" (Lukács: 1990, p.263). Rather than frame its conflict in terms of state-centred 'legal' wars, the class struggle would do better to adopt the guerrilla ethos of Mao's Red Army: "The enemy advances, we retreat; the enemy camps, we harass; the enemy tires, we attack; the enemy retreats, we pursue" (Mao: 2007, p.38).

THE RATIONAL KERNEL OF THE HEGELIAN DIALECTIC

The other title in the 'Yenan' series to which I would like to turn is *The Rational Kernel of the Hegelian Dialectic* (1978), written in collaboration with Joël Bellassen and Louis Mossot. If its form differs from that of *Theory of Contradiction*, its content—a concerted attack on Althusser's attempted break with Hegel within French Marxism—is remarkably consistent. The bulk of the book is taken up by a translation of a chapter from Zhang Shiying's *The Philosophy of Hegel*, a work of apparently 'straight' philosophical exegesis published in Shanghai amidst the tumult of the Chinese Cultural Revolution in 1972.

In truth, Zhang's reading of Hegel offers little by way of startling philosophical novelty. Its prime purpose is the dissemination throughout Mao's China of

---

11. Mao, who certainly recognised the vastness of the Chinese population as his biggest political bargaining chip on the international stage, famously dismissed the American atomic threat with the following words:
The United States cannot annihilate the Chinese nation with its small stack of atom bombs. Even if the US atom bombs were so powerful that, when dropped on China, they would make a hole right through the earth, or even blow it up, that would hardly mean anything for the universe as a whole, though it might be a major event for the solar system (Mao: 2007, p. 107)

12. The biography of Mao by Jung Chang and Jon Halliday (2006) convincingly argues that he caused the greatest famine in history, directly starving an estimated 38 million people by sending Chinese grain to Russia, even after poor harvests, in exchange for Russian assistance in constructing the H-bomb. As we will see however, Badiou cannot be accused of evading the question of the intense violence of Mao himself or the Cultural Revolution.

Lenin's revolutionary interpretation of Hegel. Zhang is clearly indebted to Karl Korsch's 1923 work, *Marxism and Philosophy*, which had already extended the materialist reading of Hegel which Lenin only adumbrated in note form. Yet in the French intellectual milieu of the late 1970s, the very fact of engaging seriously with Hegel in the wake of Althusser, but also in the wake of the pro-Kantian, anti-Hegelian positions of the *nouveaux philosophes*, constituted another act of calculated defiance on the part of the 'Yenan' collective. Beyond the narrow scholarly concerns of Hegel studies, this was an attempt to place progressive French thought under the condition of a sequence of radical conflict, i.e., the Chinese Cultural Revolution. In fact, as a text, Zhang's chapter provides little more than a typographical excuse in *The Dialectical Kernel* for the series of thirteen 'footnotes' of varying length inserted by the French authors which constitute a refinement of the arguments outlined in *Theory of Contradiction*. The philosophical 'kernel' of this book, then, is not Zhang's chapter at all, but the interventions these footnotes perform both on text, and wider inter-textual context.

Nevertheless, Badiou et al. situate Zhang's work by opening with a brief account of the French and Chinese histories of Hegelian interpretation. The implication is that the dominant reading of Hegel within a given conjuncture can function as a kind of political litmus-test. *The Rational Kernel* itself, in properly Maoist fashion, is an attempted intrusion into its own *anti*-Hegelian context in France. Regarding the French Hegel, then, the influence of Alexandre Kojève's seminal interpretation of *The Phenomenology of Spirit* is traced into the revolutionary romanticism of Malraux and the surrealism of Bataille and Breton, as well as into the parallel development, via Jean Hippolyte, Sartre and also early Lacan, of an existentialist Hegel. On this complex terrain, the encounter between French Hegelianism and Marxism was unavoidable, but also, according to the authors, impossible. This impossibility stemmed from the almost exclusive reliance on the Hegel of the *Phenomenology* at the expense of that of *The Science of Logic*, a bias that pushed French Marxism towards the master-slave drama of early Marx (say, of the *1844 Manuscripts*) and away from Marx's mature proximity to the *Logic* in the three volumes of *Capital*. Thus, the vexed Hegel-Marx, Marx-Hegel relation was always destined in the French context to chase lost causes up cul-de-sacs.

It is for this reason that Sartre stands accused by Badiou (who began theoretical life as a Sartrean) of attempting to force Marxism back into the tradition of German idealism from which, with the levers of English political economy and French socialism, it had attempted to wrench itself free. Sartre is said to invert Marx's inversion of Hegel. Thus, the central term in Sartrean existentialist Marxism is the notion of 'alienation' prominent in early Marx, with 'work' providing the nodal point at which political economy and the problem of self-consciousness intersect. Even though I would argue that it is a project proximate to early Badiou's own, and even if it provides a philosophy of conflict which might usefully supplement later Badiou's comparative silence on the question of political organisation, Badiou himself is here dismissive of Sartre's two-volume *Critique of Dialectical Reason*: "Sartre, in the same movement, salutes Marxism as the unsurpassable horizon of our culture, and undertakes to dismantle this Marxism by forcefully realigning it under the idea of origin which is most strange to it: the transparency of the cogito" (*NR*, pp. 13-14). This is perhaps a surprising analysis, given that a key term in Sartre's *Critique* is the 'group-in-fusion', emphasising the relational constitution of the 'cogito' within a totalising praxis.[13]

Yet French existentialist Hegelianism was forced to reorient itself in relation to Marxism by the combined impacts of World War II, revisionism within the PCF, and the various wars of national liberation including the brutal conflict in Algeria. According to Badiou, the most pernicious form taken by this reorientation in the 60s was Althusser's structuralist Marxism. While Althusser succeeded in stripping away the subjectivism of existentialist Marxism, returning it to a cold scientific rigour, the materialist Hegel of the *Logic* remained as foreclosed as it was with Sartre. For in his zeal to purge Marxism of all things Hegelian, Althusser had effectively thrown the baby out with the bath water. Two equally impoverished alternatives therefore presented themselves in the 1950s and 1960s. In the 50s, the Heglianised Marx of Sartre tended towards idealism. In the 60s, the de-Hegelianised Marx of Althusser tended towards "metaphysical materialism" (p.15), i.e., towards the 'objective formalism' already criticised in *Theory of Contradiction*. This parlous state of affairs was exposed by the events of May '68 when Marxists of every shade oscillated hopelessly between Sartre's Cartesianism of the cogito, and Althusser's Cartesianism of the 'ghost in the machine'. Then, feeding off this confusion, came the *nouveaux philosophes*. André Glucksmann, for example, attempted to reduce Hegel to his admiration for the Prussian State, and then link this admiration to the monstrous rationality of the Stalinist State, which, in turn, supposedly condemned Marxism *in toto* (conveniently ignoring, of course, Marx's own critique of the Hegelian theory of State). Against this, Glucksmann and his ilk promote a Kant-inspired humanitarian rights.

To arrest these oscillations, Badiou et al. advocate the maintenance of the scissional dimension of the Marx-Hegel relation: "it is necessary to return to zero, and finally to see, philosophically, that Marx is neither other than Hegel nor the same. Marx is the divider of Hegel" (*NR*, p.17). Marx manages simultaneously to identify what is valid in Hegel (the eponymous rational kernel) and to separate out what is integral to, but ultimately false in, the Hegelian system (its idealism). Badiou argues that there is no way of finally 'correcting' Hegel: rather, Hegelianism *is* the interminable conflict between the idealist-romantic deviation typical of existentialism on the one hand, and the scientistic-academic deviation typical of structuralism on the other. Nonetheless, *The Dialectical Kernel* is a valuable undertaking insofar as returning to Hegel at all in its particular context can be considered a mode of 'revolting against the reactionaries'. For it is always under the emblem of the exclusion or marginalisation of Hegel that bourgeois philosophers, such as Glucksman and Lévy, attempt to neutralise Marxism. But in order to offset the skewed nature of French engagements with Hegel, this return must be a return to the *Logic* rather than to the well-worn path that leads back to the *Phenomenology*.

---

13. It can be argued that Badiou does turn back to Sartre's *Critique* by the time of *LW*, in which the notion of the 'subject-body' surely owes a great debt to Sartre. Nina Power has identified this debt to Sartre's *Critique* in some detail (see Power: 2006).

Things are considerably simpler in the Chinese context where Hegelian scholarship is, according to Badiou et al., marked by the turning point of the 'liberation' of 1949. Prior to this date, Chinese interpretations were notable for the absence of any emphasis on the revolutionary essence of the dialectic, and for the focus on the Hegelian theory of the State—a conservatism reflected in a fascination for the *Phenomenology*, and a comparative indifference to the *Logic*. In the wake, however, of the CCP's assent to power, the whole Hegelian corpus was studied anew. A concerted effort was made, on Mao's bidding, to follow Marx and Lenin in separating the revolutionary from the conservative elements of the Hegelian system, the rational kernel from its idealist outer shell. This task divided into two distinct periods in China. Firstly, between 1956 and 1959, Mao calls for new interpretations of Hegel's work and Zhang Shiying publishes *On the Philosophy of History* (1956) and *On the Logic of Hegel* (1959). Secondly, between 1972 and 1975, there is a specific focus on a critique of the idealist interpretation of Hegel's philosophy of history. Far from being driven by abstract debates within the ivory tower (in the intensely politicised context of Mao's China, particularly after the 'Hundred Flowers' campaign,[14] no such space of neutrality existed), this second phase was in fact a direct response to Mao's attack on Lin Biao. At the 2nd plenum of the IX Congress of the CCP, held in 1970, Lin Biao advocated a deterministic conception of dialectical development that effectively turned revolutionary protagonists into little more than the automata of World History. This was an argument of which Mao—long engaged in the construction of the cult of his own personality as the leader of the heroic Long March—was less than tolerant. Thus, Mao accused Lin Biao of succumbing to a rightist deviation, subsequently inviting his scholars to rebut the reading of Hegel capable of fomenting such 'incorrect thinking'. This second phase in Chinese interpretations of Hegel, as a response to revisionism, finds its mirror-image in the project of the French Maoists galvanised by the events of May '68 to rehabilitate both Marx and, through him, a certain Hegel. For Althusser, too, was deemed by them to have succumbed to an academic version of Lin Biao's rightist deviation.

A TENTATIVE TURN TO LACAN

Far from merely introducing Zhang's Hegel into the French intellectual mix, however, Badiou et al. borrow it as a springboard for launching a refinement of the materialist dialectic. This task is now aided by a new perspective drawn from the maverick French psychoanalyst, Jacques Lacan. At first glance, this seems a surprising critical resource, given that May '68 firmly separated out the radicalism of the Maoists from the psychoanalytic clique gathered around Lacan, and from the Deleuzians who took up a third distinct position (on top of this, of course, was Althusser's own use of early Lacan). However, Lacan had long grappled with Hegel

---

14. This refers to Mao's call, in 1956, for more vibrant critical debate among China's intellectual class, under the slogan, 'Let a hundred flowers bloom, let a thousand schools of thought contend'. Historians unsympathetic to Mao and his legacy argue that the Hundred Flowers campaign was intended, from the outset, to induce critics of his regime to identify themselves so that the subsequent 'rectification campaign' (that is, execution and terrorisation of dissident intellectuals) could be conducted all the more efficiently.

throughout his renowned seminars, and in Seminar XVII in particular—in which he responds with sophistication and critical balance to May '68, often over the vociferous interventions of radicalised students—he arrived at a uniquely complex reading of the Marx-Hegel relation that would prove extremely valuable for Badiou during his Maoist phase, and beyond.

In *The Rational Kernel*, however, the authors are cautious about this psychoanalytic source, drawing primarily upon the Lacanian logic of the symbolic, specifically its reliance on the signifier as, minimally, a mark or inscription. This is evident in their very first intervention into Zhang's text, a note on 'being, nothingness and becoming' (*TC*, p.29).[15] Here, the distinction between structure and tendency from *Theory of Contradiction* is phrased in terms of mark making, repetition, and iteration. Reading Hegel through this Lacanian vocabulary, Badiou et al. immediately locate the fork within the dialectical path (conservatism in one direction, radicalism in the other) within Hegel's account of being and nothingness in the *Phenomenology*. The importance of this analysis for our purposes becomes evident if we think of the antinomy between being and nothingness as an early version of the problem of the relation, or non-relation, between the situation (being) and the event (nothingness). In this way, the origins of Badiou's increasing attraction to the philosophy of *singularity*, and the concomitant tension with regard to his dialectical proclivities, becomes apparent.

Zhang's text points out that the metaphysical tradition generally thinks being and nothingness as ontologically distinct terms. However, the elementary move in Hegel's dialectic is to insist that being and nothingness are linked in an internal and necessary fashion precisely as mutually constituting opposites. At this point, we are faced again by the non-dialectical impasse of reciprocal contradiction, and it is therefore here that Badiou et al. detect the spectre of idealism. For Hegel's dialectical solution to the impasse threatens to lapse back into metaphysics. He is aware that if being and nothingness are co-implicated as opposites, if they are dialectically transformable one into another, then the constitutive difference between the two terms dissolves. But Hegel's resolution of this deadlock by recourse to the third, synthesising term 'becoming'—which represents both a passage from being into nothingness (the fate of the old situation) and a passage from nothingness into being (the birth of novelty)—is in danger of prioritising the self-identity of being in a way incompatible with dialectics. That is, although Hegelian becoming seems to articulate two moments of absolute incommensurability, being in fact functions as the 'unmoving mover' that enables the movement of becoming itself. Being is the self-identical term which must be assumed for becoming to differentiate itself both from what it 'leaves behind' (being, the old situation) and what it 'enters into' (nothingness, radical newness from the point of view of the old situation). Crucially, this synthesis is not only in breach of the dialectical law of internal scission, insofar as it sets 'being' up as a pure, fixed, and indivisible foundation, but it also reduces the power of dialectical negativity to *mere repetition*. For if nothingness

---

15. A much more complex confrontation with Lacan, via Jacque-Alain Miller, appeared in the *Cahiers pour l'analyse* as 'Marque et Manque: A propos du Zéro' (pp.150-173, No.10, 1969). There is also a continuation of this discussion in Chapter 3 of *NN*.

is always mortgaged to being by a movement of becoming, no radical newness can ever emerge. To think nothingness in *relation* to being at all is immediately to qualify its negative power (and this anticipates the all-important conjunctive in *Being and Event*). To put it another way, if becoming equals 1 + 1 + 1 + 1, or the repetition of an ontologically eternal and unchanging being, then where will the divisive dialectical 2 come from?

It is here that the authors turn, implicitly for the moment, to Jacques Lacan in order to clarify this issue. Lacan allows them both to set aside this metaphysical understanding of being, and to re-phrase its consequences in terms of a logic of empty repetition. Thus, the double determination of becoming can be seen in precisely the opposite way, namely, as "the double inscription of identity under the form of two marks [...]: being and nothingness are two marks for the void" (*NR*, p.29). Rather than an unchanging 'essence', being arises as a recursive relation conjoining two empty marks. But even understood in this Lacanian way, Hegel merely inscribes the very weakest form of difference, the *iterative* difference between two marks separated only by their place (this 1 is not that 1 because it is minimally displaced by a repetition). This amounts to little more than a closed serial logic: the only movement within such a world would be displacement of the same, rather than dialectical transformation.

Nonetheless, the materialist side of Hegel *is* able to grasp that every inscription also produces its ground, and thus that the constitutive self-difference between, in Lacan's Saussurean terms, the signified and the signifier, is the dialectical essence of signification, or, in Hegel's ontological terms, of becoming. While serial logic is incapable of thinking its foundation in this minimal difference, Hegel recognises that a second mark is always required in order to register its effect. The ground of being can now be seen, not in some substantialist ontological sense, but rather in a relational, dialectical sense, as the repetition of the previous mark of being in a different time and place (famously for Lacan the subject is an effect of the signifier, and yet the signifier only represents the subject to another signifier). Hegel is thus able to think the engendering of an infinite iterative sequence, just as Lacan will later use Hegel's logic to think the institution of the symbolic via the unary trait that inaugurates repetition through its 'first', castrating inscription. However, warn Badiou et al., this rational kernel of the analytic is still a numerical thought of identity, not the dialectic proper: "The motor of this process is the ensemble of voids retroactively constituted by their marks [...] and not the scission of identity" (*NR*, p.31).

TOWARDS A NEW TOPOLOGY

In order to gain greater proximity to this scission, the authors follow later Lacan's concentration on the category of the real. Specifically, they pick up the thread of Lacan's 'topological turn', undertaken in order to explore the anti-narrative, anti-Symbolic capacities of formal notation as a possible pathway to this Real (Badiou's own mathematical turn will be similarly motivated). Thus, in a footnote that will be significant for the way Badiou comes to think structure and change during his Maoist phase, entitled 'On the interior and exterior: the Hegelian topology' (*NR*, p.38), Hegel is said to maintain "a new topology of knowledge" (*ibid.*). Via the dialectical intermingling of universal and particular, this new topology collapses the very distinction between inside and outside.

As ever, there are two divergent ways of interpreting Hegel's approach here. Firstly—and this is the route the authors assert Lacan himself took—there is a purely structural reading. This allows the discernment of the inside from the outside only at specific local points, while making the same distinction inapplicable at the level of the unifying Whole. While on an initial Platonic level the interior-exterior difference becomes a perspectival illusion unmasked by a higher truth (Absolute Knowledge), the proper Hegelian twist is that such illusion is the immanent and necessary form of that unfolding truth. On a certain account of Hegel's teleological historicism, this would translate into the punctual and partial manifestation of a global truth within a given moment of 'concrete universality' specifically in the form of a separation between that moment, and the truth of the Whole. The gap or split becomes the condition of dialectical truth.

Lacan, it is claimed, draws on this first interpretation. He even illustrates it with the graphic example of the twisted band of the Möbius strip. This figure similarly turns the distinction between an inside and an outside into an effect of local perspective: trace the inside for long enough around the curving surface of the strip, and it will be imperceptibly transformed into an outside. According to Badiou et al., however, the only means of escape Lacan allows from this closed loop, the only way a true Lacanian subject can emerge, is to *cut* the Möbius strip. Analysis 'cuts' the subject of the signifier, at least partially and momentarily, away from the imaginary order that imposes the *méconnaissance* of the lack at the core of being, thereby unbuttoning those *points de caption* that otherwise pin the fabric of signification. The trouble with this account, the authors assert, is its flat structuralism. It simply cleaves the inside and the outside together in a nondynamic contradiction, with subjective agency coming only from a total break with this fundamentally undecidable torsion. In fact, later Badiou's notion of the eventual subject becomes extremely close to the very Lacan critiqued here, insofar as the event will come to function as just such a 'cut' with the prevailing order. But at this stage, he asserts his distance from Lacan, ostensibly for 'political' reasons.

For if we think of the outside as a revolutionary alternative to the internal norms of a given society, then rendering the inside effectively indistinguishable from the outside amounts to a deeply nihilistic position reminiscent of some of Jean Baudrillard's more hyperbolic propositions about simulacra and hyper-reality. Such a conflation could be said to suggest the structural determination and appropriation, by capitalist society, of that which resists it: for example, the commodification of the utopian social imaginary (fair-trade shopping as a middle-class lifestyle choice that passes for 'progressive', the reduction of student radicalism to the 'branding' of Ché Guevara's face on fashion t-shirts, and so on). To avoid this structural internalisation of the exterior and its attendant politics of predetermined 'resistance'—clearly no resistance at all—the authors advocate a second way of reading Hegel's dialectical topology. On this account, the interior-exterior correlation must be rigorously thought as *scission*, with the destabilising real being "simultaneously in its place and in excess over this place, interior *and* exteri-or" (*NR*, p.39). This is the mirror-image, and therefore inversion, of Baudrillardian cynicism: what is guaranteed is not the internalisation of a (profitable) image of ex-ternality, but the *material* persistence of a *real* excess that is exterior precisely be-cause it is so intimately interior and yet so resistant.

It is this second, scissional reading of the Lacanian-Hegelian topology that en-ables the creative Maoism characteristic of Badiou's early phase. It allows him to argue that in the bourgeois situation structured by the accumulation and concen-tration of capital, it is the proletariat who carry this scissional power to its explo-sive limit. Doubly determined, the working class is at once an element integrated into the structure of capitalist society as the exploited labour power upon which it depends, and "a force heterogeneous to this society" (*NR*, p.39) insofar as it car-ries, as a 'tendency', the potential force to destroy capitalism. What is crucial in this Maoist take on Lacanian topology is that, rather than being exterior in the hard sense, i.e., something 'on the outside' of society, the proletariat is a scissional excess structural, as it were, to structure.

> In reality, only the existence of the proletariat prohibits the thought of the capi-talist 'system' as a relevant totality equipped with an inside and an outside. This is the root of the failure of all Marxist structuralism, as of all 'leftist' currents, which pretend to organise thought and action starting from an absolute comprehension of oppressive society as System (*NR*, pp. 39-40).

To think the social, even 'critically', as an autonomous system with a clear inside and outside is to indulge and indeed reinforce the fantasies of bourgeois power. The topological alternative presented by the authors is therefore intended to echo the claim in the *Communist Manifesto* that 'capitalism creates its own gravediggers', i.e., that it carries within it the seeds of its own destruction. However, and crucial-ly, they also use the concept of 'force' as a way of preventing the deterministic in-terpretation of this sentiment that would reduce the subjective dimension to an as-pect of structure.

The authors present this argument as a correction to the residually structural-ist Lacanian position: "it is necessary to oppose to the rupture-Subject of Lacan, whose fixed cause is lack, the scission-Subject of dialectical materialism, whose mobile cause is the non-adherence [*non-recollement*] of force and place" (*NR*, p.40). However, as before with Deleuze, so now with Lacan, it is quite possible to argue that this 'correction' is present in Lacan himself (which is probably why Badiou will go on to embrace Lacanian theory much more openly). From about 1969 on-wards, Lacan's notion of the Real is no longer what is foreclosed by the Symbolic, and thus a topology of constitutive lack. Far from being incompatible with it, the Real comes to suffuse the Symbolic as kind of internal limit which is also an ex-cess. Where Badiou's critique, however, does hit the mark, is in the psychoanalyst's ultimate cynicism with regard to the possibility of forcing genuine novelty without merely swapping master-signifiers.[16] Because discourse is a social link for Lacan,

---

16. Although one could argue that a version of this position emerges in *BE*, where Ba-diou denies the possibility of a stateless situation, a problem to which Oliver Feltham has adverted (2008).

this is more than simply saying that our psychological make up causes us to always yearn for father figures: it means, further, that society is necessarily structured around a phallic transcendence that grounds the law of the father. Lacan's value for emancipatory politics is therefore ambivalent. On the positive side, the Real can be thought of as a kernel of illegality at the core of this paternal law guaranteeing the possibility of social change (and it is on this that the likes of Ernesto Laclau (2001) and Yannis Stavrakakis (1999) pin their Lacanian political theories). On the downside, however, there is no longer such a thing as 'revolution' in the radical sense of an absolute beginning (although, again, Badiou is consistently critical of this notion himself): if a 'quarter turn' is always possible in Lacan's four discourses, the 'place' of mastery remains even as different terms occupy it. We will come back to these themes in more detail when we look at *Theory of the Subject*. However, it is perhaps fair to say that, at this stage in Badiou's thought, his own version of the real—force—itself remains residually 'structuralist' insofar as it is *the anti-structural power contained within, although not containable by, structure itself.*

FUNCTIONAL DIFFERENCE AND EXCESSIVE DIFFERENCE: TOWARDS THE OUTPLACE

It is clear that Badiou and his collaborators must push force beyond its ultimate determination by structure. In lieu of the re-worked topology of the interior and exterior we have just outlined, the key problem becomes the relation (or non-relation) between two types of difference. Firstly, difference thought as internal to structure, i.e., as functional to it, and secondly, difference thought as 'external' to structure, i.e., as in excess of structuration.

It is for this reason that the authors insist that in order to understand force, it must be in relation to two things: firstly, the place which it exceeds, and secondly, the structural system of placement it *destroys* (*NR*, p.44). In escaping the determination of placement, the structuring Whole is overturned. Again, force is not an excess in the sense of an addition or a superabundance—this would indeed have to come from an outside—but an excess in relation to that which it exceeds, namely, structure. It follows that the calling card of force is de-struction seen from the point of view of structure. 'Destruction' during this phase of Badiou's work refers to a qualitative difference distinguished from the *constitutive* difference upon which structuralist accounts of the social depend, and which, as 'alienation', 'scarcity', 'gap', 'lack' or 'lacuna', is lent pathos in existentialist and some psychoanalytic accounts of subjectivity. Destruction is the effect of an insubordinate differentiation that not only refuses to be placed, but contests the reigning regime of placement itself.

We can think of these distinct notions of difference through the example of trade unionism. Although a venerable and arguably successful dimension of the labour movement, trade unionism is still a functional difference to the extent that it is compensated for by the State. Trade unions and the State accommodate each other in their respective tactics. They are mutually placed and placing terms. In general, then, they are in a non-antagonistic relation to one another in Mao's sense, despite the palpable reality of their often intense conflicts. It is only by exceeding this place of functional difference that workers can be galvanised into a

proletarian force that enters into a truly antagonistic relation with the existent social system by aiming at nothing less than its destruction (see *NR*, p.44). Trade unionism ultimately subordinates itself to the State by submitting to its authority *on
certain conditions*, and it is only these conditions that account for any radicalism it
may possess (as we shall see in the next chapter, this *anti-syndicaliste* stance strongly
shapes Badiou's activism with the *Organisation politique*). Far from campaigning for
a place within it, the proletariat constitutively evades being placed by the State's
tactic of what we will call the 'parliamentarisation of difference': the reduction of
difference to an agonistic negotiation among competing self-identical interests, as
opposed to the antagonistic power of scissional difference which cleaves identity in
two from the outset.

Given that destructive force is not some kind of addition, it follows that radical change is not to be conceived of *numerically*. Cardinal numerical thought, built
upon the self-identity of the One, is precisely what enables the State to lure difference into its parliamentary trap. In Hegelese (to borrow Žižek's overused quip),
this means that the distinction between quantity and quality, so important to
Marx, cannot be captured by the numerical logic of serial identity. Quality never
emerges from the incremental addition of units of quantity,[17] as if revolution were
merely a matter of achieving a 'magic number': "the numerical increase in the
working class or the growing number of Maoist militants do not *by themselves* indicate a structural transformation of the bourgeois/proletariat contradiction" (*NR*,
p.51). Although Badiou does concede that such numerical increases may provide
the necessary if not sufficient condition for qualitative transformations, his ultimate
distinction between quantity and quality has two important ramifications: firstly, it
implies a break with any representational notion of politics of the liberal 'one person, one vote' variety, and, concomitantly, it suggests the enormous importance of
subjective commitment above and beyond numerical 'clout'. If "quantity is that by
which the variability of the considered term remains enslaved to a system of places" (*ibid.*) then neither elections, nor opinion poles, nor media-driven popularity
contests can attain to the qualitatively new. Quality is always a force of strong differentiation. Although it emerges from within placed quantitative variation, it is
an excess "which is in contradiction with quantity in the exact measure whereby
its own effect is the destruction of place" (*ibid.*). It is not therefore accurate to say
that quantity *produces* quality, even by virtue of a 'qualitative leap'. This metaphor

---

17. Badiou approaches the Hegelian dialectic between quantity and quality again in *Being and
Event*, performing the same disjunction from the perspective of number (*BE*, pp.161-170). He
points out that Hegel articulates the transition from quantity to quality around the problem of
infinity, positing two infinities, a good qualitative one, and a bad quantitative one. Qualitative
infinity is opened up by the alterity of the Other in the Same: non-being is here an *enabling* limit,
a frontier that the 'I' must pass beyond. Quantitative infinity, however, is deemed bad because
it simply repeats a Oneness without interior difference: its infinity is an empty operation of du-
plication. However, for Badiou, who is by this stage opposing to Hegel's generative ontology his
own subtractive approach, this is precisely where Hegel confronts mathematics as a potential
science of pure multiplicity. Hegel recoils from this subtractive path by uniting the two realms
through the dialectical transformation of quantity into quality. Yet this "good quantitative infinity' is a properly Hegelian hallucination" (*BE*, p.170).

cannot disguise that the notion of accumulation at work here is too linear, too non-dialectical, as if the tipping point of a set of socio-economic scales had been reached by the addition of 'one more'. In truth, genuinely qualitative change cannot be counted as an addition because it attaches itself to no pre-existing sequence of measurable elements.[18] This is also why the commitment to a politics of the radically new will always entail an ethically ambiguous romance with destruction. For, to the otherwise perfectly reasonable question, 'change, yes, but at what cost?', the genuine militant must answer, 'true change cannot be submitted to a cost-benefit analysis and remain true change'. The discarding of every moral compass, in the sense of a pre-existing codification of behavioural norms, is clearly a precondition for entering the revolutionary maelstrom. As later Badiou will underline, only an ethic of perseverance can push the pursuit of the possible to its impossible limits.

Just as the militant must subtract him or herself from the moral conventions of the society s/he overhauls, so qualitative novelty demands that its only 'place' is what the authors of *The Dialectical Kernel* call the *hors place*, or 'outplace'. It is in this concept that much of later Badiou can be discerned. It already indicates two aspects of his future trajectory. Firstly, the *hors place* represents an attempt to theorise the emergence of the radically new in *a relation of non-relation with the old*. It is therefore the first real step on the path towards the starkly singular philosophy proposed in *Being and Event*. Secondly, however, the *hors place* is simultaneously that which carries the theme of the dialectic forward into Badiou's later work, insofar as it describes immanent heterogeneity: even as it subtracts itself from the old, the *hors place* is located 'within' the old. How else could it force its transformation? As Bosteels puts it, "what is proposed is a symptomatic torsion that cannot remain on the structural level of recognising an outside within, as in a traumatic kernel of the real, but that must pass over into the destruction or disqualification of the old inside the new" (Bosteels: 2005, p.606). Despite arriving at it by thinking the immanent and thus the structural nature of force, the *hors place* begins to designate the need for an internal and yet total rupture with all the relations of difference constitutive of a situation. It is an excess not in a numerical sense, but from the point of view of the system of placement which it exceeds. Nothing 'extra' is required beyond a kind of parallax shift within the given. However, this shift is not qualitative if it does not achieve some kind of internal distance in relation to placement—in relation, that is, to relational difference itself.

This apparently abstract argument has serious political ramifications. For example, even the Maoist party can become a fixed term within the bourgeois situation. It threatens not only to be placed by the State, but to place itself (with misplaced self-satisfaction) as excessive *in relation* merely to the State's fixed place of 'resistant difference'. In this sense, being identified as radical is still at the outer limits of the logic of place, just as heretical transgressions are determined by a

---

18. In Badiou's later use of set-theory, the danger of mathematical constructivism, and its philosophical equivalent in nominalism, will be warded off with reference to the 'limit ordinal' which, like the void, is not reducible to succession and opens up, thereby, the being of number to the infinity from which it arises (see mediation 14, 15, 28 and 29 in *BE*, as well as section two of *NN*)

framework of religious belief. The real qualitative leap comes in being utterly un-placeable, immeasurably beyond good and evil, or, following Badiou's later set-theoretical turn, uncountable. One could say that the *hors place* cleaves together the later notions of the 'void' and the 'event': it is internal to a situation but un-placeable within it, and it is a radical excess that necessarily seems to come from nowhere. Whereas the void can still be thought structurally as a 'constitutive lack', the unplaceable *hors place* finally exceeds structure without relying on an addi-tion from some putative 'outside'. Deleuze, for his part, had already meditated on this very distinction between functional and excessive difference, choosing to ar-ticulate the former as 'relative deterritorialisation' (Deleuze and Guattari: 2000), the latter through neo-Spinozist 'intensity' and Nietzschean 'affirmation' (Deleuze: 2002). Badiou, however, who is still wedded to the materialist dialectic at this stage (and who will consistently oppose to Spinozist vitalism a subtractive ontology), is forced to think the passage from quantity to quality, structure to excess, place to force, as driven in some way by a version of the labour of the negative.

NEGATIVITY, NOT NEGATION

However, this labour must, in its profound negativity, produce nothing rather than something. It is for this reason that Badiou et al. critique the notion of 'negation' used in formal propositional logic, where dialectical negativity is thoroughly deter-mined by the structure of language (*NR*, p.46). This critique is also a swipe at the generalised philosophical turn to language post-May '68, which flowered in the 1970s through Derridean deconstruction, Foucaultian notions of discourse and the 'rhetorical turn' of many social sciences in the Anglophone world. In the analyt-ic philosophical tradition from Wittgenstein through to A. J. Austin especially, the category of negation has had pivotal importance in identifying the illocutionary force of statements, above and beyond their propositional content. To crudely sim-plify the argument, the Magritte-like phrase 'this is not a phrase' does not negate itself *qua* phrase, or unit of sense, despite the negation at the lexical level. It carries an illocutionary force that reveals the performative dimension of language, i.e., the merging of doing and saying in a speech-act. Insofar as the performative is a mo-dality of speech that can only be supported by social conventions and power rela-tions—the performative 'off with her head' only secures uptake if its addressor is recognised as a monarch empowered to make such imperious demands—the phi-losophers of language here intersect with some of the Althusserian arguments re-garding (discursive) interpolation. To build on Althusser's image, if the policeman who hails us then arrests us, we submit to that constraint on the basis of the social contract empowering him, effectively re-signing it by arresting ourselves. But it is precisely this nexus between language, society and power that the authors of *The Dialectical Kernel* are concerned to contest.

Thus, while they agree that one cannot enunciate a proposition that is also its negation, they further insist that "the negation of a term (of a phrase) has absolute-ly nothing to do with the dialectic, which posits that being and things are the pro-cess of their scission" (*NR*, p.46). The specific danger, brought about by Hegel's own use of the term 'negation' within his dialectical philosophy, is that a banal attribute of grammar might come to stand in for real transformation: "That which exists can certainly be destroyed, broken up, but not negated. Only speech negates, and it is on account of a linguistic idealism that it is necessary for the category of negation to carry a substantial ontological usage" (*NR*, p.47). Negation is condemned here as a logical category that has the potential to be confused for an ontological one. This conflation of merely formal contradiction in conceptual systems with dialectical contradiction in things has frequently served as a way of dismissing the Marxist philosophy of the dialectic as incoherent, for example by Karl Popper (Popper: 2002). Idealism is the right word for this slippage, since the implication is that negating capitalism linguistically somehow touches on the concrete structure of capitalist exploitation, in flagrant disregard of Marx's 11th thesis on Feuerbach. Material reality, in its dialectical truth, certainly observes rules other than grammatical ones. This critique is not only a continuation of the attack on Engels' 'negation of the negation'. It is also a broadside against the supposed pan-textualism of Derridean deconstruction, in which this conflation of being and language, under a massively expanded concept of *écriture*, becomes a fundamental move in the critique of metaphysics (Derrida: 1997). Badiou consistently asserts that language and being are *not* the same thing (faithful to his intellectual hero, Plato, Badiou carries the ancient philosophical battle against the Sophists into the present).

This critique also extends to the textual conception of History sometimes opposed to the Marxist vision of concrete world-historical progress. Thus, in a subsequent footnote, Badiou's old nemesis, André Glucksmann, is attacked for importing such textualism into his 'new philosophical' critique of the entire project of the Left. Glucksmann's seminal 1977 book, *Les Maîtres Penseurs* (The Master Thinkers), systematically undermines the philosophical wellsprings that have nourished the critical and political endeavours of the Left. His specific tactic in dressing down both Marx and Hegel is to focus on History. If the dialectical conception of History, materialist or idealist, demands that History be adduced as evidence of the unfolding of its own truth, then Glucksmann proposes to show, through historical 'facts', the ethically disastrous nature of dialectical 'truth'. In other words, historical materialism stands condemned by the human misery of the gulags and the concentration camps to which it supposedly led.

In generous mood, one might call this a form of 'immanent critique' in Horkheimer's sense, insofar as Glucksmann appears to occupy the (historical) logic of his object of critique: dialectics led, dialectically, to enormous human suffering. Yet the authors of *The Dialectical Kernel* point out that there are two ways of reading Hegel's famous notion that 'the study of the history of philosophy is the study of philosophy itself' in which Glucksmann finds the impetus for his 'immanent' argument. On the one hand, the radical, materialist interpretation understands this statement as emphasising the social conditions of emergence of past philosophies in and through class struggle, i.e., as a clarion call to the historically materialist approach to philosophical texts themselves. On the other hand, the second, idealist interpretation understands Hegel as saying that History is, ultimately, the story of the autonomous unfolding of the Concept, with mature philosophy as a mode of reflection upon this process. Predictably, it is the second, idealist interpretation of Hegel that Glucksmann utilises in his supposedly historical condemnation of Marxist theory from the perspective of the Stalinist Terror. He asserts a direct, causal line of descent that can be plotted from the Master Thinkers worshiped by the Left, including Nietzsche as well as Hegel and Marx, right down to the abject experience of twentieth century totalitarianism. Thus it is clear that the Master Thinkers whom he vilifies as philosophers of inhuman mastery are figured as effectively *making history rather than being made by it*. Even as he attacks, 'historically', historical materialism then, Glucksmann indulges "an inversion pure and simple of the materialist thesis of the primacy of reality over thought" (*NR*, p.61). When he argues that Leftists who find in Hegel the resources of a revolutionary thought are the victims of an optical illusion, and, further, that even 'left' Hegelianism will only ever realise itself in the Absolute (ir)rationality of the State, Glucksman merely touches upon the *idealist* Hegel who conceives History as a process of the realisation of Spirit—precisely what the Left, or at least Marxists, attempt to leave aside in Hegel.

THE PROBLEM OF DEVIATION

Such idealist interpretations of Hegel invariably emphasise necessity over contingency, determinism over subjective force. Badiou et al. argue that this idealism already shows itself within Hegel in the absence of any positive theory of *deviation* (*NR*, p.73). For if History is ultimately the temporal expression of Spirit's necessary self-realisation, then contingent deviations cannot truly exist: every moment is sublated in the Whole, every apparent tangent is but a point on a transcendent line. Needless to say, no Communist Party could rest on the laurels of such fatalism, precisely because the class struggle demands the cultivation of the 'excess' of politicised subjectivity as well as close attention to unfolding socioeconomic antagonisms. 'Deviation' is such an important concept, historically and theoretically, in the organisational methodology of communist and other radical parties because of the overarching need for discipline in the face of revisionist tendencies, both in the attempted forcing of a revolution, and in the maintenance of fidelity to one that has already taken place (as we will see, this apparently organisational problem of deviation takes on tremendous philosophical weight and complexity for later Badiou, coming under a panoply of terms such as 'disaster', 'betrayal', 'evil', 'occultation', 'denial', and so on).

And yet there is an obvious problem here. The very concept of deviation suggests the robust knowledge of a party line, yet this linear continuity is precisely what the dialectic proper, as a logic of thoroughgoing scission, renounces (and denounces). Only an idealist emphasis on Hegelian sublation supports this image of an unbroken 'dialectical' line that moves by virtue of contradictions but somehow maintains the sublated terms, once again domesticating destructive negativity within a totalising Whole. And surely only an inflexibly normative rather than a responsive party structure could impose and police such a line? From a Maoist perspective, the true dialectic of the masses militates against both the diachronically linear notion of the ideological 'line', and the cumbersome dogmatism of the Stalinist model of the party. This is certainly not to say that Maoism doesn't concern itself with the problem of deviation! On the contrary, deviation becomes a much more pressing, on-going issue precisely because the kind of 'line' idealistically mapped via Hegelian sublation becomes, with Mao, constantly cut up by the interiority of scission. (One feels a twinge of pity for Mao's political rivals, around whom the categories of 'right opportunism' and 'left putchism' etc. inverted and merged with dizzying rapidity, forcing them to undergo humiliating self-criticisms at any given moment).

Badiou et al.'s point here is that even if Marx's materialist reading of Hegel foregrounds a theory of deviation not to be found in Hegel himself, there nonetheless exists an *idealistic* understanding of deviation manifesting itself in two forms of opportunism: Right opportunism, which demands the repetition of an already dominant term (the ultimate authority of the party, say), and Left opportunism, which invokes a state of original purity (the party-faction that claims to be the true heirs of the revolution, say). Both of these positions represent obstacles to the politics of the radically new in which Badiou is most interested. This is because Right opportunism responds to this novelty with a reactionary reassertion of an old configuration ('party discipline at all costs!'), whereas Left opportunism subordinates this novelty to a self-declared 'special relationship' with a putative origin (in the Chinese context, the old party cadres who were 'there' at the Long March demanding to be spared humiliation at the hands of the Red Guards). However, both of these understandings of deviation are based on a non-dialectical, reciprocal contradiction sublated into the line that becomes their common measure. Both fail, therefore, to follow the scissional rupture through to its fundamentally non-linear conclusion.

Cleansed of this sort of idealism, the true materialist dialectic posits the utterly ineluctable nature of deviation. If the one divides into two, the line splits incessantly into divergent tangents. It follows that any ideological 'line' posited and policed by a Maoist party cleaving to the masses primarily has (to use an admittedly problematic binary) *subjective* value in disciplining its members for militant praxis at a given moment, rather than *objective* value in describing the immanent rationality of History as, finally, the gathering of all time into a transcendent One. At its extreme, the splitting of the Maoist scission cuts History—in the grand, monolithic sense of a majestic continuity, even one leading to communism—adrift, focussing instead upon the punctual intensity of the now. The revolutionary attitude is therefore less subordinated to the movement of History than it was with Marx himself, with the implicit 'wait-and-see' of a stagist view of the modes of production. With Mao, the revolutionary attitude draws instead on Lenin's impatient urgency between the February bourgeois revolution and the decisive Bolshevik push in Russia in October 1917 (even if the Cultural Revolution then throws into question the Leninist model of the party). It is perhaps in the knotting of these two aspects of Maoism, its unmooring from any linear notion of the 'movement of History' on the one hand and its fidelity to a 'mass line' paradoxically characterised by scissional discontinuity on the other, that persists most recognisably in what Bruno Bosteels calls Badiou's 'post-Maoism', in which he includes the later philosophy of the event (Bosteels: 2005). Certainly, the event and fidelity, or more precisely the relation between them, remain fundamentally informed by these Maoist problematics.

THEORY OF THE SUBJECT

Badiou's *explicit* Maoism finds its theoretical apogee in *Theory of the Subject* (1982). This is a sprawling conceptual montage that pastes together, scrapbook style, almost every thought Badiou seems to have had between the 7th of January 1975 and the 9th of June 1979 (the dates of the first and last seminars that constitute the entries into this 'scrapbook'). So exhilaratingly ramshackle is the book's construction that Badiou offers, in the preface, several reading strategies for tackling its 350-odd pages, ranging from a non-sequential 'thematic repertoire' to an index of the central names (Hegel and Hölderlin, Lacan and Mallarmé, Pascal and Rousseau, and of course, Marx, Engels, Lenin, Mao and Stalin). Despite these attempts at orientation, it remains a work recalcitrant of neat summary. Fortunately, there is considerable overlap between the texts we have already examined and the logic of scission radicalised in this eccentric tome. Let us therefore recap in order to outline the trajectory that leads to what is undoubtedly the culmination of Badiou's Maoist phase in *Theory of the Subject*.

As I have argued, *Theory of Contradiction* attacked structuralist Marxism precisely because Althusser's theoretical framework had failed to render Marxism equal to the events of May '68. Badiou contested the strong notion of structural determination at work in Althusser through a Maoist insistence on scission. The ontological primacy of scission makes structures internally divided and therefore given to a 'tendency' toward immanent self-dissolution: in this way, contra any hermetic understanding of structure, the possibility of change becomes guaranteed by the persistence of the splitting that cleaves every one of identity into a two of difference. Yet, arguably, 'tendency' was still too diachronic and linear a notion to carry the full implications of the logic of scission. Quite apart from flirting dangerously with economism, it says nothing about the subjective militancy required to actualise significant transformation. In its linearity, 'tendency' indicates, at most, a dialectic of discontinuous continuity, rather than continuous discontinuity. The introduction of the concept of 'force' in *Theory of Contradiction*, on the other hand, began to allow a thought of what might be called 'internal novelty', i.e., of the emergence from within structure of an anti-structural potentiality.

By *The Dialectical Kernel*, Badiou and his collaborators are attacking Althusser from another angle, this time through the resurrection of Hegel. Crucially, it is a version of Hegel that does not countenance ultimate determination by the movement of History, which, in its albeit 'dialectical' notion of Totality, effectively comes to resemble a structuralism writ large. Maoism here helps to offset the weight of such a totalized and totalising history by emphasizing subjectivity as inherently excessive in relation to historico-socioeconomic determination. Scission means that with every identity constitutively split, every moment in the present carries revolutionary potential and thus structure is punctured throughout by the minimal space of political subjectivity. What Badiou cannot allow himself, however, is to lapse back into a Sartrean decisionist subjectivism, as if the critique of Humanism (led by Althusser) had never happened. On the contrary, Badiou wants to retain the subject in the active political sense of that word without confusing it with the classical philosophical concept of the subject as, primarily, Cartesian and self-identical in the consubstantiality of being and thought. Mao, therefore, has to be supplemented by Lacan. Lacan offers two significant additions: firstly, the Lacanian psychoanalytic subject, contrasted to the individual, is constituted by and through its separation from (symbolic) determination, thereby ticking the box of 'political' subject; secondly, founded on lack it is non-Cartesian, thereby ticking the 'anti-humanist' box as well. Furthermore, the turn to Lacanian *topology* in *The Dialectical Kernel* allows Badiou to extract his guiding problem of 'internal novelty' from the inside-outside binary, which, *qua* binary, privileges either determination (inside) or an essentially mystical and passive concept of change (coming from outside). Properly complemented by a scissional materialism, then, the Lacanian topology of the subject enables a concept of force as, simultaneously, a qualitative, non-numerical and therefore unplaceable excess, and as the very material of active, transformative subjectivity. As I have argued, the key notion of the *hors place* that emerges from this twisted topology represents the minimal self-separation interior to a situation required for 'internal novelty' to become a possibility. Yet beyond any structuralism of the constitutive lack, it also underlines the forcing of this possibility by the political subject that exceeds structure.

All of this is very much repeated within *Theory of the Subject*. And yet now Badiou follows the logic of scission to its limit by folding it back upon itself. The proletariat, agent of destruction, must now destroy itself. The eponymous subject is precarious in two directions, as it were: it is not only singular and therefore rare— "[e]very subject is political. This is why there are few subjects, and rarely any politics" (*TS*, p.28)—but its only consistency lies in a subtractive destruction that envelopes even itself. An explicitly Christian dramatology therefore finds expression in *Theory of the Subject* (which contains an early 'evental' interpretation of St Paul—see *TS*, p.125): the proletariat must die that generic humanity may live, must vanish in and through its fleeting appearance for the newness it forces to be genuinely, persistently new. Already in *Theory of Contradiction* and *The Dialectical Kernel*, we saw how scission divided the rivals in class struggle from the inside: the proletariat was also the workers, the bourgeoisie both dominant reactionary class and unwitting agents of capital. However, by *Theory of the Subject*, a radicalised topology nullifies the very opposition between bourgeois and proletariat by which we intuitively understand 'class struggle': to avoid an exterior topology turning the proletariat into an internal functional difference of capital, *"we must first think the bourgeoisie's interiority to the proletariat"* (*TS*, p.130). Badiou now insists that the proletariat is a kind of immanent effect of disruption within the bourgeoisie itself: "the politics of the proletariat certainly stands in internal exclusion to bourgeois politics" (*ibid.*). Just as place creates force, so the bourgeoisie creates the proletariat, and just as place organizes itself around the containment of force, so the bourgeoisie is defined by its management of the proletarian resistance it invites. The political task of the proletariat is simultaneously to separate itself from the bourgeoisie and to continuously purge itself of the reformist bourgeois tendencies immanent to its own praxis, located as it is in the very bourgeois world it would transform. As Alberto Toscano puts it:

> Class struggle, if the term still applies, is thus not between two separate *forces*, two subjects indexed to different places within the apparatus of capital. It is an ef-

fect of the proletariat [...] expelling itself from bourgeois politics, and thus gaining its existence through the very process of organized destruction (Ashton et al.:
2006, p.343).

Whereas Badiou had previously preferred antagonism to the pseudo-democracy
of agonism, here antagonism itself seems to be swallowed up by the gathering momentum of scission: the vision of politics as a "subjective duel" (*TS*, 130) between
class *identities*, retaining as it does an essentially 'democratic' notion of difference,
must be replaced by an understanding of the inherent dissymmetry of structure.
In *Being and Event*, this will be stated clearly: "It is not antagonism which lies at the
origin of the State, because one cannot think the dialectic of the void and excess as
antagonism" (*BE*, p.110). Much of *Theory of the Subject* already revolves around the
idea that if there are two classes, it is only in the non-antagonistic sense that Lacan
says there are two sexes (**SXX**). This twoness is precisely a force of scission, and
not the fusion (or confrontation) of two identical ones. Badiou's comment in *Theory of Contradiction*, that the proletariat and the bourgeoisie have nothing in common, therefore takes on added importance here. To paraphrase Lacan, there is no
such thing as a class relation. Instead, the proletariat are to the bourgeoisie as feminine structure is to the masculine in the Lacan of Seminar XX: a *pas tout* or non-
all that disrupts masculine universality from the 'inside' without being reducible to
the exteriorizing logic of exception by which that universality attempts to domesticate excessive difference. For Badiou, the subject is always doubled: "Every subject stands at the crossing between a lack of being and a destruction, a repetition
and an interruption, a placement and an excess" (*TS*, p.139).

But it is precisely because Badiou models his notion of the subject on this
Lacanian *pas tout*, both structural and excessive, that he can say "there is only one
political subject" (*TS*, p.130). This means there is only one agency of destruction
arising from the dissymmetry within structure itself. That subject is the proletariat and "*Marxism is the discourse that maintains the proletariat as subject*" (*TS*, p.44). It is
therefore crucial not to place the normative violence of structuration on the same
level as this subjective proletarian force, as if they were opposed to one another like
gladiators in the same arena. The force mobilized by the bourgeoisie against the
proletariat, which Badiou terms 'correlation', is not a force in the strong, subjective sense at all. It is a reactionary insistence on the 'objectivity' of the given order,
whereas the essence of the subject is to break from this order. Indeed, the on-going dialectic between active and reactive forces within a situation is something of a
sideshow distracting from the truly singular subject which ruptures with that situation: "Reactive force is only determined, negatively, by the first [active force]" (*TS*,
p.49), meaning that to "to rule [*dominer*] means to *interrupt interruption*" (*TS*, 184).

Thus, by the time of *Theory of the Subject*, Badiou has come to believe that
Marx's founding insight was not into the face-off between alienated labour and
bourgeois exploitation, but into the nature of the intersection of *two* scissions: firstly, that between the forces and relations of production (generating force), and secondly, that between the bourgeoisie and the proletariat (as 'placed' elements).
Marx's genius lay in recognizing that the former leads to the weakening and ultimate ruin of the latter: class contradictions result in a diminution of capital's ability

to subdue, through placement, the proletarian force of which it is itself the recursive cause. It is this notion—that what force forces is the ultimate destruction of place—that leads Badiou to arrive at two fundamental axioms that will survive the vicissitudes of his developing thought: firstly, the political subject is the consequence (and practice) of a radical subtraction from determination, and secondly, political praxis is, from a topological perspective, an opening onto a generic (non) space disruptive of the field of placements.

It is for this reason that he now characterizes the dialectic with reference not to the model of class struggle based upon the murderous battle for recognition found in Hegel's *Phenomenology*, but to an immanent structural tension between what he now terms *esplacement* and the *horlieu*, or 'splacing' and the 'outplace'.[19] The first of these neologisms, 'splacing', refers to the fact that elements within a situation emerge at the nexus of two determinations: on the one hand, the 'in-itself' of a mark of identity consistent across iterative temporality, and on the other, the 'for-another' of *placed* identity with relationality for its mode of appearance.[20] Any 'thing' *is* the contradiction between these two determinations based on repetition and difference. Badiou writes this basic law of scission, $A = AAp$, which means that A is always both given and refused, withdrawn in and through its appearance, since it is never itself but always also its place. Furthermore, the fact of this *particular* placement of A means that the totality of its possible placements, which Badiou writes P, is constitutively excluded within this inscription of A (even as P remains its condition of possibility). In other words, A is only A insofar as it is in contradiction with P: "The dialectic divides A through the contradiction between A and P, between the existent and its place" (p.25). Against the agonistic model of difference, then, this means that "nowhere do you have a real, existing conflict between A and P as constituted and isolatable terms" (*TS*, p.14). To translate this into Lacanese, there is no other of the other from which it follows that any notion of a conceptually graspable 'social totality' in the sense used by early Lukács, for example, is ultimately idealist.

The *horlieu*, by total contrast to *esplacement*, "is repeatable only as split by inclusion in the splace" (*ibid.*). The *horlieu* results from a radical subtraction from the order of placement. This subtraction allows, through "the determination of the determination" (*TS*, p.11), the specification of a singular element, which Badiou writes Ap (A). This formula enables us to see that this is a process of purification, not addition, still less creation *ex nihilo*. The element 'A' was always already there as splaced but it now appears in its real, constitutive contradiction with P. Even in this de-differentiated form, we are not confronted by a self-identical essence. To assert such a pure identity would in fact amount to left-deviationism, a danger which Badiou now writes $A = A (A)$ (*ibid.*). Right deviation consists, on the other hand,

---

19. It is worth pointing out that, in *Theory of the Subject*, Badiou uses *horlieu* as opposed the *hors place* previously referred to in *The Dialectical Kernel*. The implied distinction between space and place is made in order to suggest that what force forces is an opening onto a universal space of politics that cannot be placed, or determined—see his terminological explanation on *TS*, p.11..

20. This concern with the recursive relation between being and being-there will return in *Logics of Worlds* where the agent of 'placing' becomes the transcendental index.

in allowing novelty to fall back into the old regime of placement, as if nothing can exist if it does not have a place: Badiou formalizes this dead branch of the dialectic, Ap (Ap) = P, where place is ultimately reasserted. Pushed toward the *horlieu*, however, A emerges not as an 'in-itself' or a 'for-itself', but as pure scissional contradiction between these two axes. This forcing of an 'outplace' is what saves 'A' from being swallowed back into the old regime as an identity either to be placed (Ap (Ap) = P), or to be rendered somehow transcendent (A = A (A)). I would add that the 'outplace' is also what prevents 'A' having particular interests which might lure it into the game of parliamentary difference. Having sloughed off the yoke of its specificity, including its class profile, 'A' attains to the generic and this is its revolutionary power. It follows that to get 'outside' of the system of assigned places that creates classes, the sociological category of the worker must be replaced by the unplaceable non-category of the proletariat whose only goal is the destruction of P.

In a certain sense, Badiou's tactic here resonates with the Italian autonomist or post-*operaismo* Marxism of Negri, Virno and Lazzarato. Their displacement of an exclusively class-based definition of the proletariat to include the immaterial labour of housewives, students and the unemployed etc. displaces also the centrality of wage labour in the Marxist account of class contradiction. Insofar as this distributes the active subjective dimension more widely across the social field, it might be conceived as a first step toward the kind of generic universal subject Badiou is pushing towards here *through* Marxist particularistic categories. Yet Badiou goes much further in his radicalization of Marxism. Where Negri's multitude is still a subject that emerges on the back of transformations in the mode of production (from material goods to immaterial information in conditions of real subsumption), Badiou's understanding of the proletariat in *Theory of the Subject* is ultimately uncoupled from any determination whatsoever, including that 'fetish' of classical Marxism, the economy. Thus, while Badiou's proletariat does define itself by escaping a narrow sociological definition of class, it also destroys the social structure that produces such individuated terms in the first place (for Negri, on the contrary, the multitude emerges immanently from *within* the globalised matrices of late capitalism and inhabits, rather than appropriates, the means of production that now, or already, produce the common *qua* substance of its social being). Lacking any predicate relating to income or education or even relations of production, the only attributable quality of Badiou's proletariat is the concentration of force against the State's regime of splacement which causes class division: "A definition: we will call *subjective* those processes relative to the qualitative concentration of force" (*TS*, p.41).

Should we conclude that class is no longer politically pertinent, then? On the contrary, class continues to matter for Badiou at this stage, but as a political *form* rather than as a social content, as a partisan activity rather than a coherent identity: "class, apprehended according to the dialectical division of its dialecticity, means partisan political action anchored in the productive historicity of the masses" (*TS*, p.27). However, does the scission of the bourgeoisie as a class not deprive the proletariat of an identifiable enemy? In fact, the 'enemy' of the proletariat does cease to be the bourgeoisie themselves—who are but a placed term within the same apparatus—but a more formidable, because ultimately unlocatable, enemy arises in their stead, in the shape of the bourgeois *world*, i.e., the totality that orders the terms it contains in such a way as to reproduce exploitation. It follows that in no way is the proletarian project the 'contradiction' of bourgeois ideology. This would be to get involved in the discursive parliamentarisation of difference. Rather, "The political project of the proletariat is communism, and nothing else. That is, the abolition of any place in which something like a proletariat can be installed. The political project of the proletariat is the disappearance of the space of the placement of classes" (*TS*, 7).

Communism, then, is not simply a confrontation with the bourgeois State aiming both to demonstrate its lack (of real power, of a true popular mandate etc.) and to turn it into a 'real' lack by destroying it. Badiou takes from Lenin the lesson that the properly communist moment comes in forcing the lack of the State, a necessarily bourgeois institution, into a second lack. If the State is first shown to lack via the insurrectional revolt of the proletariat contradicting violently with class society, then, after the State's destruction, its lack is itself made to lack by the masses, the active subjects in the new classless society, through the dictatorship of the proletariat (see p.100). The failure to take this radical communist step provides the rationale for Badiou's stark suggestion that "Socialism doesn't exist" (*TS*, 7). Socialism doesn't exist insofar as it "designates a shifting mutation of the space of the placement of classes" (*TS*, p.8) rather than its abrupt and total annihilation. To the extent that 'actually existing' Socialism retains and, as in the USSR, even intensifies the bureaucratic apparatuses of the State, it falls short of communism. Only Mao, in the Cultural Revolution, dared to attempt to realize a communism of the masses: "Mao, in the guise of a long series of cultural revolutions, for the first time has designated and put into practice the return of State's lack back upon itself" (*TC*, 81).

Yet the *agents* of this forcing of a double lack onto the State must themselves lack in a profound sense. The very concept of 'agency', often the implacable obstacle at the heart of structure-change debates, threatens—in its residual Cartesian humanism as well as its implicit pre- and post-eventual continuity—to suggest a problematic qualification of the new, as if intentional will were both the catalyst and consequence of transformation. While for early Badiou, the masses are the 'agents' of history, they must not be considered as some kind of oppressed yet coherent body-not-yet-politic. Rather, the masses must be understood as an 'evanescent term', as a kind of world-historical flash that fades as quickly as it appears: "The mass movement is the vanishing term of the eventual concatenation that is called history" (*TS*, p.63). While the masses *are* history at the level of their splacement, the masses *make* history in the spontaneous revolts that spark them into life (though, as ever, not in a manner of their own choosing). However, as mere midwives of radical novelty, they cannot hang around to appreciate their handiwork! The masses attain their being only through disappearance: "the essence of the vanishing term is to disappearance but it is at the same time that which exists the most—as Whole, cause of itself" (*TS*, p.64), i.e., as singularized, non-relational element. This sheds new light on the statement that Socialism doesn't exist. While it may have had a banal facticity in the former Soviet Union, for example, it does not ascend to the ontological intensity Badiou calls for under the phrase 'evanescent term'. Badiou can no longer countenance the notion of transition implied in socialism as a stage preparatory to communism: communism must come into being *at a stroke*, in a temporal hiatus that also resembles a cosmological 'big bang'. Revolution is the real of Marxism: it is the only form in which the non-relation between classes achieves historical manifestation (just as, for later Badiou, the event will be the sole ephemeral indication of inconsistent multiplicity and thus of Being-qua-being). Revolution is the existential appearance of the constitutive antagonism otherwise unceasingly overdetermined by the bourgeois world. Thus, correlated to the claim that Socialism doesn't exist is the insistence that it is incorrect to say that revolutions don't exist. On the contrary, they are the only things that really exist, or exist in the real, in the timeless gap the real opens up.

This preference for rupture over transition emerges, too, in Badiou's turn to the atomism of ancient Greek philosophy in *Theory of the Subject*. As the earliest known articulation of a materialist world-view, such a turn has long been a temptation for Marxist philosophers (Marx's own graduate dissertation was on the atomists and late Althusser appeals to them in his proposition of 'aleatory materialism'—Althusser: 2006), as well as for post-Marxist materialist philosophers like Gilles Deleuze. One important reason for this is that issues of structure and change, determinism and contingency, are at the very origins of atomism: Leuccipus and his more famous disciple, Democritus, are said to have devised their atomist doctrine in response to Parmenides' claim that, since something cannot come from nothing, change is ultimately illusory. Thus, the principle of the indivisibility of the atom was a way of asserting an underlying set of ontological laws that allowed for change. However, and this would be the critical basis of Aristotle's advocacy of a continuum rather than of point-like atoms, atomistic change is essentially an epiphenomenon built upon the unchanging nature of the atoms themselves. If the colliding of atoms led to new configurations of material reality, and if those configurations displayed ordered patterns because of an attraction between 'like' atoms, as Democritus claimed, there was nonetheless a fundamental stasis or continuity at the atomic level. Clearly, this aspect of ancient Greek atomism does not suit Badiou's purposes: change, although it can be said to happen, remains a matter of appearances. However, the atomist insistence on the positive existence of the void, as the empty space which makes motion possible, strikes an ontological chord with Badiou that will chime throughout his later use of set theory, in which the void becomes a fundamental category.

In *Theory of the Subject*, however, Badiou attempts to conceptualise the birth of novelty through the relation of non-relation between the Democritean concepts of the atom and the void on the one hand, and a version of the Lucretian 'clinamen' on the other. In Epicurean physics generally, 'clinamen' refers to the tiniest deviation from the absolute of a straight line, and thus the undecidable origin of a curvature. In Democritus' atomistic cosmology, the clinamen can be thought of as the veering off of an atom into the non-space of the void surrounding it, and thus the prerequisite for the clashing of atoms from which change arises. For Badiou, however, what matters is that, like the evanescent term, the clinamen is its own disappearance: it has no place, no moment. It is the flash of novelty that immediately fades. It is neither an atom nor a void, nor, crucially, the causal action of one upon the other. "The clinamen is the atom *qua* outplace of the void [...] the clinamen is subject, or more exactly subjectivation, [it] is a-specific, beyond necessity, absolutely out-of-place, unsplaceable, unfigurable: chance" (*TS*, 59). It is for this reason that Badiou insists that "*it is of the utmost importance that the clinamen in turn be abolished*" (*TS*, p.61). This is surely a version of the 'withering away of the state', the self-dissolution of the proletariat, and the evanescence of the masses, all of which indicate that Badiou is now emphasizing a comprehensive, self-reflexive destruction as a *relation of non-relation*, i.e., as a break that has to be a break *with* a past (relation), but one that simultaneously erases all the relations linking its violent act with that past (non-relation). Thus, the clinamen curves away from the rigid line of splaced identity, but this curve itself must be deleted, since it points back to what is not, by that very fact, utterly overcome. Even if the clinamen appears to act like the vector that knocks an atom off its linear trajectory and allows it to spin off into previously unknown and unknowable 'worlds', it must not act as a bridge linking the wayward atom back to its previous incarnation. In this sense, we come back to the unreconstructed notion of (political) deviation discussed earlier: just as the deviating course of the clinamen threatens to drag an atom back into its old orbit, so "the existence of deviance conditions the very existence of a combinatory" (*TS*, 61), this last term invariably denoting structural closure in Badiou's lexicon.

THE 'POST-MAOIST' DIALECTIC

So what remains of the Marxist dialectic after these baroque forays into Lacanian topology and ancient Greek atomism? At first glance, not much. Almost all of its defining traits seem to be systematically stripped away in *Theory of the Subject*, even as it insists on the 'black sheep' of dialectical materialism. Among the casualties are: the centrality of class contradiction, the economic determination of the proletariat, the scientific status of the Marxist analytic itself, the world-historical connection between revolutions, and the optimism of an emancipatory teleology of history.

Insofar as class contradiction pits sociologically 'placed' entities against one another, it does not deserve the name 'dialectical'. The properly dialectical antagonism between proletariat and bourgeoisie now takes the form of a non-relation rather than a fixed, adversarial opposition. Without general laws of social evolution driven by the economic last instance, Althusser's vision of a scientific Marxism that can pierce the veil of ideology collapses (Marxist *sociology* becomes an oxymoron). Badiou sunders the umbilical connection between politics and the economy partly to reject Althusser's own problematic critique of the humanist subject as a bourgeois fiction, so that a *political* subject can be recovered: the economy can never produce this kind of subject for Badiou. The world-historical dimension of the Marxist dialectic is also heavily reconceptualised in *Theory of the Subject*, arguably beyond recognition. Against the progressive gathering of an historical absolute, Badiou simply declares that "History does not exist" (*TS*, p.92). He replaces the Hegelian teleology of an unfolding human and spiritual destiny by a series of discontinuous explosions of mass revolt that subside as quickly as they appear. If there remains any link at all between, say, the Paris Commune and October 1917, it is certainly not of the order of historical causality. Rather, it is the retroactive conjuncture of two moments of rupture in a single sequence on the basis of a common logic or 'communist invariant': Lenin's jubilant dance in the snow outside the Kremlin when his revolution outlasted that of the Communards shows that "It is the rupture of October that periodizes the Paris Commune, turning a page of the history of the world" (*TS*, 20), not the other way around (see Chapter 5 on this concept of 'periodisation'). The Marxist dialectic understood as the philosophy of the rationality of historical evolution is discarded by Badiou then, in preference for an intense and atemporal *singularity*. If, in a profound sense, *Theory of the Subject* already implies that any relational understanding of the dialectic must now be situated on the side of placement, and thus on the side of conservatism, it also already poses the difficult question of whether one can really speak of a *non-relational* dialectic without committing a sophism?

Holding this crucial question in abeyance for the moment, it is important to point out that certain elements of the dialectic do survive the conceptual purge enacted in *Theory of the Subject*. Revolt remains the catalyst for qualitative social transformation. Negativity, in the form of scission, still guarantees the occurrence and necessity of revolt. Revolt still has a logic that can and must be formalised. The bourgeois world continues to set itself against the concentration of subjective force that revolt requires. The proletariat are still the harbingers of a society without class divisions. And faithful to the Marx of the *1844 Manuscripts*, it remains the undifferentiated, generic nature of the proletariat, having nothing to lose but its chains, which gives it its universal relevance and revolutionary power. Furthermore, in contrast to the post-Marxism associated with Laclau, Mouffe, Touraine and Gorz which also dethrones the primacy of economics, Badiou does not conclude that the category of the worker can fall into disuse or be rendered 'immaterial' without serious political consequences. *Theory of the Subject* already proposes extending the category of the worker to the illegal migrant worker in France in order to reinstate the factory as a site of politics, something which would drive Badiou's activism for decades to come. In general then—the twofold ontological assertion at the core of the Marxist philosophy of dialectics, that conflict and contradiction are inherent to all things, and that fixed identities are a transient effect of appearances, persist in *Theory of the Subject*.

A different and much bigger question is the fate of the dialectic in Badiou's work after *Theory of the Subject*, particularly given his asserted break with Marxism-Leninism-Maoism soon after. Just three years after the publication of *Theory of the Subject*, Badiou admits, in *Peut-on penser la politique?*, that "it is not an exaggeration to say that Marxism is historically defeated" (*PP*, p.48). Three years later again, he refers in the opening to *Being and Event* to the "absolute weakness [...] of the 'old Marxism', of dialectical materialism" which, in its Engels-inspired conflation with the dialectic of nature, "was, of course, still-born" (*BE*, p.4). In *Metapolitics*, he will follow his old comrade from the Yenan days, Sylvain Lazarus, in condemning the historicism implicit in the dialectics of the social sciences (*M*, p.43), and warn against regressing "to the logic of the dialectical result, to the dialectic of synthesis and the idea that the truth of a political sequence is embodied in its future" (*M*, p.126).

And yet these are never outright dismissals. In the same *Peut-on penser la politique?* in which Marxism is deemed historically defeated, Badiou finds dialectical optimism precisely in the abjection of this defeat, namely, a 'figure of re-commencement' (*PP*, p. 56) which can revitalize Marxism by breaking with the historical dialectic and insisting, instead, not on the 'there has been', or 'will be', let alone 'could be' of a revolution, but on the axiomatic 'there is' of an event. Short but transitional, *Peut-on penser la politique?* also offers a genealogy of the dialectic (*PP*, pp.84-91) in which Badiou is quite happy to locate his own new concepts of event, structure, intervention and fidelity so long as this dialectic is subtracted from notions of 'totality' and the 'labour of the negative' (*PP*, p.84). The hole that truth bores into systems of knowledge is still called dialectical (*PP*, p.89), as is anything that ruptures the order of representation (*PP*, p.90).

While *Being and Event* seems to represent the most sustained challenge to dialectical thinking, even there historical situations are defined by the inclusion of a site and thus by what a dialectician might call 'immanent contradiction'. The relation between this site and its situation is explicitly described as a 'dialectic', and the fact that this relates to the role of the 'state' of a situation clearly invokes Leninist-Maoist themes of the political State. The notion of forcing, too, formalised with reference to Paul Cohen, bears a family resemblance to a dialectical movement insofar as it 'sublates' a negative (the indiscernible multiple revealed by a truth) into a positive (an object of veridical knowledge) in a new synthesis that emerges from this determinate negation (a transformed encyclopaedia). This is why Badiou refers to "the subtle dialectic of knowledges and post-evental fidelities" and the "knowledge/truth dialectic" (*BE*, p.331).

By *Logics of Worlds*, Badiou is closer than ever to dialectical questions. Polemically opposing his own approach to what he calls 'democratic materialism'—which is to say to an unchanging world in which there are only bodies and languages, and freedom is defined negatively as the right to persist in one's banality—he privileges 'dialectical materialism'. Materialism here refers to his new emphasis on being-there or the logic of appearance of worlds, while dialectical refers to the subject's incorporation in a truth procedure that turns that logic upside-down. The possibility of truth (change) is therefore the fundamental difference between 'democratic' and 'dialectical' materialism. The new materialism in *Logics of Worlds* necessarily broaches traditionally dialectical territory. For instance, relationality is fundamentally constitutive of appearance insofar as the identity of a given multiple is transcendentally measured against at least one other multiple: being-there means being localized, a being-among-others. However, and reflecting his old worries about incorporation into a *structural* dialectic, he is careful to point out that a relation "creates neither existence nor difference" (*LW*, p.310), "[I]t does not transform the transcendental evaluations; it presupposes them" (*LW*, p.311) and therefore "[a] relation in appearing largely conserves the entire atomic logic of objects" (*LW*, p.312). This fends off two traps: one orthodox Marxist, the other Deleuzian. Orthodox Marxism of course privileges one relation in particular, that of class, while Deleuzian vitalism suggests that relation itself immanently generates change in the form of becoming (hence Badiou devoting a whole section of *Logics of Worlds* to his differences with Deleuze—see Section 2 of Book V).

In summary, I believe it is possible to claim that the dialectic, and a certain Maoist emphasis on the distinction between antagonistic and non-antagonistic conflicts, does persist in Badiou's later work, but that the labour of separation between an idealist, structuralist, economistic or even vitalist dialectic on the one hand, and a materialist, anti-structural, economically informed but not determined and subtractive dialectic on the other, continues. It continues primarily in the form of a shifting of the dialectic away from ontology or being, and towards the event. This necessitates very subtle conceptual distinctions between, say, the 'void', the 'site' or the 'inexistent', which all have a certain prima facie structuralism about them, and 'intervention', 'naming' or the 'trace', which are dependent on the disruption of an event.

2

Organising Radical Novelty

The previous chapter focussed on challenges to the materialist dialectic posed by Badiou's development, in the 1970s and early 1980s, of scissional as opposed to reciprocal difference, and of singular 'force' as opposed to relational 'place'. In this chapter, I want to focus on the political sequences of conflict already motivating these theoretical developments (we saw the importance of May '68 in this regard in the last chapter), as well as their seminal role in his subsequent philosophy of the event.

However, it is vital to point out that Badiou does not simply *interpret* these historical sequences through his philosophy, as Hegel notoriously did especially in relation to Africa (Hegel: 2006). Nor is it that he *illustrates* his philosophy through its retrospective application to them. To understand the decisive role of these sequences in Badiou's evolving work, one must keep in mind his early Maoist theory of dialectical knowledge: it is by consistently *subordinating* his conceptual framework to the logic of certain conflicts that he turns thought—his own, but also in general—into a mode of praxis engaged with real transformation (rather than with the solipsistic navel-gazing of which institutionalised philosophy is often accused).

We can discern a striking paradox here. Just as Badiou seems to be abandoning the dialectic in the mid-1980s, he could equally be said to be prioritising it. For at the very moment he turns to the notion of the event in order to break with the dialectic as a philosophy of *history*, he begins to formulate the key concept of 'conditioning' as a means of thinking the implications of innovative sequences. Conditioning refers to the imperative imposed upon philosophy by novelties outside its domain to gather together, or 'compossibilise', the truths obscured within them. As Jean Luc Nancy has pointed out, this concept has the advantage "of preventing philosophy from being understood or understanding itself as the subsumption of the diversity of experiences beneath a truth which would determine a single ultimate stake for them" (Hallward: 2004, p.40). Regarding Marxist philosophy, this single ultimate stake has been Historical: by contrast, conditioning refuses any synthetic dialectic that would sublate irruptions of 'politics' into an historical teleology. And yet, conditioning also reintroduces a relation between thought and historicity that can be described as dialectical to the extent that it is predicated both upon the material emergence of scissional difference and the conceptual discipline required to formalise its implications. Thus, philosophy itself comes to be defined through its subordination to novelties external to its habitual terrain:

> The conditioning of a great philosophy, at the furthest reaches of instituted and consolidated knowledge, is carried out by the crises, breakthroughs and paradoxes of mathematics, the quaking of poetic language, the revolutions and provocations of inventive politics, the wavering of the relation between the two sexes (*MP*, p. 38)

Oliver Feltham has referred to this move as a multiplication rather than a refutation of Maoism (Feltham: 2008, p.85). There certainly seems to be a trajectory within Badiou's development that fits with his former Maoist commitment to sharpening theory against the grindstone of practice in order to engage it in struggle, despite simultaneously shedding the triumvirate 'Marxism-Leninism-Maoism' precisely because it had, by the early 1980s, become blunt and unwieldy. First then, Badiou breaks the rusty chains of an ossified Marxist dialectic by mortgaging his own philosophy to extra-philosophical and, as we shall see, extra-historical sequences of conflict. Then he formalises this process *within* his philosophy with the concept of 'conditioning'. And finally, he re-founds the entire philosophical project on its basis so that philosophy can participate in the concentration of truths, even if it can no longer claim to produce any of its own.

'Conditioning', then, can be interpreted both as a version of the Maoist primacy of practice over theory, and as a Platonic injunction to get out of the cave and stop philosophising about mere shadows. Conditioning demands that philosophy position itself in the wake of ruptures not in the all-encompassing field of History but in the four truth-domains of art, science, love and politics. Admittedly, the domain that explicitly conditions Badiou's own philosophy by *Being and Event* is that of mathematics (science). Yet it is my risky hypothesis here that we should flirt with what Badiou calls 'disaster' by, if not prioritising the political, then at least exploring its contamination of even the rarefied abstractions of mathematics without, nevertheless, sacrificing the latter's specificity. Badiou himself effectively invites such a reading. For example, reflecting on his very first philosophical text, *The Concept of Model*, he admits that the appeal of mathematics at that time had been purely Althusserian: mathematics represented the model for a scientific knowledge that does not require transcendental or phenomenological grounding in a knowing subject.[1] Many years later, after Badiou had renounced his Althusserianism in defence of the subject, it is made very clear that the new philosophy of number elaborated in *Number and Numbers* is conceived not as either a purely mathematical or purely philosophical exercise, but as a political antidote to the 'cold calculation' that Marx and Engels ascribed to capitalism in the *Manifesto*. Paul Cohen's demonstration of the existence of generic sets in the 1960s not only transformed mathematics by 'resolving' the continuum hypothesis: in Badiou's hands, it becomes the ontological matrix underpinning a politics of axiomatic equality. By *Logics of*

---

1. Something Badiou's own student, Quentin Meillassoux, has pitted against a similar 'correlationist', primarily Kantian tradition, in his slim yet powerful *After Finitude* (2008).

Worlds, set-theory may have been largely replaced by category theory and topology, yet both are still marshalled in the service of a formal demonstration of the ever-present possibility of transformation. To this extent, one could argue that the mathematical event that explicitly conditions *Being and Event* (Cantor's set-theory and its axiomatization by Zermelo-Fraenkel) is itself recursively conditioned by Badiou's own Maoist trajectory, and its consequent openness to, primarily, political conditions.

All of which is a rather laborious attempt to justify my focus in this chapter on sequences of political rather than scientific, artistic or amorous innovation analysed by Badiou, specifically: the French Revolution, the Paris Commune, Stalinism and National Socialism, the Chinese Cultural Revolution, and May '68. It is from these profound upheavals that Badiou draws lessons inextricably linked to his philosophy of the event. Having detailed Badiou's interventions into these sequences, I will close this chapter by examining how the theory of conflict extrapolated from them has been put to work in Badiou's own activism with the *Organisation politique* group. As the group's name indicates, perhaps the most important implication to be distilled from these conflicts is the enigmatic homology between militant political subjectivity, and the problem of organisation. As Badiou moves away from the Leninist and then Maoist model of the party, a crucial question starts to loom large: how can truly radical novelty be *organised*? The absence of a satisfactory answer to this question may be the only guarantee of the singularity of politics, but it surely begs another: what is the relationship between politics and the State in the post-party era?

THE FRENCH REVOLUTION

The fraught and oscillating historiography of the French Revolution immediately demonstrates the value of Badiou's endeavour to break with history as the final tribunal of politics. There are two distinct but related trends, both problematic from Badiou's point of view: one 'revisionist', the other blindly Marxist and therefore mechanistically dialectical.

One could argue that the 'revisionist' strand begins with contemporaneous denunciations such as Edmund Burke's *Reflections on the Revolution in France* of 1790, in which the violent disdain for tradition characterising the revolution from its inception was condemned prior even to the regicide and the Great Terror. Understandable though such moral tirades are, however, for Badiou (and indeed for Burke's republican peers such as Thomas Paine and Mary Wollstonecraft) they fail to think the political truth carried by the tumultuous decade in France between 1789 and 1799. In fact, 'revisionism' proper is more than mere reactionary moral judgement in the heat of the moment. It involves cool and calculated historical reworking of the origins of conflicts with the benefit of hindsight. Thus, revisionist accounts offered in the Twentieth Century by the likes of Alfred Cobban, François Furet, George Taylor and more recently Simon Schama nullify precisely what was *true* about the French Revolution by reducing it to the particularities from which it emerged: the financial crisis of the monarchy, a series of poor harvests, the calling of the Estates General, Enlightenment utopianism and so on. And in this strategy of causal reductionism, the 'revisionists' and the Marxists reciprocally constitute one another (as the Marxist genealogy of the very term 'revisionist' suggests).

The canonical Marx-inspired account is Georges Lefebvre's *Quatre-Vingt-Neuf* written in 1939, and somewhat belatedly translated into English by Robert R. Palmer in 1947 as *The Coming of the French Revolution*. The position Lefebvre outlined there was ably defended right into the late 1970s by his successor as Professor of the History of the French Revolution at the Sorbonne, Albert Soboul. Both Lefebvre and Soboul argued that the French Revolution was a class struggle in the orthodox Marxist mould, driven by the rise of the bourgeoisie. The latter's confrontation with the feudal privileges enjoyed by the nobility and then with Louis XVI himself was, at bottom, a lurch towards a new mode of production, capitalism. The French Revolution was thus the bloodiest yet most vivid demonstration of historical materialism at work. But the extreme danger, for Badiou, of this mechanistically dialectical approach is two-fold. Firstly, it reduces what is truly novel to the mere unfolding of immanent social contradictions: nothing *radically* new takes place, only the epiphenomenal irruption of a contradiction that was already there. Secondly, this dialectical approach cannot isolate from the infinite mélange of jumbled incidents the essential truth animating the apparent chaos, since it imposes a teleological destiny that ends with the 'order' of the Napoleonic Empire (see Sutherland 1985 and 2003). This is what lies behind Badiou's righteous indignation at the following claim by Soboul: "The 9 Thermidor doesn't mark a break [*coupure*], but an acceleration" (*M*, p.138). This is clearly a choice for the dialectic rather than the event, and its implications are profound. The notion that Thermidor was an *intensification* of Jacobin subjectivity rather than a reactionary betrayal of it, plays directly into the hands of those who would conflate Virtue and Terror, and condemn all revolutions as pathological violence. In this sense, Soboul's 'radical' (which here means resolutely class-based) Marxist interpretation of the French Revolution locates its failings squarely in its bourgeois character, and yet his reading is an organic outgrowth of Thermidorean reaction itself. Any dialectic of necessity both drains history of contingency and absorbs revolution into evolution.

The bulk of revisionist responses to Lefebvre's and Soboul's dialectical account have problematised each link in the Marxist triad of economics, class struggle and revolution. With regard to the economic, George V. Taylor, for example, argues that the wealth of the bourgeois protagonists of the Revolution was in fact predominantly 'proprietary', not commercial or industrial (Taylor: 1964). In terms of class, Alfred Cobban (1967) claims that, since land and inheritance remained the form of middle-class wealth, the bourgeoisie and the nobility were effectively a single economic entity, not a social contradiction at all. Debunking the notion of revolution itself, at least understood as driven by changes in the mode of production, Michel Morineau (1970) sees no evidence of decisive economic modernization in France until as late as the mid-Nineteenth Century.[2] D. G. M. Sutherland has further argued that the truly popular uprisings of the period were led by rural peasants *against* the revolution (Sutherland: 2003). If the kind of industrial capitalism that

---

2. This brief take on the complex currents of revisionism is glossed from William Doyle's excellent *Origins of the French Revolution* (Oxford University Press: Oxford, 1999).

for Marx drives proletarianization and thus history was absent, if the class identity of bourgeoisie and nobility was blurred to the point of indistinction, and if *les peuples* were substantially opposed to the revolution at least in the provinces, what remains of the Lefebvre-Soboul thesis? Yet these 'revisionist' readings share a guiding assumption with their Marxist rivals, namely, that the origins of the French Revolution are to be found in *social* contradictions, and that historiography must proceed sociologically to arrive at causal explanations. The terrain of the socioeconomic, and thus a very crude materialism, provided the common battleground for these opposing views.

The idealistic alternative—that the French Revolution was ultimately not a social revolution but a revolution in political philosophy, one driven by the ferment of Enlightenment ideas, particularly those of Jean-Jacques Rousseau—has certainly had its proponents, notably Daniel Mornet and Roger Chatrier.[3] In fact, Lefebvre himself is happy to acknowledge the influence of Enlightenment philosophy, but only if defined as the operative ideology of the ascendant bourgeoisie (see, for example, his chapter on 'European Thought' in *The French Revolution*). In another significant overlap between supposedly rival camps, François Furet's *Penser la Révolution française* of 1987 combined an idealistic emphasis on cultural factors with a thesis of thoroughgoing continuity. Far from a disastrous derailing of a 'good' revolution at the hands of the 'bad' Jacobin faction, Furet now claimed that the Terror lay like an incubus coiled from the outset within the Idea of equality itself, so that the whole revolutionary sequence was disastrous from start to finish. Despite Badiou's criticisms of the mechanistic 'materialism' of Lefebvre and Soboul, he is even less enamoured of Furet's post-revisionist idealism, in which the Idea itself is shown to be structurally tyrannical, and from which we are invited to draw the conclusion today that it is safer to live passively *without* ideas.

There is a direct precedent for Furet's position in Hegel's critique of the French Revolution in his *Lectures on the Philosophy of World History* and the *Phenomenology*. Broadly, Hegel's critique is that the 'glorious mental dawn' of the Revolution sank into the dark night of the Terror because absolute freedom came to attain the tyranny of a pure will abstracted from the particularities of the world. That is, the Revolution tried to go too fast, bypassing the necessary passage of the universal through sensuous particularity. Although it unleashed the power of the Idea, the Revolution also deformed it into a conceptual absolutism that encountered the given only as an obstacle to be exterminated. In Kant's terminology, then, we could say that the revolution was a 'paralogism of reason': a despotic purity internal to rationality itself when left unmediated. We therefore find in Hegel's response to the French Revolution an early critique of totalitarianism that has become reformulated, in our own time via Françoise Furet, Stéphane Courtois and others, as a warning against thinking in general.

---

3. In fact, Chatrier's case is more complicated. In *The Cultural Origins of the French Revolution* (1991), he makes an important distinction between cultural shifts towards print-based intellectual exchange, the related emergence of a public sphere, secularization and the concomitant 'desacralization' of the monarchy on the one hand, and on the other, the very material conditions of possibility that enable such cultural shifts to spark into outright revolution.

Ultimately, what unites both 'materialist' and idealist' accounts of the French Revolution is an epistemology of origins in which truth is conflated with causes and with the destinies they supposedly assure. Badiou's task since the early 1980s, when revolutionary history had been successfully branded by the *nouveaux philosophes* as one of shame and failure, has therefore been to set aside this obsession with origins, causality and destiny, without, however, allowing historiography to lapse into some kind of postmodern ludic game devoid of referential grounding. Hence the inestimable value of the concept of the event. For the event is both a total *coupure* with causal explanation (it is profoundly undecideable) and a *material* irruption (it is a glimpse of the generic multiplicity of Being itself) without which no Idea can get underway (Idea in the Platonic sense of a concrete participation in truth, rather than in the Kantian sense of a regulative but ultimately normative horizon). Only asserting the French Revolution as an event of this kind enables one to suspend the vexed question of origins in order to distil from its chaos, blood and apparent defeat a political truth that still resonates today.

It is striking that the very sequence usually condemned as either the hijacking or perverse inner essence of the revolution is the one that Badiou upholds as *the* scene of its universal truth: namely, the frenetic sequence from 1792 to 1794, a revolution within a revolution, which can be summarised by the charged monika 'Jacobin'. According to Badiou, it is the fidelity of the Jacobin mode of subjectivity that forces the truth of the Revolution onto the inequities of the *ancien régime*, rather than, as is generally assumed by the History of Ideas, the abstract universalism of the *Declaration of the Rights of Man and Citizen*. The latter merely snythesised egalitarian principles which had been circulating for some time, along with the rhetoric and practical example of the preceding American Revolution: the Jacobins, by contrast, were the subjective vector transmitting the *Declaration's* potential implications throughout the *ancien régime*. The mode of articulation of the *Declaration* might have been abstractly axiomatic—'all men are born equal' and so on—but it was the concrete subjective *prescription and circulation* of this axiomatic in a complex topology of competing interests that concentrated its transformative power. Topology has become an important resource for Badiou precisely as he has begun to analyse the localised deployment in unevenly structured worlds of what Žižek, following Hegel, calls 'concrete' or 'singular' universality (see Žižek: 2000). This kind of universality does not apply seamlessly to all elements of a situation without troubling the hierarchical and exclusionary structuring of this 'all'. In the case of the French Revolution, the topology of which was immensely complex (the clubs, the Bastille, the streets, the King's tennis court, the rural regions, the movements of the Prussian army etc.), it was only the Third Estate's *localised* self-nomination as the embodiment of the entire nation, or rather of *les peuples*, that enabled the expansion of egalitarianism beyond the bourgeois boundaries in which it had been conceived. This extension would stretch all the way to the 'black Jacobins', as C. L. R. James described them (2001), of San Domingo, modern-day Haiti. A key lesson for Badiou, then, is this: only a militant form of subjectivity has the courage and fortitude to inscribe, locally but also expansively, a universal truth *into* its situation, to move from abstract declaration to concrete topological inscription.

A second crucial insight is that it falls to such a subject to ensure, invariably with some measure of violence, the *persistence* of this fragile self-constituting sovereignty. The Jacobins (and Mao would learn from their example) managed to think the immanent rationality of their *political* use of violence through the complex relation between Virtue and Terror, whose most articulate advocates were Saint-Just and Robespierre. Contrary to the conflation of these two terms, which I have tried to show is the common denominator between dialectical readings such as Hegel's, Lefebvre's and Soboul's on the one hand and Furet's motivated idealism on the other, the Virtue-Terror relation is neither identical nor reciprocally constituted. To Robespierre's infamous maxim—"virtue, without which terror is fatal; terror, without which virtue is powerless"—a third term needs to be added in order to displace the implied binarism: namely, corruption, which is the true 'opposite' of virtue. In Badiou's lexicon, 'corruption' would signal something like the appropriation of an event by worldly agendas. Virtue, as a singular, self-positing and ultimately generic sovereignty can only protect itself from the counter-revolution through a constant purging of those who would corrupt it by relegating it to competing interests. Terror is not the inherent *truth* of Virtue, then, its inner destiny or rigid telos, but the means by which, in a world hostile to it, it is enabled to pursue the implications of the truth it does carry. The Jacobins themselves phrased the Terror not as an internal logic of the revolution, but in terms of the pressing *external* exigencies of foreign wars and counter-revolutionary agitation (often presumed to have been bankrolled by the English).

Conservative narratives characterise Thermidor, inaugurated by the guillotining of the 'Incorruptible' Robespierre on the 28th of July 1794, as the end of the Terror. Badiou, however, sees it differently. Thermidor is "not so much a question of ending the terror exerted over adversaries as of bringing about a radical shift in the source and target of that terror" (*M*, p.126). In the summer of 1794, the source of terror becomes the State with a renewed monopoly over the means of violence. The target becomes insurrectionary expressions of direct popular democracy. As Badiou points out "The Directory will pursue this path right up to the—truly momentous—decision to sentence to death anyone daring to invoke the Constitution of 1793!" (*ibid.*). This shift in the control of violence is enabled by a corollary shift towards *qualified* rather than generic citizenship, with financial and cultural capital determining fitness to rule in just the way that Robespierre had railed against. Thus, Badiou deems Boissy d'Anglas to be the quintessential Thermidorean insofar as he demanded government "by the best" but connected the 'best' to "those, who, owning property, are bound to the country in which it lies, to the laws that protect it, to the peace that preserves it" (quoted in *M*, p.128). This logical chain, property-law-peace, transforms the pillars of the revolution: 'France' ceases to be a name for a generic collective and becomes the mere locus of property; the law ceases to express the general will and takes on a protective function in relation to property; and the natural right to revolt against despotism and injustice so central to Jacobinism is perverted into a 'breach of the peace' required, once again, to protect property. The Thermidorean personifies corruption in Saint-Just's sense because he exploits the fragility of virtue by bending its course towards his own interested ends. There is a quite predictable Machiavellian dimension to this.[4] Yet Badiou's more philosophical point is that the deeper goal of Thermidorean subjectivity, during the French Revolution but crucially also today, is to render *virtue unthinkable*. Divorced from interests, indifferent to property, apparently committed to terror for its own sake, virtue simply cannot make sense to the propertied bourgeoisie. In particular, the 'disarticulation' of virtue and terror, or the collapse of the one into the other (it amounts to the same thing), condemns every recourse to the concept of virtue in advance.

A very important way of recovering the truth of the French Revolution from its Thermidorean reaction, and thus to think the thought that it already was, is to analyse the ways in which its name evades Statist capture. I will be saying more about the complex question of political nomination in the next chapter, but suffice it to say here that another key insight Badiou gleans from his interpretation of the French Revolution is that the very term 'revolution' crystallizes the sequence it names. It is not ultimately a sociological categorization that refers back to thick descriptions of an assumed totality "such as 'French society in 1792' or 'the politics of the ascendant bourgeoisie'" (*M*, p.30). It is the name in its stubborn singularity that levers the event away from the old situation, yet circulates its effects within it. In *Being and Event*, this self-constituent property of events is given a detailed formal demonstration: the multiples revealed by events are the only ones that breach the so-called 'axiom of foundation' by presenting themselves. The name, which is drawn from the edge of the void, remains enigmatic for the encyclopaedia of a situation, yet it also forces its own existence on that same situation. And it is this name, 'revolution', which needs to be resurrected today if our contemporary Thermidoreans are not to snuff out all hope for significant change.

THE PARIS COMMUNE

If the French Revolution demonstrates for Badiou both the need for axiomatic equality to find local inscription through a militant subject and the inevitability of a Thermidorian reaction intent upon turning truth to worldly profit, then the Paris Commune of 1871 demonstrates two additional dimensions of political innovation: its necessary distance from the State, and its inversion of an extant 'regime of appearance'.

Before we can arrive at these conclusions, however, it is once again necessary to subtract the Paris Commune from the historiography to which it has been subjected. This is the case not only for the predictably reactionary accounts, but also for the 'radical' interpretations offered by Marx, Lenin and Mao. As we shall see, displacing such 'radical' accounts is essential if we are to avoid the neutralization of a political truth—contemporaneously in the form of cooptation, but also subsequently in the form of ritual commemoration—by what Badiou pejoratively labels the 'Left'. By this he is referring to those groups that present themselves as the

---

4. I will be returning in Chapter 6 to the obstacle that 'interests' in the colonies, precisely in the form of property, i.e. slaves, presented to the abolition of slavery even in the midst of this supposedly universal revolution.

legitimate, rational dimension of popular struggles whose (self-declared) role is to articulate the people's demands in the language of the State. This is especially problematic in the particular case of the Commune, whose force, argues Badiou, was precisely *anti*-Statist. The ambivalence of the 'Left' with regard to the State has deep roots that stretch all the way back to Marx's penetrating and timely analysis of the Commune, written just four days after its bloody denouement, in *Civil War in France*.[5] Before looking at Marx's analysis, however, it is worth glossing the basic narrative of the Paris Commune, not least because Badiou has noted that it is disappearing from the school history curriculum even in France (*HC*, p.137).

In July of 1870 Louis-Napoleon Bonaparte rashly declared war on Bismark's Prussia. Following a series of grave military defeats, the people of Paris were armed and mobilized into the National Guard, a citizen militia, in preparation for protecting the capital from the advancing Prussians. However, the utter defeat of the French national army and the capture of Louis-Napoleon himself on the 4th of September 1870 at the battle of Sedan led to the end of the Second Empire, and the declaration of the Third Republic. The Republic's so-called Government of National Defence, itself formed under siege conditions, was led first by Louis Joules Trochu and then by Adolphe Thiers whom Marx referred to as "that monstrous gnome" (Marx: 1971, p.74). Blanquists, neo-Jacobins and other socialists as well as patriots of all political leanings quickly interpreted Thiers' government as capitulationist. For Marx, this willingness to cooperate with Bismark stemmed from the new government's bourgeois character. Capitulation to the Prussians was motivated not by mere defeatism but by the perceived benefits of a class-alliance against the real internal enemy, namely, agitating workers in Paris.[6] This was confirmed by the armistice of 28th January 1871, which exposed Thiers' government as one of national betrayal rather than defence: Marx punningly called it a "Government of National Defection" (Marx: 1971, p.72). Patriotic Parisians immediately conceived of taking up their newfound arms not, or not only, against the German troops poised just to the north and the east of their city, but also against their own treacherous leaders.

Recognising that the elements of a civil war were already in place, Thiers attempted to disarm the uppity Parisians on the 18th of March 1870 by relieving them of the four hundred or so cannons set up at various vantage points around the city. But as the Commune's most colourful historian, Lissagaray, put it "[t]he execution was as foolish as the conception" (Lissagaray: 1976, p.64). National troops embarked at 3am. Encountering barely any resistance from the National Guard (sleeping like everyone else), they quickly surrounded and secured the

---

5. Marx kept up a correspondence with several active communards, and the International was indirectly influential within the Commune itself. However, it is interesting to note that he also deliberately refused to make a public offer of solidarity with the Commune while it survived for reasons which remain unclear. As early as the 6th of April, however, it *is* clear that Marx felt the Commune had missed its military opportunity to destroy the Versailles government.

6. Marx claims that Jules Favre, the Foreign Minister of the Government of National Defence, in a letter to Léon Gambetta, the-then Minister of the Interior, had explicitly avowed "that what they were 'defending' against were not the Prussian soldiers, but the working men of Paris" (Marx: 1971, pp. 73-4).

cannons. However, it was several hours before they managed to couple them to the horses needed to actually remove them from the city. By the time they had, it was approaching 8am and Paris was waking up. Spontaneous resistance by ordinary people, led in particular by women, and then backed up by the National Guard, prevented the canons being taken. This was helped by national troops, demoralised by recent defeats and by their own government's surrender, fraternizing with the Parisians: they refused to follow their commanding officer, General Lecomte's orders to shoot into the gathering crowds, and instead arrested him. Having safeguarded their weapons, the central committee of the National Guard then occupied the Hôtel de Ville as its headquarters. The inauguration of the Commune was formally declared from there on March the 28th, but in reality it had begun with the spontaneous resistance of the Parisian people on the 18th. However, it was also on that first evening, when this committee had been discussing how to replace their mandate to defend the city with one to autonomously govern it, that the leaders of Thiers' national government had been inadvertently allowed to flee to Versailles—a mistake Lenin in particular would diagnose as fateful.

Nonetheless, the following seventy two days of the Commune's existence were marked by unprecedented levels of mass political discussion on the streets, organised elections, the abolition of the standing army, egalitarian social policies on tax, health, education and political terms of office, but above all, by an experiment in direct local political organisation led by the working classes which was to provide the model for the Russian 'soviets' forty six years later. There was even relative security on the streets, at least in the first month or so. As the civil war developed, however, military sorties were made against national troops with primarily disastrous results (Dombrowski's victory at Asnières on the 9th of April was a notable exception). Some of the city's monuments to Empire, such as the Vendôme Column, were ritually destroyed.[7] Republican anti-clericalism meant that Churches were vandalised and priests and nuns victimized. And as the Commune entered April, there was growing fear and violence as it became clear that the strategy to defend Paris was failing. Finally, on the 28th of May, Thiers' troops breached the city's defences and, barricade by barricade, made their way directly to the poorest *arrondissements* of Montmartre and Belleville. During what Lissagaray calls *la semaine sanglante* (Lissagaray: 1976, p.312), they exacted a revenge on the working classes and their revolutionary sympathisers with more indiscriminate violence than anything witnessed even during the Great Terror of 1793-4. Badiou himself, drawing as usual on Lissagaray's estimates, cites the number of dead as around 20,000, with 50, 000 arrested (*HC*, p.143).[8]

As with the French Revolution, then, it is all-too tempting to judge the Commune from the point of view of its ultimate failure. Notwithstanding its simultaneous glorification, this is exactly the tendency in Marxist interpretations. From Marx himself through to Engels, from Lenin and on to Mao (albeit with some important qualifications), the Commune is essentially approached as a cautionary

---

7. Ironically, the photographs showing proud worker's posing in front of their destructive handiwork would later be used to identify communards for summary executions.

8. Tombs puts the number of dead at around 10,000 (1999: p.180).

tale regarding 'what not to do' next time. But as Badiou argues in 'La Commune de Paris: une déclaration politique sur la politique'[9] such readings miss the real import of the Commune because they are all stubbornly 'Statist', which is to say, incapable of measuring its novelty against any yardstick other than the modern nation-state. Precisely what the nature of the Commune's relation to State power was interpreted to be has varied with Marxism's own developments.

It was already ambiguous in Marx's *Civil War in France*. On the one hand, the Commune's strengths are said by Marx to include the militarization of the masses into something resembling a revolutionary army, as well as the laudable internationalism suggested by the prominence of non-French communards. Yet on the other, its weaknesses are said to stem from its lack of executive decision-making power and its failure to prioritise immediate military imperatives over and above longer-term social ideals. In other words, it was both commendably anti-Statist and not State-like enough: it was "the glorious harbinger of a new society" (Marx: 1971, p.118) insofar as it pitted the class of producers against a bourgeois government, and yet its failure, paid in blood, arose from its lack of executive authority and disciplined organisation. After Marx's death, Engels provided a new preface to the 1891 edition of *Civil War in France* in which this ambiguity was intensified. Engels criticized the Blanquists and Proudhonians of the Commune for the incommensurability between their respective ideologies and their executive decisions. Unused to wielding actual power, they failed to turn the State into an instrument for realising their commitment to centralised authority (in the case of the Blanquists) and worker's associations (in the case of the Proudhonians).

This ambiguity in the motif of the State was exponentially increased, however, by Lenin's interpretation in *The State and Revolution* (1992). There, it is quite explicit that the Commune's significance lies less in its novelty, and more in the practical lessons to be drawn from its failure. This focus on failure drives Lenin to elaborate a different slant on the State motif, one whose long shadow would stretch darkly across the Twentieth Century: the Party-State. For Badiou, this Party-State "*realises* the ambiguity of the Marxist assessment of the Paris Commune, giving it a body" (*HC*, p.146). So to the military fragility evidenced in the Commune's terrible demise, Lenin opposes centralised, punitive Party discipline. To the naïve inability to confront let alone destroy the bourgeois State, he opposes the Party-State as the means by which the *dictatorship of the proletariat* is to be facilitated. In *Theory of the Subject*, Badiou remains Leninist on this point: indeed, communism and the dictatorship of the proletariat are said to be "reciprocatable" (*TS*, p.189) because they "are *the same thing* (the subject-process of class politics)" (*TS*, p.282). Yet in the same work he also acknowledges that the "Leninist party is the historical answer to a problem that is wholly inscribed in the State/Revolution contradiction", and that, as such, it "is incommensurable to the tasks of the transition to communism" (*TS*, p.205). Badiou's Maoism makes it clear that the meaning of the 'dictatorship of the proletariat' is vague precisely because it occupies an awkwardly liminal position

---

9. This was originally a lecture in the *Rouge-gorge* series but subsequently formed the basis of the analysis of the Commune in *Logics of Worlds*, and has been reproduced in full in *L'Hypothèse Communiste*.

between anti-statism and Statism, destruction and organisation. If, as Lenin puts it in *State and Revolution*, "[t]he Commune is the first attempt of a proletarian revolution to *smash* the bourgeois state machine; and it is the 'at last discovered' political form by which the smashed machine can and must be *replaced*" (Lenin: 1992, pp.50-51), then it is the 'dictatorship of the proletariat' that cleaves together these divergent tendencies. What Stalin will exploit, however, is the State's monopoly on defining the progress of this transition between smashing and replacement.

In fact, Badiou is not persuaded by Lenin's pragmatic approach in *State and Revolution*.[10] Like Marx's before it, Lenin's reading indulges 'what if' speculations—what if the Communards had marched on Versailles to overthrow the national government straight away? What if they had seized the contents of the gold reserve at the Bank of France? and so on. Badiou sees no truth-value in such speculations whatsoever, precisely because they conceal a Statist preoccupation. Indeed, this stubborn orientation to the State situates the Leninist paradigm within the same conceptual framework as social democracy: their superficial difference resides not in ends, since the State is aimed at in both cases, but only in their proposed means to achieve them, respectively revolutionary insurrection and electoral victory (*HC*, p.146).

If we saw with the French Revolution the tendency of Marxist historiography to miss the implications of a political truth due to blind commitment to the dialectic, here, with the Commune, we see a similar blindness, this time borne of blinkered Statism masquerading as anti-statism. The Commune is thereby "reduced to two parameters: firstly, its *social* determination of the worker, secondly the heroic but defective exercise of *power*" (*HC*, p.147). Against the tremendous weight of this interpretative tradition, Badiou claims that the solution to the putative failure of 1871 proposed by Lenin and taken to extremes by Stalin, the Party-State, actually leads to the very problems that the Commune itself was better able to *think*, if we can only recover that thinking. The 'political declaration on politics' embedded in the bloody glory of the Commune, then, is not a novel relation to the State—be it bourgeois, proletarian, social democratic or otherwise—but rather the discovery of a non-relation, specifically, *a creative search for a non-Statist form of political power*.

As we shall see in a moment, it is Mao and especially the Cultural Revolution that comes closest to putting into practice this otherwise veiled truth of the Commune. Badiou goes so far as to refer to "a Chinese reactivation" (*HC*, p.149), discernible in the celebrations organised in China upon the Commune's centenary in 1971. However, in the official text accompanying these celebrations, Badiou also discerns the residues of the Statist motif. On the one hand, 1871 is calculatedly invoked in order to oppose the Soviet emphasis on the Commune as a cautionary tale justifying iron party discipline. The propagandistic goal is clearly to place China, rather than Russia, as the true heir of the communards. And at this very moment, the Cultural Revolution was attempting to organise proletarian power against the Party-State in an echo of 1871.

---

10. He had already deemed this approach, in *Theory of the Subject*, to be "much less novel" than the undertaking in *What Is To Be Done?* which "entails a silent assessment of the Paris Commune" (*TS*, p.46).

Yet on the other hand, argues Badiou, the very context of this centenary text reminds us that "*commemoration* is also that which prohibits *reactivation*" (*HC*, p.147). This commemorative text simultaneously cites the Leninist diagnosis of the failure of the Commune as originating in the absence of a small, disciplined revolutionary leadership. As Marx was split between anti-statism and Statism, so the Chinese Cultural Revolution would tear itself apart in its vacillations between mass anti-Party violence and Party-led repression. Sure enough, following through on the ambiguities of this text, which in all probability he wrote, Mao would reassert the authority of the Party (and the army) over the radicalism of the workers and the red guards he himself had unleashed. Even within the Chinese Cultural Revolution's invocation of the Commune, therefore, the "articulation of politics and the State remains unchanged in its general conception" (*HC*, p.152), as we shall see in more detail below.

To extricate the anti-Statist truth of the Commune from these Statist Marxist assessments, then, Badiou locates its novelty in the proletarian rupture even with the so-called 'Left', i.e., "the ensemble of parliamentary political personnel that declares itself alone competent to carry the general consequences of a political, popular singular movement" (*HC*, p. 156). In a declaration of the 19th of March 1871, the central committee of the National Guard declared that "the hour has arrived for us to save our situation by taking into our hands the running of public affairs" (quoted in *ibid.*). It is this rupture that encourages Badiou to undertake a simultaneously ontological and logical analysis of the Commune's truth, necessitating the introduction of some of his more technical terms: namely, 'site', 'singularity', 'event' and 'destruction'.

The concept of 'site' is a potential faux ami for readers of *Being and Event*, since it is significantly altered in the transition from that work to *Logics of Worlds*. In the former, the 'evental site' is a structural property of historical situations. In set-theoretical terms, it is "an entirely abnormal multiple [...] such that none of its elements are presented in the situation" (*BE*, p.175), a multiple, that is, 'beneath' which there is apparently nothingness: "it belongs to the situation, whilst what belongs to it in turn does not", or again "[w]ithin this situation, this multiple is, but *that of which* it is multiple is not" (*ibid.*). Occupying the very threshold of consistency then, evental sites are also said to be both "*on the edge of the void*" and "*foundational*" (*ibid.*). The void may invoke threatening inconsistency, and yet as the 'lowest' point of the counting operation that ensures consistency, it is simultaneously its 'ground'. It is when the void is exposed as scandalously foundational that the edifices built atop it falter and disintegrate. As such, the 'evental site' is a necessary though not sufficient condition for evental novelty. To the extent that there are sites, one can anticipate the potential locations of rupture amidst those abnormal, marginal figures—asylum seekers, the *sans papiers*, slum dwellers—that lack coherent predicates beyond the threat they carry of 'incompleting' national, economic, cultural and sometimes ethnic situations. In *Logics of Worlds*, however, a 'site' (the 'evental' part is dropped) is far from being structural or locatable prior to an event. Instead, the 'site' is now that rare existent characterised by *auto-appearance* and enabled by an event. Rather than being indexed by the given 'transcendental regime', the site now "counts itself in the referential field of its own appearance" (*HC*, p.158). This means that the site exists, vividly but briefly and precariously, by producing its own non-relational and therefore entirely exceptional being-there.[11]

According to Badiou, the 18th of March 1871 conforms to this second definition. It occurs in a world, 'France at the end of the Franco-Prussian war of 1870', which is already divided. On the one hand, there is the 'legitimate' government of Thiers, the national army, and also the Prussian forces that recognise them; but on the other, there are the Parisian workers, the national guard, the political clubs, the influence of the International and so on. The 'inexistent' term in this divided world is the worker's capacity for self-governance, which appears to everyone, workers included, only as incomprehensible. But into this world bursts the site of the 18th of March, spontaneously producing its own conditions of appearance and, for the first time, exposing "the worker-being [...] in the space of political and governmental capacity" (*HC*, p.161). As we noted above in relation to the French Revolution, the site breaches the ontological axiom of foundation by belonging only to itself. Its name is not an index of something else, but a catalyst and support of its own being. Thus, Badiou points out that in Lissagaray's seminal history of the Commune, the resonant term '18th of March' composes and participates in the very sequence it designates: formulations such as 'women of 18th of March' and 'people of 18th of March' explore linkages between existing multiples and the exceptional appearance of this site. In this way "'18th of March' comes to appear, under the injunction of being, as an element of the situation which it is" (Badiou: 2009, p.163). Even on the evening of the 18th of March, there remained 'Leftist' tendencies within the committee of the National Guard, i.e., moderates who hesitated before claiming the immediate legitimacy of their 'mandate' to govern. Strictly speaking then, as a site, the 18th of March really begins with the break with this Leftist tendency through the declaration of that day as (already) inaugural.

Now, in both *Being and Event* and *Logics of Worlds*, the site is an ontological concept but in a paradoxical sense. Even in the former, the site registers a limit within ontology as a counting operation: before the enigma of self-belonging, ontology is dumbstruck.[12] By *Logics of Worlds*, the site comes to emphasise the effect of this flash of pure multiplicity or the void upon appearance. Like the evanescent cause in *Theory of the Subject*, it is an ephemeral anomaly whose destiny is to disappear in an instant, just as the remarkable day 'March the 18th' passed in an incandescent moment. However, it is vital to move from an ontological to a logical register here, from Being to being-there, since what really characterises a truth *sequence* is the con-sequences set off by the appearance of an unprecedented possibility—in the case of the Commune, 'working class political organisation'.

To think the logic as opposed to the onto-logic of the Paris Commune, then, Badiou defines it as a 'singularity'. This means, first, that it is not reducible to the

---

11. The complex relation between the purely ontological concept of the evental site and the logical concept of the site is elaborated in *Logics of Worlds* in the section on atomic logic—see Section 3 of *LW*.

12. This does not mean, however, that set-theory does not offer incomparable resources for formalising the 'matheme of the event'. See Meditations 17 and 18 of *Being and Event*.

relational mode of appearance governing the world in which it arises, but secondly and more subtly, that it is nonetheless constrained to appear in *this* world and no
other, and thus to be ascribed a value of existence peculiar to it. The point had already been made in *Being and Event* that the void that emerges from a site with an
event is not trans-situational Being-qua-being or underlying Spinozan substance.[13]
For this reason, a void is always a void *for and of* a particular situation. Singularity,
then, describes the mode of appearance of a site in *its* world, not of pure Being in
general. However, the intensity of this appearance can be weak or strong. A 'site'
can have such a weak value of existence in a world as to barely appear at all, quickly being eclipsed by its incorporation as a 'fact' continuous with the worlding of
that world.

Badiou gives as an example of such a weak fact the final, despairing declaration
of the Commune hurriedly pasted up on the walls of Paris even as the Versailles
army overran the barricades on the 23rd of May 1871. This declaration invokes
the beauty of 'March 18th' and measures the subsequent failings of the Commune
against this sublime point. And yet it simultaneously retains enough confidence in
the Commune's political authority to make demands in the very throes of abject
defeat (dissolution of both the Versailles Assembly and the Commune itself, armistice, the retreat of the army). This declaration is certainly an element of the sequence 'Paris Commune', but what it registers is its moribund decomposition. One
can well imagine that amidst the carnage of *la semaine sanglante*, its absurdity must
have inspired contemptuous laughter among the vengeful soldiers. The 23rd of
May declaration, then, marks the moment at which the singularity of worker-being was swallowed back into the network of quotidian 'facts' that had previously
made its appearance impossible: 'the working class has no aptitude for politics', 'all
they can organise is barbaric violence', and so on. A form of 'I told you so' rhetoric
re-imposes the previous logic of appearance by retrospectively rendering the site
once again impossible. Singularity, by complete contrast to worldly facts, cleaves
to the novel consequences that persist precisely because the impossible *has* happened, thereby shifting forever the co-ordinates of the possible. Thus, what matters for Badiou is not so much the brief ontological intensity of the self-constituting site, but rather, the persistence of the "glorious and uncertain consequences"
(*HC*, p.171) that it enables and whose modes of appearance are invariably singular.

Despite its attempted 'factual' erasure, the Commune for Badiou remains a
strong rather than a weak singularity. It is therefore an event. There are three aspects of the Commune that support this conclusion. Firstly, its protagonists were
completely anonymous. Far from being either career politicians or even professional revolutionaries, they were ordinary working people politicised by the circumstances in which they found themselves. To the official government in Versailles,
accustomed to politics as procedural negotiation among legitimate representatives
(this was, after all, their approach to Bismarck), such anonymity was maddeningly
enigmatic. Yet for Badiou, it indicates an invariant property of truths, namely, that

---

13. For example, in Meditation 16 Badiou refers to "the question of 'what-is-not-being-qua-
being'—with respect to which it would not be prudent to immediately conclude that it is a question of non-being" (*BE*, p.173).

absolutely anyone can participate in them. Secondly and relatedly, the Commune, as founded upon the site of the 18th of March, was an event because it transformed an inexistent of the old situation (working class political organisation) into a maximally intense existent in the new situation which Versailles was forced to confront. Indeed, the paradoxical effect of any event is that "the inexistent of a site exists absolutely" (*HC*, p.173). Thirdly then, this absoluteness endows singularity with infinite or eternal duration. Because of the eventual trace it leaves to posterity, legible in the very blood spilled in the attempt to efface it, the Commune unendingly authorises new beginnings. This can be seen, for example, in the grassroots soviet councils of the Bolshevik revolution, in the Shanghai People's Commune established in the midst of the Chinese Cultural Revolution in 1967, and arguably in the *comité d'action* of the May '68 movement in France.

It is only thanks to the eternal nature of singularity that the anti-Statist truth of the Commune can be extracted from its Statist historiography today. However, it is crucial to note—and I shall be exploring this in more detail in the final chapter—that this possibility is also predicated upon a *destructive* dimension of events. While Badiou is no longer, as in his explicitly Maoist days, flirting with destruction as intrinsically progressive, it is here acknowledged as nonetheless fundamental to permanent change. What is destroyed is not, as in the Leninist model, the bourgeois monopoly on the political apparatuses of State, and subsequently the State itself, but rather the bourgeois logic of *appearance* that had ensured the impossibility of working class political organisation. The "Commune-event [...] certainly did not have as its consequence the destruction of the dominant group and its politicians; but it destroyed something much more important: the political subordination of the workers and the people" (*HC*, p.175). What was destroyed was "of the order of subjective incapacity" (*ibid.*). Following the Commune, it could never again be claimed that the working classes have no capacity for autonomous political mobilisation.

THE BOLSHEVIK REVOLUTION, STALINIST 'DISASTER' AND FASCIST 'SIMULATION'

With both the French Revolution and the Paris Commune, we have seen that Badiou mines from historical failures gleaming nuggets of political truth that transcend the very category of 'failure'. Particularly in the case of the Commune, we have also seen that this mining involves digging away at the foundations of the State, as the supposed locus of power with the capacity to neutralise truths by, as it were, re-Stating them. It should therefore come as no surprise that Badiou is ambivalent about that apparently exemplary Communist *success*, the Bolshevik Revolution of October 1917. Accordingly, the lessons to be learnt from this conflict are quite different from those discussed so far.

As with Hegel and Marx, one must view Badiou's Lenin as split. We might think of this as a split between Lenin himself and Lenin*ism* as an overdetermined Marxist doctrine. Badiou's hesitations centre on the latter, whereas the professional revolutionary offers many valuable lessons. We already saw in the last chapter that it was Lenin's Hegel that inspired Badiou's scissonal dialectic of the mid-to-late

1970s. But Badiou has also consistently taken Lenin's emphasis on 'iron discipline' seriously (see *M*, p.75). For early as for late Badiou, a dis-organised subject is entirely oxymoronic. He also applauds Lenin's insistence that insurrection is an *art*, in the classical Greek sense of *phronesis*, rather than a science in the crudely positivist sense (see *TS*, p.170). Against Menshevik parliamentarianism but also ponderous elements within the Bolshevik party itself (Zinoviev and Kamenev), Lenin argued in the crucial weeks of Autumn 1917 that insurrection is a willed creation rather than a passive anticipation of the 'right moment'. The latter will never arrive, it must be *made*. His impatient but insistent question-cum-demand, what is to be done, is exemplary for Badiou in combining practical analysis with political urgency: following "Lenin, every Marxist text bears the title: "The Current Situation and Our Tasks" (*TS*, p.82). Yet no analysis of 'objective' social conditions will ever answer the question 'what is to be done' *on its own*. Identifying a conjuncture as ripe for intervention is not intervention itself, indeed the gap between these is the infinite gap between a Marxist sociology and a Marxist politics. Something else must be added, a supplementary decision founded on an excess of subjective will: as Lenin had written enthusiastically in the margins of Hegel's *Logic*, "Leaps! Leaps!". In 'The Crisis Has Matured' of September 1917, Lenin upbraids his party for its shameful hesitancy before the necessity of such a leap (see also MP, p.75). For the Badiou of *Theory of the Subject* at least, the leap that *was* subsequently taken in the following month undoubtedly "opens onto a new stage in the history of Marxism" (TS, p.204). In particular, October 1917 'periodizes' the failures of 1848 and 1871 by demonstrating a new dimension of emancipatory struggle: the crucial role of the party in organising an enduringly *"victorious* insurrection" (*ibid.*).

But this is also the limitation of Lenin*ism*. For to the same extent that it is adapted to the task of insurrection against the State, Leninism is also, as we have already seen, incommensurable with the transition to a classless, Stateless society. Leninism "makes no real place [...] for the problem of communism as such. Its business is the State, the antagonistic victory" (205). The history of the USSR, with its expanding State bureaucracy, its Five Year plans, its rhetoric of transition coupled with its Siberian gulags, is the unfolding of this very contradiction, underlining the dialectical adage that "[e]very victory is the beginning of a failure of a new type" (91). So even though Badiou draws on Lenin's insight into the bourgeois nature of any State in order to assert the need for the 'lack of its lack',[14] he simultaneously distances himself from doctrinaire Leninism, by calling for "the post-Leninst party, the party for communism" (205). At this stage, this post-Leninist party is the Maoist party, yet subsequently the *Organisation politique* will refer to itself as a post-Leninist *and* post-Maoist group because it abjures the model of the party altogether. This trajectory is already clear in Badiou's disagreement with the representational link forged in Lenin's 'ABC of Marxism', where it is asserted that the "masses are divided into classes, the classes are represented by parties, and the parties are

---

14. "Lenin [indicated that] any State was at bottom bourgeois, so that, in coming to lack under the effect of the first insurrectionary assault, which clears the ground for the proletariat, the State—always bourgeois—must necessarily lack a second time, now clearing the path for the communist masses of the classless society" (*TS*, p.82)

run by leaders" (quoted in *TC*, p.108). To be sure, this rigidly authoritarian version of Leninism is probably a retrospective construct courtesy of Stalin, who never hesitated to quote this same 'ABC' in spelling out his Party-State. Yet there was in Lenin's own 'Leninism' sufficient reification of the Party to make the Stalinist perversion of "generic communism" (MP, p.79) into repressive State socialism possible. For this reason, *Theory of the Subject* argues that Leninism, if not the example of Lenin himself, must be left behind.

Indeed, in strictly organisational terms it should be acknowledged that the novelty of the Bolshevik sequence is to be found not in the Party, especially as it ossified after 1917, but in the local grassroots Soviet Councils consciously modelled on the Commune. These were the unprecedented *places* of innovative politics that dislodged the topology of centralised power in imperial Russia. Yet, according at least to Badiou's friend and major influence, Sylvain Lazarus, this novelty was abruptly marginalised by the Party vanguard prior to the revolution per se: "as soon as the Soviets, which are one of the places of Bolshevik politics, disappear (thus from autumn 1917), the Bolshevik political mode, whose thought Lenin names, ceases to exist" (*M*, p.34, see also Lazarus: 1996, p.40). The radically democratic form of organisation in the Soviets was subsequently erased further by the rapid merger of Party and State, formalised in the 'union' that led to the Congress of Soviets becoming the USSR in 1922. This was a process driven both by the Statist model of power already embedded in Leninism, and arguably by the civil war which forced the Bolshevik's to use the State as a war machine in extremely traditional ways.[15] From this point of view, and contrary to what we have said about the catalyzing role of the term 'revolution' in the French Revolution, it may well be that the so-called Russian 'Revolution' actually marks the end rather than the beginning of what was truly revolutionary about the Bolshevik sequence.

This only goes to show that no particular signifier, not even 'revolution', possesses a global singularity, and in fact it would be more properly dialectical to insist on the 'torsion' or 'involution' of the terms 'end' and 'beginning' with reference to October 1917 precisely to avoid the typically Statist obsession with discrete chronologies and causalities. Yet we have undoubtedly crossed a chiasmus now. Whereas the previous conflicts we have looked at extrapolated victories from apparent failures, here we discern failings intrinsic to apparent victories. By far the most important question to be asked of October 1917 and its aftermath, therefore, is just how an event—Badiou never denies that this is what it was—can start so well, yet end so badly. How can Lenin's glorious insurrection become degraded into the bloated State-apparatuses of Stalinism? How can the USSR, "despotic grey totality", become the "reversal of October '17 into its contrary, [...] the police-run blindness of the State" (*IT*, p.127)? Already in *Theory of the Subject*, Stalinism is

---

15. Lenin himself, in his thesis on imperial power, had argued for the distinction between war and revolution yet also the dialectical links between them, such that the former enabled the latter. The same problem of the State's Hobbesian role in quashing civil war arguably appears again in the Chinese Cultural Revolution, when Mao mobilises the army and then the authority of the Party-State following the incident at Wuhan in 1967.

vilified as the antithesis and thus target of Maoism. If Mao recognised the party's role as one of (self)purification, Stalin mistook this as implying that the party itself is pure, absolute, infallible: "On this bloody path" claims Badiou, "Stalin arrived at nothing but disaster" (*TS*, 38). Lenin's revolutionary discipline, vital in the insurrectionary phase, was corrupted by Stalin into suffocating social conformity during the endless 'transition' that was State Socialism.

An absolutely key issue here is that of legitimation. Stalinism explicitly drew on the supreme cause of the revolution to justify the very State-Terror that quashed every possible novelty. Using the term 'revolution' against what was revolutionary, it was therefore a political sequence that came to suppress truth *in the name of the truth*. One of the most important questions to ask not just of Stalinism, but also of Badiou's analysis of it, is 'how can we tell the difference between a true revolution and one that merely ab-uses the name of revolution'? Or again, how can we know when the force of a truth has dissipated, leaving in its wake merely an empty *discourse* of fidelity? There are various answers to this. In *Theory of the Subject*, it would seem that Stalinism represents an example of both left and right deviation: left deviation in the sense that it constantly harks back to the self-identical purity of October '17 to claim a privileged connection to it, right deviation in the sense that generic communism is soon 'placed' by the very structure of placement, the State, which changed hands but was not destroyed. In *Being and Event*, in its legitimating appeal to an idealised Leninism, the left deviation of Stalinism is phrased as 'speculative leftism', "any thought of being which bases itself upon the theme of an absolute commencement" (*BE*, p.210). In this sense, the unimaginable misery and starvation caused by collectivization was justified insofar as the Party-State that imposed it was both embodiment and guarantor of the legacy of October '17, of what is proper in the proper name 'revolution'.

And yet the Soviet State functioned like any State in ascribing irruptions of resistance to "the *hand of a stranger* (the foreign agitator, the terrorist, the perverse professor)" (*BE*, p.208). That this designation of an external cause is a general function of States can be confirmed by a tropology common to both sides during the Cold War. While McCarthyite America subjected 'Pinkos' and 'Commies' to their own public trials, Stalin's USSR wielded terms such as 'Kulak' (every resistance to collectivization was ascribed to these affluent peasant landowners), 'wreckers', 'counter-revolutionaries' and so forth. But what is specific about the Stalinist sequence is that it carried out this Statist labelling of excrescent multiples in the name of an eventual fidelity (although one might make an analogous claim with regard to America's fidelity to the *Declaration of Independence* as well, and perhaps most nationalisms have a similar pseudo-eventual structure or at least narrative). We therefore need conceptual tools for identifying the point of 'saturation' of a truth-procedure when its novelty has been exhausted, and for separating this out from merely rhetorical fidelity to an inactive truth.

Such tools are adumbrated in Badiou's book *Ethics: An Essay on the Understanding of Evil* (2002), where the driving ethical problem is precisely the fate of a truth procedure. Having critiqued the essentially religious notion of absolute evil underpinning neo-Kantian visions of human rights, as well as the equally theological 'ethics of alterity' inspired by Levinas, Badiou opts to nonetheless retain the category of evil. He does so by defining it not as *opposed* to the Good, but rather as a possible consequence or outcome of it. The Good is conjoined neither to a concept of the ideal society nor, therefore, to a putative good life, but rather to a resolute commitment to an event. In the extremely grandiose (and in fact semi-theological) language of this book, Badiou argues that only events reveal truths and thereby allow human animals to discover the Immortals that they are. It follows that evil is whatever interrupts, suppresses or terminates such fidelity, reducing human immortals back to their quotidian animality. This mode of evil, claims Badiou, takes three forms: terror, betrayal and disaster.

True to his previous verdict in *Theory of the Subject*, Stalinism seems to conform most closely to disaster. Disaster ensues when the subject-language of a truth-procedure asserts total power, as if it could "name and evaluate *all* the elements of the objective situation from the perspective of the truth-process" (*E*, p.83). In fact, somewhat disconcertingly in a book on the ethics of commitment, Stalinism is not mentioned directly, yet it is impossible not to sense its presence between these lines: "Rigid and dogmatic (or 'blinded'), the subject-language would claim the power, based on its own axioms, to name the whole of the real, and thus to change the world" (*ibid.*). Arrogating to itself the exclusive right to name those Immortals participating in the Bolshevik truth, the Soviet State does not hesitate in naming, and extinguishing, those mere mortal animals *un*faithful to that truth. In fact, Badiou argues in *Ethics* that genuine truth-procedures invariably leave at least one multiple "which remains inaccessible to truthful nominations, and is exclusively reserved to opinion, to the language of the situation" (*E*, p.85). Something, that is, must remain, like the 'navel' of a dream according to Freud, resolutely unnameable. It is this ethic of the unnameable, including a prohibition against any exclusive authority to name, that prevents the ethic of militant perseverance from assuming the authoritarian mastery wielded by Stalin (who, not coincidentally, advocated a dogmatically *scientific* Marxism).

However, what is perhaps more significant, and arguably underdeveloped, in Badiou's analysis of evil is the implicit connection between Stalinism as disaster, and Nazism as Terror. The latter, to use the vocabulary of *Being and Event*, involved the 'ontologization of the void'. What does this mean? We have already seen that the void is not an unmediated experience of either pure being or pure non-being, but rather a situation's encounter with *its* particular in-consistency. The void is a jamming of the counting operation such that the boundless multiplicity of *what* is counted briefly makes itself felt. But insofar as what is counted is the void as "absolute neutrality of being" (*E*, p.73), it evades all ontological predication per definition. What Nazism does, however, is to deliberately invoke a void endowed with a fully localisable presence, a plenitude of being, naming it with the term 'Jew'. The evacuation of this ontologized 'void' then becomes coterminous with the projected completion of the German people in their Aryan purity. As a closed abstract set, the Aryan race defines itself by its extermination of the Jewish void that only temporarily and contingently blocks its destined closure. Terror, then, is the inevitable outcome of a political community rooted in blood and soil, which must cut into its own flesh to cut out the void contaminating its otherwise perfect body-politic. It is not as clear as one would hope why this self-directed Terror is distinct from the properly political form of Jacobin Terror, but Badiou insists it is. His suggestion seems to be that with the Jacobins Terror was targeted in the specific defence of the Good of the Revolution and was thus ethical fidelity in process, whereas in Nazism, Terror was structurally indiscriminate because death was universalised across the entire German situation on the back of the logic of the void it utilised (the void, as predicateless, is also everywhere, it cannot *not* belong) (*E*, p.77). Badiou diagnoses this Nazi mobilisation of "terror directed at everyone" (*ibid.*) as the "return of the void", the real void (*E*, p.76-77).

Yet a more perplexing proximity exists between this ontologization of the void in Nazism and October '17. For Badiou points out that, notwithstanding the explicit ideological differences, Nazism presents itself as an eventual sequence echoing October '17 (specifically, it seems to me, its Stalinist figuration): not only lexically in its self-description as National *Socialism*, but also in the generalised appeal to "the break with the old order, the support sought from mass gatherings, the dictatorial style of the State, the *pathos* of the decision, the eulogy of the Worker" (*E*, p.72). Although he is willing to concede that there was "a radical break" (*E*, p.73) in Germany in the 1930s, Badiou does not consider this an event, mainly because it was always 'German' in an exclusive, non-universal sense. This means that the Nazi sequence is the *simulation of an event*. The verisimilitude of this simulation is indeed ethically worrisome: 1933 in Germany is "formally indistinguishable from an event" (*ibid.*), "all the formal traits of a truth are at work" (*E*, p.74), it convincingly "mimics an actual truth-process" (*E*, p.75). Perhaps in this very specific sense, there is value in the term 'totalitarianism' insofar as it teases out a common deployment of what we might term eventual appearances in both Nazism and Stalinism. In the case of the former, there is no event whatsoever, only the propagandistic construction of an image of one. From the point of view of truth, Nazism is simulacral 'all the way down'. But appearance is also key in the case of Stalinism, where the fidelity to a genuine event took the form of 'disaster' following the dwindling of that event's truth, perhaps, as Sylvain Lazarus suggests, as early as the incorporation of the Soviets *prior* to the so-called revolution. So with Nazism, the Jewish void is a fake from the outset, yet the 'real' void returns in the ultimately self-destructive universalisation of death. With Stalinism, the 'real' void of the Russian masses *had* appeared in October '17 and nominal fidelity to it continued to define the Soviet situation. Yet with the 'Statification' of the Soviet Councils and the consolidation of the Party-State, the truth unleashed by the proletarian void petered out and, precisely because of this, the void became absolutized as an object of dogmatic Party knowledge. This second Stalinist void is arguably a fake too. These are both logics of totalitarianism to the extent that appearances are manipulated in order to construct an impossible totality: Stalinist mastery over the truth and recovery of lost Aryan plenitude.

In terms of bloodshed and repression then, one might be tempted to argue that disaster and terror, absolutization and simulation of the void respectively, are 'worse' than the third of Badiou's categories of evil, betrayal.[16] And yet in terms of truth rather than its attendant violence, betrayal is actually more brutal. Beyond merely giving up on a truth, betrayal is the utter denial that any truth in fact took place. For example, ex-Maoists who want to become elected politicians renounce their former youthful errors, 'mature' artists turn their backs on previous avant-garde experiments, and ex-lovers, reconstituting their egos following a breakup, persuade themselves they were never in love but only infatuated, and so forth. Stalinism is not a betrayal in this sense. On the contrary, it is a disastrous form of fidelity. But this is the gamble of any evental decision: while it is the condition of possibility for any Good, it simultaneously unleashes unprecedented modalities of potential evil. October '17 can be rigorously said to 'condition' Nazism because "a simulacrum is possible only thanks to the success of political revolutions that were genuinely evental (and thus universally addressed)" (*E*, 77). No Bolsheviks, no Hitler. It would be entirely erroneous, however, to conclude that because Nazism could not have come about without October '17 the former retrospectively condemns the latter (this would be something like an inversion of 'periodization'). A more difficult conclusion is more appropriate: events would not be events if they offered guarantees regarding their outcomes.

For this reason, Badiou's work has shown an on-going preoccupation with disentangling Communism from its disastrous Soviet overdetermination. In response to the collapse of the Soviet Union, for example, he quickly refuted the conflation of the Soviet State and Communism underlying the gleeful assertions, on the part of neoliberal triumphalists, of the 'death of Communism' (*IT*,pp.126-140). Back in 1990, however, his argument struck a tone of melancholy resignation which more recent work has alleviated. In essence, he claimed that Communism did not die with the unravelling of the USSR because collective forms of subjectivity, the true source of genuine Communism, had been deceased for some time: "the dismantling of the Soviet Party-State is nothing more than the objective crystallization [...] of the fact that a certain thought of 'we' has been inoperative for more than twenty years" (*IT*, p.95).[17] Once again, 'world-historical' appearances notwithstanding, the collapse of the Soviet Union was not an event. Nor was the putative 'death of Communism', whose funeral knell it allegedly tolled. Since everything dies, death cannot be an event. But by no means does it follow that Communism proper is alive and kicking. On the contrary, the 'second death' of the Soviet State represented delayed confirmation that the militant form of subjectivity required to support Communism is, if not dead, at least currently in less than rude health. At bottom, Badiou was trying to prevent the name Communism from going down with the rusting Soviet ship. Stalinism had already perverted the name of 'revolution'. Neither the Soviet Union, nor indeed any State, should be allowed to monopolise the historical, political and above all subjective reach of the term 'Communism'.

---

16. Already in *TS*, Badiou had proposed that "betrayal is the proper opposite of ethics" because we must "equate ethics and partisanship" (*TS*, p.312).

17. As we shall see later, this disjunction between the apparatuses of a nation-state and the collective national *subject* is key to the analysis of the breakup of the former Yugoslavia put forward around the same time in *La Distance politique*, the journal of *Organisation politique*.

Almost twenty years later, Badiou returned to this theme but put a more affirmative slant on it. At the end of his polemical book on Sarkozy, during a 2009 conference at Birkbeck and a follow up event in Berlin in 2010 (see Douzinas and Žižek: 2010 and Badiou and Žižek: 2011), in his *Seconde Manifeste pour la philosophie*, and in the fifth volume of the *Circonstances* series, Badiou (re)advocates what he calls the 'communist hypothesis'. An historical foundation for this hypothesis had already been laid with the appeal to 'communist invariants' as early as *De l'idéologie* (1976): the notion of transhistorical invariants obviously cuts across any privileging of the Soviet reference. But the more recent appeal to the communist hypothesis seems to be geared towards re-activating the collective subject today. As part of this project, he makes the surprising proposal of Communism as an 'Idea', not in the sense of one idea among others in the history of ideas, but as a particular logic of change. We will be returning to this proposal in the latter half of Chapter4.

THE CHINESE CULTURAL REVOLUTION

The final sequences of conflict I want to look at continue the 'deconstruction' of the success-failure binary. For the lessons that emerge from the Chinese Cultural Revolution and May '68 in France cannot be said to be affirmative in any simple sense. On the contrary, the shared truth borne by them seems to remain essentially negative: if it warrants the adjective 'evental' at all, it is only to the extent that this negativity inescapably conditions all subsequent emancipatory politics. In brief, both the Chinese Cultural Revolution and May '68 pose the problem of the *saturation*[18] of the very term 'revolution', at least when conceived as a transformative articulation between politics and the State. After 1968, this articulation is utterly exhausted. In a slightly more positive register, however, this saturation or exhaustion does demand, in its turn, repeated local and provisional solutions to a corollary problem: namely, the non-Statist organisation of radical political novelty. Nonetheless, in a sense which actually sits very uncomfortable with the logic of the event, both of these sequences are negative, primarily in relation to the (Statist) history of Marxism.[19]

This is especially vivid in the case of the Chinese Cultural Revolution. But which Cultural Revolution? Not the one portrayed by liberal Western historians who tend to see in it further 'proof' of the inevitability of revolutionary Terror and the evils of totalitarianism. Nor the version put forward by the Chinese Communist Party itself under Deng Xiaoping which presented it as Mao's unorthodox bid for power *within* the party following his marginalisation after the costly failure of the Great Leap Forward. Nor, finally, is it even the version that Mao himself undoubtedly shaped in both word and deed after September 1967, when he began to impose Statist order upon the whirlwind of destruction he himself had unleashed. Since 'officially' the Cultural Revolution lasted until the arrest of the

---

18. The term is actually Sylvain Lazarus', although in his work it is both a diagnosis and a methodology (see Lazarus: 1993, pp. 37-47).

19. Žižek has pointed out that it is "difficult to miss the irony of the fact that Badiou, who adamantly opposes the notion of the act as negative, locates the historical significance of the Maoist Cultural Revolution" (2009, p.399), and, I would add May '68 too, in failure.

'Gang of Four' soon after Mao's death in 1976, it is imperative to specify the dates of Badiou's more focussed referent.

As a truth sequence, the Chinese Cultural Revolution stretches from November 1965 to July 1968, with its most intense and 'eventful' period being May 1966 to September 1967 (see *HC*, p.94): these sixteen chaotic months contain the novelty of the red guards, of rebel factory workers, of occupations, of the proliferation of unprecedented political places and declarations. Rather like Lenin picking over the sad bones of the Paris Commune, however, Badiou is arguably more intent on the failings of this sequence than its novelties. His analysis traces an incommensurability, internal to the Chinese Communist Party, between its guerrilla insurrectionary past in the long battle with the Kuomindang, and the cumbersome form it took following its acquisition of State power in 1949. This trajectory echoes the 'good' Bolshevik phase and its 'bad' Stalinist perversion in the Russian sequence, with State power playing a similarly corrupting role. However, Mao certainly represents an important advance on Stalin. For to the two 'alternatives' presented by Stalin's Party-State—a perfectly functioning bureaucratic obedience on the one hand, and Terror 'liquidating' all resistance to the State on the other—Mao added a third option: mass popular mobilisation *against* the oppressive Party-State. He deemed this necessary because, like Lenin in *State and Revolution*, he argued that even in conditions of socialism the bourgeoisie inevitably reconstitutes itself as the Party bureaucracy, implying a political rather than socio-economic definition of the bourgeoisie that Badiou would push to its limits in *Theory of the Subject* (see *TS*, p.42).

So if the Stalinist State used the legitimating moniker 'revolution' to paradoxically quash revolutionary activity, Mao briefly revitalized this term by generating a revolution against the covertly bourgeois State. However, the real lesson of the Cultural Revolution, according to Badiou, is that Mao ultimately failed to disentangle himself from the dominance of the Party-State form. From the outset, he demanded control over that defining instrument of State domination, the army, in order to 'guide' the anarchy of revolution not towards the outright destruction of the party, but towards its dialectical rejuvenation. This became clear after September 1967, demonstrating that, in the end, Mao remained a man of the party. It is for this reason that Badiou's analysis of the Chinese Cultural Revolution arrives at an affirmative answer to his own weighty question, 'The Last Revolution?'.[20]

The ambiguity that would lead in this terminal direction is already clear in the text that launched the Cultural Revolution, the 'Decision in 16 Points' adopted by the party's Central Committee on the 8th of August 1966. Portentously, this text had a liminal status with regard to legitimate party authority. Using a tactic he had perfected prior even to the Long March, Mao had used the threat of force to shape the composition of this committee in his favour. Conservatives and bureaucrats

---

20. Last, but also, according the *Theory of the Subject*, the first (so presumably the only): "The Chinese Cultural Revolution deserves [...] to be named the first communist revolution in history" (*TS*, p.185). Perhaps this radical singularity is only to be expected of an event, but this only increases the enigmatic negativity of the Cultural Revolution: if it was the first and last, and yet also fundamentally negative, how does it support the communist hypothesis?

were excluded in preference for the very radicals and militants from the universities to whom the 'Decision' extended unprecedented powers. As a political declaration then, the 'Decision' is both inside and outside the party, 'illegal' yet made in the name of the party. If its Machiavellian context reflects a strategic ambiguity vis-à-vis the Party-State, its *contents* turn this ambiguity into an audacious but contradictory programme for radical change. The text of the 'Decision' enables us to draw up a clear 'ledger' of assertions that conform to the two sides of this fundamental contradiction: scissional anti-State 'force' on the one hand, and reactionary Statist 'placement' on the other.

In the column marked 'anti-State force', we have points 3 and 4 of the text which agitate for mass mobilisation, point 7 which explicitly grants impunity to the student red guards, and point 9 which, referring directly to the Paris Commune, invites novel forms of organisation to counter the congealed cadres of the party. In the other column of this 'ledger', however, marked 'Statist placement', we have point 8 which distinguishes between good and bad cadres and suggests that the latter are few in number (so cadres are not bad per se), point 11 which ensures that the Party-State has a veto over media coverage of the revolution, and perhaps most significantly, point 15 which declares that the army must remain subservient to the central authority of the party. The symmetrical tension between these contradictory statements accounts for the extraordinary outburst of iconoclastic violence that followed, and also, according to Badiou, for its doomed fate.

The Red Guard, predominantly composed of university students, clearly embodied this animating tension as they took on the role of Mao's revolutionary 'shock troops' against the old order. Armed with catechisms from the Little Red Book and other declarations by Mao—"without destruction, no construction", "the struggle of the new against the old" etc.—they were the primary vector of anti-State force, unleashing against manifestations of bourgeois 'culture' within the party hierarchy a campaign of humiliation, intimidation and often senseless violence. Badiou acknowledges the excessive nature of much Red Guard cruelty, but it is important to point out that this is measured not against a normative moral ideal, but rather against the *political* criterion of effective social transformation. Thus, the excess of Red Guard violence was an expression of the fundamental contradiction driving the entire revolution: Mao 'let them loose' against the party, but simultaneously restrained them by his insistence on the party in the final instance. Like a dog goaded into anger yet also leashed, much of the brutality perpetrated by the Red Guard became inwardly directed in the form of armed factionalism. Badiou speculates that if, by contrast, a space outside or 'at a distance from' the State had offered the young militants a venue for political affirmation rather than mere iconoclastic destruction, the carnage could have been, not eradicated, but more efficiently directed toward genuine change. At any rate, it is clear that once they had served his purpose, Mao did not hesitate to criticise the Red Guards for their arrogance and 'ultra-leftism', thereby subjecting them to Statist placement.

This absence of singularised political spaces outside the placing power of the Party-State is well illustrated by the brevity of the Shanghai Commune of 1967. By late 1966, Mao had become exasperated at the ability of local party cadres to mimic Maoist rhetoric and even offer hollow self-criticisms in order to stay in power. He therefore re-invoked the Leninist theme of the direct "seizure of power by proletarian revolutionaries" already mentioned in the 'Decision in 16 Points': this was a direct invitation to the Red Guards to physically oust local party officials no matter how Maoist their mere rhetoric. In Shanghai, this invitation was accepted by an alliance of workers, Red Guards, and a faction of the army which together deposed the city's party officials in January 1967. The extremely fragile unity of this alliance led Zhang Chungqiao, a member of what would later be called the 'Gang of Four', to propose a model of organisation inspired by the Paris Commune: the Shanghai Commune was therefore officially formed on the 5th of February. Like its eponymous French predecessor, the Shanghai Commune had all the appearances of an innovative organisation opposed to the (Party)State. Yet, as Badiou points out, this "counter-model" (*HC*, p.111) never truly had the scope to pursue an anti-Statist politics since the wider revolution, of which it was an experimental moment, was simultaneously committed to the maintenance of minimal State *continuity*.

Within the group of party leaders orchestrating the revolution, it was clearly the role of Zhou Enlai (in truth, never fully committed to the revolution) to balance Mao's intuitive capacity for destabilisation by ensuring minimal economic functioning. His unenviable task was often to mediate between numerous factions with a view to establishing both unity with the (renewed) party and relative social order, and Mao never discouraged him from this work. Although, formally speaking, similar 'seizures of power' did take place around China after the Shanghai Commune, with Red Guards occupying party buildings and imposing public humiliations on deposed officials in various provinces, such actions remained within the horizon of the Party-State. For Badiou, despite this geographical proliferation of 'communes', their "political space was too narrow" (*HC*, p.111). Sure enough, after February 1967, the word 'commune', with its deep anti-State resonance, disappears from Mao's discourse, to be replaced by the more obviously Statist expression 'revolutionary committee'. These committees were then conceived of as a 'triple alliance' between the new cadres, the workers, and the army, an essentially vertical line of authority that led back up to the party. Unlike the Paris Commune, then, the Shanghai Commune ended not in *une semaine sanglante* but in the apparently anodyne non-event of a name-change recommended by Mao himself. And yet, concerning the possibility of non-Statist political organisation, this name-change is arguably the more final of the two terminations.

Two further incidents illustrate Mao's hesitancy before properly non-Statist politics, the so-called Wuhan incident and the intervention into the Red Guard occupation of the University of Peking. We need not go into the detail of these complex episodes here. Suffice it to say that Wuhan demonstrated that, confronted with the possibility of revolutionary unrest tipping over into civil war, Mao was determined to deploy the army to restore enough order to save the Party-State. Similarly, Mao's mobilisation of the worker's *against* the Red Guards occupying the University of Peking under the slogan "nothing essential divides the working classes" was a way of reasserting the State's very classical role of Leviathan-like harbinger of order. Far from simply confirming the infinite cunning of Mao himself, as if he had planned this volte-face all along, the Wuhan and Peking incidents should be viewed as exemplary of the revolution's fundamental contradiction (in which Mao was no doubt unwillingly enveloped himself at times).

As a truth sequence, then, the value of the Chinese Cultural Revolution lies in its excessively zealous push towards an impassable limit. It demonstrated in no uncertain terms that political innovation constrained within the strictures of the State, irrespective of whether that State has been brought to the very brink of self-dissolution, can only lead to destruction of the old, rather than construction of the new. There is an almost Christian narrative here. It is as if, for Badiou, the immense bloodshed and upheaval of the Cultural Revolution constitutes an historical sacrifice of which we, contemporary militants, are the heirs. As he puts it in *Logics of Worlds*: "For the sake of all the world's revolutionaries, the Cultural Revolution effectively explored the limits of Leninism" (*LW*, p.518). That is, Mao killed State-based revolution that non-Statist revolution should live!

But are we happy to receive this particular inheritance? In fact, Slavoj Žižek (2009, pp.399-401) has brought out a subtle shift in Badiou's position on the Cultural Revolution between 'The Last Revolution?' (originally a conference paper delivered in 2002), and the version of this same argument that appears in *Logics of Worlds*. In the former, the Cultural Revolution is a clear failure that "bears witness to the impossibility truly and globally to free politics from the framework of the party-state that imprisons it" (quoted in Žižek: 2009, p.400). In *Logics of Worlds*, however, we find that "the Red Guards [...] prescribed for the decades to come the *affirmative realization* of this beginning" (*ibid.*) of a non-statist form of political radicalism. In the first account, politics cannot escape the party-state framework, whereas in the second, politics cannot be conducted within this framework. Žižek is right, I think, to point out that this represents a serious impasse. Moreover, he is also right that Badiou's solution—that politics should be conducted at an 'internal distance' from the State (the dialectical 'torsion' of *Theory of the Subject* was already at pains to elaborate this 'extimate' topology)—has potentially worrying consequences.

The problem itself is implied within the very rigour of Badiou's set-theoretical ontology, where there is no option of a 'stateless' set. Consistency relies on the count of the count performed by the state: all the ones of the first count of presentation must be recounted within an overarching One. Quite simply, every set *qua* set is ordered, and the state is what orders it. This is perhaps where the 'analogy' (but of course, much of the burden of Badiou's project depends on it being far more than an analogy) between mathematical sets and 'actual' worldly situations may impose limitations on the politics he advocates. Thus, the semantic slippage Badiou openly courts in *Being and Event* between the set-theoretical 'state' and the political 'state' prevents him thinking of the latter as anything other than fundamentally apolitical. 'State' in Badiou's sense is almost entirely homologous with 'status quo'. It may well be that a peculiarly French historical experience has led him to this stubborn conviction: from Thermidor to the June Days of 1848, from the Paris Commune, through May '68 and on to *Mitterandisme* in the early 1980s, the French State has indeed found numerous ways to both quash and incorporate radical movements in defence of the status quo. But can we simultaneously '*do* without the State' on the one hand (in the bivalent sense of both abjuring representational politics and innovating outside the State's sanctioned authority) and resign ourselves to its structural necessity on the other?

Žižek phrases just the kind of questions Badiou is ill-disposed to even consider: "if the space of emancipatory politics is defined by a distance towards the state, are we not abandoning the field (of the state) all too easily to the enemy? Is it not crucial *what* form state power takes?" (2009, p.402). There seem scant resources within Badiou's *philosophical* system to even pose the question of whether, say, a welfare state is preferable to a totalitarian party-state, a 'nanny' state to a laissez faire liberal state. But even a cursory glance at the recent swing to the left in Latin America (to take only the most obvious example) surely counsels us against dismissing the politics-state relation *tout court*. Is it not difficult to see how Evo Morales' redistributive wealth and land reforms in Venezuela, or Hugo Chavez's economic resistance to the Washington Consensus, flawed and limited though they may be in many respects, could be implemented through anything other than State-based means? Let us not forget, either, that these figures buck the Latin American trend of gaining power by means of military coup d'état (although not for want of trying in Chavez's case): both have gained the position to implement significant change by way of the very ballot box that Badiou sees as a poisoned chalice. Likewise, Jean-Bertrand Aristide's profound challenge to the Haitian ruling class and its supporters in the US is inconceivable without the electoral process and the power of state legislation to, for example, disband the army (see Hallward: 2007).[21] Aristide's use of grassroots networks to ground the Fanmi Lavalas movement in the real concerns of the Haitian people demonstrates the crucial importance of Badiou's favoured political localism. But equally, it is hard to see how such local horizontal networks alone could challenge IMF restructuring and the consequent debt-cycles without operating on the vertical axis of the State. We will come back to these questions, but they are worth signalling here because it is from the

---

21. Peter Hallward is of course an exemplary Badiou scholar, yet his meticulously researched book on Haiti presents an implicit challenge to Badiou's rigid anti-Statism, as is clear in the following:

> Aristide was a threat because he proposed modest but practical steps towards popular political empowerment, because he presented widely shared popular demands in terms that made immediate and compelling sense to most of the Haitian population, because he formulated these demands within the constraints of the existing constitutional structure, because he helped to organize a relatively united and effective political party that quickly came to dominate that structure—and in particular, because he did all this after eliminating the main mechanism that the elite had relied upon to squash all previous attempts at political change: the army (Hallward: 2007, p.xxx)

Consensual, building on common-sense, constitutional, and based on an elected political party: these are at complete odds with, say, the activism of the *Organisation politique*. No doubt Badiou would acknowledge that everything that happened in Haiti, up to its suppression by American-backed military coups, was very important and valuable, but simply would not come under the heading of 'politics' in his very stark sense. Does this not indicate a weakness in his deliberately limited concept of politics?

Chinese Cultural Revolution above all that Badiou deduces the need for a politics subtracted from the Marxist-Leninist, but also social democratic, obsession with the State. These sorts of questions about Badiou's relation to the State also have implications for the value of his work as an intervention into debates about, and resistance to, globalisation. Does his insistence on the structural necessity of the state fly in the face of the demonstrably deterritorializing effects of late capital? Perhaps, but only if we continue to conceive of the state as the nation-state, whose territorial and juridical sovereignty has certainly been eroded by trans- and supra-national entities. In this sense, the value of Badiou's notion of the State may end up being precisely its formalism, which allows us to see the continuity of its structural necessity even in the, as it were, de-nationalised and deterritorialised forms of sovereignty attendant on economic and political globalisation.

MAY '68

Related questions are raised by the other episode of conflict central to Badiou's personal as well as intellectual biography: his 'road to Damascus' experience, the movement of May 1968 in France. In fact, there are numerous uncanny overlaps between May '68 and the Chinese Cultural Revolution that extend far beyond the direct influence of French Maoists (who, anyway, often had little idea what was actually taking place in China). Among these overlaps are: the centrality of militant university students, their creative alliance with industrial and agricultural workers, the proliferation of new political spaces by means of occupations, the suspension of conventional social hierarchies as a condition of politics proper, the dialectics of active and reactive violence, the truly mass nature of mobilisation, the omnipresence yet increasing inadequacy of brittle Marxist rhetoric, and above all, the ultimate incompatibility between radical political novelty and the party form of organisation.

One crucial difference, however, and one of the many reasons for examining it on its own terms, is that the real enemy against which the May movement mobilised was not, as in the Chinese context, an ossified revolutionary party, but what Badiou calls 'capitalo-parliamentarism'. By this he means the way in which the increasingly corporate state facilitates capitalist exploitation by hiding behind the electoral fetish of liberal democracy. In the wake of the rise and rise of neo-liberalism and globalisation (with China now very far down the 'capitalist road' Mao so feared), it is clearly this complex and subtle machinery of governmentality that constitutes the 'State' of our contemporary situation, not the forced (and false) choice between totalitarianism and democracy characteristic of the Cold War period. In this sense May '68 holds a relevance outside the history of actually existing State Marxisms, with which it was seen by many at the time to be a decisive break—this is what the 'new' in 'new social movements' and the 'post' in 'post-Marxism' meant after all.

But, once again, which May '68? Kristin Ross (2002) has done an exemplary job in delineating the impoverished versions that initially offer themselves in answer to this question. She also makes it clear that these have been made to congeal around the May movement as part of the commodification of historical, political and cultural memory intrinsic to capitalo-parliamenta-rism (a process much in evidence in the plethora of publications, media discus-sions, art exhibitions and film screenings which marked the 40th anniversary of *les événements* in 2008). Even more damaging than the frequent denial that anything significant actually took place in those tumultuous months is the now wide-spread argument that May '68 *was* a radical rupture, but one that broke from the staid moralism and bureaucratic hypertrophy of Gaullism in order to pave the way for precisely the kind of libertarian individualism sustained by capitalism! In the consumerist 1980s in particular, it was claimed that the true legacy of May '68 was today's market-based model of individual freedom (see Lipovetsky: 1983 for just one example).

This vision of May '68 as the irruption of unregulatable desire—which man-ages to fuse Deleuzian vitalist anarchism with the anti-Soviet individualism of the *nouveaux philosophes* and even elements of Freudo-Marxism—involves a series of massive elisions, reductions and simplifications. The time and space of what was in reality a sprawling mass movement touching every part of the French na-tion is reduced to just a few elements: to the young, to students, to Paris, and even to the barricades around the Sorbonne. In this way, the French May, rath-er than what was happening in China, is depicted as the truly *cultural* revolu-tion, specifically, a counter-cultural idealism that burst asunder the patriarchal rigidity of Gallism and enabled a wider, sexier range of lifestyle choices .... Of course, as Ross admirably demonstrates, this narrative of May '68 as a kind of Woodstock with attitude has to erase another, much more radical May '68 to even begin.

This alternative May does not emerge spontaneously from sexually frustrated students in the segregated dorms of Nanterre. Rather, it comes out of an honour-able if slower burning prehistory that stretches back to the politicizing effects of France's 'war'[22] with Algeria between 1954 and 1962. The progressive identification with the 'wretched of the earth' established during the Algerian crisis was, accord-ing to Ross, resurrected during the war in Vietnam. Indeed, it was thanks primar-ily to Vietnam that all the Leninist, Trotskyist, Maoist, anarchist and Situationist factions of the May movement could unite in their shared opposition to US impe-rialism. Even more importantly, this alternate May centralises the figure not of the student activist, but of the worker, and the space not only of the Parisian university, but of the provincial factories and farms, thereby teasing out the importance of the prehistory of radicalism in the French labour movement as well. In particular, for Ross this radical May differs starkly from its libertarian cousin in superimposing the colonial other upon the figure of the worker within a critique of capitalist impe-rialism (which is partly why Maoism played such an important role). The *overthrow* of capitalism, then, and not a clearing of the way for its affective free play, was the real goal for most of the May protagonists. Ross's contextualisation of May with-in anti-colonial struggles and the consequent tricontinentalism of many activists in

---

22. Thanks to the very colonialism that was being resisted, and the *departement* system of French colonial administration, the anti-colonial freedom fighters of the Algerian FLN were technically a 'police' matter internal to France and therefore not a war in the traditional sense.

Europe and elsewhere, combined with the spark of Vietnam, goes a long way to-wards explaining the truly international scope of the upheavals of that year.[23]

Because of its figurative overdetermination and perhaps his own involvement in it, Badiou has in fact been very ambivalent about May '68. In *Theory of the Subject* he presents it as a reciprocal rather than scissional contradiction, and thus as a "revolt without a future" (*TS*, p.11). He also writes of its "enormous weakness", of "the insurmountable dilution of the revolt into peaceful, protesting, infrapolitical figures", and of the ultimate return to "the fixity of splace" (*TS*, p.42). His hesitant conclusion is that "May '68 is really only a beginning, and continuing the combat is the directive for the long run" (*ibid.*). In an interview with Lauren Sedofsky in *Artforum* in 1995 Badiou even admitted in relation to May '68 that "it's entirely pos-sible there was no event at all. I really don't know".[24] Clarifying this, however, in the interview that appears at the end of *Ethics*, Badiou explains that May remains an 'obscure event' in Sylvain Lazarus' sense, i.e., one that has yet to find its proper evental name: "the name 'revolt'" he argues "wasn't the right name [...] if we say the event has 'event' as its name, it means we haven't yet found its name" (*E*, p.127). As recently as *Logics of Worlds*, he continues to argue that "May '68 is an ambigu-ous episode" (*LW*, p.564).

His most systematic attempt to clear up this ambiguity can be found in 'May '68 Revisited, Forty Years After', a conference paper reproduced, along with two other May-related texts, in *L'Hypothèse Communiste*. There Badiou, like Ross, is en-gaged in the retrieval of a May capable of inspiring us to believe that another world is possible. Yet he immediately acknowledges that this is an extremely dif-ficult task: "May 68 is itself an event of great complexity" (*HC*, p.40). Its simulta-neous novelty and obscurity lies in the concurrent explosion of not two, not even three, but of four truths. As we saw with the ethics of commitment, this fourfold complexity multiplies the forms of betrayal and disaster to which May '68 has in fact proved susceptible. This accounts in part for the political blurriness that per-sists behind its arguably sharp-edged *cultural* iconicity (41). Shifting the lens to re-verse this field of political vision requires, according to Badiou, a clear understand-ing of the four different 'Mays'.

The first May is composed of the familiar elements of the iconic version: stu-dents hurling paving stones through clouds of teargas at *matraque*-wielding CRS, overturned, burnt-out cars in the rue St. Jacques, Blanchot-like 'crowds' in the Place Denfert-Rochereau, but also semiotic echoes of all this in images from Italy, Germany, America and Mexico, as well as the dominant role of Marxist revolu-tionary discourse in the banners, slogans and graffiti. This is certainly a seductive iconography. And thanks to the subsequent role of the students themselves as writ-ers, journalists, film makers and academics, it is extremely visible. Nonetheless, Badiou is quick to point out that, proportionally, students represented a tiny

---

23. See the chapter entitled 'The Police Conception of History' in Ross: 2002 in particular. It is interesting to note that she describes May as "an event, in the sense Alain Badiou has given to the term" (p.26) yet her own assiduous attention to the pre-history of May is precisely the oppo-site of Badiou's punctually ahistorical event.

24. See 'Being by Numbers' in *Artforum*, Vol. 33, No. 2, from October 1994.

fraction of the young who were swept up in the May events (indeed, it is arguable that it was precisely by leaving behind their student status that students became militants at all). It is this first May of *engagé* student radicalism that is packaged as glossy nostalgia with each passing anniversary, ending up on the coffee tables of university-educated 'liberals'.

The second May Badiou identifies is the one I have already invoked via Ross: that of "the biggest general strike in all of French history" (42). Badiou, however, sees the terrain of this May as being that of the 'classical' left, drawing primarily on a trade unionism dominated by the CGT (the *Confédération générale du travail* which had close links with the perfidious PCF). Nonetheless, he finds three aspects of this second May that introduced radical innovation even into the State-dominated field of trade unionism. Firstly, the young workers propelling the strike were of a generation only partially inculcated into the unions, and thus partially distrustful of them: hence the wildcat nature of what the French, as melodramatically as the English, call *grèves suavages*. (Significantly, Badiou notes that these strikes actually began in 1967, giving the lie to the image, embedded in the first May, of politically illiterate workers being led by the intellectual student vanguard). The second element of innovation was the occupation of the factories. Although an old tactic, this was creatively generalised during and after May.[25] Such occupations were an effective strategy during wildcat strikes when unions were liable to oppose the disruption. Seizing the 'means of production' meant the management could not keep the machines running even with non-union members or strike breakers. The third element of innovation involved a willingness to kidnap top-level factory management themselves in order to achieve national media visibility. For Badiou, this indicates an acceptance of violence as a political strategy that the workers shared with many of the students. These innovative dimensions within the otherwise Statist terrain of traditional *syndicalisme* account for the split caused by the Grenelle agreement hurriedly negotiated by de Gaulle with the unions. Those familiar with the protocols of unionism were happy to settle for very little (a rise in the minimum wage and a modest extension of union rights within the factories), whereas younger workers recognised that such compromises were 'small beer' indeed when judged against the backdrop of the massive national disruption their strikes had caused.

The third May is arguably the one of which Badiou is least fond. Overlapping at least semiotically with the first May of student radicalism, it is the 'libertarian May' of free love, individualism, and the 'new social movements' associated with women's rights and gay pride etc.: it is thus the May most amenable to cooptation by the apologists of liberal, multicultural capitalism. But more specifically, it is also the 'cultural' and even 'aestheticised' May whose Situationist origins can be heard in the title of Andrew Feenberg and Jim Freedman's book, *When Poetry Ruled the*

---

25. Ross, who draws on Rancière's account of the May movement as a contestation of the spatialisation and specialisation of 'police' order, argues that, in fact, both the barricades around the Sorbonne and the occupation of the factories could have inhibited the truly novel dimension of the movement, namely, the physical as well as intellectual interaction between students and workers. Both of these tactics arguably lapse into what Peter Starr calls 'specular doubling' (1995, p.3), i.e., a staging of the confrontation between the 'resistant' and the 'repressive' within a covertly shared logic of space which the latter were, above all, desperate to uphold.

Streets: The French Events of May 1968 (2001). Indeed, culturalist accounts often identify as the "incubator and test run for the May events" (Crow in Hambourg: 2006, p. 18) the dismissal, in February 1968, of Henri Langlois, the eccentric but groundbreaking director of the Cinémathèque Française. One epicentre of this third aesthetic May is therefore the occupied Théâtre de l'Odéon of May proper, outside which hung a banner reading 'When the National Assembly becomes a bourgeois theatre, all the bourgeois theatres should be turned into national assemblies' (quoted in Knabb: 1995, p.446). The other epicentre, whose importance is acknowledged by Badiou, would be the *Atelier populaire* resulting from the occupation of the École des beaux-arts. It was from here that the iconic posters which have come to summarise the graphic fusion of art, politics and desire characteristic of this third May were designed and mimeographed at a frenetic pace.[26]

Three different 'Mays' then: one of student activism, one of worker radicalism, and one of counter-cultural aestheticized libertarianism. However, and this is what makes May '68 both unprecedented and extraordinarily fragile as an event, Badiou argues that these three strands remained fundamentally distinct, "lacking important intersections" (p.44).: thus "forty years later, three different assessments" (p.45) whose 'compossibilization' remains elusive. The most important, although chronologically vague, 'May' is therefore the fourth and final one. Not only is this May irreducible to the month of May itself (already a reduction which sidelines the second 'May' of the general strike which in fact spills over into the whole of June), but Badiou refers to it as the *"décennie '68"* (p.45), the '68 decade'. It therefore encompasses the long and arduous post-May struggles leading up to the fateful year of 1978, which culminated in the absorption of the event's most inventive fidelities into the parliamentary Leftism of *Mitterandisme* and, more generally, the mainstreaming of ex-*gauchistes* within traditional trade unionism, journalism, the cultural industries, conventional academia and official politics.

In this period, then, there was a painful break with the representational fallacy animating all the revolutionary factions of the May movement. This was the fallacy that there was a privileged agent of historical change, whether it be the Algerian, the Vietnamese, the French worker on the Renault assembly line or indeed the student; that such agents must be organised to unleash their transformative potential; and finally that the most appropriate, indeed the only, form to do that was the party. Within this broad assumption, of course, there was massive and heated disagreement, not least between anarchists and Leninists. Nonetheless, during May itself the language of class, class struggle, proletarian consciousness and so on managed to encompass such disputes and thus operate as the hegemonic vocabulary of more or less all the participants. However, rather like the furiously paradoxical nature of contiguous events in China, Badiou argues that this

26. There is a nice story which summarises the disinterested immediacy of what Badiou would call a 'subject-language' and which we can extend to these posters. Early on, an attempt was made to take them to an art gallery with a view to selling them and ploughing the proceeds back into funding the May movement. However, the posters were snatched out of the would-be revolutionary entrepreneur's hands in order to be pasted up and disseminated in the streets where politics was taking place without the need for the mediation via the abstract exchange of money.

shared vocabulary carried a growing inadequacy: "May '68 presents a fundamental ambiguity between a unanimously shared language and the start of the end of the use of this language" (p.48). The representational assumption embedded in such Marxist vocabulary was in fact contradicted by innumerable examples of revolt for revolt's sake. Of course, students transgressed the authority of de Gaulle's government and perhaps thought themselves Leninists for doing so, but many also ignored university authorities, the police and sometimes parents. Striking workers repeatedly stuck two fingers up at the trade unions. And both students and workers displayed contempt for the PCF's attempts to first appropriate, then mediate, and finally dissipate the movement as a whole (for a particularly vibrant account, see Quattrocchi and Nairn: 1998). Already during May itself, elections were widely recognised as a trap. One piece of graffiti read 'Referendum: whether we vote yes or no, it turns us into suckers' (quoted in Knabb: 1995, p.447). This was put into vivid relief by de Gaulle's extremely effective method for drawing a line under the unrest: the referendum that he called on his authority in June granted him a landslide victory. This nonetheless also demonstrated, once and for all, that parliamentary democracy was "an apparatus for the repression of movements, of novelties, of ruptures" (*HC*, p.49). If the Cultural Revolution exposed the limits of Leninism then, May '68 exposed the limits of parliamentarism. The '68 decade' that followed is one caught in a kind of limbo: it slowly accepts the inadequacy of classical Marxism on the one hand, yet it is still too bogged down in the latter's conceptual framework to fully imagine an alternative on the other. Badiou himself is exemplary of the fact that the decade was engaged in the most basic question: what is politics, now that it cannot be *that*? [27]

In a similar vein to Jacques Rancière, Badiou argues that the '68 decade' answers this question in the following way: the new politics must be one of the suspension of the assigned places that make both social order and exploitation possible. It must, that is, evade Statist placement. This immediately poses the question of organisation. While the libertarian individualist May is presented as the explosion of uncontainable and therefore disorganised desire, the militant May in fact produced an important organisational innovation in the form of the *comité d'action* (see chapter two in Ross: 2002). These were small cells of ten to fifteen people, local, open, non-prescriptive and therefore dialectically supple in the face of rapidly changing circumstances. Some of them remained active for several years after May. Maoist *comités* in particular not only discussed tactics and produced and distributed agitprop to fuel the wider movement. They also adopted a subversive spatial politics that deliberately contested the dominant topology of the division

---

27. Peter Starr has traced the impact of the 'logic of failed revolts' exposed by May in the theoretical elaborations of Lacan, Althusser, Derrida, Barthes and Kristeva as well as lapsed Maoists such as Guy Lardreau and Christian Jambet during Badiou's '68 decade'—in fact, it is a long 'decade' covering the twelve years from the "resurgence of leftist activism in 1965 and ending with the massive abandonment of Marxist models exemplified by the "New Philosophy" debates of 1976 and 1977" (Starr: 1995, p.2). For Badiou, however, most of these thinkers of the 'logics of failed revolt' themselves failed to articulate a viable post-party politics, primarily by giving up on politics in preference for ethics.

of labour.[28] Just as Mao had attempted to loosen the distinction between town and country with his 'exchange of experience' programme, so French Maoists as well as Trotskyists attempted to close the gap between intellectual and manual labour by entering the factories and learning from the workers (in fact, the strategy of *établissement* whereby intellectuals took jobs in the factories preceded May '68 by several years). Conversely, the university began to be conceptualised as a factory of ideas. Easily criticized as condescendingly worthy, these exchanges nonetheless represented genuine attempts to merge the first and second 'Mays' identified by Badiou.

However, the *comités d'actions* notwithstanding, it is the fourth May that poses the problem of organisation with greater clarity than could be expected from within the maelstrom of May itself, offering, as Badiou puts it, a "diagonal of the three others" (p.59). The '68 decade' allows us to see that it is ultimately *as* 'student' and 'worker' movements that these two threads remained sociologically placed and, for all their topological intertwinings, conceptually divorced. The post-May period has confirmed this. With rare exceptions, student radicalism has been simultaneously appropriated by the culture industry and nullified by the rise of what Lacan called (in a seminar delivered just after the turmoil) 'university discourse', in which techno-scientific knowledge, rather than the hysterical structure of critique, occupies the position of the master in the social link (see *SXVII*). Even more profoundly, the figure of the worker has receded from political view, as has the factory as a site of political subjectivity. If, culturally, the figures of the students and the workers of May have enjoyed a vibrant afterlife in the stylized shots of Jean-Luc Godard's *La Chinoise* or the photographs of Serge Hambourg (Hambourg: 2006) and so on, politically they are so dead as to rarely appear even as ghosts. The *comités d'action*, even in their attempt to unite workers and militant students, did not offer a durable solution to the question of organisation.

The challenge, then, of a truly singularised, unplaceable politics and an appropriate organisational form remains today because of the 'failures' of May 68 and in particular the closure of the '68 decade'. Precisely as such, however, Badiou argues that we remain contemporaries of May '68. We, too, must search for a new way to organise significant change in the wake of the exhaustion of classical revolutionary politics. For all its confusing complexity then, one thing is certain about May '68 and the decade that followed: it presents us with a stirring antidote to contemporary cynicism and defeatism. As the anonymous graffiti artists of Paris famously put it: 'be realistic, demand the impossible'.

Organisation Politique

Stirring sentiments. Yet if politics demands the impossible, it is only in order to extend the scope of the possible within a given, necessarily constrained situa-

---

28. This is somewhat reminiscent of Situationist tactics of *dérive* although much more successfully subtracted from the bourgeois trope of the *flâneur*. Henri Lefebvre, a thinker closely linked to the Situationists, offers a similarly space-based account of the May 'explosion' (Lefebvre: 1969). For accounts of the Situationist influence on May '68, see Viénet: 1992, Dark Star: 2001, the section entitled 'May 1968 Documents' in Knabb: 1995, and chapter three of Ford: 2005.

tion. To distinguish itself from the kind of inchoate social movement May '68 has been discursively reduced to, politics proper must be analytical, disciplined in some way, and above all organised. In closing this chapter, I want to briefly review the post-May, post-Leninist, post-Maoist group co-founded by Badiou whose very name indicates the centrality of this issue, *Organisation politique* (*OP* from here onwards).[29] By reviewing its declarations, interventions and tactics, I intend to demonstrate its direct connection to the lessons Badiou draws from the historical sequences of conflict we have been following. However, this will also allow us to nuance the critique of Badiou's anti-Statism mounted, via Žižek, above, since a much more complicated relation between politics and the State emerges from the activities of *OP*.

OP formed in 1983 as a splinter-group breaking from the Maoist *Union des communistes de France marxiste-léniniste* (UCFML) which lasted from 1966 until its self-dissolution in 1985. Differentiating itself from the UCFML by adopting a post-classist (post-Marxist) and even post-party (post-Leninist) politics, *OP* nonetheless retains from its origins in the UCFML the Maoist commitment to a small, effective 'cell' of dedicated militants. Its key founding members were only four in number: Alain Badiou himself, Sylvain Lazarus, Natacha Michel and Catherine Quiminal. And in typically Maoist fashion, it has conducted numerous *enquêtes* or 'investigations' into concrete situations, mostly in factories or the 'foyers' where undocumented workers are housed. Its first journal, *Le Perroquet*, was published until 1992. This was then replaced by *La Distance politique* which increasingly became less a theoretical journal and more a functional bulletin for circulating slogans and organising demonstrations. Until recently, *OP*'s analyses and statements were also made available online.[30] Although it is a genuine collective and its declarations must be taken as such, it is probably fair to say that it is the thought of Sylvain Lazarus which is most palpably influential at least in *La Distance politique*: it is his terminology of 'saturation', 'historical mode of politics' and 'politics in interiority' that characterise the group's initial self-descriptions.[31] However, *OP* is not defined by the thought of one individual or even by its small kernel of militants. There are absolutely no criteria for 'membership' beyond involvement in a given cause, since—and this is what accounts for its truly *post*-Maoist character in the wake of both the Chinese Cultural Revolution and May '68—the model of the party is fiercely abjured. If *OP* aims to defend the worker, or rather to resurrect the *figure* of the worker (as we shall see, this is an important distinction), it is without recourse to the parliamentary form of the Socialist Worker's Party or, indeed, the trade unions. Like the Paris Commune, *OP* dissociates itself from all forms of 'Leftism'.

29. Peter Hallward's account of *Organisation politique* (Hallward: 2003) remains the most comprehensive available in English, although we still await the detailed history of the group he calls for.

30. The first *OP* weblink was www.organisationpolitique.com. This was subsequently moved to www.orgapoli.net. However, neither link is live at the time of writing: I have included references to the latter in the hope that it will be active again by the time this book is published. Nonetheless, back issues of *La Distance politique* can still (again, at the time of writing) be found at http://membres.lycos.fr/orgapoli/collection.htm

31. In fact, excerpts from Lazarus's then forthcoming *Anthropologie du nom* appeared in early issues of *La Distance Politique* (see Number 7 for example).

One of the limitations in our conceptualization of organisation is topological. We tend to assume the importance of fixed places and boundaries, of territory and its defence. Yet in the absence of a party and at a distance from the 'corridors of power', it is in fact the scattered, entirely unpredictable and temporary places of politics that become 'central' in a practical rather than spatial sense. Following Lazarus then, the *lieux* in which *OP* intervenes are by definition outside of 'official' State-based politics. This is especially true when the space of State politics is apparently extended to polling stations during elections. *OP* constantly reiterates its proud refusal to vote: "The vote is an anti-declaration organised by the State. As our politics requires the declaration, it is, necessarily, a politics of non-vote. We do not abstain […] We declare our politics according to the places where the vote is absent" ('Europe' in *La Distance Politique*, issue number 8). Places are determined by politics then, not the other way around. They *can* be, and have been for *OP,* the streets, the factories, the schools, whichever building happens to house a meeting, the Parisian foyers, even churches[32] but they can just as easily emerge in entirely unforeseen places.

Nonetheless, if *OP* is concerned to avoid the parliamentary trap, it is just as keen to avoid the fetishization of mass spontaneism (another lesson from May). It therefore maintains *some* organisational forms. Among the more permanent of these are the various 'noyaux' or small groups which have been located in factories such as Billancourt, Flins and Bourogne. These noyaux are not connected to unions and indeed do not 'speak up' for worker's rights per se. Rather, in specific moments, they cooperate with the militants of *OP* to sustain a political subjectivity proper to the factory as a place where, quite simply, workers exist (and not just salaried employees seen only through the statistical lens of capitalist production). The noyaux's activities can be in the form of distributing OP statements or organising informal reading groups for studying militant texts. But also, in a more grassroots manner, it can involve generating prescriptions that crystallise the stakes of a confrontation and help towards agitating for walkouts and stoppages. These last may sound like the traditional tools of trade unionism, but the noyaux in fact provide a radical alternative to the unions. A noyau at the Renault factory in Flins, for example, refused to speak of 'strikes' precisely in order to distance themselves from the unions. The noyaux in general testify that "there exists a political will which is governed neither by worker interest, nor by workerist democratism, but by the decision to face the politics of which we disapprove" without mediation ('La politique des noyaux' in *La Distance Politique*, issue number 8). This strand of the *OP*'s activism arguably stays faithful to its roots in the Maoist interventions into May '68 when the factories were clearly sites of politics.

However, during the 1990s a more transient form of non-factory based organisation, *rassemblements* or 'gatherings', began to play an increasingly prominent role

32. In the summer of 1996 three hundred immigrants of mainly African origin occupied Saint-Bernard church in an attempt to contest the 'illegal' status imposed on them by the Pasqua immigration laws, and to show the French public that their plight was essentially an administrative construct. In this sense, the adoption of the term 'sans papiers', with its clear reference to bureaucracy, was an advance on the previously dominant 'clandestin', with its implication of shadowy evasion. The families were nonetheless forcibly removed from the church after several months.

in *OP* activism. The group claims, however, that such *rassemblements* are removed from the limited goal of run-of-the-mill protest marches, which is generally to demonstrate the numerical weight of opposition to a governmental policy or act (such as Juppé's welfare reforms in the case of the massive December 1995 protests, arguably the largest such movement in France since May-June 1968). Although some have in fact been quite sizeable, *OP*'s *rassemblements* aim instead to demonstrate the qualitative, rather than quantitative, existence of truly political subjects (see 'Rendez-vous de Billancourt: briser l'encerclement' in *La Distance politique*, issue number 3). To take one example, presenting just twenty or thirty *sans papiers* to the public not as an administrative problem for the French government, but as ordinary people with families who are working, or trying to work, just like everyone else, is a way of challenging the divisive Statist nomenclature of '*clandestins*'.

This emphasis on context-specific interventions and the ephemeral nature of the places of politics might seem to make summarising the work of *OP* intrinsically problematic. But would it not be a reification of pure spontaneism to imagine the ghostly disappearance of *OP*'s 'real' work behind the ponderous weight of the mere words it leaves behind? In fact, 'mere' words are absolutely central to its practice in the form of axiomatic declarations forged in the heat of conflict and confrontation. From the outset, *OP* have insisted that the politics they envision and encourage proceeds by means of prescriptions which are "always relative to a concrete situation" but are "neither ideological nor expressive of a party line" (Badiou in E, 96, see also 'Connaissez-vous l'Organisation Politique' in *La Distance politique*, issue number 29). If there is a lingering commitment to something like Leninist discipline then, it is a discipline of rigorously articulated thought rather than of adherence to the party. Indeed one of *OP*'s peculiar gifts is its capacity to formulate simple yet deeply challenging assertions that get to the heart of urgent issues. By examining some of these prescriptions, arrived at through a typically Maoist combination of direct struggle and theoretical reflection, we can get a sense of what might be termed the *OP*'s logic of conflict.

To the extent that one of *OP*'s goals is the recuperation of the abjected figure of the worker, it has formulated prescriptions such as 'in the factory, there are workers', 'without its workers, there is no country', 'workers count!' and simply 'work counts!' (see *La Distance politique*, issue number 1). Worker here means not the sociologically inert category defined by management and the State, but the political *figure* of the worker capable of generating thought of his or her own. In this sense, the term 'worker' can be opposed to 'employee' insofar as the latter is statistically triangulated by salary budgets, attendance records, and productivity measures. In a manner reminiscent perhaps of early Marx and the discourse of 'species-being', the term 'worker' tries to bring out the intrinsic, non-monetary value and dignity of work itself. Thus, when, in 1991, workers at the soon-to-be-closed Renault factory at Billancourt were offered a redundancy package whose conditions included a signed admission that they left 'voluntarily', 130 people refused to sign (see 'l'Ouvrier qui ne signe pas' in *La Distance politique*, issue number 1). The refusal to sign up was a refusal to conform to capital's demands for an anonymous and flexible army of mobile labour. It was also a refusal of the implicit erasure of years of

loyal service by means of the 80,000 Franc pay-off. Where capital wanted to reduce these workers to a redundancy package—an 'outlay' fully justified by the increased productivity gained at the new site—*OP* helped the workers assert their
subjectivity *qua* workers which was, in part, the sedimented result of many years
of labour within a shared habitus. Again, the notion that the abstract, objectifying
time recognised by capital and something closer to the living, subjective time of
sensuous labour are in antagonistic contradiction is reminiscent of early if not late
Marx.[33] So the notion that 'workers count' and that 'work counts' is a demand for a
mode of counting other than that of technocratic capital. This is much more radical than a *syndicaliste* call for recognition, which would suggest the goal of improved
integration. It constitutes a call for a completely different regime of evaluation.

Probably the most sophisticated and insightful analysis put forward by the *OP*
connects the disappearance of the political figure of the worker to the rise of the racialised discourse surrounding the *sans papiers*. Of course, workers have long been
subject to a zoological tropology comparing them to rats and so forth. Yet *OP* traces the emergence, particularly during strikes in the 1980s, of a specifically xenophobic discourse in which militant workers became first 'immigrants', then 'illegal
aliens', then 'clandestines' and more recently 'sans papiers'. An oft-cited example in
the pages of *La Distance politique* is the description, by then-Prime Minister Pierre
Mauroy, of striking workers at Talbot and Flins in 1983 as "Shiites and strangers to
the social realities of France" (see 'Conditions pour la conscience démocratique' in
issue number 1). This divisive rhetoric has found legal support in France through
a series of reactionary pieces of legislation vociferously opposed by *OP*: the Pasqua
laws of 1993, the Debré laws of 1996, the Weil-Chevénement laws of 1997-98, and
the Sarkozy-CESEDA laws of 2006. Presented as immigration acts, *OP* maintain
that these are also anti-worker acts, not least because most *sans papiers* are economic migrants seeking work. This is arguably another echo of the Maoist influence
on May '68. For just as the Maoist critique of the imperialist nature of capitalism
enabled a critical link to be forged between the colonial other abroad and the exploited French worker at home in the run up to May, so *OP* recognise the attempted *erasure* of this link through the marginalisation of the worker by the figurative
centralisation of the ex-colonised 'alien'. In this way, the contradiction between labour and capital can be phrased as a bureaucratic problem of immigration relevant to the diasporic impacts of economic globalisation. But whereas the solution
proposed by most of the activists in May was class-based, *OP* maintain a strictly
post-classist, egalitarian and generic vision.

Hence the profound power of a prescription such as 'everyone who is here
is from here'. This offers a major challenge to any State attempting to define itself in terms of ethnic, religious or cultural specificities and to police its borders

---

33. In his *Anthroplogie du nom*, Lazarus opposes the temporal unicity of Statist nomination to the
'homogenous mulitiplicity' of the political name: to take a simple example, he opposes the factory as a place of measured time to the timeless demand of the political figure of the worker. For a
complication of this opposition, see Antonio Negri's *Time For Revolution* (2003) in which any use-
value outside of exchange, and thus any measure for labour-time as an externality in relation to
production, is encompassed within 'real subsumption'.

accordingly. RTo the extent that the French State does this, Jean-Marie Le Pen's xenophobic nationalism is the fundamental truth of its so-called 'democracy'. Laurent Fabius admitted as much when in 1985 he openly said that "Le Pen poses the true problems". But from the notion that 'everybody who is here is from here' follows the necessity of naturalising the *sans papiers* who are very much present in France. *OP* argue that they should be naturalised on the basis not of asylum claims or religious, ethnic or cultural compatibility with the host nation, since it is precisely this communitarian vision that cultivates the likes of Le Pen, but simply on the basis of work.[34] If they are already working and contributing, they should be given papers. What therefore also follows from the declaration 'everyone who is here is from here' is the intimate connection between anti-racist activism and support for the worker's struggle. a strictly complimentary prescription is "Strengthen the workers, and thereby limit Lepenism" ('Conditions pour la conscience démocratique' in issue number 1).

This leads us to examine the *OP*s changing relation to charged terms like 'country', 'nation', 'State' and particularly 'Nation-State'. Perhaps in an effort to escape its Marxist-Leninist origins in the UCFML, one of the most startling and certainly insistent claims made by *OP* early on was that its politics was 'at a distance from the State' (this is the central meaning of its journal's title). At the level of its trenchant critique of parliamentarism and the illusory agency of the vote, 'distance' initially seemed to mean haughty aloofness. However, over time—and I would argue that this change is also reflected in Badiou's philosophical work in the all-important transition form *Being and Event* to *Logics of Worlds*—it has taken on a more complex meaning, arguably driven by the practical exigencies of *OP*s activism with workers and *sans papiers*, both of whose interrelated plights are unavoidably connected to the State. Interestingly, the other significant prompt for reflecting in a more nuanced manner on the question of the State seems to have been the collapse of ex-Soviet states in the early 1990s, and the break-up of former Yugoslavia in particular. In issue 4 of *La Distance politique*, a critique is formulated of the ethnic and religious lines along which the NATO powers seemed happy to patch together the post-Tito situation. Consistent with their disdain for the two-state solution to the Israel-Palestine conflict, *OP* argue that such a parliamentarisation of essentialised differences leads to war, not peace. But in the course of this analysis, a series of distinctions are made that come to have an impact on how *OP* view their own relation to the French State.

Firstly, the concept 'country' is separated from that of the State to the extent that the former *can* be a place prescriptively produced by its people (as in the constitutional 'we the people'), and thus a generic collective rather than a multiplicity of unequal differences. The contemporary State, by contrast, is an apolitical mechanism of control and order that operates primarily through a form of 'divide and rule'. Not only does it try to govern without the people that make up the country, but more than ten years after their analysis of Yugoslavia, *OP* refer to the

---

34. For related reasons, *OP* also agitate for equality in schools under the slogan 'A child, a student' specifically to oppose the powers, granted under the Sarkozy-CESEDA laws, to take the children of undocumented parents out of school often to execute deportation orders.

"fascism of the State" which wages war *against* the people by distinguishing them as 'foreigners', 'youth', 'the unemployed', 'Muslims' and so on (see 'Déclaration sur la situation actuelle dans les écoles' at www.orgapoli.net). In contrast to Badiou's set-theoretical and therefore *structurally* apolitical character of the State, however, in the analysis of the Yugoslav war the problem is historicized. A more prescriptive understanding of the State as emerging from the generic collectivity of a people is possible, and history demonstrates this: the underlying referent here is obviously the role of the term 'France' in the revolutionary Republicanism of 1789-1799, but I would add the emancipatory role of nationalism in anti-colonial struggles in the first half of the Twentieth Century. Yet, argue *OP*, today this possibility has become "*périmé*", it has passed its use-by-date. Indeed, attempts to resurrect this generic nationalism have led to massive bloodshed precisely because they have failed to separate out the territory administered by a State apparatus and the purely political subject constitutive of a 'national character': the example given is the ultra-nationalism of the Khmers Rouge. Again, to counter this essentialist nationalism, *OP* offer clear prescriptions: "'Country' must be a political place', and 'The country is the people who live there'.

Two issues later in *La Distance politique*, and after clarifying their reading of ex-Yugoslavia, *OP* begin to confront the implications of this reading of the State for their own activism: as if anticipating Žižek's critique, it is now asserted that the separation of State and politics does not lead to the "banishment of the State outside the field of the thought of politics" and moreover that "in order that 'country' be a political place, prescriptions on the State are necessary" ('Au sujet des prescriptions sur l'État' in issue number 6). By issue 11, a full-scale "adjustment" of *OP*'s position is explicitly announced in 'La politique et l'État'. While the doctrine of the strict separation of the State and politics had been essential in establishing the specificity of the rare and singular nature of the latter, it was now just as essential to renew the State on the basis of this reconceptualised politics. It is recognised that the democratic space is always *internal* to the State rather than being opposed to it or outside of it. It is further recognised that the very possibility of politics is predicated upon a "non-dialectical" relation between the "subjective and the objective" which it is the role of the State to cleave together. What this seems to acknowledge is a Gramsci-like hegemonic link between popular consent and State power, and the importance of traffic between the two. But to escape the very classical model of sovereignty suggested by this binding of governance (objectivity) to the governed (subjectivity), and the liberal parliamentarism it suggests, two further elements need to be added. Firstly, that of the *pure* subjectivity of singular politics which, as Badiou would later put it, unbinds the social bond maintained by the State (see chapter 4 in *Metapolitics*). But secondly—and this is really the crux of the 'adjustment'—that there is no truly pure, extra-Statist subjectivity that can afford not to address its prescriptions to the State. *OP*'s approach now is therefore not one "where it would be necessary to oppose the State, as sole objectivity, to politics, as unique subjectivity". Instead, it involves a recognition of two interrelated facts about the State. Firstly, that in attempting to 'structure away' the impossible (parliamentarism is defined by its erasure of political innovation) the

State simultaneously opens up unregulated pockets of possibility. that is, the State imposes its objectivity but both needs the subjectivity it creates, and, despite itself, proliferates sites of possible novelty and thus politics. But secondly and just as importantly, that the kind of politics it thereby makes possible must maintain a principled distance from the notion, fatally present in orthodox Marxism-Leninism, that the State *itself* can be a political place, and thus a goal in a programme: "The place is not political, the prescription is. The State is a non-political place which, even politically prescribed, does not transform itself into a political place [...] that the State can never be a political place is that in which its essential objectivity consists".

A key prescription *on* or even *against* the State, which cannot come *from* the State in anything other than empty rhetorical form, is the fundamental axiom of egalitarian democracy: 'everyone counts as one', or perhaps more precisely 'every one counts as one'. This is the opposite of saying everyone counts as One, i.e., a closed and unified set such as a totalizing nation-state, but it is also not homologous with liberal individualism, since it articulates a right to sameness rather than difference. To take the paradigmatic example for the *OP*, the demand of the *sans papiers* is precisely not to be considered in their Senegalese or Algerian specificity, but to work and enjoy the health care and education enjoyed by other citizens of France. In the terminology of *Being and Event* the prescription 'every one counts as one' confronts Statist representation with presentation, the hierarchical count of the count with the count as such, the putative One with the multiplicity of ones it encompasses. In a context like France then (but the same could certainly be said of Britain), the notion that every one counts for one continually challenges the unruly mass of predicates gathered under the term 'French'. France then, as a generic category, must be opposed to the exclusivity of Frenchness, and this must be done via prescription *on* or *to* but never *through* the State.

If our first chapter exploring Badiou's explicitly Maoist phase demonstrated his conceptual progress beyond reciprocal contradiction (with the State as a necessary component of antagonism) and towards scission as an internal and constitutive splitting of what the State attempts to order, we glimpse with the activism of *Organisation politique* a theory of conflict which neither takes the State as its inevitable and exclusive terrain, nor ignores the State's logic of inclusion. From *Being and Event* onwards, it becomes clear that the politics of conflict involve both an anti-Statist process of subtraction and a truth-procedure which is itself State-like. In the next chapter, we will look at the name as an indispensable site of this play of anti-State subtraction and State-like nomination.

3

The Conflict of Names

We already saw in the last chapter the complex importance of the names attached to political sequences. We saw that the term 'revolution' in the French Revolution continues to resist revisionist interpretations by carrying the challenge of egalitarianism into the present. But we also noted that the very same term in the Russian sequence arguably serves an exactly opposite role, that of petrifying the memory of past innovation in order to suppress its potential emergence in the (Stalinist) present. Likewise, the name 'Paris Commune' becomes, after Lenin's intervention and Stalin's distortion of it, an historical cipher for the necessity of iron party discipline. Yet in Mao's China during the Cultural Revolution, the same referent morphs into the precise inverse: a call to arms *against* the Party-State. As for the name 'May '68', we saw that it perpetuates many of the ambiguities of the tumultuous episode it designates. Chronologically, 'May' brackets out both the militant pre-history that made it possible, and the largely post-May General Strike which made it so significant. Moreover, the culturalist reworking of the 'May' signifier has more or less successfully transformed an anti-capitalist insurrection into a capitalist 'revolution'. Even more worryingly, we saw with Nazism the dangerous possibility of a completely simulacral name with only the appearance of a grounding in truth, as well as the deadly violence consequent upon a naming of the unnameable void.

From these examples, it is already clear that names in themselves are fragile ('revolution' can mean diametrically opposed things), site-specific ('Paris Commune' in Soviet Russia and Maoist China), and susceptible to both 'saturation' ('revolution' after May '68) and apparent erasure ('Communism' following the collapse of the Soviet Union). Yet the previous chapter also demonstrated that the task of rescuing truths from reactionary historiography can have no other starting point, indeed no other material on which to work, than names. We also saw, in the activism of the *Organisation politique*, that the name 'worker' needs to be endowed with a subjectivity that the objectifying Statist nomination eradicates. The fate of the name is therefore at the core of the conflict over truths. In a sense that is only *prima facie* idealist then, the name appended to an event determines in a very fundamental way the modes of possible fidelity to it. Without a name, quite simply, there can be no event (although as we shall see, Badiou changes his position on this by *Logics of Worlds*). This issue is of such significance for evaluating Badiou's philosophy, particularly as a potential contribution to the theorisation of conflict, that this chapter will be entirely devoted to it.

COUNTER-NOMINATION

Before looking at Badiou's theory of the evental name and some of the sources upon which it draws, it is important to emphasise something to which Badiou himself arguably pays insufficient attention: the State's power of what I will call 'counter-nomination'. Given that in the absence of a name an event cannot be said to have happened at all, it follows that the names imposed and circulated by the State in response to an event constitute a profound threat to evental transformation. Counter-nomination, then, can be defined in the following way: it is the Statist strategy of obscuring the implications of a fundamental disruption by appending to its traces an existing Statist label. Such names bring with them three interlinked elements anathema to the logic of the event:

1. An implied causality and origin: the counter-nomination links the disturbance to a network of banal names that structure the world as it is
2. A reactionary judgement: the counter-nomination ascribes a negative value to the disturbance as measured by a Statist norm
3. An asserted legitimacy: the counter-nomination both enacts the State's authority to name and encodes the appropriate (read: exclusively Statist) response

Nomination in general, as opposed to counter-nomination, can be understood as *the* Statist operation. The State names individuals as belonging or not belonging to a national or other community, as occupying such and such a position within the hierarchy of that community, as performing such and such a role, as enjoying such and such rights, and so on. To the extent that the *polis* is a rational ordering of individuals and institutions, activities and capacities, functions and movements, it is inherently taxonomic and topological: it both produces types, and distributes them in a productive spatial assemblage. For Jacques Rancière this is the function of the 'police', understood in an expanded sense as "the set of procedures whereby the aggregation and consent of collectivities is achieved, the organization of powers, the distribution of places and roles, and the system for legitimizing this distribution" (Rancière: 1998, p.28). The police, then, is not simply "the truncheon blows of the forces of law and order" (*ibid.*), but "an order of bodies that defines the allocation of ways of doing, ways of being, and ways of saying, and sees those bodies are assigned *by name* to a particular place and task" (Rancière: 1998, p.29—my emphasis). The police therefore enforce, through naming, what Rancière calls 'the distribution [*partage*] of the sensible', which is to say, the hierarchical unity of what is both common and divisive in a community (he plays here on the double meaning of *partage*: a sharing that creates the common, but also a sharing *out* that unevenly distributes this supposed common). Such policing is akin to the divide and rule tactic of colonialism, in which names divide a space and its inhabitants for the purposes of administration. All States practice internal colonialism of this kind. Yet this is not a simple process, Rancière argues: "the police order thus defined cannot be turned into that dim leveller in which everything looks the same" (*ibid*, p.30). One of Rancière's key points is that the 'distribution of the sensible' determines what is visible and invisible, sayable and unsayable, in the policed domain, so that parts that remain nameless in a society literally have no visible or audible part or role within it. So if this police mode of nomination can be considered the *sine qua non* of Statist rational ordering, what Rancière calls, simply, politics is the subjective transformation of this nominal matrix through the poetic invocation of the "part of no part", the nameless.

However, what I want to underline through the notion of *counter*-nomination is the fact that the State is eminently capable of responding to the irruption of politics in this rarefied sense. In Rancière's terms, we could say the State is adept at reducing politics to the police. Unlike the poetic novelty of the names of politics (as we shall see in the next section), counter-nominations are drawn from an array of *existing* terms, including 'politics' itself, though kept for the most part in reserve for 'emergency' situations. It is vital to note here that, as we have seen post 9-11, it is often in the interests of the State to declare something like a permanent state of emergency precisely to turn a *rhetoric* of counter-nomination into the quotidian duty of the State, as if banal nomination were in fact exceptional counter-nomination. In this instance, I would argue that we are dealing with simulacral counter-nominations that correspond to simulacral events. As with the event, then, much depends on being able to distinguish true 'political' names from false Statist names.

Although I will argue in Chapter 5 that it has an important historical dimension, counter-nomination is nonetheless predominantly an urgent task in the present because its aim can be described in the following elliptical way: *to turn the event into instantaneous history.* That is, counter-nomination reduces the event to something causally connected to the world, something perhaps noteworthy and significant, but in the end, internal to the policed order and not therefore political in Rancière's very Badiouian sense. The event can only threaten the policed world if it can found its singularity upon a *non*-Statist name that gives it form and force despite the fact that what it reveals is invisible, unsayable and undecideable. Conversely, counter-nomination makes the disruptive appearance of an event visible, sayable and entirely decidable by assigning it an existing name, even if that name nominates, in Schmittian fashion, the exception itself. And the urgency of counter-nomination includes a framing of the 'legitimacy' of the immediate response from the State. If an outbreak of unrest is named an 'insurrection', and thus categorized as a direct challenge to constituted authority, it obviously meets with proportionally severe measures. The almost immediate description by the Bush administration of the terrorist attacks of 9/11 as 'an act of war' clearly categorized it, inserted it into a certain historical narrative, and laid the foundations for a military response modelled on the very image of wars between nation-states that transnational terrorism cuts across.

If Badiou is insistent that the event is undecideable, he is equally insistent that this is simultaneously a weakness and a strength. It is a weakness to the extent that the State can do its utmost to 'decide' it away by naming it otherwise, but it is a strength to the extent that, as constitutively excrescent, something will inevitbaly escape the State's taxonomic capture. I would argue, however, that ultimately, the accent falls on the weakness of the event since the appearance of this excrescence relies on the prior success of the eventual name and has no existence apart from it (as long as we do not imagine the name abstracted from the subjects that declare it). The Badiouian twist is that this weakness is a call to arms for the subject who can turn it, jujitsu style, into a strength. But if the State succeeds in getting there first, then it is initially difficult to see how an event can get underway without also countering counter-nomination.

Moreover, as well as keeping in reserve a panoply of names which counter-name the event as a possible 'incident', the State also deploys a similarly rich vocabulary in counter-naming the subjects who attempt to be faithful to the event, and without whom an event's truth has no 'body', no material impact on the world. Clearly, a 'people's liberation army' or 'freedom fighters' become, from the State's point of view, simply 'terrorists' whom they are obliged to eliminate. Likewise, politico-legal terms such as 'illegal immigrant', 'refugee' and 'asylum seeker' police the movement of bodies across sovereign territories by appending to those bodies names which are functions of bureaucratic control. Illegal immigrants are illegal because they duck under the border controls that regulate entry and exit, except that, so named, they are of course fully ensconced within those controls (what else are visas but names that police the 'proper' of a territory and its narrative of legitimate belonging). Once absorbed into this bureaucratic machinery, 'refugees' and 'asylum seekers' are made to incorporate their own very particular stories into crude, State-driven templates of narratives of human rights abuses, templates that are notoriously bad at encompassing the low level abuse of humans that is massive structural economic inequality. Now, the rarity of events means that one can never assume that illegal immigrants are somehow always subjects of a truth, but it is certainly the case that being named as such reduces their practical capacity to become subjects in the Badiouian sense. Counter-nominations are a particularly intense form of policing: taxonomy and topology are reduced to, respectively, 'types' defined exclusively by their constitutive need to be policed (the asylum seeker), and the absolute restriction of movement and interaction (the detention centre).

Related to nomination as the policing of a now global sovereignty, the designation 'underdeveloped', attributed to countries in the Southern hemisphere particularly, imposes a linear model of development always relationally connected to both the history and the geography of Euro-America. The very term 'underdeveloped' thereby justifies, in an apparently neutral or even benevolent descriptor, a dubious neo-colonial development discourse that reinscribes the North/South divide and produces the very 'illegal immigrants', 'refugees' and so on we have just been discussing. In this sense, something like the Non-Aligned Movement in the 1970s was, at the level of its name (which, I am trying to show, is quite a 'deep' level), an attempted counter-counter-nomination. But again, where a certain emancipatory discourse might defend 'anti-colonial activists', 'the non-aligned' or 'alter-globalists' etc., the (World) State always has at its disposal terms such as 'failed' or 'rogue states'. It is crucial to note, too, that the *Index of Failed States* published annually by the American think-tank 'Fund for Peace' does not include Palestine or Kosovo at all: to recognise them as 'states', even if only to fail them, would paradoxically endorse their struggles for national self-determination as in some way legitimate.

As we shall see below, Badiou points out that many counter-nominations for would-be subjects construct a narrative of pernicious foreign influence. This is a way of covering up the founding interiority of the void by externalizing its destructuring power. So the inefficiencies of collectivization for Stalin were really due to the nefarious influence of saboteurs and Kulaks who allegedly hoarded grain rather than surrendering it to the State in order to speculate, like capitalists, on higher prices. Similarly, we saw in the last chapter that the figure of the Jew, as a sort of included enemy that needs to be purged helped to cover over the indiscriminate death-drive of National Socialism. The malleable, because ultimately empty, term 'terrorist' provides such alarming scope for what I am calling 'counter-nomination' because it encapsulates this logic of 'the enemy within'. It is one of the key problems of our times.

But let me be clear about what, precisely, the problem of counter-nomination is. The point is *not* that political subjects must engage in a tit-for-tat war of discursive position with the State, as if what mattered was the hegemonic fate of the name itself. There is a danger here of getting caught up in the infinite strategic regress of a binary vision of the State and radical politics, with the name as the terrain of this confrontation. This is arguably the impasse of the politics of democratic articulation expounded by Laclau and Mouffe (2001). Concentrating on the name alone, and limiting politics to a terrain staked out in advance by the State, potentially leads to two apparently opposed but actually intimately interlinked outcomes: parliamentarism, and what Mao used to call 'ultra-leftism'. Instead, what I want to emphasise is the delicate role of the eventalname in evading both of these traps. The practical problem of the interplay between both Statist nomination and evental nomination on the one hand, and evental nomination and Statist counter-nomination on the other, must be attended to closely if the fragility of the event is to be ameliorated. I begin with this problem of the interweaving of these three orders of nomination—banal, evental and reactionary—in order to see if Badiou's theory of the eventalname provides an adequate solution to the challenge posed by counter-nomination.

LAZARUS' ANTHROPOLOGY OF THE NAME

However, a further detour is required before we can address this question. It is vital to first acknowledge one of the major influences on Badiou in the form of the thought of his old comrade in arms, Sylvain Lazarus. In *Metapolitics*, Badiou openly acknowledges that Lazarus' 'historical mode of politics' is equivalent to his own 'truth-procedure', even going so far as to declare that "My thought on this point is sustained, purely and simply, by that of Lazarus" (*M*, p.52). It is therefore worth looking in some detail at Lazarus' *Anthropologie du nom* which, although it appeared in 1996, crystallizes an approach that had been developing in the pages of *La Distance* from its inception.

What, for Lazarus, is a name? And what is a name such that it requires, of all things, an anthropology? Since Lazarus' use of the term is almost the exact contrary of our usual understanding, it is perhaps easiest to begin by outlining what a name is *not*. The name is not a simple label for a thing in the world. Nor is it, conversely, a mere discursive construct with no purchase on 'reality'. It is not a concept which mediates perception. It is also not a description of a state of affairs which adheres to logical form. It is not even, as Saussure would insist, arbitrary and produced by means of purely relational difference. So the name in Lazarus' sense is so exceptional that it does not conform, respectively, to naïve nominalism, postmodern constructivism, transcendental phenomenology, formal logic in analytic philosophy, or even synchronic linguistics.

To take each of these in turn, the name is not a label for a thing in the world because it does not index a pre-existing referent, a coherent given object. Lazarus is very far indeed from being a 'nominalist', if by that we understand someone who advocates a correspondence model of language based on the foundational role of noun designation. In fact, for him, a crucial property of the name is that it has no *object* whatsoever. He means this in both the empirical sense of 'something out there' to which the name points, and in the more Foucaultian sense of a discursively triangulated construction filtered through power (in the way that disciplines of knowledge construct 'objects' of study). The name is not a mere discursive construct because it actively subtracts itself from discourse, precisely as the nexus between power and knowledge. Yet it is not without purchase on 'reality' either, as if it were 'merely' linguistic. The name is produced within and from reality, but it supports a subjectivity that, by confronting that reality with its real in the Lacanian sense, actively opposes the processes of objectification that structure it. For the same reason, the name cannot be a concept either, because it does not proceed by adequation, by the subsumption of a perception or phenomenon under an a priori schema of intelligibility. In fact if it names any*thing* in the mundane sense it is that which evades a priori discernment. This evasion is not due to some flaw or glitch in the mode of discernment itself. Rather it is the consequence of an active practice of thought that pursues a novelty incompatible with quotidian conceptual capture.

But if it is not a concept in the Kantian sense, nor is it a concept in the Foucaultian sense of an anchoring point in a field of statements that make up a discursive formation (Foucault: 2003). Whereas Foucault accounts for the movement of concepts between disciplines (how medical expertise can carry weight as expert testimony in the field of law for example), Lazarus insists that names are utterly "distinct" and, in that sense, un-disciplined (Lazarus: 1996, p.119). Far from circulating in easy discursive transactions, names are rooted in both finite historical 'modes' (such as the Bolshevik mode or the Leninist mode) and in the discrete *places* of their enunciation, whether that be the soviets, the factories, the streets or the universities. This emphasis on place also explains why the kind of name invoked by Lazarus does not conform to the structuralist formalism of

Saussurian linguistics. While it is arbitrary in the ontological sense of having no essential connection to its 'referent' (it doesn't have one), it is nonetheless 'motivated' in the same sense that Roland Barthes, drawing on Saussure, speaks of a second-level mythological order at which arbitrariness is ideologically overdetermined (Barthes: 1993). Like Bathesian myth, the name also *reworks* an existing conceptual field. The name that comes to be deployed within a politics has to be taken from that field in order to materially affect it—a point Badiou, too, will insist on when he argues that the name must be 'drawn from the edge of the void' (Meditation 20 of *BE*). So Lazarus's notion of the name is not reducible to Saussure's axiom of relational difference since it must withdraw itself from the conventional fixity of *la langue* in order to *parole* otherwise, and always from a concrete context or place.

Thus—and now we must start speaking more affirmatively of what names *are*—the power but also the fragility of the name according to Lazarus resides in its ability to suspend the circulation of mere words. In the normal course of things, these words are sustained by exhaustive definitions and technical protocols of usage, and together make up what Lazarus calls 'heterogeneous multiplicities', a term which corresponds to something like Badiou's 'encyclopaedia of knowledge': a systematic way of categorising and differentiating phenomena for ultimately conservative ends. By suspending the hold that such 'heterogeneous multiplicities' exercise over everyday discourse, the exceptional name upon which Lazarus focuses carries the thought constitutive of what he calls a 'homogeneous multiplicity'. Again, this term has a rough equivalent in Badiou's lexicon. It resembles what in *Logics of Worlds* is called a 'subject-body', a rare and singular subjectivity that has self-constituent *interiority* as its mode of existence and action, rather than the exteriority of 'heterogeneous multiplicities' which demand that names become instrumentalised, institutionalised, productive.

To do its work then, the name cannot be like an ordinary name in any way. It actively refuses to be defined by an object. We saw in the last chapter an example of why this might be important in the activism of the *Organisation politique*, for whom the name 'worker' must be recovered from its reduction to an impoverished signifier of employment or productivity statistics. In the mobilisations organised at Bilancourt etc. *Organisation politique* turned the name 'worker' into a catalyst for a subjectivity that not even the trade unions, with their discourse of rights, could recognise. So this kind of name manages to open up a space both of subjective political action and, simultaneously, of that subjective action's 'thinkability', since politics 'in interiority' is necessarily a form of thought for Lazarus. Thought here means something like an active exploration of the possible that does not draw on the external resource of the given, but only on itself, on thought's inner reserves. In this way, the name, conjoined with the place of its enunciation and the subjectivity it supports, is *a prescription of possibility* rather than, indeed opposed to, a description of actuality.

It follows—and again, this will be important for Badiou—that Lazarus's version of the name is itself unnameable. Naming in the everyday sense "opens onto a generalisation, a typology, or onto a polysemy [...] which denies singularity" (p.16).

Indeed, the delicate balance to be struck in Lazarus' project is to *think* political sin-gularity without naming it, as other disciplines such as history or political science attempt to do. The name, as catalyst of subjectivity, must remain unnameable by any 'objective' criteria. Given that these kinds of names must remain unnameable, we might be forgiven for accusing Lazarus of using a misnomer, as it were, in uti-lising the term 'name' at all. However, the whole point of his intervention is that only an exceptional kind of name can keep open this crucial place of the unname-able, and ensure its thinkability both in the present of its 'taking place', and in the historicity of its 'having taken place'. As for Badiou, the value of the name lies in its capacity to act as a torsion between the actual and the potential, the old and the immanent new.

We have addressed the first part of our question, but not the second: why does this non-objective, prescriptive rather than descriptive, and ultimately unname-able name require an anthropology rather than a semantics, a rhetoric, a prag-matics or, indeed, a philosophy? Lazarus's is certainly a strange kind of anthro-pology, one in which the content of *anthropos* is deliberately boiled down to an extreme minimalism. He founds his 'anthropology of the name' on two fundamen-tal enunciations:

1. 'People think' (Lazarus: 1996, p.15)
2. 'Thought is a relation of the real' (*ibid.*, p.17)

The term 'people' here is resolutely empty. It does not designate a culturally or ter-ritorially bounded community with a particular identity. Instead, Lazarus refers to 'people' as a *certain indistinct* (p.17) which only points to the existence of a 'there is' of thought without ascribing predicates to its thinkers. Strictly speaking, the thinkers of a thought, in the proprietorial sense of a thought's 'originators', are erased along with the subject-object distinction. Thought comes 'before' its thinkers in the same sense that, for Badiou, there can be no subject without a prior event. But Lazarus also wants to prohibit the lapse into an idealist, disembodied thought or Spinoz-ist rational substance. Even if there are no 'people' without thought, the necessity of the 'people' that think roots subjectivity in concrete contexts. In Badiou's hands, this minimal philosophical anthropology is used much more clearly as a coun-ter to the prevailing cynicism of our times. A sort of article of faith, it grounds an optimism in the permanent human *capacity* for thought even in its contingent ab-sence. The name needs an anthropology, then, simply because unnameable names emerge from thought, and thinking is what people do.

The first assertion that people think is constrained by the second, that thought is a relation of the real. Badiou himself comments on the oddity of this formulation: '"Relation of" is clearly opposed to 'relation to'. Thought is not a re-lation *to* the object, it is an *internal* relation of its Real, which taken 'in itself' re-mains indistinct" (*MP*, 28). Any discourse constructs its own category of the real, so that, as Lazarus puts it, philosophy is a thought-relation-of-thought, and his-tory is a thought-relation-of-the-State, but only the anthropology of the name is a thought-relation-of-the-real itself (Lazarus: 1996, p.17)—and as such, it is only the anthropology of the name that insists on exposing a "non objectal real". The notion that 'people think' on its own could remain immured within the realm of the imaginary, of 'reality' as it is. The second enunciation is required to link thought to the real as the kernel of impossibility that *prescribes* its own possibility, and thereby opens up a horizon of potential change.

As an anthropology, this approach resembles a discipline of knowledge, but it is a paradoxical one reminiscent of late Lacan's call for a 'science of the real' (see *SXX*). It is only possible as a knowledge-like practice because, although the name 'itself' is unnameable and thus unknowable, a politics that mobilises such a name will deploy its own 'intellectuality' (its own way of thinking the thought that it is). This intellectuality *can* be analysed and known. Furthermore, it will contain 'categories' which orient its unfolding—so the category of Jacobinism was 'virtue', while the category of Leninism was 'revolution' etc.—and whose subsequent fates can be historically and politically mapped. To avoid reducing the name to an objective definition, the anthropology of the name has to think the thought of a politics by inhabiting the interiority of its intellectuality, naming its categories and their deployment, whether it is an 'historical mode' that has come to an end, or whether it is a singularity in the present. One of Badiou's major debts to Lazarus, in fact, is to the notion of 'saturation', referring to the decline of a category which is foundational for a political sequence, for example, the 'Party' after the Cultural Revolution, 'revolution' itself after May '68, or indeed 'Communism' after 1989 (p.37). This sounds like a melancholy task, but what Lazarus refers to as the 'method' of saturation actually involves an investigation of the possibilities for *new* categories that open with the demise of old ones: the 'method of saturation' asks what, out of this failure, do we inherit that can be made into a success? Lazarus makes a distinction between the 'redoubling' of names, which simply reinscribes the symbolic order, and their 'reiteration', which creates a gap or separation between "thought and the thought of thought" (p.80)—say between a political sequence and an investigation of the categories that sequence deploys—and it is this iterative gap that resists symbolic redoubling. If he refers to the 'simple name' this simplicity must be conceived in the sense that physics or chemistry gives to that term: something irreducible, elemental. The simple name resists both the banal nominal matrix that places all the components of a given situation, and the metalinguistic analyses of so-called political science that would claim to 'name the name', thereby abstracting it from its places and neutralising its interiority. The anthropology of the name is not a distanced contemplation, then, but a participation in both the historicity of a sequence and the prescriptions active in the present.

THE EVENTAL NAME

Much of Lazarus's work in *Anthropologie du nom* is carried over into Badiou's own theory of the eventual name. Like the keystone in a roman arch, this theory bears a decisive weight in Badiou's entire system. For it is the torsion of the name that links the pre-evental situation to its post-evental reconfiguration. It is, in other words, Badiou's answer, at least in the first volume of *Being and Event*, to his guiding question about how novelty can emerge from within a situation without being absorbed back into default schemas of intelligibility. The name of the event is the very mark of that aleatory decision which gambles on the event's existence. It is therefore the necessary condition of subjective intervention. As we have already observed, no name, no event; no event, no subject; no subject, no truth. À la Lazarus then, the name of the event must be, from the point of view of the situation, exceptional, enigmatic, unplaceable. This is because the name indexes a decision on the indiscernible that resolutely refuses Statist modes of, precisely, discernment. And yet the name is very far from indulging a merely poetic invocation of the ineffable, of the tantalizing but foreclosed far side of representation. On the contrary, the name must come from somewhere within the situation (what Badiou calls the 'edge of the void') in order to unfold a rigorously *implicative* logic, in the mathematical sense, one that challenges the state of a situation to count an excrescent or impossible multiple as one of its own elements. Thus, as the orienting point of the truth-procedure and, ultimately, of forcing, the name of the event is the prerequisite for genuine, radical transformation. What is often overlooked, however, is that Badiou also incorporates into his theory of the eventual name a series of provisos and qualifications that amount to a kind of ethics of the name. It is imperative, then, that we look at it in some detail.

Perhaps one of the biggest misconceptions about Badiou's theory of the name is that the event boils down to 'something happening' and the struggle to give that 'something' adequate representation. In the end, this characterisation involves a simplistic before-and-after temporality and the supposed extension of the State's nominal reach to cover the enigmatic point articulating the two. This obdurate image has at least two negative consequences. First, the notion that 'something happens' all-too quickly sidesteps Badiou's insistence that the event is non-ontological, that, in a very important sense, events do *not* happen, but must be made to happen precisely because they leave no ontological trace. Second, it turns events into an essentially juridical problem of historical 'justice', as if the only thing preventing events being recognized as such is the dearth of encyclopedic evidence. Such claims simply imply a more 'detailed' encyclopedia, an improvement of the given framework of representation. In fact, the accent of Badiou's analysis falls not on turning an event into a 'fact' that finally finds its place among the others that represent a situation's history to itself, that is, on finding a Statist name for it. It is not at *inclusion* in Statist representation that the eventual name aims. Instead, the emphasis is very much on the event as an axiom that maintains the militant will of a transformative subject, whether or not the existing State accords it any factual value whatsoever (structurally, of course, it cannot), now, or at any time in the future. The result of forcing is not at all the recognition, by *this* State, of an element it did not previously include. On the contrary, the result of forcing is another State, a new State. Unlike certain deconstructive elaborations of a politics *à venir* then, future recognition or inclusion of eventual names would not represent 'justice' but the very opposite. The future is a form of continuity, whereas the event demands the discontinuity of a break.

Equally, however—and this is a second major misconception regarding Badiou's theory of the name—if the name must evade Statist inclusion in order to force novelty, it must also avoid ontologization at a second level, as if the name *itself* inaugurated the event and was homogeneous with it. Best exemplified by

Daniel Bensaid (Bensaïd: 2004), this kind of reading leads directly to the criticism of Badiou as an absolutist, voluntarist and/or theological thinker. Absolutist because it invokes ungrounded, unjustified power; voluntarist because naming here is an effort of sheer will; and theological because it is a grace-like act of pure creation or donation. Yet it is quite possible, and indeed vitally important, to characterize the vast majority of Baidou's work as an attempt to evade this fetishization of the self-constituting, radically autonomous name (Bruno Bosteels has done the most in this direction—see Bosteels: 2009). One can find direct and severe criticisms of this orientation scattered throughout Badiou's oeuvre, as for example the non-dialectical focus on 'force' to the exclusion of 'tendancy' in *Theory of the Subject*, as 'terrorist nihilism' in *The Century*, and as 'speculative leftism' in *Being and Event*. Each of these refer to the temptation to appeal to a miraculous, ex nihilo nomination which directly gives birth to novelty through its very assertion, and whose subsequent incantation becomes the form of a tautologous, unquestionable authority. It is as if, in order to avoid the banal nominations of the State, the speculative leftist can only invent a name out of the blue, and invest that name itself with a utopian zeal in fact destined to consume only itself.

Both of these visions of the eventual name—as a belatedly adequate label for something that happened, and as the essentially divine creation of something altogether new—miss what is most difficult, yet most significant, in Badiou's philosophy: that it is infinitely more important that the eventual name be internally riven by a necessary duality (or dialectic) than that it either 'rest in peace' in a lifeless realm of representation in the near future, or live eternally in some otherworldly space beyond materiality. So what form does this split within the name take? Meditation 20 of *Being and Event* insists that, like the notion of scission in *Theory of the Subject*, such a split must be present from the beginning of the subjective intervention as its very form. Quite simply, for a subject to intervene in a situation of undecidability by naming a multiple as eventual, s/he must already have decided, without any justification, on its belonging to that situation. Naming the event adds to this groundless decision something like an empty formal notation which nonetheless allows the consequences of this asserted belonging to be unfolded within that situation. Of course, the name of the event gives consistency to the subjects faithful to it (it names their faith), but it does not belong to them alone. As subjects, their role is to extend the name to every multiple of the situation without qualification.

But which name? And why that one? We can initially identify three negative answers to these questions. Firstly, the eventual name cannot be transposed from the existing range of Statist names: "No presented term of the situation can furnish what we require, because the effect of homonymy would immediately efface everything unpresentable contained in the event" (*BE*, p.203). Since the mechanical action of the State is to count as one, or 'name', the elements of the situation, it is incapable of naming the unpresentable part exposed by the event. However, and secondly, this prohibition against redeploying existing Statist names to designate the event must extend also to the eventual site from which the event emerges. This is because although the site is abnormal (none of its parts are elements of the situation), it is still a recognizable element of the situation: it counts as one, albeit as the 'emptiest' one within the situation. Badiou does not bring this out, but in view of my discussion above regarding counter-nomination I would add that, because there is always an oppressively 'policing' discourse focused on the abnormality of the site, the State is in fact fully poised to localize the disruption of the event at its site, thereby obscuring what is truly troubling *within* the site (and thus the entire situation itself, as the truth procedure attempts to demonstrate). For example, it will always be easier for the State to explain away a serious strike as a local issue pertaining to a particularly militant trade union rather than as symptomatic of a generalized contradiction between labour and capital. To choose as the name of this potential event the name of the factory from which it first emerged would potentially be to become complicit with the existing matrix of Statist nominations. Thirdly, and related to this, it is vital that once the name of the event is settled on it retains an anonymous singularity that resists, resolutely, any attempted attribution of predicates. For a truly generic politics, predicates are invariably a link back to worldly interests. To retain the ghost of class analysis, we might even add that the 'property' ascribed by a predicate should be understood in both an ontological and an economic sense: to have (a) property is to be located within a hierarchical ensemble. Only by presenting to the powers of predication a sheer surface upon which Statist names can get no purchase whatsoever is it possible for the generic subset that the name comes to designate to remain of universal significance for all inhabitants of the situation. Just as we saw Lazarus insisting that the name is unnameable, so Badiou asserts, perhaps more precisely, that the "event has the nameless as its name [...] Its proper name is thus the common name 'belonging to the site'" (*BE*, p.205). If with Lazarus we have an essentially epistemological concern regarding the naming of the name by the social and political sciences, here, thanks to Badiou's use of set-theory, this nameless quality of the political name becomes a positive declaration of pure belonging rather than a negative limit in relation to positivist knowledge.

A triple prohibition then: against drawing the eventual name from an existing Statist name; against naming the event after its site; and against allowing the name to carry any predicative dimension beyond generic belonging. The positive alternative to these deadends is provided by Badiou in an extremely dense formulation: "The initial operation of an intervention is to *make a name out of an unpresented element of the site to qualify the event whose site is the site*" (*BE*, p.204). The phrase 'to make a name out of an unpresented element' does not mean to name that element in the referential sense. That is precisely what the State, which can only count what has been presented, cannot do. 'Making a name' here designates the invention of a formal notation upon the basis of which an implicative process can begin.

Far from being a proper name linked to a system of properties and proprieties, this kind of name is more akin to the elementary algebraic operator '=', that is, to a function which reveals certain relations when put to work in an equation but which has no intrinsic 'meaning' or referent of its own. We can pursue this analogy a bit further. Before an algebraic equation is balanced, this '=' is both a positive hypothesis (these elements *are* equal), and a signifier that enables the work of exploring this hypothesis to begin (*are* these elements equal?). To put this differently, it is an assertion of equality which paves the way for the labour of proof required to retrospectively confirm, or not, its validity.

So in Badiou's matheme of the event, if X designates a site, and if this X must not itself be the name of the event because it counts as one in the situation, then the name of the event will have to, be $x \in X$, with x here indexing the evental multiple itself—a totally unpresented, uncountable, impossible multiple from the point of view of the situation. The wager which allows this unpresentable multiple to have any bearing on the situation whatsoever is '$\in$', the assertion of belonging. If this assertion of belonging can be demonstrated, then x, though it has no properties that the State can ascribe to it, is nonetheless shown to belong to its situation. Henceforth, the State will have to count its elements differently. This is what makes the State new in Badiou's sense: no longer the Leninist vision of the seizure of the State apparatus by the proletariat, but rather a genuinely new state almost in the sense that physicists use that term: an altered condition of matter. If x is made to belong, the State alters its relation to the void whose denial is its very foundation.

At this point, however, the peculiar ambiguity of the evental name has to be stressed in order to avoid the twin traps I have already identified of parliamentarism and speculative leftism. On one side, the evental name is the basis of an ontological inference that echoes the Statist count: like '$=$', it is the basis of a claim for equality with the other terms of the situation at the minimal level of co-belonging. But on the other side, the very anonymous formalism of the name "indexes the event to the arbitrariness of the signifier" (*BE*, pp.204-205), reminding us of the persistence of the Saussurean bar between signifier and signified. The former allows the inference of a presence or a belonging, the latter simultaneously invokes the absence, for the *current* situation, of this inferred belonging other than as an empty name. So parliamentarism, which can be defined here as the impossibility of non-Statist nomination or the putative omnipotence of inclusion, is avoided because the evental multiple with which the existing State is confronted is constitutively impossible for it to count (as Badiou says, "one cannot refer to a supposed *inclusion* of the event in order to conclude in its *belonging*"—*BE*, p.202). But the other side of the evental name, its arbitrariness, also militates against the kind of speculative leftism that would try to make of the event a local miracle belonging only to a chosen few. It is precisely the mistake of speculative leftism to treat x as if it were *a name with a confirmed referent, a new, but fully present term of the situation*. Speculative leftists forget their Saussure, and lapse into a metaphysical conflation of signifier and signified, evental name and being.

Saussure notwithstanding however, there *is* a mutual dependence between the event and its name. A key question, then, is how can the leftist tendency to mistake this dependence for an absolutely circular equivalence be evaded? As Badiou puts it, "there is actually no other recourse against this circle than that of splitting the point at which it rejoins itself" (*BE*, p.209). He introduces this splitting through the concept of 'evental recurrence'. Evental recurrence refers to the principle, which we have already touched upon, that a precondition for naming an event is the prior event of an ungrounded decision on the belonging of the evental multiple to the situation for which it is an event. In other words, every event is played out in the interval between itself and a 'previous' event, it is a diagonal between the name of the event and the decision founding the intervention. This is in fact a resolutely materialist hypothesis: it is the insistence that an exceptional nomination cannot take place without being conditioned by an exceptional event. While commentators on Badiou such as Žižek and Johnston have had recourse to the notation Event1 and Event2 to designate the intervallic logic of eventual recurrence, it is important to be cautious about the causality this inadvertently implies. As both Žižek and Johnston certainly know, the 'first' event is the retroactive effect of the 'second', as Badiou's syntactical nod towards Lacan's famous dictum regarding the subject in the following assertion suggests: "An intervention is what presents an event for the occurrence of another" (*BE*, p.209). As with the retroactive fantasy of a full jouissance lost upon castration, the simplistic before-and-after temporality, and the apparent certainty of the ego that separates them, is in fact an imaginary screen projected onto the gap or interval of the real. The name is what blocks this imaginary projection by circulating the real.

But what prevents the State's counter-nomination from negating or obscuring the evental nomination in its turn? If it were only a matter of different names attempting to attach themselves to the same incident, the event would not stand a chance, given that the State secures for itself sovereign hermeneutic rights. But for ontological reasons relating to the State's incapacity to count its own void, the apparent irrationality of the 'supernumerary name' of the event *is* a profound challenge that cannot be named away, even by drawing on the existing resources of counter-nomination. Badiou points out that the only parts of the event the State can get any purchase on at all are the site, already counted as an element, and the multiple formed out of the consequences emerging from that site. So for example, the closing of Nanterre would be the 'site' of May '68 on the one hand, and the subsequent alliance of students and workers across Paris and then France on the other would be the 'multiple' that emerged from it. Yet the State can get no further than this in its efforts at counter-nomination. As we saw above with reference to Rancière's notion of the 'police', and this is even clearer in *Logics of Worlds*, nomination always polices *relations* between elements. But the site and what Badiou calls its 'singleton' have no discernible relation from the State's point of view. This is why the State encounters the event as "an excrescence whose structure is a Two without concept" (*BE*, p.209). It is worth quoting Badiou at length on the State's response to the evental name:

> Every time that a site is the theatre of a real event, the state—in the political sense, for example—recognizes that a designation must be found for the couple of the site (the factory, the street, the university) and the singleton of the event (strike, riot, disorder), but it cannot succeed in fixing the rationality of the link. This is why it is a law of the state to detect in the anomaly of this Two—and this is an avowal of the dysfunction of the count—the *hand of a stranger* (the foreign agitator, the terrorist, the perverse professor). It is not important whether the agents of the state believe in what they say or not, what counts is the necessity of the statement. For this metaphor is in reality that of the void itself: something unpresented is *at work*—this is what the state is declaring, in the end, in its designation

of an external cause. The state blocks the apparition of the immanence of the void by the transcendence of the guilty (*BE*, p.208)

Given the importance of this conflict of names between the State and the subjects of a truth at this stage in his work, it is remarkable to note that by *Logics of Worlds*, Badiou is castigating his former obsession with evental nomination, and celebrating the ways in which his new logic of appearance leaves that problematic behind (*LW*, p.361). Language is more clearly identified there as the enemy insofar as it is central to the dominance of democratic materialism. Thus the turn to logic is one in which the object is "wholly alien to any doctrine of representation or reference" (*LW*, p.38). The new emphasis on an albeit 'objective' phenomenology of appearance allows change to show itself without the mediation of a mysterious name. Naming is no longer required because the key process in evental singularities is the shift from the minimal to the maximal appearance of previously inexistent worldly objects: so the appearance of Paris, and certainly the role of workers in it, was already transformed before the declaration of the Commune itself which, as we saw in the last chapter, came some ten days into the occupation of the French capital.

Nonetheless, as the vexed relationship between language and perception in the phenomenological tradition itself attests, no appeal to a pure efflorescence of auto-appearance in the form of the site can set aside the problem of naming. In fact, I would argue that in *Logics of Worlds*, much of the burden of the previous centrality of evental naming is taken on by 'evental statements', insofar as these still support the subjective exploration of an event's implications, contemporaneously but also in the future (as the new category of 'evental resurrection' developed in Book I indicates). For the Paris Commune, such a statement would be something like 'workers can autonomously organize their own mode of politics'. While the efflorescence of the 'site' is indeed a matter of an inversion of the aesthetics rather than linguistics of the given, what enables the transformation of the ephemeral site into the durability of a singularity with maximal consequences remains the irreducibly linguistic pivot of the evental statement. And as we shall see in the next chapter, it is even clearer in *Logics of Worlds*, in the elaboration of reactive and obscure subjects, that the conflict around evental names/statements remains central in the second volume of *Being and Event*.

THE NAME JEW

Perhaps the clearest demonstration of the stakes involved in this conflict between Statist and evental names is the vitriolic debate sparked in French media and intellectual circles by Badiou's 2005 work, *Circonstances 3: Portées du mot 'juif'*. In the wake of this publication, the pages of everything from *Le Monde* to *Les temps modernes* demonstrated a significant refusal to actually read Badiou. Attacks on him, some of which included the accusation of anti-Semitism, came from Roger-Pol Droit,[1] Fédéric Nef,[2] Claude Lanzmann, Jean-Claude Milner and Eric Marty,[3] and Meïr

---

1. 'L'universel, avantages et impasses: *Circonstances 3. Portées du mot 'juif'* d'Alain Badiou' in *Le Monde des livres*, 25th of November 2005.

2. "Le 'nom des Juifs' selon Alain Badiou' in *Le Monde des livres*, 23rd of December 2005.

3. All in *Les temps modernes* between November 2005 and January 2006.

Waintrater.[4] One could summarise Badiou's project in this short work as an attempt to criticize the Statist *word* Jew in order to restore its properties as an eventual *name*. More precisely, it tries to transform the word 'Jew' from its current entanglement with Zionist particularism into a generic name for the universal. To be sure, few of Badiou's critics actually grasped that this was his aim, which only demonstrates the weight of the Statist semantic. Yet his own evident astonishment as this wave of often violent reaction crashed over him and his supporters, such as Natacha Michel and Cécile Winter, arguably bespeaks a problem I have already noted: the tendency for Badiou's infinite philosophical disdain regarding Statist nomination to overlap with an apparent naiveté before its stubborn, practical resilience.

But because the word 'Jew' has, since the Second World War, offered an open surface for the inscription of numerous and diverse agendas, Badiou's disdain could not remain merely philosophical during this very Parisian squabble: he was forced to confront the power of counter-nomination as it attempted to shout out his own argument. The key moments of this debate are collected and translated into English in *Polemics* (2006). One can see there the extreme difficulty of separating out truly political from merely Statist nomination, and the danger of being drawn into counter-counter-nomination. But what is particularly useful for our purposes here is that one can also see the specific difficulties that stem from the fact that the Statist word 'Jew' has taken on the outward appearance of an *exception*, and therefore bares more than a passing resemblance to the name of an event. In many ways then, with the discussion of the word 'Jew' we are back to the problematic of simulacral names identified in Badiou's previous book on ethics. But with the wider controversy that followed the publication of *Circonstances 3*, we also witness the State's power to re-inscribe this simulacral name.

Badiou's argument in *Circonstances 3* was as simple as it was controversial. He put his finger on a widely deployed rhetorical topos with four key interlinked elements: firstly, the claim that the Shoah was an event not only for European Jewry, but for Humanity as such; secondly, the insistence that thenceforth the word 'Jew' must be treated as exceptional in relation to all other names; thirdly, the injunction that it must simultaneously testify to the unrepresentable horror of 'Auschwitz' and the aporia of Enlightenment hyperrationality that causes it to collapse into its barbarous inverse; and fourthly, the related demand that it must stand as a cipher for the ethically imperative existence of the State of Israel, to which individual Jews, as victims *par excellence*, have the transcendental right. This rhetorical topos is sustained in numerous ways, which Badiou does not hesitate to identify. In the media, there are the diverse activities which could be gathered under the provocative but perhaps perceptive heading of what Norman G. Finkelstein famously termed 'The Holocaust Industry'. In academia and wider intellectual circles, there have been numerous so-called poststructuralist philosophers, such as Emmanuel Levinas, Jacques Derrida, and Jean-François Lyotard, who provide theoretical sustenance to this line of thinking by means of an ethical critique of the violence of representation. And these currents have found concrete and consistent State backing. We can

---

4. 'Alain Badiou et les Juifs: Une violence insoutenable' appeared in the journal *L'Arche*, number 574 in February 2006.

see this in the form of State legislation against anti-Semitism. While obviously welcome in itself, such legislation often partakes in the elevation of the signifier 'Jew' to a unique and, in the end, unequal status without in fact curbing emergent forms of anti-Semitism or indeed the worrying rise of far right groups across Europe. But we can see the State's backing for this topos of exceptional victimhood most clearly in the State of Israel itself, and in its alliances with the United States and therefore with neoliberal versions of globalisation. In France in particular, notes Badiou, all three of these strands—media, intellectual life, and the State—come together in the rise of the *nouveaux philosophes* who have played such a role in policing (in Rancière's sense) this particular(istic) figuration of the word 'Jew'.

Before moving on to look at Badiou's challenge to this narrative and its supports, it is important to point out the extent to which its account of the word 'Jew' initially resembles an evental name. After all, it is exceptional, in that no other name is like it. It is grounded in a ruptural novelty, the 'Shoah'—a term which as Badiou himself suggests has come to indicate a kind of ethical solidarity with what is otherwise referred to as the Holocaust (and this remains capitalized, trace of its transcendentalisation). Moreover, it is clearly the focal point for a militant subjectivity in the case of Zionism. The whole burden of Badiou's intervention, then, rests on parsing a distinction between the virulent particularism which has been appended to the word 'Jew', and the generic universalism upon which a politics of axiomatic equality can be based, of which 'Jew' has also been the name in a philosophical tradition deeply influenced by Jewish thinkers and Jewish thought. This distinction therefore necessitates a subtle differentiation between simulacral counter-nomination and true evental nomination. "[W]hat is at issue", Badiou states, "is to know whether or not, in the general field of public intellectual discussion, the word 'Jew' constitutes an exceptional signifier, such that it would be legitimate to make it play the role of a final, or even sacred, signifier" (*P*, p.158).

Not surprisingly, the key differentiator between this kind of exceptional signifier and a truly evental one is "the intrusion of [an] identity predicate into a central role for the determination of a politics" which, in line with his position in *Ethics,* Badious here claims "leads to disaster" (*P*, p.163). One such predicate is that of 'victim'. For Badiou, the entire logic of human rights has this figure of the victim at its core. He is against it because it reduces what is properly human to the animal, to a kind of bodily fragility determined by a juridically recognized crime. In *Polemics*, he asserts explicitly, "I cannot accept in any way the victim ideology" (*P*, p.161). Reminiscent of Nietzsche's grudging recognition of Christianity's transvaluation of weakness into a will to power, Badiou discerns in the Israeli State's deployment of this victim ideology—historically with reference to the Holocaust, of course, but also currently with reference to Palestinian mortar attacks and suicide bombers—a justification of what is effectively the colonial occupation and subjugation of Palestinian land and peoples.

Nonetheless, he is very far from taking up the extreme position of Iran's Mahmoud Ahmadinejad who famously called for Israel to be 'wiped from the map'. Israel, simply as a State, has as much right to exist as any other. What Badiou does object to is the way in which the word 'Jew' is attached to it as a communitarian predicate supposedly carrying innate ethical legitimacy. His problem with Israel, then, is with "its exclusive identitarian claim to be a 'Jewish State', and with the way it draws incessant privileges from this claim, especially when it comes to trampling underfoot what serves us as international law" (*P*, p.163). There is a deep historical irony here, which Badiou does not emphasise enough. International law was primarily the fruit of the Nuremburg trials and the prosecution of Nazis for crimes against the Jewish people. The Holocaust would then become the paradigm for crimes against humanity and the invention of the albeit disputed legal category of 'genocide' in 1948. The paradox, then, is that the paradigmatic case of Jewish victimhood is actively being used by the Israeli State *against* the would-be universalism of international law to excuse what ought to be recognized as crimes against Palestinian humanity. The general volatility of the Middle East region is often cited as a reason for apparent international tolerance for this Israeli exceptionalism, which mirrors so conveniently its American counterpart, but Badiou isn't buying: "The claim is sometimes made that this state is the only 'democratic' state in the region. But the fact that this state presents itself as a 'Jewish state' is directly contradictory" (*ibid.*). Democracy is generic for Badiou, or it is a sham.

Furthermore, he is balanced enough to find the same discursive strategies on the other side of the West Bank wall equally repellant. Thus, "the signifier 'Palestinian' or 'Arab' should not be glorified any more than is permitted for the signifier 'Jew'" and "there is no question of tolerating the anti-Jewish diatribes [made by] a number of organizations and institutions that are more or less dependent on identitarian words such as 'Arab', 'Muslim', 'Islam'" (p.164). For this reason, Badiou is against the two-State solution favoured by most Western liberals as well as moderate Israelis. As with the analysis of the break-up of former Yugoslavia that we briefly encountered in the pages of *la Distance Politique* in the last chapter, so, here, with the Israeli-Palestinian conflict, Badiou advocates not the partitioning of indentitarian differences but their dissolution within a generic, and thus cosmopolitan nationalism. For him the Israeli-Palestinian conflict can only be resolved by a single secular State that does not base itself on the Old Testament or putative links between territories and ethnicities. But for this to happen, the word 'Jew' must become a *name*. Badiou therefore calls on individual Jews to undertake a subjective break with Israel to reclaim the name 'Jew' from what he calls the "dictatorship of predicates" (p.166). For "this name can have no meaning unless it is radically extricated from the State of Israel, and unless it is proclaimed that, in its current form, this state is incapable of tolerating, or meriting in any way, the label 'Jew'" (pp.166-67). As so often around the topic of the transition from individual to subject, the figure of Saint Paul is at work behind this call from Badiou. After all, Saint Paul was the Jew who transcended his Jewish placement by challenging the Greek-Jew binary but, crucially, who also returned the power of the universal back to the Jewish people insofar as Pauline Christianity welcomed them, as well as all others, unconditionally. This last move is essential to bear in mind if Badiou's call for a subtraction of the word 'Jew' from its Statist inscription is not to be conflated with the phenomenon of the so-called self-hating Jew.

Polemics also includes an extract from Badiou's 1997 novel, *Calme bloc ici-bas*, which shows the persistence of his interest in rescuing the name from the word. In the reproduced scene, the character in the novel who takes on the, significantly, invented name of Ahmed Aazami (previously he had been known as Simon Symoens) converses with a Jewish mathematician named René Fulmer. Unsurprisingly, it is the mathematician who has a privileged insight into the generic destiny proper to the name of his faith and his people. Clearly echoing St. Paul, Fulmer says "[l]et's call 'Jew' the one who says in the name of all others that there is no law separating them" (*P*, p.184). In an extremely novel interpretation of European anti-Semitism, Badiou has Fulmer asserting that "The Jew is not hated because he is the Other. The Jew is hated because he is the Same" (*P*, p.185), i.e., he is not hated because his ethnic, cultural and religious identity is different from that of European gentiles, but because he is the unwelcome harbinger of a generic universality that sweeps away such distinctions.

A hint of this notion that the Jew is hated for being the Same rather than the Other is present in Jean-Paul Sartre's famous *Anti-Semite and Jew*. There, Sartre relates that a classmate of his from the lycée described a scenario supposedly justifying his anti-Semitism:

> A Jew passed the *agrégation* the year I was failed, and you can't make me believe that that fellow, whose father came from Cracow or Lemberg, understood a poem by Ronsard or an eclogue by Virgil better than I (Sartre: 1995, p.12)

As Sartre notes, this classmate explained his own lack of preparation for the *agrégation* on the basis of precisely the kind of conspiracy of Jewish infiltration and influence out of which Hitler had already made much mileage: "he will in time manage to justify his past laziness on the grounds that it really would be too stupid to prepare for an examination in which Jews are passed in preference to good Frenchmen" (*ibid.*). The Jew is subjected to a process of Othering here precisely because he threatens to perform the 'same'—being 'French', understanding the best of French literature—better than the anti-Semite. Hence Sartre's aphorism, "If the Jew did not exist, the anti-Semite would invent him" (Sartre: 1995, p.13). This aphorism can be read in conjunction with another by Frantz Fanon, whose dissection of the overlapping structures of anti-Semitism and anti-black racism in *Black Skin, White Masks* led him to declare that "[f]or the black man there is only one destiny. And it is white" (Fanon: 1986, p.12). This is not fatalist resignation on Fanon's part. He is recognising the same problem that Badiou identifies for the individual Jew confronted by the word 'Jew' by which he is nominated. Fanon is arguing that to fight under the banner of a category given to him by the white man, without turning this word 'black' into a *name*, is to inadvertently consolidate the trope of 'uppity native' that has long legitimised the imposition of white discipline. Neither the Jew nor the black man serves his cause well by collaborating with the invented word that securely places him in his position of subordination. Fanon's appeal, at the emotive conclusion of *Black Skin, White Masks*, to the universality of 'man' is the same solution as Badiou's, perhaps because of their common Marxist referent: "The Negro is not. Anymore than the white man" (Fanon: 1986, p.231).

SOVEREIGNTY AND NOMINATION

In the last part of this chapter, I would like to continue to interrogate this all-important separation between counter-nomination and the evental name by exploring overlaps and differences between Badiou's notion of the event, and Carl Schmitt's notion of the exception. As legal theorist to the Nazis, Schmitt's work is clearly relevant to the specific question of the word 'Jew', and we have just seen that Badiou's intervention into the uses of that word in *Circonstances 3* was, in part, motivated by an attempt to separate Zionist exceptionalism from the evental message of generic universality carried by the name 'Jew' in the philosophical tradition. And just as this intervention lead to accusations of anti-Semitism, so Badiou has been suspected of echoing aspects of Schmitt's position.[5] By disentangling Badiou's event from Schmitt's exception more clearly, I hope in this section to demonstrate the value of Badiou's philosophy of conflict precisely in the context of a post-9/11 world in which the exception (and Schmitt) seem to have returned with such vengeance.

This has become an urgent task because a strategic ambiguity within Schmitt's *Political Theology* has led to a pseudo-'evental' interpretation of the exception post 9/11. Long before Schmitt's particular intervention, the exception was already understood as soething like an unprecedented occurrence exceeding the norms governing all procedural legal codification, and therefore calling forth a power of decision outside or beyond the law. Schmitt follows his philosophical mentor, Hobbes, in resolving this apparent aporia through the transcendent power of a sovereign: hence the infamous dictum, "Sovereign is he who decides on the exception" (Schmitt: 2005, p.5). There is part of a very long tradition—running from monarchical absolutism, through Jacobin theories of the autonomy of the political, and on to dictatorial authoritarianisms—that understands sovereign power precisely as the capacity to decide in the context of radical undecidability. This tradition insists that when the state is in imminent and unprecedented danger, only the Hobbesian Leviathan, the Rousseauian Legislator, or, indeed, the Caesar, Tsar or Führer, is authorised to make the decisions required to restore law and order, and to save the kingdom from destruction. As such, this tradition figures the exception as both descriptive of, and responsive to, an exceptional empirical event such as a siege, epidemic or civil war.

There are thus two overlapping 'states' discernible in this logic of the exception, which account for Schmitt's insistence that sovereignty is a "borderline concept" (*ibid.*):

1. The exceptional state, which refers to the transcendental condition of being outside or beyond the law
2. The state of exception, which refers to a contingent situation supposedly justifying the suspension of the rule of law

---

5. By Badiou's own admission, Jean-François Lyotard was among the first to label him "a sort of new Carl Schmitt" (*IT*,p.172). Under the provocative subheading 'Badiou *Absolutiste?*', Peter Hallward has also indicated overlaps between Badiou's notion of the subject of truth and absolutist theories of sovereignty (Hallward: 2004, pp.285-286). And Nina Power has also explored common elements between Badiou's and Schmitt's critiques of Rousseau (Power in Ashton et al.: 2006. pp.309-338).

These two dimensions are linked because the sovereign power to decide what constitutes the state of exception already presupposes an exceptional state with regard to the law that is being suspended. There is thus a fundamental ambivalence around the calling forth of the sovereign by the exceptional event, and the calling exceptional of the event by the sovereign himself. The sovereign is the necessary embodiment of this ambivalence, yet draws his legitimacy from his supposed power to resolve it.

However, for Schmitt, this strange double articulation remains prey to the tendency of constitutional liberalism to mortgage the exception to a provision *within* law for unprecedented circumstances: the state of emergency. In contrast, the real novelty of Schmitt's *Political Theology* is that it distinguishes the exception from any contingent state of affairs whatsoever. The true specificity of Schmittian sovereignty, then, lies in the structural necessity of the first dimension of 'state' described above, which only justifies itself through the second. The apparently 'evental' component that indicates an empirical irruption of disorder is thoroughly subordinated to the prior topological necessity of what Agamben has called an 'included exclusion' (Agamben: 2005). In this way—and this is the key difference with Badiou—Schmitt posits the exception as *a structure, and not an event*. It is in this way that the notion of a 'permanent exception' with which Hardt & Negri and others have described globalised forms of postmodern sovereignty is only apparently paradoxical. Qua structural, it was always permanent. Schmitt shows that law can never found itself, because it cannot immanently generate the authority required to enforce its decrees. Law therefore always has an outside, yet this extra-legal exterior is by no means illegal, since it is the very condition of possibility of all law, irrespective of whether it responds to a perceived emergency or mere day-to-day social order.

Thus, constitutional liberalism's attempt to constrain the personalism and absolutism of Hobbesian power by exhaustively legislating for extraordinary circumstances misses the point entirely. For Schmitt, the tendency to deny the exception by attempting to codify it within the jurisprudence of emergency is a risible denial of politics itself, insofar as politics *is* the necessity of the sovereign decision (see chapter 4 of Schmitt: 2005). Moreover, he is perfectly clear that this decision, even in its extra-legal ambivalence, nonetheless remains governed by a 'we' which constitutes itself as an 'us' only in a relation of enmity to a 'them'. It is through the friend-enemy distinction that organises *The Concept of the Political* (Schmitt: 1996) that Schmitt reworks Hobbes' state of nature, as a war of all against all, by transposing it onto an international politics of relentless antagonism and conflict. The sovereign's role on this international stage is to act in accordance not with *a* constitution, but with *the* on-going constitution of a unified 'we' in and through conflict with an adversarial Other. As such, Schmitt rightly stands as the dark prophet of the War on Terror and its reactionary consequences.

The most pressing political problem that Schmitt bequeaths to us today, then, is what I would call the 'tourniquet' of the logic of the exception. This tourniquet refers to the fact that, after Hobbes and particularly Schmitt, conflict itself becomes the legitimating precondition of sovereign power. In Hobbesian terms, we give up our right of resistance so that the sovereign can police conflicts with a violence we implicitly endorse. However, in such a context, any exercise of the liberal right of resistance can always be presented as an 'evental' exception justifying the other kind of exceptionalism that is extra-legal violence, concealing the fact that this violence is structural and foundational rather than responsive to an indeterminate emergency. It is a tourniquet because the more one fights to free oneself from it, the more it tightens. Worse still, through the dominant paradigm of (international, national, and individual) security, this tightening *is* the source of its legitimacy, suggesting a kind of exponential double-binding of the contemporary politics of resistance. How can we escape this diabolical dialectic of power? How can resistance evade the logic of the exception and challenge the new Imperial sovereignty without inadvertently legitimating it? Is it possible to formulate this problematic without advocating an exception to the exception, a counter-counter-nomination, *ad infinitum*?

Badiou's philosophy, I believe, answers these questions, but it is important initially to acknowledge the apparent overlaps between the event and the exception, because they demonstrate the often blurred line between Statist counter-nomination and evental nomination which we have already seen in relation to the word/name 'Jew'. I will identify five such apparent overlaps, before going on to explore the differences.

Firstly, both the event and the exception evade every calculus of prediction. For Schmitt, the exception "cannot be circumscribed factually and made to conform to a preformed law" (Schmitt: 2005, p.6): it is "that which cannot be subsumed; it defies general codification" (p.13). It follows that "no pre-existing set of rules can be laid down to make explicit whether this situation 'is' in actual reality an 'exception'" (Strong in Schmitt: 2005, p.xiv). Just as for Schmitt the exception is in excess of all constitutional attempts to predict it or know it ahead of time—which is why "[a] jurisprudence concerned with ordinary day-to-day questions has practically no interest in the concept of sovereignty" (Schmitt: 2005, p.12)—so for Badiou the event is completely indiscernible from the point of view of the encyclopaedia of knowledge and its routine machinery of verification. Consequently, for both thinkers a certain theory of the liberal 'state' is conceived from the starting point of the denial or repression of the very truth that sustains it. For Schmitt, this truth would reveal the necessity of a transcendent sovereign power with an absolute and therefore uncodifiable capacity for decision. For Badiou, on the contrary, it would be the forced revelation of an in-existent because inconsistent multiple that belongs to, but is not included in, a situation. Nonetheless, Schmitt's description of the incalculable irruption of the exception could be transposed more or less intact onto Badiou's rhetoric of the event: "[i]n the exception the power of real life breaks through the crust of a mechanism that has become torpid by repetition" (p.15).

Secondly, as a result of this incompatibility with all forms of knowledge, both thinkers appeal to the figurative power of a secularised version of the Christian concept of 'grace'. Thus, in Badiou's analysis of Saint Paul (which revolves around the distinction between law and truth), he insists that "the event's sudden emergence never follows from the existence of the evental site. Although it requires conditions of immanence, that sudden emergence nevertheless remains of the order of grace" (*SP*, p.71). Arguably straying onto the territory of the speculative leftists he himself criticises, Badiou echoes Schmitt's invocation of a divine agency beyond mere law when he says "Evental grace governs a multiplicity in excess of itself, one that is indescribable, superabundant relative to itself as well as with respect to the fixed distributions of the law" (*SP*, p.78). Compare this, too, to Schmitt's blunt assertion that "[t]he exception in jurisprudence is analogous to the miracle in theology" (Schmitt: 2005, p.36). Indeed, in tones reminiscent of Badiou's diatribe against 'democratic materialism' in *Logics of Worlds*, Schmitt criticises the deist world-view that conspires with the modern constitutional State precisely because the former excludes the possibility of divine miracles beyond natural laws, just as the latter legislates against exceptions beyond the remit of positive law. Such a State presents what Badiou would call a static 'atonal world', one devoid of the points from which change can arise. Schmitt prefers instead "a form of fundamentalism in which the exception plays the same role in relation to the state as the miracles of Jesus do in confirming the Gospel" (Hirst in Mouffe: 1999, p.13).

This appeal to miraculous grace is much more than a mere analogy for Schmitt then. Even the constitutional State's interventions are often represented as "the graceful and merciful lord who proves by pardons and amnesties his supremacy over his own laws" (Schmitt: 2005, p.38). Yet grace really comes into its own when it can be deployed as a counter-revolutionary philosophy of the exceptional state, as in the conservative responses of Catholic philosophers de Maistre, Bonald and Donoso Cortés to the French Revolution. Schmitt's so-called secularisation thesis actually advocates the restoration of a political transcendence which is structurally theological but distanced from doctrinal religious dogma.[6] According to Schmitt, this politico-theological structure, present in Sixteenth and Seventeenth century political philosophy and practice, has today been lost amidst the horizontal bureaucratization of politics.[7] This same tension between the secular and the theological is discernible in Badiou's account of the situation and the event respectively, not least in his decidedly secular engagements with just as decidedly theological thinkers such as Pascal and Saint Paul, as well as his often ecstatic rhetoric of conversion to militant fidelity.

This shared appeal to grace foregrounds a third proximity: both the exception and the event inherently demand a decision. Moreover, insofar as they constitutively exceed law and the encyclopaedia respectively, the kind of decision they demand lacks all comforting precedents. It must be a decision that is radical, absolute, *ex nihilo*, even 'mad' in Kierkegaard's sense. The evental/exceptional decision must be a de-cision, a cut or rupture with everything calculable and knowable. Thus, for Schmitt, in the state of exception "[t]he decision frees itself from all normative ties and becomes in the true sense absolute" (Schmitt: 2005, p.12). To Schmitt, what matters is not at all the substantive issue that is resolved (or not) by a given decision, but rather the bare fact of the "genuine decision" (p.3) being taken

6. For a detailed discussion of Schmitt's notion of secularisation, see Norris: 2000.

7. Tracy Strong makes this argument in her foreword to Schmitt: 2005.

at all. The primordial structure of competence that allows for such a decision renders the decision itself "relative, and in certain circumstances absolute and independent of the correctness of its content" (p.31). It is for this reason that Schmitt defines state power as not simply "the monopoly to coerce or rule, but as the monopoly to decide" (p.13). While many see this as an endorsement of fascistic absolutism, for Schmitt himself this possible political outcome is secondary to the more fundamental fact that the immanent authority of the decision itself, as a pure form subtracted from any content, must be the basis of all law. His claim, oddly recalling Badiou's set-theoretical vocabulary, that "all law is situational law" (p.13), is really a claim that the sovereign power of this pure decision must be re-invoked *every time* a legal declaration is uttered. This is why Schmitt opens *Political Theology* by asserting that "the exception is to be understood to refer to a general concept in the theory of the state, and not merely to a construct applied to any emergency decree or state of siege" (p.5). We have already seen, in the concept of 'eventual resurrection' at the heart of his theory of the name, that Badiou also bases the event on a founding decision.

Finally then, and perhaps most importantly, there is a fifth overlap between the event and the exception in their shared reliance on naming. For in neither case is it possible to imagine the 'existence' of an event or an exception without an accompanying declaration or naming of this existence. This is because both are shrouded in uncertainty from the point of view of everyday business as usual, the resources of which for determining 'what happens' are by definition inadequate. Without the support of a powerful intervention in the form of a nomination, the exception, just as much as the event, threatens to evaporate in the passing enigma of its evanescence. For both Badiou and Schmitt then, there is an indispensable performative element in their respective logics. For Schmitt, it is clear that there is not an exception until a sovereign says there is. All the constitutional devices for specifying conflict, disorder and unrest fall short of this identification, which is also an instituting, of transcendence. Why? Because ultimately absolute sovereignty is not dependent on the kind of empirical variables legislated for by the jurisprudence of the state of emergency from which the logic of the exception has historically evolved. Like Lazarus' 'anthroplogical' name, Schmitt's sovereign exception is not referential and therefore not subject to veridical scrutiny of the kind that might determine whether the conditions of war or insurrection justifying a declaration of martial law actually exist. On the contrary, the sovereign exception is purely performative. However, it can also be said to be reliant on this performativity to the extent that the declaration of the state of exception is, simultaneously, the actual exercise of sovereign power. This is why there is a reciprocal production between the two dimensions of the logic of the exception, with sovereignty itself being called into being by the exception it names (just as the social contract presupposes the Leviathan it claims to institute). This conflation of saying and doing which also produces the enunciative 'I' of the enunciation itself is the quintessence of the pure performative, an apparent merging of logos and ethos in an absolute Law. From this tautological circle, the veridicality of positive law is thoroughly exiled.

If for Badiou, as we have seen, the event and its naming by a subject are *almost* inseparable, so for Schmitt the sovereign delcaration has the primary function of designating the "point of ascription" (Schmitt: 2005, p.32) which localises the transcendental competence to decide. Naming the exception points at the sovereign, while the name itself cannot be encompassed by any lexicon or taxonomy because it designates an exception. Just as the name of the event cannot be incorporated into the situation and remain an event, so the Schmittian exception cannot submit itself to protocols of proof and remain truly exceptional. Evental and exceptional nominations, then, share a fragile bridging function: they interweave the old and the radically new, the normal and the abnormal, the legal and the illegal. Like the Schmittian sovereign utterance that founds the law by both 'being' and naming the exceptional, the Badiouian evental name seems to be both radically autonomous and catachrestic. Both rely on a singular, non-referential mode of nomination that also sustains an exceptional subject.

WHY THE EVENT IS NOT THE EXCEPTION

Having noted these overlaps, it is important now to qualify them. Quite obviously, Schmitt appeals to a conservative tradition of authoritarian absolutism, whereas Badiou's inspiration is drawn from the Jacobin tradition of radicalism. While the two thinkers may have in common a venomous critique of parliamentary liberalism, they certainly come at this from opposing sides. One way to conceive of this difference—and this is a theme I will come back to in my final chapter—is in terms of the venerable battle over the legitimacy of extra-legal violence. In the Hobbesian camp, we have the transcendent right of the sovereign to operate above the law. In the Lockean camp, we have the immanent sovereignty of the people's right to resistance. Using this notion of extra-legal violence as an operator of differentiation, one can quickly contrast the exception with the event by suggesting that Schmitt pulls out all the philosophical stops to ensure only the sovereign State has the right to, and the monopoly over, the means of violence. In contrast, Badiou, in his residual Maoism, is intent upon the preservation of a certain legitimacy for revolutionary, anti-State violence. Post-9/11, the prevarications around this constitutional endorsement of 'people power' and transcendent discipline have manifested themselves in the shifting discourses around martial law, emergency powers, and the logic of the exception. This is because the common object of such discourses is a certain right to an extraordinary form of violence.

Agamben, in his seminal meditation on the state of exception, describes the stakes around the question of violence in the exchange initiated by Walter Benjamin's famous 'Critique of Violence', and Schmitt's—according to Agamben—response to Benjamin in *Political Theology* (see Agamben: 2005, pp.52-64). Agamben claims that Schmitt's superimposition of the norm and the exception is an attempt to counter Benjamin's argument that separates the exceptionality of a law-making violence which grounds the law, from a revolutionary, law-breaking violence which dissolves every relation to existing law. On this account, we can immediately say that the logic of the exception and the logic of the event can be distinguished in terms of their relation to the conservative violence that maintains the status quo, and the revolutionary or, as Benjamin describes it, the 'pure' violence that over-turns the status quo respectively.

So the logic of the exception *consolidates* state power by violently positing not the count per se, but the State's absolute right to count, to perform what Badiou calls the "count of the count" (*BE*, P.96). The law is clearly a vital mechanism of the State's count insofar as it legislates upon the border between inclusion and exclusion, and attempts to police the dangerously indistinct but 'singular' cate-gory of belonging-without-inclusion through, for example, asylum and immigra-tion law. The state of exception, as an apparent suspension of the legal count, is in fact a kind of zero in which the right to the cardinal ordering of the social struc-ture is simply asserted and imposed. By no means does this suspension extend to the foundational count that determines the parts that belong to a situation (pres-entation). On the contrary, the exception only touches on the level of intensity of appearing (to use the vocabulary of *Logics of Worlds*) of elements on the level of representation. Schmitt's exception therefore only relates to a secondary ordering internal to the national situation and its maintenance through control of the means of violence, even though an aspect of this ordering may involve the re-configura-tion of legislative definitions around inclusion (for example, in citizenship and ex-tradition laws, as we have seen post-9/11). There is thus a legal matrix determining inclusion that would have us believe that inclusion is coterminous with belonging.

Badiou's analysis therefore enables us to recognise law, as Marx did long ago, as a kind of superstructural justification for, and reproduction of, an existent sta-tus quo. The logic of the exception always mortgages itself to the *perpetuation* of a configuration of power which preceded the declared state of exception, even if, on a discursive level, a 'new paradigm' may be posited precisely in order to pursue and intensify the hegemonic maintenance of an 'old' social formation (e.g., the so-called 'War on Terror'). Radical novelty for Schmitt can only mean chaos and an-archy. Because "there is no norm that is applicable to chaos" (Schmitt: 2005, p.13) and no exception without a norm, it follows that "the exception is different from anarchy and chaos; order in the juristic sense still prevails" (p.12). Indeed, the an-archist who believes in the inherent goodness of humanity and corruption of gov-ernments is forced, according to Schmitt, to "decide against the decision" and be-come, like Bakhunin, the "theologian of the anti-theological" and the "dictator of an anti-dictatorship" (p.66). This indicates the paradox within Schmitt's position noted by Paul Hirst: "For all its stress on friend-enemy relations, on decisive po-litical action, its core, its aim, is the maintenance of stability and order" (Hirst in Mouffe: 1999, p. 14). In the terminology I have been developing in this chapter then, *the exception is nothing other than a simulacral counter-nomination.*

Schmitt's infamous aphorism—'sovereign is he who decides on (and thus names) the exception'—should be seen as exactly asymmetrical to evental naming. Not only is it the quintessence of Statist nomination, but it also arrogates to itself the exclusive right to its declaration, as opposed to Badiou's generic truth which has no privileged delegates and excludes no one. For in Schmitt's performative ab-solutism, the exception is indeed coterminous with its declaration by the sover-eign. This is despite his insistence that "what is inherent in the idea of the decision is that there can never be absolutely declaratory decisions" (Schmitt: 2005, p.31). In this disingenuous statement, declaration is understood in terms of the positivity of content, not form—"Looked at normatively, the decision emanates from nothingness" (pp.31-32)—whereas the burden of Schmitt's argument falls on pure form. The exception as an 'event' both happens all at once, in the very instant of its nomination, and doesn't happen at all, or has always already happened, in that the exceptionalism of the sovereign is timelessly because structurally presupposed. Thus, the tautology of sovereign power means that the exceptional 'event's' existence cannot be doubted: it is, quite simply, because the sovereign says it is. In this sense, Schmitt's claim that the exception defies general codification is only partially true, for it is essential that the sovereign himself be nominated *prior* to the exceptional 'event' as the figure or entity delegated with the power of absolute decision. This nomination is designed precisely to avoid the fatal uncertainty of *competing statements claiming sovereign status*. Such a scenario, resembling the parliamentary discussion against which Schmitt rails so vehemently, describes a lapse back into the state of nature, into a kind of discursive civil war. Hence Schmitt's injunction that "[i]t cannot be just anybody who can execute and realise every desired legal prescription" (p.32). Truly faithful to Hobbes, Schmitt remains ensconced within social contract theory.

By complete contrast, the evental name has no natural, pre-existing, pre-ordained addressor in the form either of privileged agents of historical transformation, or of their State-like representation by a party structure, or, indeed, of some kind of figurehead or leader. The subjects of a truth may be considered sovereign in relation to their immanent fidelity, but they are certainly not recognised as sovereign by the situation they challenge because theirs is a revolutionary or 'pure' mode of extra-legal violence. Whereas the speech of the sovereign's juris-*diction* (from *dictiô*) is imperious within his domain, what Badiou calls the *langue-sujet* that systematically pursues the implications of an event must begin from a localised and singularised evental site, expanding outwards only haphazardly. The evental name therefore has a much more complex structure than the tautological nomination of the sovereign. The latter has a stark semantic simplicity. Recalling its origins in martial law, it functions as a command in a quasi-military sense: a pre-existing hierarchy of *ethos* endows the sovereign *logos* with unquestionable rhetic force. The evental name, however, is 'poetic', an act of invention. Evental truth *is* isomorphic with the effects of its naming upon the State of the situation, but this should not lead to the conflation of the event with its name, and thus to the drawing once again of the parallel with Schmitt's exception.

IN WHOSE NAME?

To conclude this chapter, I am going to undertake an analysis of the 'Not in Our Name' anti-war movement because I believe such an analysis can do two things: firstly, it can indicate the basic logic of a generic politics, but secondly, it can also suggest the weaknesses of an exclusive focus on the exception in the absence of a real conditioning event. From our characterisation of the Schmittian exception as a modality of *simulacral* counter-nomination, it follows that engaging in the infinite regress of a counter-counter nomination is a Statist trap to be avoided since it constrains conflict within reciprocal contradiction. Initially however, I want to tease out what can be considered to have at least an 'evental' form in this movement.

The 'Not in Our Name' (henceforth NION) movement has its origins in the United States, where it was largely the initiative of the Maoist-oriented 'Revolutionary Communist Party', but which, since its inception in March 2002, has taken on a global scope and complexity in keeping with its proclaimed adversary: the War on Terror. Alarmed by the warmongering of the newly formed 'coalition' powers and their rhetoric of 'regime change', the movement crystallised around the attempt to gather visible and vocal public opposition to the post-9/11 militarisation of Western foreign policy, in the Middle East and elsewhere, and the assault on civil liberties at home. An initial 'Pledge of Resistance' was written in April 2002, and this was followed a couple of months later by a longer and more programmatic 'Statement of Conscience'.[8] While the former did not seek signatories, the latter did, and has, to date, attracted tens of thousands. It has made its presence felt in the American public sphere via *The New York Times* and the *San Francisco Chronicle*, as well as having a strong global presence on the internet. An Australian off-shoot of the American campaign has gathered over 58,890 signatories and been tabled in the Australian parliament.[9] In a more diffuse but still significant sense, the statement itself, 'Not in Our Name', has become a widely used slogan within many anti-war movements.[10] As an explicit response, therefore, to the reactionary political sequence that has today creatively redeployed the Schmittian logic of sovereignty, this movement is particularly suited to my differentiation between the politics of the exception and those of the event. But if the War on Terror can be said to distil the politics of the exception par excellence (one need only mention Guantánamo Bay to illustrate this), how can the NION movement be said to evade the exception? And is it successful? I will coordinate my analysis around the four elements of the movement's name itself.

Firstly, the 'Not' in NION clearly indicates a negation of popular consent, and thus an immanent withdrawal of the democratic mandate. Its syntax of refusal effectively attempts to un-sign the social contract in order to contest the legitimacy that contract supposedly lends to sovereign violence. Indeed, in seeking its own signatories, the 'Statement of Conscience' of the NION movement could be viewed as an alternative social contract, one that eschews the need for the towering authority of a Leviathan. That NION is firmly anti-State is apparent in both the 'Pledge', which promises "to resist the injustices done by our government", and the 'Statement', which rails against the Bush administration for unleashing "a spirit of revenge", creating "two classes of people", and bringing "down a pall of repression over society". More specifically, NION is critical of the model of parliamentary liberalism by which the State generates the illusion of popular legitimacy: "No

---

8. The 'Pledge of Resistance' can be found at http://www.notinourname.net/ and the 'Statement of Conscience' can be found at http://www.notinourname-seattle.net/statement.html (both accessed 15/04/10).

9. See http://notinourname.org.au/, accessed 15/04/10

10. For just one example, see http://www.stopwar.org.uk/

election, whether fair or fraudulent, can legitimize criminal wars on foreign countries". This is clearly a direct challenge to the democratic State's particular mechanism for garnering legitimacy in its exercise of the means of violence.

In this anti-Statist aspect, NION shares with Badiou's truth-procedure a starkly divisive power. The supposed One of the State is shown to be a Two, split between electorate and the sovereign allegedly mandated by them. Bush's infamous 'with or against' rhetoric is in this way actually intensified into a logic of internal scission, cleaving the represented from the putatively representing. However, this negation of consent and withdrawal of legitimation is not simply a renunciation. It is also, positively, an attempt to constitute a new political subjectivity. This ambivalence between negation and creation is reflected in the rhetoric of the movement's founding 'Pledge of Resistance', in which we find a kind of visceral rejection of the body-politic: "Not by our will", "Not by our hearts", "Not by our hands", "Not by our mouths". This distancing from the State could be said to attempt to separate the *res* from the *res publica*, the body from the body-politic, in order to constitute the kind of 'subject body' Badiou calls for in *Logics of Worlds*.

Ontologically speaking, however, this trans-individual but subjectivised body is not radically new, in that it emerges as a result of subtraction, of the stripping away of the specifying differences by which the State individuates and controls its citizens as *these* types of bodies speaking *those* languages. The only predicate that can be rigorously assigned to the signatories of the NION Statement of Conscience is 'anti-State citizen'. The liberal ideal of a vibrant civil society enjoying freedom of speech necessarily incorporates this otherwise apparently paradoxical figure. And yet, in times of war, particularly in liberal democratic polities dependent upon the construction of consent, such an anti-State citizen becomes a significant problem. This problem is all the more acute when the war in question justifies itself as the creation of exactly such freedoms for another people. The 'Not' in NION is therefore simultaneously destructive and creative insofar as it destroys (or at least challenges) the citizen-as-unit-of-consent counted by the liberal warring State on the one hand, and creates the citizen-as-subject-of-resistance on the other. The State *must* count its citizens, but it cannot count them in this manner.

Secondly, the 'in' of NION not only contests, through its negation, the apparently transparent transfer of consent in the democratic mandate. It can also be read as foregrounding this generic belonging of the citizen, its location *within* the American situation *as* the American situation (or, given that the NION movement spills over national borders, in and as the Western liberal democratic situation). For the crucial point about the Lacanian *pas-tout* upon which Badiou draws is that it is not some kind of mystical substance outside the universalising One-All. [11] It is not, therefore, something which could provide the adversarial difference posited and policed by the sovereign exception. The 'in' of NION confronts inclusion

---

11. Lacan elaborates the logic of the pas-tout or not-all in Seminar XX in the tables of sexuation where it is aligned with feminine structure and opposed to the phallic logic of the exception on the masculine side. It can be seen as an attempt to move beyond Freud's Oedipal account of civilization's origin in the primordial father who acted as the exception to the prohibition against incest.

with pure belonging, reducing citizenship to its genericity but potentially exposing, thereby, a pure inconsistent multiplicity whose very existence challenges the post-9/11 situation. That is, the 'in' of NION prevents the situation from projecting its void into a threatening externality (Osama Bin Laden, Saddam Hussein etc.), or into an even more threatening interiority (home-grown terrorist cells etc.) by forcing it to confront the structural interiority of its own impossible kernel of the real, as Žižek might put it. For liberal democracies that define themselves by the consent given to their exercise of sovereign violence, the de-individualised citizen-of-dissent is, indeed, impossible to count without transforming the situation.

Thirdly, then, and despite its origins within the US and the apparent specificity of American belonging, the 'Our' in NION articulates a radically inclusive universalism that brooks of no exception. This is implicit on the level of practical activism in the expansion of the movement well beyond America's national borders to become something of a nodal point for global anti-war movements. However, it is also evident in the universal rhetoric of its 'Pledge': "We pledge to make common cause/ with the people of the world/ to bring about justice,/ freedom and peace". The 'Statement' further declares that "[w]e extend a hand to those around the world suffering from these policies", exhorting "let the world hear our pledge!". However, it is vital to note that this appeal to global humanity necessarily passes through the particularity of a specific situation—not a national 'set', but the transnational War on Terror and its consequences. NION embraces an open truth to which literally anybody can 'sign up', yet it is a truth only for the Western Liberal democratic situation (although interestingly, one could imagine beleaguered Iraqi's adding their names to the growing list, precisely because liberal democracy is being imposed upon them). And yet, it retains the power of the universal to the extent that the 'Our' in NION can be considered an empty or floating signifier available to all those 'in' the situation. Rather than embroiling itself in the hand-wringing moralism of identity politics by attempting to 'represent' African-Americans, Hispanic-Americans or, indeed, Arab-Americans, NION invokes a universal belonging immanent to the movement itself. The word 'Our' expresses and galvanises a solidarity without fixing boundaries which might determine protocols of inclusion.

Fourthly, the 'Name' in NION also operates on both destructive and affirmative levels. On the side of destruction, it is a pure function of erasure, deleting the individuated citizen's name as it operates as a unit of popular legitimacy. If 'Name' here names anything at all, it is only this immanent resistance to State nomination. However, it does not designate a stable referent or sub-set of the situation. Naturally, this hardly prevents the logic of appearance of this 'world' from attempting to impose such a referent—'whining liberal', 'peacenik', 'anti-patriot' etc.—in order to subdue the name's disruptive power. But such specified labels fail to incorporate the movement to a politics of petty differences. 'Name' instead resonates in enigmatic defiance: drawn from the edge of the void of the liberal democratic situation, it turns an indiscernible into an undecidable that challenges the reigning veridical order. On the side of affirmation, therefore, the 'Name' in 'Not in Our Name' is in excess of the negation at the level of the statement's propositional content because it is also the supernumerary name of a political movement, and as such, it is a catalyst. Not despite, but precisely because of, the negation of the name at this semantic level, the term 'name' breaches the axiom of foundation by becoming an element of the resistant political sequence it itself 'names'. This affirmation is creative to the extent that the subject is constituted in and through its de-individualising self-(un)naming. It cannot be said to precede such a subtractive/creative act. Prior to this act, which is also a decision, there are only individuals as putative units of the State's consensual legitimacy.

These four operations relating to the four elements of the movement's name—subtractive negation ('Not'), forced internalisation of the void ('in'), generic universality ('Our'), and attempted nomination of a body separate from the state ('Name')—indicate, in Badiou's parlance, the truth of a void. But let us be clear about what this void is, and of what it is the truth. The void indexed by the NION movement is that of the generic citizen radically separated from its individuation by the State, proclaiming nothing but a pure belonging and the right arising from that belonging to challenge the State that doesn't include it. In the situation to which this belonging pertains—the Western liberal democracies declaring and orchestrating the War on Terror—this citizen of pure belonging carries the truth of a void because, at the level of the count of the count, the citizen can only be included as a unit of legitimating consent for such military adventurism. What Badiou, in *Logics of Worlds*, calls the 'transcendental regime of appearance' is configured in the liberal democratic world in such a way as to privilege the citizen of consent. However, the citizen who withdraws or subtracts themselves from the degraded parliamentary pantomime itself, and yet who insists, as the NION movement does, that not even a fair election can legitimise the State's extra-legal violence, cannot appear in this 'world' as such.

These four operations escape the tourniquet of the logic of the exception in the following ways. Firstly, subtractive negation is not *dialectically* antagonistic in relation to a dominant term within a situation, but radically immanent to a situation's entire 'being'. Secondly, the forced internalisation of the void may resemble, formally, the topology of the Schmittian sovereign as an included exclusion, yet in its disruption of the order of appearance, it is more like an excluded inclusion: the denial of its 'existence' is what gives the situation its founding consistency, in contrast to the maximal existence of the exceptional sovereign that merely structures its hierarchical ordering. Thirdly, generic universality is opposed to exceptional universality insofar as it is thoroughly inclusive, recognising no other qualifying predicate than belonging: it is exceptional only in relation to the situation it exceeds. Fourthly, the subject-body supposedly nominated by the 'Name' is a configuration of that which the body-politic cannot incorporate *in that form*: it is a trans-individual body that escapes the State's atomising, differential count of the count.

All of this is an extremely generous interpretation of the NION movement which underlines its proximity to the kind of politics of the name Badiou advocates. However, it is important now to signal the major weaknesses of this movement, only one indicator of which is that the national office and organisational structure of NION in America was closed on the 31st of March 2008. Why did this movement run out of steam? The simplest way to address this question is to pose another: to what event was it faithful? The answer clearly identified in NION statements is the terrorist attacks of 9/11 and the subsequent declaration of a war on terror. But what if 9/11 was not an event but an exception, which is to say, what this chapter has emphasised as a simulacral counter-nomination? For his part, Badiou has made it very clear that he does not believe that 9/11 was an event at all. Indeed, in 'Philosophy and the 'War against Terror'' (*IT*, pp. 141-164), he argues that the name 'terrorism' has "played a decisive role [...] it has cemented a world coalition, authorized the UN to declare that the US is in a state of 'legitimate defence', and initiated the programming of the targets of vengeance" (*IT*, p.142). Echoing a genuine evental name, the name terrorism "has a triple function [...] It demarcates a subject [...] supports predicates—on this occasion terrorism is 'Islamic'. It determines a sequence—the entire current sequence is from now on considered as 'the war on terror'" (*IT*, p. 142-143). But the 'war on terror' is *not* an evental name: what it designates is "*the disjunctive synthesis of two nihilisms*" (*IT*, p.158), combining as it does both the obliteration of the dignity of everyday life beneath an essentially religious zeal (on both sides of Huntington's clash of civilizations) and that "nihilism of virtual equality" (*IT*, p. 161) characteristic of late capital, which reduces humanity to the impoverished commonality of consumerism. Nothing radically new emerged on that day then, although something found a newly intense form of visibility.

But if 9/11 was an exception, a simulacral counter-nomination, rather than an event, it follows that although the logic of the NION movement broadly resembles that of a generic or subtractive politics, without the ontological rupture of an event, without the emergence of a genuine novelty, it in fact lacked conditioning in a truth, and thus the possibility of a coherent subject-body. In attempting to condition itself on a simulacral counter-nomination, the 'name' it attempted to mobilise did not ultimately name anything. It is in this sense that the NION movement could be said to have become entangled in the infinite regress of counter-counter-nomination inherent to an exclusive focus on the un-conditioned name, the truly ex nihilo name. It remained stuck in the logic of negation. Once again, this is where speculative leftism and parliamentarism coincide at the extremes of a vicious circle. While NION appears to have a radically anti-Statist politics, in fact it is perfectly containable within the logic of abstention built into the parliamentary vote. Under the hegemony of a militarised neoliberal democracy, one is even supposed to feel lucky that one is free enough to be able to abstain.

4

Active and Reactive Subjects

Arguably Badiou's most impressive achievement is to have successfully challenged the hegemony of those various theoretical movements—poststructuralism, deconstruction, postmodernism—which, emerging from the critique of Humanism, share a common rejection, or at least a severe qualification, of the category of the subject. Of course, the subject persists in these movements, but always as an effect of structure. So for early Althusser, the agential, rational subject is a bourgeois fiction concealing the last instance of the economic behind naturalised class domination: better to seek potential change in structural nodes of overdetermination than in strategic class alliances or consciousness-raising (Althusser: 1969). Similarly for Foucault, the 'Man' of Humanism is an historico-discursive construct specific to the modern episteme beginning in the Eighteenth Century, but palpably waning in the Twentieth (Foucault: 2000). With Foucault then, the subject is no longer the Kantian rational autonomous agent (which it only ever was epistemologically rather than ontologically): again, it has today become a kind of nodal point arising from the triangulations of power. As for Derrida, his subject loses the instrumental relation to language-as-tool inscribed in Humanism and becomes, on the contrary, a mere side-effect of language as a generalised textuality. Specifically, the metaphysical subject-effect arises from the aporetic logic of the proper name, which both assigns putative presence and is promiscuously iterable (Derrida: 1997).

In these three seminal critics of Humanism, the subject is always determined: interpellated by ideology for Althusser, discursively produced for Foucault, and woven from language as a differential structure for Derrida. Nor is it a coincidence that these three thinkers have been seminal points of reference for the diffuse cultural and philosophical movement known as 'postmodernism'. With its natural home in the American epicentre of late capital, postmodernism has found a way to turn this structurally determined subject into a ludic consumer of multiple lifestyles. Schizophrenic and short on cognitive maps, it is even endowed with a semblance of agency in the form of a capacity for cultural collage and parodic performativity. Freedom for the postmodern subject seems to be achieved primarily through creative consumption. This is arguably how

Althusser's anti-capitalist critique of the bourgeois subject has been comfortably re-appropriated by Capital itself.

Only Lacan—Badiou's 'master-thinker' (and not generally 'cool' for postmodernists)—stubbornly maintained an undetermined, exceptional notion of the subject right in the midst of the structuralist and then poststructuralist revolutions: "[Lacan] holds steady with regard to the subject effect, when all the others will understand that it must be relegated to the museum of dying humanist ideology" (*TS*, p. 225). Desire and the unconscious ultimately demonstrate the fantasmatic nature of the *imago* of total determination, of the complete subjection of the subject. This is why Lacan has long served as the necessary anti-philosopher to Badiou's philosophy. But as a philosopher, Badiou argues in *Theory of the Subject* that even the enfant terrible of psychoanalysis stops at the brink of the limit of structural subjectivity. Early Lacan in particular focuses on the 'subject of the signifier' or even a 'subject of the combinatory', and thus on the its castrating entanglements in an almost machinic Other of language qua social link—this, after all, is what Althusser draws on in his notion of interpellation.[1] In the last meditation in *Being and Event*, Badiou accuses Lacan of never fully escaping this structural subject, of always "localizing the void" (*BE*, p. 432) on the side of language rather than of being. Badiou's effort then has been to push Lacan beyond this anti-philosophical limit towards a subject in sustained excess over structure, including over structure's constitutive lack, as we saw in Chapter 1.

Very much against the grain of intellectual fashions then, Badiou has managed to resurrect for the 21st Century questions that many had deemed dead and buried in the third quarter of the 20th. In many ways, he has resurrected a Sartrean thematic, inescapably political in character, for our supposedly apolitical or post-political times. Debates about freedom, decision, action and militant cohesion are back on the theoretical table. However, the term 'resurrection' here must be understood in the technical sense introduced in Chapter 1 of *Logics of Worlds*: the revival of an 'old' truth in a new situation conditioned by a second event. That is to say, there is nothing to be gained from resuscitating the dead 'Man' upon whom Foucault performed his meticulous autopsy. On the contrary, Badiou's thought emerges from the same anti-Humanist philosophical and political conjuncture as Althusser, Foucault and Derrida, carrying many of their insights into his new theory of the subject. Ed Pluth's claim (Pluth: 2010), that Badiou ultimately conforms to Althusser's dictum of 'theoretical anti-humanism plus practical humanism' is perfectly defensible, as long as this is not perceived as a loop back to Humanism, but rather as the spiral with which Badiou describes the black sheep of dialectical materialism in *Theory of the Subject*: a circle that moves forward precisely because it never intersects with itself.

Alongside Slavoj Žižek then, Badiou has genuinely changed the co-ordinates of debate about political subjectivity. However, now that Badiou himself is almost

---

1. Later Lacan (*SXXIII*) develops a quite different subject, a subject of jouissance and the related singularity of the *sinthome*, which is not a symptom enslaved to the 'defiles of the signifier', but rather a kind of creative affirmation that lends a consistency to the subject without relying on the Other.

embarrassingly fashionable, my aim in this chapter is to off-set that version of the radically singular, un-worldly, and apparently miraculous subject which many are still inclined to present as *the* Badiouian subject. This is not a misreading per se, but a partial reading, one based too heavily on the admittedly foundational first volume of *Being and Event*. If the Badiouian subject is to be inscribed in a philosophy of conflict, this absolutely singular subject represents a very serious obstacle. As Peter Hallward has convincingly argued (see Chapter 13 of Hallward: 2003), a non-relational, quasi-divine subject ends up being too external to the world with which it breaks to truly effect it: it becomes extra-worldly. Insofar as Badiou's re-founding of the subject is a fundamentally political act, intervening into the de-politicised context of deconstruction, postmodernism, the ethical turn and what he now calls 'democratic materialism', it may be that *Being and Event*, with its punctual and rather heroic vision of the subject of truth, actually limits the efficacy of this intervention.

There is an unavoidable overlap here between a polemical requirement imposed upon Badiou by the context into which he intervenes, and that context's capacity to read him against himself. He *must* emphasise this radically singular subject, given what he is opposing: biopolitical control, internalised surveillance, micro-technologies of capillary power, and the consumerist mobilisation of affect, all of which have incrementally increased the reach and grip of normative individuation. In such a context, with its inadvertent theoretical reflection in the 'death of the subject', Badiou's insistence on a (self)determining rather than determined subject is bound to sound shrill and possibly archaic. But this shrillness threatens to become an example of the kind of 'ultra-Leftism' that Capital is perfectly happy to appropriate in the form of what I would call 'rebel chic': cool but ultimately harmless rebellion at the level of rhetoric. In mock Žižekian style, we could say that the radicalism of this miraculous, singular and probably impossible subject channels the nostalgia for real political stakes into a Christ-like purity, satisfying to the precise extent that it cannot be encountered in the real. It is an *objet a* for lacklustre postmodern subjects who fantasise about being the troubadours of social transformation, but who actually remain ensconced in the logic of courtly love Lacan analysed in Seminar VII, where desire is sustained by maintaining the unattainability of the object of desire (in order to keep it as cause).

Certainly, any reading of Badiou which allows one to imagine that there could be anything radical about sitting around waiting for an event and the possibility of becoming a subject completely misses the axiomatic basis of subjectivization. For reasons that will become clear, I prefer the more declarative formula, 'there *have been* events, and there *can always* be subjects'. My goal in this chapter, following Bruno Bosteels' example in particular (Bosteels: 2009), is to demonstrate the extent to which such subjects are in the world, enmeshed in relationality, and inseparable from conflict, confrontation, and controversy.

ONE OR MORE SUBJECT?

Let us begin by dispelling some illusions. In *Being and Event*, the subject is not an organic unity that would fall under an entry in the encyclopaedia of the situation.

Although Badiou will speak in *Logics of Worlds* of 'subject-bodies', these are by no means bodies with 'natural' or even socially constructed forms. The reference to bodies is intended to place an emphasis on the material dimension of a subject that exceeds pre-given taxonomies, and not, therefore, on the subject as a determinate biological unit. Despite being made up of recognisable multiples of the situation, taken globally, the subject is utterly indiscernible because the parts it composes have no recognised rule of composition. The subject's mode of collective appearance is entirely irrational. In this way, the subject is only rarely and contingently a 'biological' individual in the intuitive sense.[2] However, it is just as important to point out that, certainly with regard to political truth procedures, subjects necessarily in-corporate or em-body 'biological' individuals as the physical supports of a truth. This immediately suggests that the subject is always a mixed subject, a knot between truth and world.

Nor, on the other hand, is the subject a kind of irruption of pure Being-qua-being from behind the façade of an essentially fake 'objectivity' or 'reality'. The subject does not reveal a hidden, deeper being concealed beneath appearance. In Badiou's own parlance, the subject is not the avatar of the void, as if the void were a unified substance beneath worldly dissimulations. As we have said repeatedly, the void is only void for a particular situation: it is certainly not a kind of Leibnizian divine and universal substance underlying all possible worlds. If the void were such a divine substance, and the subject merely its local avatar, the messianism sometimes imputed to Badiou would be entirely justified.[3] Indeed, the trap of speculative leftism, which shares with its religious counterpart the tendency towards dogmatism, lies in this temptation to conflate the subject with a fuller being than quotidian appearance can possibly convey. One of the most important roles of the event, therefore, as a break with ontology, is to condition a subject that can never claim trans-situational or extra-worldly plenitude, divine or otherwise.

So the subject is not an individual (although it can be composed of individuals), and it is not the upsurge of unmediated Being-qua-being (because it is a break with being as a particular regime of counting). But nor is the subject the locus of a privileged experience, such as the ecstasy of an epiphany or a conversion. While, as we shall see, experience in the form of affects is a secondary dimension of subjectivization, it is inaccurate to see these affects as direct indexes of truth (as if 'ex-stasis' in both the Heideggerian and Sartrean senses were indicative of access to the authentic).[4] Related to this distance from mysticism, Badiou's subject does not

---

2. The one exception to this is love, which Badiou calls the 'Scene of the Two' and which necessarily involves individual subjects (see Badiou's contribution to the collection *De L'amour*. Flammarion, 2000, pp177-190).

3. Following Alberto Toscano's work on fanaticism, I will myself be recuperating the value of a certain millenarianism of the political subject through the example of Rastafari in Chapter 7.

4. Heidegger refers in *Being and Time* to the "'*ecstases*' of temporality" (Heidegger: 1998, 329) by means of which temporality is essentially futural: time is constantly "outside-of-itself" (*ibid.*) in the sense that the existential present is the result of the conjuncture between the having-been and the future. Sartre, in *Being and Nothingness* (Sartre: 2006) dialogues with Heidegger's notion of ek-stasis and offers three modalities of nihilation which can be considered as progressively ek-static, moving as they do from being-in-itself to being-for-itself (see section 1 of Part 11). Both

serve as the mouthpiece of a revelation, of a new, divine meaning. The truth does not have a meaning, only effects. And so far is Badiou from the Cartesian trope of the isolated, rational subject that he insists that it may not even be conscious of being a subject at all: the subject is "neither consciousness nor unconsciousness of the true" (*BE*, p.407). It will certainly be in a position of ignorance vis-à-vis the truth it carries, because it is of the world with which that truth is incompatible. And precisely due to this ignorance, it must have an exorbitant faith in the truth. Faith, we could say, is the only way to radically affirm what one cannot know.

Finally, and this is very important, the subject is neither the origin nor the result of an event. The subject is not the origin of the event for the simple reason that it is totally conditioned by its occurrence. The materialist axiom of conditioning effectively prohibits the intuitively valid question 'can a subject *will* an event?', since the subject presupposes the event and must be, albeit in a complex sense, temporally subsequent to it. To ask if the accumulated and concentrated will of *individuals* can play some role in paving the way for, or resurrecting, an event is a subtly different question, and one I will be broaching later in this chapter. But we are faced here with the difficulty of thinking just what kind of necessity binds a subject to events and vice versa. This necessity cannot be thought of in the reductively Newtonian terms of cause and effect. Whereas the universal laws of gravitation necessarily induce as one of their effects the falling of Earth-based apples, there is no objective, mechanistic determination operating between events as causes, and subjects as effects. Just like Lacan's then, Badiou's subject is constitutively split: the event conditions its very possibility, yet the event also requires its subject's supplementary intervention. The subject was already referred to as a 'torsion' in *Theory of the Subject* for this very reason, and still in *Being and Event*, where words such as 'liason' and 'juncture' are used, the subject is a kind of chiasmus crossing the infinite gap between an evental truth and the situation in which it arises.

In *Logics of Worlds*, Badiou will make this even clearer when he writes the symbol for the faithful subject-body as $\cancel{C}$, in graphic distinction to the apparent fullness of the obscure body, written simply C. Again, this split nature of the subject reflects the all-important 'disjunctive synthesis' (to borrow a term from Deleuze and Guattari) of the 'and' in *Being and Event*. It is essential to the argument there that the subject is not "transitive to being" (*BE*, p.392), in other words, not guaranteed in any way by structure. The 'and' is deliberately distinct from 'as' (which would ontologize the event) as well as from 'or' (which would transcendentalise the event). On the contrary, the 'and' of *Being and Event* is the disjunctural space of subjectivity itself, both in its opaque excess over being or structure, and in its process of putting that excess to work. The technique of forcing intrinsic to the truth procedure will reintroduce the legitimate *con*junctural dimension of this 'and' by constructing a situation in which the eventual multiple will have belonged to the situation. But it follows from the conditioned nature of the space of this forcing—and this is what those impatient for a radical cause to immerse themselves in lament—that subjects

thinkers have in common with Badiou an interest in the subject's extraction from the essential inauthenticity of determination by being ('throwness into the They' for Heidegger, 'bad faith' for Sartre), but both provide what Badiou cannot: a nuanced phenomenology of this extraction.

are *rare*, and that we should never simply assume their existence. It does not follow, however, that we should indulge wait-and-see quietism. I would argue that the stress on the rarity of true subjects constitutes the precise opposite. It implies unceasing vigilance in the recognition of simulacral subjects so that when evental subjects do arise, they cannot be so easily nullified.

Even with these careful qualifications regarding what a subject is *not* (a biological individual, an avatar of pure being, the receptacle of an ecstatic experience, the origin of an event, the causal consequence of an event, transitive to a situation or world), the dominant critical reading of *Being and Event* still tends to ascribe to this subject an absolute, transcendental singularity, i.e., one that is decidedly extra-worldly. *This* singularity emphasises the stark completeness of the ontological break with the count of the situation (or with the being-there of appearance and the transcendental of worlds) and also the punctual temporality of this complete break. The singularity of the event, on this account, is then problematically conflated with the subject itself, overemphasising two motifs. Firstly, an apparent voluntarism insofar as the decision is indeed utterly decisive for subjectivity, secondly, the militant durability of this conversion as 'disciples' cohere around an internally generated (unworldly) 'confidence in confidence'. Thanks both to the complete and point-like rupture of the event and the subject's voluntaristic autonomy, this subject appears to be the distillation of a complete subtraction from all worldly individuation and thus relationality. It is at this point, as Peter Hallward rightly points out, that the subject starts to become problematically abstract: punning on Marx's 11th thesis on Feuerbach, he writes "[t]hough it will have long since ceased merely to describe the world, its promise to change this world will always remain unduly abstract" (Hallward: 2003, p.322).

So the kind of singularity which gets read back into Badiou in general and *Being and Event* in particular, not without ample evidence of course, and folded into his notion of the subject, is:

1. Purely Ruptural
2. Utterly Punctual
3. Starkly Voluntarist
4. Militantly Durable
5. Completely De-individuated

Each of these spells doom for the philosophy of conflict I am trying to tease from Badiou's wider work. A rupture that 'just happens' and seems irreversible is not a terrain of conflict, but simply the origin of ineluctable consequences. If a rupture is deemed to be localisable in a specific point, one moreover recognised by the existing state of things, this opens the door to speculative leftism where, rather than conflict, we simply have dogmatic assertion by an already counted multiple. If the subject could be freely willed into existence, conflict would be reduced to a battle of wills rather than embraced as a process of contingent emergence from complex systems in which will is but one force amongst others. If the subject, once 'converted', retained unshakable conviction in the face of all evidence to the contrary, there would be no doubt or uncertainty, only the recklessness of fanaticism.[5] And finally,

---

5. See Toscano: 2010 for a counter-history of the role of fanaticism in political movements to

if the subject were completely de-individuated, deprived of all worldly predicates, it would not appear in the world at all, and no change would be carried by it. It would remain indiscernible.

It is true that this kind of extreme singularity seems to be exacerbated in *Being and Event* by the fact that Badiou follows through there on an assertion he had arrived at, albeit tentatively, in *Theory of the Subject*, namely, that there is only *one* subject. In the early seminars, Badiou had developed his notion of scissional contradiction within a fairly orthodox model of class antagonism which ascribed historical agency to *two* entities, the bourgeoisie and the proletariat: "The bourgeoisie" he initially claimed, "makes a subject" (*TS*, p.42). But by later seminars, he had nuanced his position to the point of disagreeing with his former claim: "Does the bourgeoisie make a subject? I affirmed as much in this very place, in April 1975. Let me contradict myself [...]. The bourgeoisie has not been a subject for a long time, it makes a place. There is only one political subject ...." (*TS*, p.130). *Being and Event* represents the set-theoretical formalisation of this radical singularisation of the subject. In Part VIII, it is made very clear that there is only one subject of truth, the militantly faithful one. As his engagements with Saint-Paul and Pascal as well as with Kierkegaard demonstrate, Badiou is perfectly aware of the Christian imagery behind the lone subject as something like a soldier of truth. This has allowed 'strong' theological readings of Badiou, such as that by Frederiek Depoortere (2009) who—'miraculously' I am tempted to say—finds in Badiou's recourse to set-theoretical notations on infinity, not a resolutely secular fidelity to the death of God, as Badiou himself would have it (see *MP*, p.43), but, rather like Descartes, a kind of mathematical deism.

This lone subject-as-soldier-of-God also gets ascribed a kind of Cartesian anthropocentrism by some commentators. Of course, on one level, Badiou is thoroughly anthropocentric insofar as he is adamant that events and truths are distinctly *human* affairs. However, we should immediately qualify this by adding that he describes truth as "undoubtedly an experience of the inhuman" (*LW*, p.71). For Badiou then, humans are thinking beings, but thought puts them in contact with the radically generic and therefore the non- or inhuman. The specifically human faculty is the capacity to transcend, through thought as active participation in truth, what he provocatively calls in the *Ethics* book, the 'animality' of humanity. Yet the anthropocentrism that limits the reception of Badiou's subject is residually Cartesian in that it conceives the human in a wholly different register, at once psychologistic and theological. It persists in imagining the self-identical individual as the fundamental substrate of subjectivity, and thus coincides with the worst excesses of narcissistic consumer individualism. It is from this perspective that all five dimensions of this already excessively 'singular' subject are measured, whether by critics eager to dismiss Badiou, or advocates mistakenly misrepresenting him:

---

the one offered by liberal historiography, which attempts to maintain a binary between 'irrational' fanaticism and rational political consensus. I am not using the term 'fanaticism' in the sense bequeathed to us by this liberal political historiography, but precisely in Toscano's sense of a failure of emancipatory politics.

Self-identical Singularity	Individualising Reinscription	Consequent Subject Figure
Pure Rupture	… with the individual's habitus or lifeworld	Extra-worldly ascension
Punctual Emergence	… from an individuated and individuating *place*	Localisable privilege of the generic (speculative leftism)
Stark Voluntarism	… of the individual as rational decision-maker	Idealist autonomy of the will
Durable Militancy	… as individual determination	Defence of identity (rightist dogmatism)
Complete De-individuation	… as a kind of individual freedom	A singularity predicated on individuality

These figurations of the subject of truth nullify precisely what is so important in Badiou's re-conceptualisation of the category. They skirt dangerously closely to notions of 'downsizing', 'escaping the rat race', even 'joining a commune' or 'starting a cult'! The heroic individualism embedded in such images paradoxically turn the generic into a privilege. More importantly, they miss the thoroughgoing *formalism* of Badiou's theory of the subject. Ultimately, it is only this last that can exorcise the ghost of individualism and its correlate, identity politics. In a deeply Lacanian sense, only the matheme can prevent singularity from being individualised (which also means imaginarised).

Luckily, there are plenty of resources within *Being and Event* itself, and more still in Badiou's wider oeuvre, to counter this troublesome tendency. For one thing, it is not strictly accurate to say there is only one subject in *Being and Event*. In fact, the number of conditioning truth-domains and thus the kinds of subjects that can be faithful within them, multiplies by a factor of three when compared to *Theory of the Subject*. Whereas the latter had only one type of subject, the political one, *Being and Event* adds to this the possibility of artistic, scientific and amorous subjects. Immediately, the existence of artistic and scientific subjects in particular helps to off-set the residual Cartesian anthropocentrism I have referred to. This is because artistic subjects are not artists per se but 'configurations' of their works (see *HI*). Scientific subjects are not scientists but the mathematical formulae or theoretical axioms they produce. Furthermore, the fact that such truths pertain only to the realms from which they irrupt, and not to their global context, also immediately suggests that singularity is not generalisable, even in the form of radical non-relation. To put it somewhat elliptically, we could say that non-relational singularity is nonetheless non-relational in relation to that which it singularises itself *from*. More simply, artistic truths are singular *for* art, and not for, say, politics,[6] and scientific

---

6. This, of course, is where Badiou radically diverges from Jacques Rancière. Badiou's affinities with and differences from Rancière can be found expressed in Chapters 7 and 8 of *Metapolitics*, while Rancière's critique of Badiou's concept of 'inaesthetics' can be found in Rancière:

truths are non-relational only in relation to pre-existing science, not in relation to anything and everything. Badiou's rigorous formalism, evident in the definition of the subject as "any local configuration of a generic truth procedure from which a truth is supported" (*BE*, p.391), emerges precisely as he is distilling the invariant properties of not one but *several* kinds of subjects across divergent and, indeed, incompatible truth-domains. Formalism is needed to make sense of this multiplicity, not to abstract it away.

This trajectory, whereby singularity is, as it were, multiplied, is clear in *Logics of Worlds*, where he enacts something of a volte-face regarding the axiom that 'there is only one subject'. Returning to the more antagonistic aspects of his ostensibly Maoist phase, he now posits three subjective figures that can emerge in all four truth domains. Far from insisting on the lone, heroic subject of fidelity then, this new comprehensive taxonomy of the subject has no less than twelve modalities of subjectivity. To the faithful subject are added the reactive and the obscure subjects, both also conditioned by an event but responding to it in ways diametrically opposed to the faithful subject. The reactive subject says 'no' to the event and cleaves to the familiar norms of the old world. However, this 'no' does not succeed in being a logical negation without remainder, for "in order to resist the call of the new, it is still necessary to create arguments of resistance adjusted to the new itself" (*LW*, p.62). In his matheme of the reactive subject, Badiou places the new present generated by the event under the Saussurean-Lacanian bar of the unconscious. Rather like a psychoanalytic symptom then, denial operates as an unwilling index of what is repressed, opening up the space for a symptomatic reading of the work of the reactive subject. A more violent and formidable enemy of truth, however, is the obscure subject. Whereas the reactive subject subordinates the faithful subject but in so doing creates a new (negative) present that can be read as a reaction-formation around what it denies, the obscure subject pursues the occultation of the new present itself. It obliterates the implications of an event by offering a monstrous alternative body, built, unlike the generic body of truth, from identitarian and particularistic notions of community, nation and race—the paradigmatic example here is Fascism and its occultation of the Bolshevik event.

Because there are, or can be, faithful, reactive and obscure subjects in the realms of love, politics, art and science, *Logics of Worlds* confronts us with a much more complex strategic field of intersubjective relations which influence the outcome of an event. The alliances and oppositions between these subjective figures begin to resemble a battlefield in which concrete strategy, rather than a semi-transcendent notion of 'singularity', becomes crucial. Badiou hints that reactive subjects often pave the way for, and perhaps even do the dirty work of, obscure subjects for instance: "the reactive and obscure subjects are already at work, as rivals and accomplices in weakening the substance of this present or occulting its presence" (*LW*, p.62). And yet the faithful subject must not get drawn into a war of worldly position with these enemies of truth, lest she simply consolidate the

2010, pp. 205-218. My own notion of an 'evental culture' sketched in Chapter 7 suggests a certain rapprochement between these positions.

commutative "diagram of the world" (*LW*, p.314), which we will examine later in this chapter when we treat of 'relation'.

SUBJECTIVIZATION

> It is not the singularity of the subject that validates what the subject says; it is what he says that founds the singularity of the subject (*SP*, p.53)

The image of the self-identical, singular subject can be further mollified if we stress its composite nature. That the Badiouian subject is a mixed or compound entity has been evident since *Theory of the Subject*. Already there, Badiou makes a distinction between 'subjectivation' on the one hand, and the 'subject-process' on the other (*TS*, pp.243-247). 'Subjectivation' refers to the sudden, out-of-the-blue emergence of a novel force that interrupts the reigning regime of splacement. 'Subject-process' refers to the more productive work, over time, of constructing a new situation. If the former is punctual and ephemeral, a vanishing cause, the latter endures as a labour of organised transformation. However, the key point for our purposes is that the subject is neither one nor the other. Neither the historical flash of insurrection, nor the organisation of force over time, the subject is the torsion or knot that holds both together. Indeed, this is arguably *the* Maoist problematic in *Theory of the Subject*: how to ensure organisational consistency following the insurrectionary explosion of proletarian historicity. As we saw in Chapters 1 and 2, Badiou's answer to this problem used to be the Maoist party. It was tasked, conceptually and practically, with the job of holding together these moments of subjectivation and the subject-process, and thus of destruction and recomposition. But to repeat, the subject is not one of these poles in isolation, or even both at different stages of a teleological unfolding. Rather, it is the dialectical (which also means contradictory) *cleaving* of the two. The bivalence of the verb 'to cleave' is extremely useful in describing this mixed subject, since it means both separation or division and convergence or imposed unity, mapping neatly onto the all-important hyphen connecting destruction-creation.

In *Being and Event*, this same logic of cleaving is evident in the relation between the concepts of 'intervention' and 'fidelity'. As we saw in the last chapter, intervention is an illegal and exceptional moment when the event is given a name. Fidelity, on the other hand, describes the drawn out process of maintaining the subjective confidence needed to keep going with the laborious task of pursuing the implications of this name. Their temporalities are different, but inextricably intertwined. Both are equally divorced from quotidian time, being born, we could say, of *kairos* rather than *chronos*.[7] But intervention is clearly a brief intensity, whereas fidelity unfolds in the dimension of duration. As the Bergsonian resonance of the term 'duration' suggests, there is a sense in which the time of fidelity enfolds within itself the time of intervention, but also that there is a recursive effect travelling in the opposite direction, from fidelity 'back' to intervention: the notion of 'periodisation' in

---

7. This distinction between *kairos* and *chronos* is important in Antonio Negri's meditation on the Marxist theory of time and its fate in conditions of real subsumption (see Negri: 2003).

Theory of the Subject had already outlined something of this recursive temporal folding, the Deleuzian resonances of which Badiou has been careful to forestall (see pp.381-387 of *LW*).

Despite being published long after Badiou's break with the party model of politics, there is a category in *Being and Event* that essentially plays the same cleaving function that the Maoist party had in *Theory of the Subject*. I am referring to the 'operator of fidelity' (see Mediation 35 of *BE*). Written $\square$ by Badiou, the 'operator of fidelity' refers to institution-like structures that accommodate truth enquiries exploring an event's effects on its situation. In a starkly divisive way, these operators separate out every element of a situation that connects positively to the name of the event ($ex \square y$) from those that do not ($\sim(ex \square y)$), gradually, if haphazardly, building a generic set out of the former (*BE*, p.394). Badiou mentions the Church as well as the Party as examples of such 'operators', insofar as they cleave their worlds into faithful and unfaithful sets. But as both of these examples also suggest, the operators of fidelity are themselves prone to a kind of corruption when they are taken to be subjects themselves. Just as infallible Papal authority is divorced from the Christ-event, so the bloated apparatus of the Stalinist State is disjoined from the Lenin-event. The more encompassing term, therefore, that now cleaves together intervention and fidelity (with the operator as no more than the organisational means of this cleaving) is "subjectivization" (*BE*, p.393). Far from designating something external to the situation, something radically singular in some global sense, the term 'subjectivization' clearly faces inwards, into the complexity of the situation itself: "Subjectivization is interventional nomination *from the standpoint of the situation*, that is, the rule of the intra-situational effects of the supernumerary name's entrance into circulation" (*BE*, p.393).

Significantly given our discussion of the role of the evental name in the previous chapter, Badiou goes on in Mediation 35 of *Being and Event* to emphasise the importance of the proper name in holding a place within the symbolic so that subjbectivization can get underway. This is needed precisely because the subject is split between its situation and the truth it carries. So, the proper name has both the emptiness required to enable a generic enquiry, and the worldly consistency to allow this enquiry to be 'properly' intra-situational and not merely abstract. In this sense, the Christian church needs the proper name 'Saint Paul', Bolshevism needs 'Lenin', set-theory needs 'Cantor' and so on, in each case to cleave together intervention and fidelity, preventing either being unduly reified:

> What the proper name designates here is that the subject, as local situated configuration, is neither the intervention nor the operator of fidelity, but the advent of their Two, that is, the incorporation of the event into the situation in the mode of a generic procedure (*BE*, p.393)

Reading this closely, one senses the levels on which the bivalence of the logic of cleaving inherent to subjectivization operates. Within the generic procedure itself, it performs the divisive function of separating out the generic set attributable to the evental name, and it thereby forces truth and situation together—separation and unity. But to the extent that the subject is in and of the situation, the logic of cleaving ultimately emphasises separation, insofar as it attempts to prevent the subject's absorption into the ever-present temptations of left opportunism (which fetishizes intervention) and dogmatic rightism (which reifies the operator of faithful connection, as Stalinism did the Party-State): earlier in *Being and Event* (p.238), Badiou had rightly worried about 'spontaneist' and 'dogmatic' as well as 'generic' forms of fidelity.

Nonetheless, it is obvious that the role of the proper name in anchoring a generic procedure comes with a considerable risk of hero worship, or even of the rise of a cult of personality. To offset this danger, Badiou reminds us that the subject is never reducible to an individual, but only to that part of an individual that participates in a much larger process of transformation. One of his most insistent definitions of the subject is as a finite fragment of an infinite truth. What he means by this rather hyperbolic formulation is that the subject is finite because, in its situational dimension, it is *also* a mundane and mortal individual. Even in the case of artistic events, in which we have suggested that anthropocentrism is held at greater distance, the subject is an empirical work that not only must pay for its sensuous presentation of truth at the price of its tendency towards physical decay, but must also stake a claim to being categorisable as 'art' in the everyday sense, and thus prey to the whims of artistic fashions. Truth on the other hand is infinite because what it unveils is uncountable for the situation. It is not infinite in a temporal sense per se, but in a non-denumerable sense, as a limit of formalisation. In the *Ethics* book, this composite combination of the infinite and the finite is phrased in terms of the human and the animal, and the immortal and the mortal respectively. Once again, the emphasis is certainly not on a permanent ascension from one to the other, but on a difficult intermixture, as the concept 'some-one' conveys in the following quote:

> The "some-one" thus caught up in what attests that he belongs to the truth-process as one of its foundation-points is simultaneously *himself*, nothing other than himself, a multiple singularity recognizable among all others, and *in excess of himself*, because the uncertain course of fidelity *passes through him* (*E*, p.45)

Far from being singular in a pure way then, "[e]very subject is qualified [...] there are some individual subjects inasmuch as there is some love, some mixed subjects inasmuch as there is some art or some science, and some collective subjects inasmuch as there is some politics" (*BE*, p.392). Some subjects, not *a* subject. This 'some' indicates that each subject is a matter of degree or intensity in relation to the residual animality they will also inevitably carry. But, simultaneously, they are some-*one* in something like the sense of the One that Lacan develops in Seminar *XX*, where he coins the aphorism 'Y'a de l'un', there is some Oneness, and then Seminar *XXIII* where Borromean consistency makes a One by adding a fourth 'suppletion' to the three rings of the trefoil knot. These late seminars develop a One of internal consistency uncountable by the seriality of the Symbolic Other. It is a One of indiscernible excess, then, which clearly resonates with Badiou's 'ultra-one' and the truthful dimension of subjects. Later in this chapter, we will explore whether this resonance allows the distinct kinds of singularity dealt with by psychoanalysis and philosophy to converge or overlap.

But this 'some' also indicates that there are more than one (in the banal sense). We already know that there is more than one subject insofar as there are four truth-domains in which they can appear. We also know that, by *Logics of Worlds*, Badiou concedes that there can be three subjective responses to the event in these four realms. But that concession has not yet been made in *Being and Event* where he remains committed to the notion that there is only one subject. And yet he declares there that "in the same situation, and for the same event, different criteria can exist which define different fidelities [...] there are many manners of being faithful to an event" (*BE*, pp.233-34). This is a 'more-than-one' that pertains neither to the plurality of truth domains, nor to the later plurality of subject figures (obscure, reactive, faithful). Rather, he is hinting at the possibility of multiple types of faithful subject, all sustained, presumably, by different evental names and distinct operators of fidelity. Now, the abstract openness of Badiou's formalism of the subject means that he might well claim that such different names and different operators are ultimately subsumed within the larger subjective forces that catalyse change. What's in a name, he might say. But 'on the ground', this surely complicates the picture quite seriously? Aren't these divergent forms of fidelity likely to end up lapsing into mutual enmity? How does forcing work when the generic multiple being included in an altered encyclopaedia has two (or more?) names with two (or more?) groups of equally militant adherents? Ontologically, it may well be that they are disputing the self-same multiple and simply appending it with different names. Ontologically, this difference may be of no more import than the differences between algebraic notations. But since this dispute must be phrased in the language of the situation if it is to change it, different subject-languages surely open onto a more Lyotardian universe of competing phrase regimes? The necessarily animal aspect of every subject, as well as the role of the proper name in subjectivization as a whole, opens the way for this risk of in-fighting and a return, of sorts, to the impasses of identity politics. Badiou might protest that truth is no longer operative at this point of impasse, when a kind of saturation has set in. Yet the above quote implies that multiple faithful subjects are possible *as part and parcel of an active truth-procedure*, irrespective of its subsequent decline. At the very least, this makes the task of distinguishing between simulacral and genuine subjects much more difficult.

With these kinds of questions, we are now touching on the difficult concept of forcing developed in Meditations 33 and 36 of *Being and Event*. Although this concept only poses these questions more acutely, it does make it very clear both that the absolutely singular subject cannot be maintained, and, relatedly, that conflict is unavoidable in any truth-procedure. Badiou takes the term directly from the mathematician Paul Cohen, who proposed it in 1963 as a technique for, not so much resolving, as working *with* the undecideability of Cantor's so-called 'continuum hypothesis'. Much is at stake in this hypothesis, since it relates to the dominance of either an infinitely constructible universe or an incomplete and paradoxical one; thus to mathematical ontology as exhaustively descriptive of the pure multiplicity of what is, or the persistence of a certain real even within mathematics. We do not need to go into the labrynthine technical details of Cohen's concept of 'forcing', and others have done so for us.[8] Suffice it to say that its inestimable value for Badiou lies in its ability to offer a formally coherent language for describing a completely generic extension of a situation *in that situation's own terms*, thereby logically imposing that extension's eventual addition.

Because a generic set is devoid of all predicates as far as a situation is concerned, it is invisible, impossible, ineffable: no change can arise from such an absolutely indiscernible status. Implicitly echoing Lacan's aphorism that woman is not-all, Badiou writes the generic set with the feminine symbol, '♀'. What this means is that, if there is, as Lacan insists in his tables of sexuation in Seminar *XX*, no relation whatsoever between this feminine position and the phallic logic of the male side, we are left with a static stand-off. This is the equivalent, within sexuation, of Badiou's ontological opposition between presentation and representation. What forcing does, however, is allow Badiou to demonstrate how, in his set-theoretical version of the Lacanian not-all, the represented situation can be *made* to relate to the non-relation of the unrepresentable generic set. If 'S' stands for the existing situation, and '♀' for its generic extension, then forcing enables both the inscription of 'S♀'—or the hypothesis of the belonging of the generic set to the situation—and a series of logical operations such that this hypothesis of originary belonging *will have* been true in a new, supplemented situation. In short, forcing is the logical process of transforming an indiscernible into an undecidable: it turns something utterly uncounted into a very visible challenge that forces a decision onto a situation, precisely because it is phrased in its own terms (rather than the easily dismissed appeal to the ineffable in the discourse of mysticism or messianic politics etc.). By demonstrating first that certain axioms are true for an initially hypothetical generic set, and then that that set was always already included in the initial set, though without belonging to it, forcing creates both a new set incorporating its generic extension, and a new regime of veracity in which the 'new' generic truths must also be incorporated. As a knowledge-like process, it opposes to the Statist count something resembling a rival Statist count, albeit one entirely illegal from the point of view of the former. Forcing is therefore the privileged means for articulating being and event, situation and subject, in such a way as to irrevocably transform both.

More than a logical process, however, forcing is also "the trace of the being of the Subject" (*BE*, p.428). You will recall that Badiou's theory of the subject includes its structural ignorance vis-à-vis the 'content' of the truth. Crucially however, forcing provides what might be called a coherent writing of the indiscernible. This writing of the indiscernible both sustains the subject's fidelity, and becomes the logical weapon it turns on the situation:

> [A]lthough an inhabitant of the situation does not know anything of the indiscernible, and so of the extension, she is capable of thinking that the belonging of such a condition to a generic description is equivalent to the veracity of such a statement within that extension (*BE*, p.411)

Importantly, Badiou adds a few lines later, if "she forces veracity at the point of

---

8. See chapter 3 and the appendix entitled 'On the Development of Transfinite Set Theory' in Hallward: 2003; chapter 3 of Gillespie: 2008; pp.128-151 of Norris: 2009.

the indiscernible", she "does so with the nominal resources of the situation alone" (*ibid.*). In other words, existing names are drained of their quotidian referential value and turned into empty formal letters. It is these letters that designate a hypothetical multiple that will be shown to have been present in the situation from the outset. As we already noted with Badiou's early turn to topology in his Maoist work of the 1970s, everything rests on the addition or supplementation of the generic extension *not* coming from a putative outside, *not* inaugurating an absolute commencement, but emerging immanently from the incompleteness of the situation itself.[9] But to expose and impose the real of this truth, once again the subject must serve a complex cleaving function. Let us quote Badiou at length:

> A truth, forced according to the indiscernible produced by a generic procedure of fidelity, can definitely support *supplementary* veridical statements […]. However, this supplement, inasmuch as the fidelity is inside the situation, cannot cancel out its main principles of consistency. This is, moreover, why it is the truth *of* the situation, and not the absolute commencement of another. The subject, which is the forcing production of an indiscernible included in the situation, cannot ruin the situation. What it can do is generate veridical statements that were previously undecidable. Here we find our definition of the subject again: support of a faithful forcing, it articulates the indiscernible with the decision of an undecidable (*BE*, p.417)

Once again, there is a certain continuity between this impure nature of forcing in *Being and Event* on the one hand, and the distinction between 'bodies' and 'subjects' in *Logics of Worlds* on the other, where bodies emphasise the worldly side, subjects that of truth: "The body is a composite element of the world; the subject is what fixes in the body the secret of the effects it produces" (*LW*, p.47). This split between body and subject is another precautionary measure against ontologizing the subject. It means that the body cannot be 'full' of truth even as truth can only have any 'fullness' at all *through* bodies. For this reason, Badiou breaks the body itself down into at least two parts, the part that is transcendentally indexed by the world, and the part that is not. Confronted with the necessity of a decision which will either extend novelty or deflect it back into the world as it was (what Badiou defines as a 'point'—see Book VI of *LW*), a body has an 'efficacious part' that decides positively in relation to a truth, *and* an inefficacious part which, though contained within the same body, might well decide negatively. A body is divided on the one hand into "an efficacious region, an organ appropriate to the point being treated, and, on the other, a vast component which, with regard to this point, is inert or even negative" (*LW*, p.52). In fact, Badiou breaks the body down further still. To the extent that a body *persists* in enabling, within appearance and point by point, the maximal intensity of an inexistent, it must, so to speak, organ-ise its efficacious part: that is, it must turn its internal capacity to stay 'true' to an evental site and its unfolding consequences into a

---

9. This is assured by the axiom of excess, which demonstrates both the measureless difference between the state of the situation and the situation itself (thereby dispelling the liberal reification of political representation), and the 'unruly' errancy of the event with regard to being (thereby making the ultra-one of the evental multiple uncountable). In both cases, excess is rigorously immanent. See Mediations 7, 8 and 26 of *BE*.

functional (named, conceptualised) element of its own structure. Organs, explains Badiou, are "the immanent synthesis of the regional efficacy of bodies" (*LW*, p.470). Far from being a self-identical singularity then, a subject body is a fluid intermixture of site-objects and traces, of efficacious and inefficacious parts, and of new presents and organs. Whether such a body appears in the realm of politics, where it is called an 'organisation', art, where it is a 'work', love, where it is a 'couple', or science, where it is a 'result', it will have this impure, compound structure.

RELATION

At this point, I would like to take a step back from Badiou's theory of the subject in order to outline his examination of the concept of relation in *Logics of Worlds*. This is valuable because it brings us to the all-important dividing line between individuals who may be engaged in certain kinds of conflicts, and subjects who are, precisely, vectors of qualitatively different conflicts with genuinely transformative implications. For the obvious danger of our approach here is that, by pushing the subject back into the world in order to ameliorate the image of its transcendental singularity, we end up falling into the opposite trap: that of encouraging its 'worlding', its reduction to a 'fact' that entirely nullifies it. Having qualified singularity then as being neither pure nor generalisable, I now want to defend the different kind of singularity the Badiouian subject *does* have. One way to do this, then, is by contrasting it to relational determination or individuation itself. This helps to distinguish not only the singularity of the subject from the relationality of the individual, but also their differing relations to conflict.

Book IV of *Logics of Worlds* deals with the question of relations, while Book V deals with the 'Four Forms of Change'. In other words, the issue of relation closes the Greater Logic that examines the modalities of appearance of 'objects' in essentially stable worlds, and opens on to the analysis of worlds riven by the bursting into appearance of an evental site. This expository proximity between relation and novelty, however, should not fool us into imagining any kind of transitivity between the two. Badiou is just as concerned here as he was as far back as *Theory of Contradiction* to escape the essentially conservative model of dialectics that would see in relation itself—paradigmatically the antagonism of the relation between classes—the very motor of history qua change. The mistake of this kind of dialectics is to ascribe ontological agency to relationality itself. For this reason, Badiou is extremely careful to spell out at the beginning of his meditation that "it is not in effect possible to accept that relations between objects have a power of being" (*LW*, p.301). Relation must be understood, then, from the perspective of the objects related, not from a 'being' of the relation that connects them. Part 1 of the Greater Logic had established the operations of the transcendental of a world (there are three: minimum, envelope, conjunction) which govern being-there, while Part 2 explores the articulation between pure being-qua-being and appearance. But this last section, dealing with relation, presupposes both the being of a multiplicity and the being-there of its appearance rather than somehow generating them. One cannot reverse-engineer appearance, arriving at the atomic trace of being within objects through the relations between two or more such objects. This is what Badiou expresses when he writes, concisely enough, "a relation creates neither existence nor difference" (*LW*, p.310).

Far from being an event therefore, a relation presupposes the transcendental of a world, and appears within the world thanks to it. Furthermore, Badiou sets out to prove that every relation within a world is *universal* for that world: in other words, relation is fundamentally conservative because it is constitutive of the process of worlding itself. What makes a world a world is its capacity to encompass any relation that can be established between the elements it contains. Thanks to Cantor, we know that these elements and therefore the relations between them are infinite: for example, he showed that the power sets generated from the sub-sets of an initial set are 'bigger' than that initial set. The same goes for worlds, such that any object can be shown to have infinite numbers of atomic parts that belong to a world, even as they seem to exceed it. Relation, then, can be roughly defined as *a power of the envelopment of infinity*.[10] So what Badiou calls the 'logical completeness of worlds'—which does not at all mean their totalisable, cardinal denumerability— entails that any relation therein, is a relation 'for all', and thus universal.

Significantly for our purposes, Badiou offers, by way of an illustration of this universal dimension of relations, an example of conflict: the so-called 'Oka crisis' of 1990 in Quebec, Canada. This crisis involved armed clashes between, on the one hand, Mohawk Indians who protested first against a proposed golf course planned for their ancestral lands and subsequently against their generally marginalised position in Quebecois culture, society and civil life; and on the other, the Quebec Provincial Police and eventually the organs of Canada's State. The relation that Badiou investigates is that between the two objects 'Mohawks' and 'Quebecois administration'. But because of the world these objects inhabit, he is also led to examine the relations to this relation amongst the myriad other objects constitutive of Quebec (indeed, he will also touch on the relations of 'Quebec' to the other world that would subsume it, the nation of Canada). Now, this stand-off between the Mohawks and the Quebec authorities might seem to have an event-like appearance: there seems to be a site, normality is disrupted, militants seem to be conducting a variety of anti-State politics and so on. However, Badiou cautions against rushing in to an 'evental' reading of this conflict which would describe the revolt by the Mohawk Indians as the ascent to a maximal intensity of appearance of a multiple with a previously minimal value in the transcendental of the world 'Quebec'. In fact, although the object called 'Mohawk Indians' has historically been given a very low value of appearance in the Quebec world—it has been marginalised in and of itself, but also in its subordinate relation to another conflictual relation, that between Francophone Quebec separatism and Anglophone Canadian federalism—it is precisely *as* marginalised that the object 'Mohawk' does appear as an already existing apparent of the Quebec world. Just because the Mohawk cause takes on added intensity during the conflict, it does not follow that this intensity indexes anything new. On the contrary, the entire conflict plays itself out on the basis of this *pre-existing relation*, governing the various alliances and

---

10. See p.584 of *LW* for a definition of the envelope as "the smallest of the elements greater than all the elements of" a subset.

antagonisms between the police authorities, non-rioting Mohawks, non-Mohawk Quebecois, whether supportive of their resistance or resistant to it, and so on.

A relation to a relation (for example, how do the wider Quebec community relate to the conflictual relation between the Mohawks and the police?) is clearly a relation to two things: both the objects related (Mohawks, police), and to the relation connecting them (the current crisis itself). Badiou has recourse to the diagram of the 'commutative triangle' to illustrate the mutually reinforcing conservatism of such relations. A commutative triangle is one in which each of the three axes describes an enclosed circuit, such that no matter where one begins, one is 'directed' along the same lines and led to the same result. What this shows when applied to this example is that relations are conservative, *especially* in apparent conflict situations. It is here that the doctrine of the rarity of the subject cautions us not to assume their emergence from any conflict whatsoever.

Thus, the relation of a progressive Quebecois citizen to the relation between the Mohawks and the Quebecois administration respectively can be seen to be mutually reinforcing: the more they support the Mohawks, the more they vituperate the Quebecois administration. Moreover, if one were to add to this triangle a second triangle, this time illustrating the *reactionary* citizen's relation to the same relation between Mohawks and the Quebecois administration, we find the inverse pattern: the more the reactionary vituperates the Mohawks, the more they support the administration. Finally, if we examine the relation between the progressive and the reactionary citizens at the apex of these two triangles, we discover the logical necessity of mutual vituperation. To put it the other way around, if the progressive were suddenly to support the reactionary or vice versa, the diagram would cease to be commutative and the triangle of this conflict would lose all coherence as a world.

It is in this sense that Badiou defines the 'Oka crisis' as a relation that is, as he puts it, "universally exposed" (*LW*, p.317) in the world 'Quebec in 1990': it effectively exposes the mutual relations, already conflictual in themselves, that constituted that world's enveloping exposition. The only new thing about this conflict is the level of visibility this exposed relation meets with during this sequence. The reader will sense that, with this analysis, we are not at all far from Badiou's early use of Mao's distinction between non-antagonistic and antagonistic contradictions. He takes this deeply conservative dimension of relationality even further by asserting that the axiom of the logical completeness of worlds, which we recall also entails their infinity, implies that *every* relation belonging to that world is universally exposed. He makes the same point using a galactic example, our own Milky Way (*LW*, pp.317-319). As a world, which is to say as a logic of appearance, its power arises not simply from its sheer size (since no concept of 'biggest' functions as an upper limit in a non-denumerable infinity), but rather from its capacity to encompass an infinity of objects and the infinity of possible relations between them. The world 'Milky Way' contains or envelopes *x* number of Helium molecules as well as Alpha Centuri, Blue whales and all the novels of Balzac![11]

_____

11. Given that this universality of relations invokes the image of an infinitely interconnected web of co-constitutive inter-relations, it should come as no surprise that the next section of *Log-*

If the analysis of relationality so far seems to reduce it to the tyranny of all-encompassing structure, it is important to qualify this. For Badiou also argues in Book IV that every object (i.e., the result of a pure multiple falling under a transcendental regime in order to appear in a certain way in a world) carries within it a trace of the 'real' multiplicity that it is, and thus the contingency of its particular mode of appearance. In short, every object has an inexistent whose value of existence is nil. This is in direct contrast to our example of the Mohawks above which had a low value, but a value nonetheless, and moreover one 'universal' enough to expose the foundations of the entire Quebec situation. Whereas a universal relation is 'exposed' and thus extremely visible, an inexistent is visible only in the impoverished form of a nullity (and this can only be changed by an event). Thus, Badiou returns in his analysis to the object 'Mohawks', but explores it in a different world, Quebec between 1918 and 1950. In this period, putatively 'universal' suffrage in fact excluded Native American Indians, including the Mohawks: thus, "[t]he object 'civic capacity of the Quebecois populations' admits as its proper inexistent, during this temporal sequence, the set of 'Indians'" (*LW*, p.323). It follows, and this obviously prepares the way for the 'Oka crisis' of 1990, that 'Indians' are without rights, and therefore without any relation whatsoever, within right, to those with rights: "within right [...] 'to be outside of any right', establishes a juridically non-differentiable category" (*ibid.*). To the extent that this notion of the inexistent is doing here the theoretical work borne by 'evental site' in *Being and Event* (whereas 'site' in *Logics of Worlds*, as discussed in Chapter 2, becomes post-evental), a certain generic power can already be discerned in this non-differentiable character. "To have no rights" Badiou says, "is to be transcendentally identical to an Indian" (*LW*, p.323).

However, he is as adamant as ever that this generic power can only be unleashed by an event, since the inexistent is still 'contained' (just barely) by a world's logic, even if it registers its internal limit. In essence, we are back at the fine distinction between a structural lack and a dynamic lack elaborated in *Theory of the Subject*. Despite the violence of the 'Oka crisis' then, despite the 'progressive' mobilisation behind its cause, and despite the appearance of divisiveness, at no point was this crisis animated by a truth or by subjects by Badiou's criteria. On the contrary, it was a conflict that laid bare the relations between objects fundamentally constitutive of the world 'Quebec, 1990'. The Mokawks were not subjects then, but merely individuals engaged in antagonistic relations with the world that made them appear as marginal, unimportant, and in some sense 'less' Quebecois.

This is where the starkness of Badiou's notion of truth and consequently of politics demonstrates both its strengths and its weaknesses. On the side of strengths, it helps us to parse out structurally contained conflicts from genuinely disruptive ones, and, as part of this, it also cautions us against the mere appearance of

---

ics of Worlds is a mediation on that great thinker of the monadic universe, Leibniz. Badiou praises him for recognising the infinity of worlds but criticizes him for his "desperate retention of the power of the One" (*LW*, p.329), which is to say, for trying to impose a divine limit on the infinite dissemination of infinite worlds.

'progressive' struggles. We learned this lesson at the end of the last chapter, in our analysis of the Not in Our Name movement.

On the side of weaknesses however, there is still as yet no way of positing any kind of causal relation between such struggles, and the outbreak of evental sequences. But is it really the case that the Oka crisis simply *reinforced* the 'Quebec' world? Or is it possible that it inaugurated a sequence of changes that might have coalesced, or might yet, into an evental situation? Strictly speaking, the utterly aleatory and unpredictable nature of the event means that we are in no position to rule this out simply because it is unknowable. Arguably, it is because this possibility is unknowable that we should 'rule it in'. Adrian Johnston has asked similar questions when speculating as to whether "specifically evental times immanently arise within and out of broader, longer currents of non-evental times" (Johnston: 2009, 12).

Marxist dialectics was able to answer this question in the affirmative, and the Communist tradition includes the project of creating and sustaining militant subjects precisely in order to foment the *future* event of revolution. For all its awkward historicism, 'DiaMat' is at least capable of positing some kind of link between ongoing anti-State resistance and a destabilising of the existing system that may one day prove decisive. Not only does Badiou's analysis of relation, in attempting to escape this politics of transitivity, end up suggesting that antagonistic resistance to the prevailing world *will not*, in and of itself, induce such a tipping point. It strongly implies that such antagonism actively solidifies the world as it is.

AFFECT

We have so far argued that the subject is more enmeshed in the world it challenges than a pure notion of singularity would suggest, but also that it is not so enmeshed as to become reducible to an existing relation constitutive of that world. But we still face the problem we have just touched upon (one that has been noted by Peter Hallward, Adrian Johnston, Sam Gillespie and Alberto Toscano among others): namely, that Badiou's anti-Cartesian formalism effectively bars him from developing a phenomenology of the *emergence* of transformative subjectivity.

This problem is tacitly acknowledged in *Logics of Worlds* when Badiou refers to his methodology there as an "objective phenomenology" (*LW*, p.277). This apparent oxymoron holds together three contradictory aims: firstly, the continued refutation of dominant understandings of the subject (Cartesian, Neo-Kantian and Althusserian); secondly, the emulation of Lacan's recourse to a *formal* theory of the subject precisely as a way of opposing these dominant versions; and thirdly, a confrontation with the problem of the *appearance* of a truth without relinquishing this commitment to formalism. 'Objective', then, is really an anticipation of the theory of objects developed in the Greater Logic rather than a truth-claim opposed to merely 'subjective' knowledge, while 'phenomenology' addresses the problem of appearance in the absence of the perspectival anchoring point of a perceiving subject in the Husserlian tradition. In fact, it is not at all clear that Badiou's various examples actually escape this perspectival trap, and his repeated assertions regarding its danger come close to an example of protesting too much. At any rate, while both terms in 'objective phenomenology' are used in an idiosyncratic way, their conjunction does nothing to bridge the gap between individual and subject: Badiou has, and arguably can have, no category of 'experience' with which to affectively map the narrow and fluid space between them.

And yet as anyone who has been involved in political activism knows, affects predominate in any sequence of conflict, from defiance, fear and hostility, to commaraderie and enthusiasm, from elation to exhaustion and back again. Moreover, are not people's passionate attachments to the way things are, their fervent defence of their own interests, fundamentally constitutive of the recalcitrant dimension of the status quo? Similarly, are not timidity and doubt instrumental in both preventing individuals from taking the leap into subjecthood in the first place, and in rendering subjectivity, once embarked upon, extraordinarily fragile? In short, is the absence of a theory of affect not a serious lacuna in Badiou's system, particularly if we wish to push it towards a theory of conflict?

In fact, despite the general 'coldness' of Badiou's abstract emphasis on formalism, he does not entirely ignore the role of affect in subjective militancy. The most complex and arguably most useful engagement with it comes in *Theory of the Subject*, where he enhances his concept of 'subjectivation' by including within it the various permutations among four essentially affective categories: 'superego', 'anxiety', 'courage' and 'justice'. According to Badiou, and despite Lacan's own dislike for the notion of affect (engaged as he was in a polemic against the biologism of American ego-psychology),[12] the two terms 'superego' and 'anxiety' represent those aspects within Lacan's work that gesture beyond structural lack, and towards the possibility of the dynamic lack of destruction.

This is surprising with regard to the 'superego' in particular, insofar as Freud's *Civilization and its Discontents* famously makes of it a monstrous entity feeding off the repression it imposes, a kind of feedback loop destined to instil and exacerbate an irrational guilt in the neurotic subject of modernity. However, Badiou finds in Lacan's early account of the superego in Seminar *I* a glimmer of 'hope', precisely to the extent that the superego indexes a kind of irrational excess. In an extremely Schmittian reading that also foreshadows his later discussion of Kant and the Marquis de Sade in the *Écrits* (Lacan: 2006, pp.645-668), Lacan declares that the "superego is at one and the same time the law and its destruction" (quoted in *TS*, p.145). In other words, the superego is that kernel of irrational force that inheres in the core of law as an otherwise rational system of codified placing. It is the pure authoritarian command that founds the procedural legitimacy of law, "the part of nonlaw that adheres destructively to law itself" (*TS*, p.155). This is 'hopeful' in the sense that the subject is illegal too, and similarly draws its legitimacy from, or asserts it on the basis of, the extra-legal (we

---

12. In Chapter 8 of *SVII* entitled 'The Object and the Thing', Lacan refers to "the confused nature of recourse to affectivity" which "always leads us toward an impasse" (pp.125-126). However, he also refutes the notion that his position is "a matter of denying the importance of affects" (p.126). They are important, but precisely in parsing out the distinction between affectively invested imaginary objects on the one hand, and the real of objet a or *Das Ding* on the other. Badiou's reservations are close to Lacan's here.

already noted in the last chapter why this creates a certain proximity between classical notions of sovereignty and the Badiouian subject).

With regard to anxiety, Badiou draws two key aphorisms from Lacan's Seminar *X*: firstly, that anxiety is "that which does not deceive" (*SX*, p.85), and secondly that it is "the lack of lack" (*SX*, p.105). Anxiety does not deceive insofar as it registers a more direct encounter with the real, one relatively unmediated by semblance. So confronted with the superegoic excess of the law, for example, the anxious response is predicated on a recognition of it as pertaining to the real as constitutive excess, rather than its misrecognition as a mere 'glitch' or 'blip' in the normal functioning of the law. In this sense, anxiety is what one feels when the façade of the fantasy support slips for a moment and exposes the real: Badiou even defines it as "the trouble with seeing clearly" (*TS*, p.155). Hence Lacan's second aphorism regarding anxiety, that it is 'the lack of lack'. As we know, for the Lacan of the 1950s and early 1960s, the subject finds its albeit divided place in the symbolic order by dint of the fact that that order is constituted around a lack. The symbolic compensates the castrated subject by giving it the signifier of a retroactively constructed loss, around which a fantasy of that loss's contingency (rather than its traumatic structural necessity) can be woven. Anxiety, however, causes this essentially compensatory, even reassuring lack to lack in its turn. Anxiety thus exposes the phallus—essential pillar of the consistency of the Other—as impotent, and it is the (unconscious) sight of its detumescence that causes such intense affect. But this anxiety is also a source of hope for Badiou to the extent that it indexes a certain failure of law-as-placement, and thus the possibility of the emergence of a dynamic lack: "Anxiety is that excess-of-the-real (excess of force) over what can be symbolized (placed) thereof in a certain order, from whence a subject emerges already divided" (*TS*, p.155). Schematically then, we could say that the superego implies the Other's illegal excess, or, in Badiou's terms, a kernel of force intrinsic to placing, while anxiety is capable of experiencing this excess *qua* excess, or, again in Badiou's terms, qua dis-placement of the lack into the *hors-place*.

The other two terms in Badiou's theory of subjective affect, 'courage' and 'justice', are taken not directly from Lacan but from the two Greek tragedians, Sophocles and Aeschylus. Badiou's broad claim is that psychoanalysis, even in Lacan's unorthodox hands, remains broadly Sophoclean and therefore locked into an Oedipal dialectic between law and its transgression.[13] Specifically, Sophocles gives us literary figures of the superego and anxiety in *Antigone* with the characters of, respectively, Creon and Antigone herself. But taken in isolation, these two figures are tragic in the sense of being bound together in a reciprocal contradiction that can only have death as its outcome. For this reason, Badiou instead "proposes that we must be Aeschylean" (*TS*, p.161), taking as his guide Aeschylus' play

13. I would argue that Badiou is in fact wrong about this. *SVII* pushes beyond this dialectic precisely by showing that Sade's perversion remains implicated in the logic of Kant's categorical imperative, perversion effectively consisting not in transgressing the Other as law, but in repetitively staging the effort of making it exist. Lacan's analysis of Antigone is intended to carve out a figure of the criminal that exceeds the closed Oedipal dialectic, and can therefore be considered an Aeschylean reading of Sophocles' play. I would like to thank my former PhD student, Luca Bosetti, for bringing this reading of Seminar VII to my attention.

Oresteia. Leaving aside the details of the plot of this play, we can simply note that from it, Badiou develops his notions of 'courage' and 'justice' as the crucial supplements to the superego and anxiety, in just the way that we have already seen that subjectivation must be supplemented by the 'subject process'.

Courage moves beyond the anxious recognition of the Other's illegal excess in order to affirmatively produce "something the existence of which Lacan denies—the existence of an Other of the Other" (*TS*, p.156)[14]: "Courage positively carries out the disorder of the symbolic, the breakdown of communication, whereas anxiety calls for its death" (*TS*, p.160). This is courage not as mere audacity, which would still be determined in a relation of defiance with regard to the Other, but as *fortitudo* (*ibid.*), which is to say, as strength of mind in the face of adversity. Again, this would not be adversity defined by the symbolic, but rather as the difficulty of turning towards (ad-verse) an excess ex-timate in relation to the Other. *Fortitudo*, in its self-positing autonomy, is therefore approximate to what Badiou calls, also in *Theory of the Subject*, 'confidence'. Both terms carry the same simultaneous meanings of internally generated affective cohesion on the one hand, and of a holding out, over time, against the imaginarisation of the real imposed by the Other on the other hand. Courage then, is "the destructive tipping of the scales in which the truth is *sustained* in its division (*TS*, p.174—my emphasis).

The final affect in Badiou's quartet is 'justice'. Justice is what tips the superego over into a progressive rather than repressive form. It does so by suspending the legitimacy of the law, *not* in order to assert Leviathan-like authority over and above the letter of the law, but instead to give consistency and legitimacy to the necessarily illegal pursuit of an egalitarian social redistribution. Thus, "justice names the possibility—from the standpoint of what it brings into being as subject-effect—that what is nonlaw may function as law" (*TS*, p.159). Clearly, in-justice here is conceptualised as the merely nominal 'justice' offered by an enclosed system of codified, procedural law whose application to novelty could only ever be a form of reductive violence. To the extent, then, that true justice must oppose 'justice' in this official form, it must include "a dialectical precariousness of the law, susceptible of being shaken up in the process of its scission" (*ibid.*). Only in this way can the violence of the symbolic order be met with another which is just precisely because it is outside the law. In sum, justice tries to hold open an affirmative space for this extra-legal legitimacy.[15]

These four affects can be mapped onto the phases of, and possibilities internal to, a sequence of conflict. Anxiety does represent a disruption of business as usual, but a passing and inarticulate one: it is thus analogous to a riot in which property is destroyed, roads barricaded, police engaged in combat, but which passes fairly rapidly, leaving only the wreckage of destruction in its wake. This is the limitation

---

14. This is a strange claim by Badiou, given that one could see his recourse to Cantorian set-theory as a mathematical demonstration of Lacan's dictum of the inexistence of the Other of the Other, and its corollary, 'there is no such thing as a metalanguage'.

15. See Bruno Bosteels' revealing comparison of Badiou's justice with Derrida's take on it in both the 'Force of Law' and the engagement with Schmitt in *Politics of Friendship* (Bosteels: 2009, pp.90-95).

of anxiety. It can only oppose to order a disorder measured against the very order which, precisely in being challenged, ends up being underlined. "Anxiety", explains Badiou, "as we see in the mute and suicidal riots (June 1848, for example) implies in effect the death of destruction itself" (*TS*, p.292). It is at this point, post-riot, that anxiety can come into a relation with the superego which is unmistakably conservative insofar as it "puts excess back into place" (*ibid.*). Rioters are arrested, incarcerated, publically punished, normality is forcibly resumed. One could put it simply: the law of the father is reimposed. Borrowing from Hegel's response to the French Revolution, Badiou names the superegoic placement of anxious excess after another affect, 'terror'. Courage, however, would consist of a different response to the same conflict, emerging from the same place as anxiety but unbowed by the threat of terror. Let us suppose that during this riot, a group of rioters decide that they do not simply want to destroy everything, but rather to transform their neighbourhood with a view to *sustaining* their acts of defiance. Suppose that they occupy a building, draw up a strategy, divide out roles and begin to articulate what might constitute a justice to erase the injustice against which they are struggling. Far from inducing the riot police to simply do their job and quell the riot, as was the case for the merely anxious outburst, this courageous stand "puts the law to the test, instead of calling for its restoration" (*TS*, p.295). It is from this courageous because illegal place that a new justice, one more just than the nominal kind offered by the powers that be, can be demanded.

In the broader history of Marxism, then, anxiety would generally refer to the numerous revolts and riots that express blind opposition to oppression but are easily crushed, whereas courage would refer to more durable insurrections such as the Paris Commune and Mao's battles with the Kuomindang. The superego would correspond to the dictatorship of the proletariat, particularly in its Stalinist guise, although this should not imply that Badiou sees the superego primarily negatively—it is a necessary part of subjective organisation. Justice, finally, would be the Idea of Communism itself. There is a scissional dialectic between these two strands, with the anxiety-superego axis forming one strand, which emphasises destruction and is therefore 'closer' to the world as it is, while the 'courage-justice' axis forms another, which emphasises recomposition and the sheltering of an unfolding novelty. The subject could be conceived as the braiding of these two strands.

But if the pairs 'anxiety-superego' and 'courage-justice' can be compared and contrasted, what of the remaining 'diagonals' between 'anxiety-justice' and 'courage-superego' that cut across these two strands, destructive and recompositional? Badiou treats of these in the session dated May 11th, 1979, entitled 'Diagonals of the Imaginary' (TS, 297-303). Given that the subject for Badiou is a relation to the real, the term 'imaginary' is just as negative for him as it is for Lacan. This title therefore forewarns us that these particular affective linkages threaten the subject's very survival. Sure enough, Badiou argues that when courage links up with the superego in its conservative dimension, it can take the form of a kind of internecine violence amongst militants. Imagine that our courageous rioters occupying their building, articulating a cause and formulating a strategy around it, suddenly turn on their own in a fever of paranoia, beating up suspected police 'moles' or potential informers and casting them out. Something similar could be observed in the Chinese Cultural Revolution, insofar as the courage of the Red Guards was ultimately linked back to Mao's (superegoic) authority. As we saw in the last chapter, it was this tension that led to so much bloodshed. This violent diagonal between courage and the superego is also the 'fraternity-terror' that Sartre diagnosed as a tendency within the group-in-fusion in his *Critique of Dialectical Reason*. Badiou aptly chooses, then, to call this particular diagonal 'dogmatism'. It is imaginary in the sense that it inscribes a limit-point for the excess of force in a superegoic absolute, and in this way simultaneously unleashes and shackles innovation.

Conversely, when justice links up with anxiety, we get a situation which should be familiar post-9/11, insofar as this configuration is typified by an attempt to recodify the uncertainty intrinsic to true justice (which, as we have said, is in excess over procedural justice). In such a scenario, anxiety quickly morphs into doubt about the legitimacy of this illegal principle of justice. The imaginary responds with the false reassurances of, effectively, constitutional liberalism: "Everyone agrees to overcode justice with ideals, to subject future nonlaw to some rule, to name indefinitely [...]. This is because everyone *essentially* doubts the real autonomy of justice" (*TS*, p.300). Perhaps this would correspond, in our hypothetical example of the self-organising rioters, to a collective decision to give up on the pursuit of their singular justice in favour of surrendering to the legal 'authorities', so as to pursue their goals in more 'official' (reformist) ways. Badiou chooses to call this final affective diagonal 'scepticism'. To the extent that, in the history of Marxism, Communism is the name for justice, today's scepticism has involved nothing less than the replacement of the Communist notion of freedom with its liberal free-market simulacrum (freedom of the private individual from the interventions of the state, freedom to own property and to consume goods, freedom of the market to regulate economic and social life through the invisible but ultimately benevolent hand of the price mechanism etc.). Scepticism is imaginary in the sense that it deflects the demand for the impossible real that *is* the courageous pursuit of justice back into lawful reality, where it cannot survive.

THE PSYCHOANALYTIC SUPPLEMENT

Having explored the affective dimensions of subjectivization in *Theory of the Subject*, it is important to point out that they are of no use whatsoever in addressing our guiding problem here: the absence of a phenomenology of subjective *emergence* in Badiou.

For twice in *Theory of the Subject*, he categorically affirms that these affects are purely formal properties of material processes and not experiences belonging to individuals. They "refer neither to subjective experiences nor to parts of the subject, but rather to [...] processes whose combination defines that region of practical materiality that we would do better to call the 'subject-effect'" (*TS*, p.154); and again, "the four concepts are neither virtues nor abilities. Better yet: they are not even experiences [...] they are only names for certain processes, nothing else" (*TS*, p.291). The anti-Cartesian, anti-phenomenological gesture here is palpable. Thus, all four affects are properties of entities that are *already* subjects to the extent that they are engaged in subjectivation. We are no closer to imagining what might be termed, albeit awkwardly, a pre-evental pro-evental affect: in other words, to an individual (pre)disposition towards subjective truth.

Anxiety and the superego provide a modicum of potential insofar as they are more 'internal' to the situation. But for precisely that reason, they are also prone to blind and wanton destruction. Moreover, they still depend entirely on some kind of irruption of the real into the situation, some kind of event. Courage and justice would seem to be even further removed from the affective realities of the pre-evental moment insofar as they are clearly engaged in the maintenance of a conditioned but already extant fidelity. None of these affects-without-experience are in any way *transitive* to individuals with passions and interests. They therefore shed absolutely no light on the latter's mode of incorporation into a subject. A similar pattern emerges in the first chapter of *Logics of Worlds*, where the newly complex taxonomy of subjective figures includes distinct affects for each truth domain. These are 'enthusiasm' for politics, 'pleasure' for art, 'happiness' for love, and 'joy' for science. These are only the "local signs" of a new evental present, signs which, "in their anthropological form" (i.e., for humans) "are affects" (*LW*, p.76). But again, the enthusiastic participant in politics is already a subject, just as the happy couple are already part of an amorous sequence. These affects in no way *cause* subjects. They are secondary consequences of the existence of subjects.

Badiou, it seems, has absolutely no interest in the passions or fears of individuals. Within his system, there is a good reason for this. Such passions and fears are merely the emotional glue binding the old to itself. But what he *should* arguably be interested in is the role of such passions and fears in the unbinding of that glue, their transformation into solvents of the given, and bearers of the transition towards the new. Understandably, several commentators have attempted to fill in this glaring omission in Badiou's work with recourse to a psychoanalytic supplement. Adrian Johnston, for example, similarly dissatisfied with the absence of a pre-evental subject or mode of forcing in Badiou's work, calls for

> a metapsychological investigation into the affective, libidinal, and identificatory features of the pre-evental human psyche with an eye to discerning what, within these features partly tied to what could be designated a sort of "constitution" or "nature", harbours the possibility for a readiness or responsiveness to the transformative effects of eventual interpellations (this would involve a Badiou-inspired reassessment of psychoanalytic metapsychology and its accompanying theory of subjectivity, a reassessment with real political stakes) (Johnston: 2009, p.79)

One can quickly see how this appeal to what is essentially a psychoanalytically informed philosophical anthropology, on the basis of which to build what seems to be a political philosophy (rather than a metapolitics in Badiou's sense), represents considerable dangers from an 'orthodox' Badiouian perspective. It sucks the subject back into the social, and thus ultimately suggests a social science approach to the kind of 'animal' that we are. Rather than being an aleatory exception to everything objective, the decision that inaugurates a subject would emerge, on this account, from a 'constitutional' or even 'natural' psychological inclination (although that assumption does rather beg the question of why subjects do in fact seem to be so rare, to which Badiou has a rigorous ontological answer). But was this not the trap of the Freudo-Marxism of the first generation of Critical Theorists, with their overly substantialist conception of both social and individual repression?[16]

What saves Johnston's own argument from this slippery slope is his appeal, not to psychology per se, but to psychoanalysis, and particularly its Lacanian variant, which is militantly suspicious of generalised notions of a 'human psyche' fuelled by organic libidinal instincts,[17] as well as of the autism of many of the social and indeed hard sciences.[18] And in fact, although it is embedded in a detailed critique of Slavoj Žižek's rather Badiouian take on the *passage à l'acte*, Johnston does invoke, as a wedge to drive between both Žižek and Badiou, a 'third' Lacan, one whose version of materialism is less prone to that nostalgia for the absolute that we have been fending off in this chapter. This is the later Lacan who begins to think of the real not as something foreclosed from the symbolic via castration (as the early mirror-stage essay and the postulate there of an imaginary body displacing the 'animal' body of unmediated instincts suggests), but rather as saturating the symbolic itself, foregrounding a necessary materiality that is at once support and obstructive residue. To phrase this in Badiou's terms but against his entire philosophical project, Johnston wonders whether it may just be that the 'encyclopaedia' of a situation (essentially the symbolic) does not actually need a seismic event that irrupts from nowhere in order to be transformed, if, that is, it always carries its own internal real distributed throughout its very fabric. This is helpful to Johnston's attempt to outline a pre-eventual subject, insofar as a speaking subject always has a capacity, albeit via the necessary detour of a transferential relation with an analyst, to intervene in the language that constitutes them, even if it is a difficult labour that involves subjective destitution rather than the exercise of will in any straightforward sense. There is no need to wait for an event, only the emergence of a *demand d'analyse* precisely from that which constrains the subject in their situation: it is the experience of dissatisfaction or disorientation with their world that brings the analysand to the couch (strictly speaking, the symptom only emerges once the analysand articulates it in the analytic setting). Needless to say, however, Johnston's argument largely

---

16. This tendency is arguably typified by Herbert Marcuse in *Eros and Civilization*, or rather by its dumbed-down deployment in the so-called sexual revolution, which assumed an authentic or 'natural' sexual instinct only contingently repressed within the capitalist mode of production. But much of the sociological approach of Adorno and Horkheimer to the authoritarian personality also draws on the problematic image of a kind of sexual pressure cooker model of society. In mapping this libidinal economics onto historical materialism, the Frankfurt School arguably lapsed into an affectively supplemented, but essentially unchanged, model of dialectics. Lacan is the most useful antidote to this aspect of Freudo-Marxism.

17. Lacan's insistence on James Strachey's error in translating Freud's *triebe* as 'instinct' rather than 'drive' bears precisely on the political implications of psychoanalysis. Instinct points in the direction of biological determinism and thus developmental and even evolutionary psychology, with the consequent 'animalisation' of the human.

18. See Seminar XI, particularly session 17 entitled 'The Subject and the Other: Aphanisis' where Lacan mockingly describes experiments that model stimuli-response mechanisms of the kind that underpin behaviourism—for example Pavlov's famous dogs—as exercises in finding merely what one is looking for: "we interrogate the animal about our own perceptions" (*SXI*, p.228).

allows Badiou's ontological restrictions on the event, and the event itself in a certain fashion, to fall by the wayside. For Badiou I suspect, Johnston simply brings us back to a real confined to structure, a void that is not yet an eventual multiple.

Sam Gillespie, too, has appealed to Lacan in order to further explore "the question of affect as a principle of the subject" (Gillespie: 2008, p.116). Gillespie's argument, like Johnston's, also passes by way of a critique of Žižek, specifically of his tendency in *The Ticklish Subject* (Žižek: 2000) to fall into the very trap identified above, of reducing subjective acts to "a way of regulating primordial psychic drives" (*ibid.* p.117). "Žižek's move", asserts Gillespie, "is to ground *all* subjective action in impulses or interests that are applicable only to a psychoanalytic subject" (*ibid.*), one that is ultimately animalised in its psychic determination. Of course, Žižek is well aware of the Lacanian critique of the instinctual reading of Freud. Yet Gillespie implies that because Žižek imposes a rather rigid psychoanalytic framework on contemporary culture, in the end his incipient formalism threatens to swallow the subject into the very behaviourism Lacanian psychoanalysis opposes.

In order to carve out a more positive path, Gillespie has recourse to Lacan's tenth seminar on anxiety, *L'angoisse* (though, surprisingly, without referencing Badiou's similar strategy in *Theory of the Subject*). He immediately notes that "in contrast to emotions like fear and pity, anxiety is distinct from the ordinary passionate attachments that define a subject's relation to the world" (*ibid.* p.119). From his earliest work with hysterics with Breuer through to *Inhibitions, Symptoms and Anxiety*, Freud distinguished anxiety from fear on the basis of the presence or absence of a triggering object in the empirical sense. Fear, Freud argued, is a somatic response sparked by an object localisable in 'reality', something perceived as dangerous. It is thus an adaptive, animal reflex that is not, properly speaking, relevant to the domain of psychoanalysis. Anxiety, on the other hand, is a more acute affect precisely because it lacks an empirical object and is, as a result, omni-directional and apparently sourceless. As such, anxiety is actively incompatible with the animal instinct for flight that characterises fear, resulting more often in a paralysis that in empirically dangerous situations would hardly assist survival.[19] By implication, anxiety is a pre-eminently psychoanalytic concept. Moreover, in this subtraction from (animal) reality, anxiety is already closer to the (distinctly human) real. Gillespie points out that this non-objective nature of Freudian anxiety means that the anxious subject is seized from all directions by something unplaceable for which s/he has absolutely no name. Anxiety can overwhelm precisely because it has no referent, either empirically or symbolically.

In fact, Lacan will directly challenge this Freudian reading in his tenth seminar when he asserts that anxiety *does* have an object, or more precisely, it is not without having one.[20] This object remains neither empirical nor symbolic as it

---

19. In *Inhibitions, Symptoms and Anxiety* Freud also ascribes to anxiety an anticipatory dimension: expectation heightens anxiety, so much so that in certain circumstances, the arrival of an object rationally worthy of our fear comes as something of a relief. Think of those scenes in horror films in which the eventual appearance of the monster the viewer *knew* full well was coming is greeted with both a sharp intake of breath, and then a drawn out sigh of relief.

20. This odd syntax is a quite deliberate ploy by Lacan to avoid the forced choice imposed

had been for Freud, but now becomes real: *L'angoisse* fills in the outline of Lacan's famous *objet a*, first sketched in Seminar VII as *das Ding*. Initially conceived as a partial-object left over as a residue following Oedipal separation from the primordial Other (essentially the Mother), the *objet a* is increasingly connected by Lacan to the circulation of the drives in the subject's relation to fantasy (hence its place in the matheme of the fantasy, S ◊ a). Thus, in Seminar X anxiety comes to be understood as an encounter with the unbearable jouissance of the real, once the mediating fantasy of this *objet a* is exposed as an empty, meaningless function. Although Gillespie does not bring this out, in Lacan's account of this affective seizure by anxiety its temporality is not of the order of anticipation (as it had been for Freud) but of *tuché*, to be contrasted to that of *automaton*. In other words, anxiety is a sudden encounter with something that has no place and that nothing in the automatic workings of the symbolic, whose role is to ascribe place, could have prepared one for. Lacan illustrates this via a Chekhov short-story, in which terror is invoked by utterly harmless triggers (see *SX*, pp.185-198). By contrast, Freud's notion of anxiety-as-anticipated-fear passes through the symbolic insofar as the designation of an object as dangerous and therefore fearful relies on recollected experience, and thus signifiers. Gillespie does note, however, the general resonance here with the subject's sudden incorporation into an unknowable truth in Badiou, in which an affect sweeps an individual up into a process without a clear and distinct referent or goal.

Nonetheless, Gillespie is quick to acknowledge the serious limitations of these analogies between Lacanian anxiety and the emergence of the Badiouian subject of truth. The key one is that the real in Lacan must be a subjective category, whereas for Badiou it has to be ontological. Ultimately, this represents a decision on Badiou's part for philosophy and against psychoanalysis. Much of his system depends on it, for only by making the real an intimation of the pure inconsistency of being 'beneath' or 'before' the consistency of presentation can Badiou go on to define the subject as a vector of the *generic*. It is this ontological claim about the generic nature of being that makes the real trans-individual for Badiou, opening up his very traditional philosophical preoccupation with truth, and also with a collective subject in the Communist tradition. By contrast, for Lacan, the intimation of a real outside linguistic presentation comes in the form primarily of an individual experience of *jouissance*, an upsurge of intense but ambivalent and non-signifying pleasure/pain. Moreover, from a Lacanian perspective, it is the specific way in which an individual has learnt to live with this *jouissance* of the real that endows them with singularity. Clinically, it is crucial that psychoanalysis respect this singularity insofar as the analytic setting cultivates an ethics of receptive listening on the part of the analyst, one very much opposed to rapidly subsuming individuals within pre-existing nosological categories such as those gathered in the *Diagnostic and Statistical Manual*. So we are undoubtedly dealing with two different kinds of

---

by ontological discourse between being or non-being. It appears, for example, in the dialectic of being and having that determines the sexuated relation to the phallus, in which the man is 'not without having' the symbolic phallus. The logic behind this syntactical ploy finds its fullest development as the logic of the not-all in Seminar *XX*.

singularity here. With Lacan, singularity seems to be one of isolated difference, whereas the generic aspirations of Badiou's philosophy attempt to push singularity towards the universal.

In fact, Gillespie tries to negotiate this impasse as we have in this chapter, by conceptualising the subject as a kind of knot, but one that now tethers the individual real of non-universalisable *jouissance* on the one hand (Lacan), to the generic real exposed by a universal truth on the other (Badiou): "The Real, as I see it, names that part of a truth that the subject operates in the service of, at the same time that the subject's action traverses the individuality of the real" (Gillespie: 2008, p.120). This is arguably a too-rapid answer to Jacques-Alain Miller's question, posed to Lacan during Seminar XI, regarding whether his notion of the subject implies an ontology (*SXI*, p.29), and one, moreover, that sidesteps Lacan's own nuanced response along the lines that the unconscious is neither being nor non-being, and is better approached as having an ethical status (*ibid.* 33). Nonetheless, this move allows Gillespie to go on and elaborate this knot between individual and universal singularity by mapping the significant overlaps between Lacan's theory of the *objet a* on the on hand, and sublimation on the other. In combination, these allow him to sketch an answer to a question that is indeed common to both Badiou and Lacan: how can a subject give form to its own existence when that existence must be based on nothingness?—on the real of castration for Lacan, on the void of the evental multiple for Badiou.

With regard to the *objet a*, one has to be extremely cautious. What Gillespie is getting at is really the formal object-cause-of-desire indexed by the matheme 'objet a', certainly *not* the infinitely substitutable series of mundane objects which occupy its place precisely to plug up the real, and stem the flow of anxiety emanating therefrom. These endlessly substitutable 'good objects' (to pun on Melanie Klein) are the imaginary basis of the mobilisation of affect characteristic of consumer culture. The matheme that writes the logic of imaginary desire, however, underscores a real: namely, the psychoanalytic insight into both the emptiness of consumer culture, and that which, in the individual consumer, exceeds his or her (a)cculturation. It is just this distinction between imaginary and real objects that the process of analysis gradually helps the analysand to subjectivise. During analysis, she is guided away from the structural impossibility of desire (no concrete object, whether it be a new lover or pair of designer shoes, can 'fill' the place of the *objet a* since it is a function and not a thing), and towards the circularity of the drive which, *qua* drive, is partial. Jacques-Alain Miller has usefully distinguished desire from the drive by pointing out that the former is predicated on lack and thus an imaginary loss that might one day be redeemed, while the drive is organised around a hole that punctures any image of a possible Whole. [21] As Gillespie succinctly puts it, the drive "gives form and determination to the empty ground of [the psychoanalytic subject's] causality in and through the formation of an object (a)" (Gillespie: 2008, p.111).

---

21. See Miller, Jacques-Alain, 'Commentary on Lacan's Text', 442-426 in Richard Feldstein, Bruce Fink and Mairie Jaanus (eds.), *Reading Seminars I and II: Lacan's Return to Freud*, SUNY: New York, 1996.

Clarified as an empty function then, and pushed towards the drive rather than desire, *objet a* can be seen, like Badiou's subjectivization, as a subject's way of relating to the indeterminateness of being as pure inconsistent multiplicity. *Objet a* both founds the subject on something indiscernible and positively orients the subject's behaviour towards what Gillespie rightly calls, following Lacan, an ethics. As Seminar *VII* makes abundantly clear, this must be an ethics based neither on *les service des biens*, goods in the sense of commodities, nor on the Good in the sense developed within Aristotelian moral philosophy. If late capitalism has specialised in the superimposition of these two conceptualisations of the good, both nonetheless remain entrenched in the model of biological needs, and the assumed possibility of their satisfaction. Because Lacan's emphasis is always on the fact that, for speaking beings, full satisfaction is impossible (desire is irreducible to need), ethics takes on a quite different meaning: its dictum becomes the very Badiouian sounding "never give up on your desire". Far from constituting a clarion call to individualised hedonism, this ultimately means adhering, militantly, to one's particular mode of 'making do' with *nothing*, precisely—albeit the nothing by which one is intimately animated.

Nonetheless, one could argue here that the nothing for Lacan is still a nothing *for* a perceiving subject: it is an experience, 'intensional' in the phenomenological tradition. This implies a residual Cartesianism incompatible both with Badiou's formalism of the subject, and his generic, subtractive ontology in which nothing is, as it were, for all. Gillespie attempts to address this problem by drawing a link between *objet a*, as a drive which orients an individual subject's relation to the indeterminateness of being, and sublimation, as "a means of instantiating the forms of indiscernible being that *can be met with recognition from other subjects*" (Gillespie: 2008, p.121—my emphasis). That is to say, he follows Lacan closely in retaining from Freud's orthodox definition of sublimation—the redirection of desexualised libido towards socially validated activities—only the trans-individual dimension, the opening onto a shared lifeworld. Freud's rather normative elitism, whereby high cultural forms are the only ones that receive validation, is undercut by Lacan when he famously re-defines sublimation as "the elevation of the object [...] to the dignity of the Thing" (*SVII*, p.138).[22] This elevation is not an accident that haphazardly befalls the object. It is a subjective act, a creation. Unlike the Kantian theory of the natural sublime, then, in which passivity before the awesome spectacle of Nature is transformed into the 'activity' of the free play of the faculties (Kant: 1987), psychoanalytic sublimation must be the result of a certain subjective labour: "if the object is to become available in that way [i.e., as sublimated], something must have occurred" says Lacan (*SVII*, p.139). This something necessarily involves a subject.

The odd anecdotal example Lacan gives in Seminar VII is of seeing, winding around the mantelpiece of his friend, Jacques Prévert, a 'snake' of interconnected matchboxes, each linked to the next via the insertion of its opened 'drawer' into its anterior counterpart (a form of linkage which of course reminds him of

---

22. Unlike Freud's taste for the renaissance art of Leonardo Da Vinci for example, Lacan's own thought on sublimation is arguably 'conditioned' by more iconoclastic art movements such as Dadaism and Surrealism, as his friendships with André Breton and Salvador Dali suggest.

the signifying chain). Subtracted from banal utility, these matchboxes foreground that which is 'in them more than them', the thingness that supports their utility but also infinitely exceeds it. But these matchboxes did not spontaneously organise themselves in such a quirky configuration. They needed Jacques Prévert's whimsical intervention. Significantly, this definition of sublimation paves the way for the next session of Seminar VII, entitled 'On Creation *Ex Nihilo*'. Here, sublimation is further illustrated by the well-known trope, avowedly borrowed from Heidegger, of the potter creating a vase by cupping his hands around emptiness, thereby implying that art can give a kind of visible, shareable consistency to that emptiness or nothingness. The vase, then, is at once a utilitarian object *and* an enigmatic signifier, one of the first in mankind's history, of the nothingness that makes 'somethingness' in general possible, the lack that gives birth to fullness. Despite the existentialist tones of these references to emptiness, therefore, the emphasis in Lacan's account of sublimation is not on the quandary of the lonely Cartesian cogito reflecting on the ultimate emptiness of its own being. On the contrary, it is on the power of art to *transmit* this human dilemma to other humans: "the human factor will not be defined otherwise than in the way that I defined the Thing just now, namely, that which in the real suffers from the signifier" (*SVII*, p.154). Because of its transit through the signifier, this suffering is at least a suffering shared. As Roberto Harari points out, this is what separates sublimation from the symptom: "in the sublimation [...] an ability for symbolic exchange different from the privacy of the symptom is circumscribed. [...] The subject, furthermore, wants (in principle) to be cured of the symptom. Of this other type of circumstance, he doesn't" (Harari: 2004, p. 224). That sublimation represents a more 'public' mode of inscription than the private idiom of the symptom is hinted at by Lacan's much later claim, in Seminar *XXIII*, that James Joyce achieved the best that can be hoped for from the end of analysis without needing to go through it. In the same seminar, Lacan points out that Joyce's writing 'made a name' for him, implying that Joyce's utterly idiosyncratic practice of nomination could nonetheless rebound on the wider world in a way that the Badiouian subject could only hope to emulate.

Although he points out that art is probably the most problematic truth-domain in Badiou's philosophy, it is in such sublimated artistic creation that Gillespie sees a kind of affective bridge between subjects and individuals, and thus a certain resonance with pre-evental subjects-to-be. For neither the Dada-inspired manipulator of matchboxes, nor the Bronze Age sculptor of vases, needed an event to undertake their affirmative subjective act. It remains to be seen, however, whether sublimation *prepares* individuals to become subjects of the event to come. It also remains to be seen whether sublimation is circumscribable within the realm known as 'art', and whether, therefore, any truths forced by sublimation can resonate with others in other realms.

PRE-EVENTAL SUBJECTIVE RESOURCES

In closing this chapter, I would like to turn now to the moment in Badiou's work where he gets closest to considering what I will call 'pre-evental subjective resources', i.e., those tools—conceptual, affective, identificatory, practical—that might force as close a proximity as possible between resistant individuals that precede events, and singularised subjects that emerge from events.

This moment comes from a surprising source, but one that links directly to Gillespie's argument about sublimation: Badiou's engagement with the literary innovations of Samuel Beckett. Beckett is among that pantheon of artists esteemed by Badiou because of their shared commitment to a subtractive aesthetic. Keeping him company are, among others, Rimbaud, Mallarmé, Pessoa, Proust, Celan and, in music, Wagner and Schoenberg. All of these in one way or another pare their medium of expression down to a minimalist metaphysics. According to Badiou at least, they get close to capturing being as pure inconsistency, and even to articulating a poetic relation to the event (maintaining its undecidabilty in Rimbaud for example, presenting the wager of chance in Mallarmé). But Beckett specifically seems to have exercised an enduring fascination for Badiou, who refers to a "forty-year passion for this author" (*OB*, p.40), one that culminated in the publication of several overlapping studies of the Irish-French writer in the 1990s. These have been translated into English and collected by Nina Power and Alberto Toscano in their 2003 volume, *On Beckett*.

As the editors point out in their excellent introduction, to many literary scholars as well as sensitive lay readers, Badiou's approach to Beckett initially seems typical of philosophy's generally violent appropriation of the literary text. Heidegger, for example, in the very name of a 'hearkening' to the Saying of being within language, arguably yokes the works of Goethe and Rilke to his own preferred conceptual framework without really considering either the subtle cadence of the language itself or the wider critical debates about alternative interpretations (Heidegger: 1982). This is clearly true of Badiou's idiosyncratic intervention which completely ignores Beckett scholarship. But unlike the simultaneously neurotic and pious gesture prevalent in that body of literature, whereby Beckett's texts are said to represent a sacrosanct exception to the very possibility of knowing commentary, Badiou's 'reading' (if that is what it is) has the merit of being honestly and openly that of a philosopher. His forty-year passion (actually more like 60 now) stems precisely from his intuition that Beckett's literary output constitutes a rigorous form of thought in its own right, to which philosophy has an obligation to respond.

What is shocking, however, about Badiou's philosophical intervention is his bold and counter-intuitive claim that "all of Beckett's genius tends towards affirmation" (*OB*, p.41). This flies directly in the face of the prevailing view in Beckett scholarship, much of it coloured by the coincidence of Beckett's turn to the French language in the mid-1950s and the dominance in the France of that period of Sartrean existentialism (a conjuncture in which Badiou himself was caught up, causing him to refer to his former Sartrean self as a "young cretin" (*OB*, p.39)). For the bulk of post-war continental criticism from thinkers as diverse as Adorno, Blanchot and Bataille has bequeathed to us the image of Beckett as an author exploring the empty absurdity of existence, our tragicomic incarceration in the prison house of language, the meaningless search for meaning, the laughable human proclivity for groping in the mud and slime of abjection whilst waiting for … nothing. Little in the poststructuralist and then postmodernist Anglo-American interpretations of Beckett in the 1980s and 1990s fundamentally challenges these images: rather, they reinscribe them into a narrower linguistic problematic of *différance*.[23] Badiou in fact recognises all of these themes, but condenses them into an earlier phase, one that according to him is eventually but decisively surpassed. There is a shift, he claims, from claustrophobic inevitability to what might be called the possibility of possibility: "Beckett's trajectory is one that begins with a blind belief in predestination and is then directed towards the examination of the possible conditions, be they aleatory or minimal, of a kind of freedom" (*OB*, p.55).

To support this provocative claim, Badiou constructs two thematic and stylistic phases in Beckett's literary output as a whole, with the second emerging from—surprise surprise—an event-like *coupure* with the first. The first phase includes the famous 'trilogy' of *Malloy* (1951), *Malone Dies* (also 1951), and *The Unnameable* (1953). Here, the Cartesian subject's attempt to use language to escape language and merge with the unmediated authenticity of silence is shown to be both impossible and burdened by a counter-veiling "imperative of saying" (*OB*, p.81): we are doomed to compulsively narrate, though stutteringly and pointlessly, our all-too human predicament. This phase culminates with *Texts For Nothing* (a collection of works written between 1950-53), which, as the title implies, bumps up against the impasse of this "Cartesian terrorism" (*OB*, p.55) and can find no way through. This impasse provokes both a creative and an existential crisis for Beckett, as well as nourishing his dominant reception as a nihilist.

However, according to Badiou, this crisis (and this nihilism) is surpassed with the composition, between 1969-70, of *How It Is*. Stylistically, this work announces an even more pronounced move away from novelistic devices such as character and narrative, and towards a fierce exactitude, the cutting edge of which is used to pare away the inessential in order to arrive at an affirmative writing of generic humanity. Yet for Badiou, what really makes *How It Is* such a literary 'event' within Beckett's *oeuvre* is the conjuncture of this stylistic shift with a thematic one moving away from the unbearable Cartesian imperative of the saying of nothingness, and towards an exploration of the possibility of the Other, the encounter, the chance exit from solipsism—in other words, of the event.

Prominent Beckett scholar, Andrew Gibson has cast considerable doubt upon Badiou's rather stark before-and-after chronology, pointing out that "Badiou has a quite un-Beckettian attachment to the clarity of narrative sequence" (*OB*, p.134). It is certainly extremely suspicious that Badiou's reading of Beckett echoes so closely the structure of *Being and Event*. This is clearest in the essay entitled 'The Writing of the Generic' (*OB*, pp.1-36). There, he effectively argues that early Beckett is a literary rather than a mathematical ontologist exclusively concerned with being, whereas later Beckett is a thinker of the event. Thus, in early Beckett, his tragic

---

23. Andrew Gibson (in Ramond: 2002, p.424) cites the following as exemplary of this Anglo-American criticism: Thomas Trezise's *Into the Breach: Samuel Beckett and the Ends of Literature* (New Jersey: Princeton University Press, 1990); Steven Connor's *Samuel Beckett: Repetition, Theory and Text* (Oxford: Blackwell, 1988); Leslie Hill's *Beckett's Fiction: In Different Worlds* (Cambridge: Cambridge University Press, 1990); Carla Locatelli's *Unworlding the World: Samuel Beckett's Prose Works after the Nobel Prize* (Philadelphia: University of Pennsylvania Press, 1990); and Richard Begam's *Samuel Beckett and the End of Modernity* (Stanford: Stanford University Press, 1996).

characters are located at the deadlock between an intuition into the "grey black" of pure being on the one hand, and the "shades" of appearance which forever bar them access to this being on the other—a dilemma exacerbated, as I have already suggested, by the compulsion to repeatedly enunciate it. Thus, the suffocatingly closed worlds of many of Beckett's texts (the cramped room in *Endgame*, Mr Knott's house in *Watt*, and, though a later piece, the hermetically sealed cylindrical universe of *The Lost Ones*) can be seen as figurative invocations of the utterly closed and determined world of set-theory: both give intimations of the pure "grey-black" inconsistency of being 'beneath' the shades of presentation.

However, Badiou then presents us with a Beckett focussed, after 1961, not only on the theme of the encounter (for example, the sudden attack of a 'tormentor' in *How It Is*, which, though apparently aggressive, nonetheless constitutes a relief from the Sisyphean task of slithering alone across an endless expanse of black mud), but also on the theme of the naming of this event (the title of *Ill Seen Ill Said* invokes, for Badiou, the meaninglessness of the name as a way of fixing a trans-Cartesian experience). This repetition of the structure of *Being and Event*— first being, then event—in Badiou's version of Beckett's literary trajectory is convenient to say the least. It is also true that his extremely 'strong' reading is based entirely on a relatively small number of de-contextualised and rather terse quotes. From the point of view of the disciplinary expectations of literary criticism then, including a certain ideal of 'sensitivity' to the text, Badiou comes across like a bull in a china shop. He ransacks rather than reads, mugging the texts for what he needs.[24]

Nonetheless, as Power and Toscano suggest in their introduction, this undeniable violence is not without a certain recursive effect, a certain rebounding. If Badiou's Beckett is "by no means a mere 'application' of [his] doctrine to a figure writing (ostensibly) in another discipline" (*OB*, p.xii), there is a case to be made that, aggressive as it may be on one level, Badiou's intervention is nonetheless 'sensitive' enough to the specificity of Beckett's texts to constitute, precisely, a Beckettian encounter for his own philosophy. Rather like the 'tormentor' that pounces on a 'victim' in *How It Is*, it is a meeting that leaves both parties changed. And the direction of this change in Badiou's own conceptual system—seemingly induced by the fact that, after all, it cannot fully contain or tame Beckett—is of extreme significance for our purposes in this chapter, since it *pulls him in the direction of a pre-evental subject*. It is here that what I have called 'pre-evental subjective resources' make their appearance. Moreover, like Badiou's notion of the truth procedure, this has a retrospective impact on how Beckett's work as a whole is to be understood. The 'event' of *How It Is* causes the earlier work, conventionally characterised by relentless hopelessness, to be seen in a new light, one that reveals powerful subjective

---

24. In his contribution to Ramond: 2002 (pp.407-420), Dominique Rabaté argues that even within Beckett's oeuvre, Badiou's reading is very partial. For example, the optimistic reading of the theme of love in later Beckett is predicated upon the exclusion of *Company* (1977), the last word of which is, simply, 'Alone'. More generally, Rabaté argues that Badiou conflates Beckett's texts with Beckett's thought, thereby ignoring the wider intertextual literary context from which his work emerged. This is reflected, Rabaté argues, in the serious underdevelopment, in Badiou's *Inaesthetics*, of the notion of 'artistic configuration'.

resources supporting, precisely, hope. Waiting for Godot, in other words, ceases to be comic in its absurdity, [25] and becomes instead an epic ode to resilience.

In short, Badiou begins to acknowledge the value of both phases of Beckett's literary enterprise in terms of its exploration of *courage*. As Gibson rightly points out, this courage is definitely not homogeneous with Badiou's own notion of fidelity (*OB*, p.133). We should not be misled, therefore, into imagining that it is the same 'courage' elaborated in *Theory of the Subject*, which, as we saw, was an early version of Badiou's constitutively *post*-evental fidelity. Beckettian courage, by contrast, is the courage to keep going in the ungrounded, unreasonable, indeed irrational anticipation of an event, an encounter, or an arrival that *has not yet happened*. Neither being in its inertia nor the event in its singular rupture, courage outlines the subject *in potentia* harboured within the individual. By no means is this a merely passive hope then, a stoicism sustained by prayer. Courage has nothing to do with faith in the exclusively religious sense of a final meaning that will be donated, one fine day, by a supreme Other. This sort of faith necessarily waits on this Other, who, like God-ot, will surely never arrive. By contrast, courage must be thought of as an urgent and ongoing labour on and through language itself, a work that is in 'our' hands rather than those of an Other. This work on language is a 'worsening' or 'lessening' of meaning precisely to prepare the way for the advent of the radical non-meaning that is the chance encounter. Is this not akin to the resistant individual who, far from passively waiting, actively creates the conditions, in himself and in his world, for the emergence of subjectivity?

The key reference for Badiou on Beckett's notion of courage is the very late novella, *Worstward Ho* (1983), from which he extrapolates the following lesson:

> For Beckett, courage comes from the fact that words have the tendency to ring true […] courage pertains to a quality of words that is contrary to their use in worsening. There is something like an *aura* of correspondence in words from which (paradoxically) we draw the courage to break with correspondence itself, that is, to hold worstward (*OB*, p.97)

I take this to mean, quite simply, that language, used in a certain way (sublimated, to recall Gillespie's Lacanian argument), can promise access to the generic, even if this promise cannot be fulfilled: for Beckett as for Badiou, entering the silence of the void itself is impossible. And yet, *qua* promise, language provides a resource for courage, not only a reason to go on in the sense of the telos of a utopian Idea, but also a work, a labour, a task in the here and now which opens language up to that Idea. This moves beyond the superegoic dimension of the "imperative of saying" in the earlier work, retrospectively adding a hopeful timbre to the famous last line from *The Unnamable*: "you must go on, I can't go on, I'll go on" (Beckett: 2006, p.407).[26] One can detect here the literary counter-part of forcing, but one that crucially *precedes* the event. For like forcing, it operates with the extant language of the situation (the English and French languages in Beckett's case) but twists it in such

---

25. Martin Esslin famously based his notion of the 'theatre of the absurd' on *Godot*—see Esslin, Martin, *The Theatre of the Absurd*, London: Methuen, 2001.

26. This could be linked to the even more famous line from *Worstward Ho*: "No matter. Try Again. Fail Again. Fail Better" (Beckett: 2009, 81).

a way as to open it up to the generic. And like forcing, the 'writing of the generic' is not only a logical operation, but the very being of the subject: insofar as Beckett dramatizes his very method in and through his characters and their extremely restricted worlds, he performs the notion that courage is not at all deluded patience or religiously inspired passivity, but an activity that allows one to "hold worstward", to maintain fidelity.

That this link between an aesthetic activity (writing as the 'worsening' of meaning) on the one hand and courage on the other ultimately points in the direction of Gillespie's sublimation is confirmed when Badiou further connects courage to *beauty*. "When it is seized by beauty" he argues, "this acceptable material of a life without meaning [...] attains a super-existence [...] in which the weakness, repetition and obstinacy of life, disappears" (*OB*, p.77). One should not hear in this quote an argument for a compensatory aestheticisation of the meaninglessness of life: the emphasis is not on abjection compensated, but on affirmation enacted. As we saw, there is something of this affirmation in Lacan's account of sublimation. Beckett's profound achievement, therefore, is to have written "the poem of the tireless desire to think" (*ibid.*).

One can see how this tireless desire animates and structures the ant-like business within the cylinder of *The Lost Ones*. The 'vanquished' are effectively at the bottom of the hierarchy of this world, insofar as they have given up on the search for their 'other', a search which alone gives this world meaning. While entering the category of the 'vanquished' is irreversible for the individual concerned, it is not terminal for the general possibility of possibility, for, in other words, the "tireless desire to think": becoming a vanquished non-seeker *remains* a choice that continues to testify to the possibility that it could have been refused. As Badiou succinctly puts it

> what is not possible (such as recommencing one's search if one has renounced it) is not definitively and properly speaking impossible, but only temporarily 'no longer possible'. That means that the choice of renunciation destroys everything. But the *possibility* that inheres in choice remains mysteriously indestructible (*OB*, p.63)

Thus, *The Lost Ones* suggests that it is exactly when the individual is reduced to a kind of abject unfreedom that one can see its amazing tenacity not simply as absurd and meaningless, an irredeemably bad faith, but also as beautiful. Perhaps here, just as we have embraced the bivalence of the term 'cleaving' in describing the knot of the subject, we can now embrace the bi-valence of term 'determination' in describing the potential emergence of the subject from the individual. That is to say, determination in the sense of objectification (the stultifying rules that exhaustively govern the squirming in and out of niches and the ascending and descending of endless ladders in *The Lost Ones*) ultimately foregrounds determination in the subjective sense of an empirically unjustifiable yet indestructible will. Resonating, moreover, with Badiou's conviction regarding the infinity of truth, subjective determination can be heard as de-termination, the refusal of an end, a terminus, where life would come to a standstill, becoming permanently vanquished. This is why Badiou discerns in Beckett "a powerful love for human obstinacy, for tireless desire, for humanity reduced to its stubbornness and malice" (*OB*, p.75). Again, waiting is no longer passive or pointless: "Doubtless, we will never know 'who' Godot is, but it is enough that he is the emblem of everyone's obstinate desire for something to happen" (*ibid.*).

Courage and the beauty with which it endows the human animal connect to one final category in Badiou's analysis, an affect significantly, but one that, without the encounter with Beckett, I very much doubt he would ever have praised, so at odds is it with his own emphasis on novelty. I am referring to *nostalgia*. Surely nostalgia simply paints a gloss of sentimentality over a (mis)remembered past, often to sugar-coat the bitter pill of the present? Surely nostalgia is an affect that binds the old rather than paving the way for the new? Indeed, Badiou is in general vehemently opposed to the politics of memory and of memorialisation (see the conclusion in *LW*). Nonetheless, here, thanks to the power of Beckett's prose by which Badiou's thought comes to be conditioned, nostalgia is recognised as a potent pre-evental subjective resource. This is signalled by Badiou's characterisation of Beckettian nostalgia not as a "metaphysics of time as in Proust, but as a 'voluntarism of remembrance'", one that "constitutes an experiment with alterity" (*OB*, p.67). 'Voluntarism of remembrance' invokes not an 'objective' determination by one's past, even less by one's egoic narratives of that past, but a subjective determination that makes creative use of the fabric of recollection to re-collect the historical world in a new configuration. Thus, 'experiment with alterity' signifies the Othering of the historicised present determinant of the self. The primary literary support for this argument comes from *Krapp's Last Tape*, in which an old, apparently dying man listens to tape recordings of his younger self, not to look back on his life from the sad vantage of a terminal point, but to reconstruct the present he still occupies, courageously, in the face of death. It is worth simply citing three quotes that convey what Badiou draws from *Krapp's Last Tape* in terms of a redemption of the category of nostalgia:

1. "[With nostalgia] we are dealing with another world, with the hypothesis whereby the grey-black is juxtaposed, in an improbable and distance [sic] place, to a colourful and sentimental universe. The narrative of this universe puts solipsism to the test and forces literature to reflect upon the theme of pure differences (or of the 'other life')" (*OB*, p.68)

2. "No true link is established between nostalgia and the course of things. Memory is not a saving function. But, once it is captured in a story, memory is simply what attests to the immanent power of the Other" (*OB*, p.70)

3. "The force of nostalgia lies in giving us the power to suppose that one day (before, afterward, time is of no importance here) the eye will open, and, under the astonished gaze, in the nuances of the grey black of being, something will lighten" (*OB*, p.71)

The first quote shows the power of nostalgia to challenge the present to live up to its alternative vision: it opens a critical subjective space. The second makes it very clear that nostalgia does not in fact ruminate bitter-sweetly on a bygone era that supports "the course of things" in the present, but rather, that it testifies to the *current* (immanent) potential for change. The third and final quote demonstrates the imaginary resource of nostalgia as an openness precisely to the futural (even on the verge of death, as is the case in *Krapp's Last Tape*). The key point, however, is that nostalgia is something like a re-appropriation of individuation from the Other which pushes towards subjectivity even in the absence of an event: nostalgia can actively support courage. Returning to psychoanalysis, although there has been a post-Freudian tendency to understand analysis as the recovery of repressed memories and the reparative completion of a narrative of the self, Lacanians make a key distinction between the return of the repressed as rememoration, and a more Deleuzian repetition which instantiates difference (see Harari: 2002). In fact it is the symptom that is on the side of the return of the repressed, whereas repetition is on the side of an othering of the self in order that "something will lighten". Beckettian nostalgia can be seen as this process of exposing memory to repetition-with-difference in the form of a work of de-individuation or, in one of Lacan's formulations of the goal of analysis, 'subjective destitution'.

To sum up then, the interconnections between courage, beauty and nostalgia all 'force' Badiou to admit something that elsewhere in his philosophical work, but particularly in *Being and Event*, is rigorously excluded: "we can say that every event admits of a figural preparation, that it always possesses a pre-evental *figure*" (*OB*, p.111). The italicization of *figure* here signifies, still, its distinction from the subject *stricto sensu*, and the term suggests a virtual mode of existence. However, such a pre-evental figure is arguably the closest we ever get in Badiou's work to a productive proximity between the individual and the subject, and thus to a phenomenology of the emergence of the latter from the former. The fact, too, that he speaks of a "figural preparation" indicates that the resistant individual is *not* condemned to twiddling his thumbs in idle anticipation of an event, and the birth of a radically singular, extra-worldly subject. He must prepare. As we will see in the next chapter, this casts a whole new light on the importance of the historical maintenance of a resistant political imaginary.

This chapter has helped to relocate the subject within the problematic of conflict. We can now see that far from being other-worldly, the subject is constitutively in conflict not only with the world but with its own animality through which the world exerts a gravitational pull that would absorb the subject back into the individual. We can also see that subject are necessarily in conflict with other subjects, certainly with reactive and obscure subjects that respond negatively to the event, but perhaps even other faithful subjects whose subject-languages draw on divergent sources and articulate different truth-claims. We saw that Badiou's insistence on the subject's separation from relation helps to parse out structural from anti-structural conflicts, but we also recognised that this was at the cost of any phenomenology of the emergence of subjectivity and its affective dimensions. Turning to psychoanalysis and Beckett has enabled us to outline pre-evental subjective resources in affects such as anxiety, courage and nostalgia, thereby rescuing the importance of resistance from the starker aspects of Badiou's approach, and perhaps indicating some kind of connection between resistant individuals and subjects proper.

5

Towards an Evental Historiography

In this chapter, we will continue to undermine the account of the event as an abstract, extra-worldly singularity in order to situate it more centrally within a theory of conflict. We will do so by focussing not, as in the last chapter, on the phenomenology of the transition from individual to subject, but on the vexed question of the relation between the event and history. And yet we are far from leaving behind subjective concerns. We will argue that history continues to shape not only the individual in its worldly 'thrownness', but even the subject in its exceptional subtraction. Despite the widespread reading of the event as utterly ahistorical in the purity of its rupture, we will claim that historical factors are intrinsic to the event. Nonetheless, risking this heterodox assertion must involve a considerable complication of a position we have already traced, as well as a clarification of what 'historical' can mean in this assertion.

For as we saw in Chapters 1 and 2, the notion of the event in Badiou's own intellectual trajectory clearly *does* mark an attempt to break free from the oppressive weight of dialectically determining History. More specifically, Badiou explicitly hopes that the event will liberate philosophy from its subsumption within the Hegelo-Marxist paradigm, and the consequent dominance of the historico-political 'suture' (see the chapters on 'Conditions' and 'Sutures' in MP). This move not only allows philosophy's conditioning by other, non-political truths, but it also supports Badiou's subtractive theory of the subject, insofar as what the subject is subtracted from is, precisely, historical determination broadly conceived. If the notion of the event does mark such a break, however, some precision is needed regarding what, exactly, it breaks with. For far from championing the abandonment of history, *the event is specifically a weapon in Badiou's polemic against historicism.*

The term 'historicism' gathers a 'rogue's gallery' of Badiou's philosophical foes. We can briefly list their profiles: the metaphysical form of Hegelian historicism, in which World Spirit unfolds in a temporal becoming; the economistic form of Marxist historicism, in which the modes of production guarantee a communist future; the Heideggarian variant, in which there are distinct epochal modes of the unveiling of Being and thus the 'destining' of philosophy; the strategic historicism of the *nouveaux philosophes*, in which 'actually existing Marxism' is condemned by reducing it to the purges and gulags, and by grouping Stalin and Hitler under the single banner of 'totalitarianism'; the so-called 'new historicism' associated with 'poststructuralist' accounts of history such as that offered by Foucault, in which epistemes govern the discursive protocols of the knowledge-power nexus; and the related 'postmodern' historicism, in which the emphasis is on the relative, socially constructed nature of scientific and other truths, and the essentially fictional status of historical discourse. Behind the diversity of these 'mugshots' of Badiou's historicist foes lies the common assumption that truths, or truth-claims, are relative to the contexts in which they are produced, insofar as those contexts are historically determined. In general then, historicism combines, in a mutually reinforcing way, two tendencies utterly anathema to Badiou's entire project: it both nullifies the possibility of radical novelty and thus the formation of a subject, *and* it confines truth (including our conceptual access to it) to the spatio-temporal location of its emergence. To the extent that the historicist model of History functions as a *container* of events, consigning them to 'history' in the colloquial sense of destroying them, it is no surprise that Badiou should want ardently to break with it.

However, what we will try to clarify in this chapter, building on Chapter 2, is that *Badiou's anti-historicism by no means implies ahistoricism*. To leap to such a conclusion would simply be to repeat the dominance of the historicist account of History (rather as pessimistic accounts of the omnipresence of domination collude with and extend that domination). The term 'ahistoricism' implies a complete indifference to historical factors, a pure and uncompromising rejection of their relevance, or—given that it is most frequently used as an insult—an outright ignorance of supposed historical facts. Badiou cannot be justly accused of any of these things. What is required, then, is an investigation into the possibility of anti-historicist conceptualisations of history. Such an investigation paves the way, explored in the latter half of this chapter, for the affirmation of a mode of historiography that is integral to the transformative labour of the subject. Such an affirmation prevents us from adopting the essentially idealist position of viewing history *tout court* as something to be definitively broken away from. As we shall see, recently Badiou has allowed for a relation to History that sustains a radical, because historically informed, political imaginary, something surely relevant to the possibility of pre-evental resistance.

HISTORY, HISTORICITY

It is not difficult to discern this attempt to articulate anti-historicist conceptualisations of history in Badiou's Maoist phase.

In *Theory of Contradiction* (1975), he explicitly criticizes the tendency of bourgeois historiography to disguise dialectical necessity as mere contingency. Thus, irruptions of mass revolt are explained by the bourgeois historian with reference to everything *except* the social relations of production required by capital's exploitation of labour. Peasant revolts are put down to grain shortages, worker's movements are ascribed to foreign interference, slave uprisings are explained away as expressions of racial difference, and so on. It is this façade of misleading contingency that

prevents the dialectical momentum of class struggle from appearing as an historical *necessity*. The fetishization of the notion of 'causality' in bourgeois historiography is by no means a commitment to historical truth and its origins, then. It is,
rather, a motivated attempt to incorporate true novelty into a narrative form. With
bourgeois historiography, it is as if one version of chance, essentially synonymous
with randomness, is deployed to obfuscate another version, chance as the positive
opportunity for political innovation. Symmetrically, we could say that it is also as if
one version of necessity, synonymous with the naturalisation of the 'given' (for example, Capital itself), is deployed to obfuscate another version, the dialectical necessity of class struggle. It is to sustain the conjuncture of the second forms of both
chance and necessity against the first that Badiou argues that it remains "deeply
necessary to render the rationality of this persistence of [revolt]" (*TC*, p.22). Such
a rendering remains historical. This is why, in *Theory of the Subject*, he will gnomi-
cally declare that "it is always Marxist to say that history is the chance of political
necessity" (*TS*, p.60). But already in *Theory of Contradiction* it is clear that History is
being split into two. On the one hand, a reactionary bourgeois history that subdues
revolt by explaining it away as avoidable contingency, and on the other, a counter-history that opens on to, and indeed galvanizes, the necessity of revolt as guaranteed by the dialectic of class struggle. Nonetheless, this counter-history is still a
history, an arc of temporal coherence. Without this, the multiplicity of particular
revolts threatens to disperse in a cloud of discontinuous particles rather than coa-
lescing into a universal logic: "the essence of the proletarian position lies in its historical project, not in particular revolts" (*TC*, p.9).

This proletarian 'historical project' is given a more positive elaboration the
following year in the book co-written with François Balmès, also in the Yenan series, entitled *De l'idéologie* (1976). It is in this work—a polemic with the Althusserian
and Deleuzian responses to May '68, based primarily upon an analysis of Thomas
Münzer's role in the Peasant's War—that Badiou suggests a *timeless link* between
past revolts through the notion of 'Communist invariants'. Flying in the face of
postmodern cultural relativism (which binds truth to time and space), this notion
insists that no matter which historical juncture or cultural context, whether in ancient Rome, the European Middle Ages or Russia in the early 20th century, all
true revolts display a set of common characteristics. "Our hypothesis is the following", write the authors, "all the successive major revolts of the mass of exploited
classes (slaves, peasants, proletarians) find their ideological expression in egalitarian formulations, anti-property and anti-Statist, which constitute the lineaments of
a communist programme" (*DI*, p.66). These common characteristics include the
attempted dissolution of the 'state', the pursuit of an end to private property, the
egalitarian distribution of social wealth, and the deliberate dismantling of the machinery of domination (*DI*, p.67). In a much later work, *D'un désastre obscur*, Badiou
extends this list to include:

> The egalitarian passion, the Idea of justice, the will to break with the compromis-
> es of the *service des biens*, the deposing of egoism, the intolerance of oppression, the
> wish to end the state. (*DO*, pp.13-14)

By describing communism as 'invariant' in this way, Badiou is clearly extracting it from history in the teleological sense, even as he wishes to present the proletariat as the heirs of past revolts. They are the bearers of "ideological invariants of the communist type constantly regenerated through the process of the unification of the major popular revolts of all time" (*DI*, p.67). However, 'invariant' here does not mean that these communist traits endure uninterruptedly in some subterranean way. The emphasis is rather on timelessness, at least with regard to the historicist understanding of Time: 'invariant' really means actualised communism is the same not 'all the time', but *each time*. This 'each' invokes completely discontinuous, isolated revolts with no 'world-historical', progressive connection between them. If each revolt, taken singly, carries certain traits discernible in other revolts, it is not because they are metaphysically linked across time, but because all revolt necessarily touches on the generic, on the real of politics. But the whole question for Badiou is how this isolated flash of the invariant generic can be made to illuminate a broader historical logic. In order for discrete, point-like revolts to demonstrate their invariance, they must be put into some kind of non-causal relation with other revolts. They must be gathered into the proletarian 'historical project' that focuses their logic into a transhistorical universality. *De l'idéologie* makes it clear that the exploited groups of all historical periods have produced resistant ideologies that are simultaneously forms of knowledge (*DI*, p.15). It also shows that, while necessarily drawing on the dominant ideologies of their times (for example, Münzer's egalitarianism had to be phrased in the religious form of heresy, one radical enough that even the religious reformer Luther railed against it), these resistant ideologies also contributed to, and drew upon, the timeless invariance of communism. However, the real message of *De l'idéologie* is that it is only with the emergence of the proletariat, as the last and most universal of history's exploited groups, that the invariance discernible in past revolts can be concentrated into a revolutionary praxis (*DI*, p.74).

If this sounds precariously close to the very Hegelianism that underpins much historicism, including its Marxist incarnation, *Le noyau rationnel de la dialectique hégélienne* (1978) is Badiou's effort to distil from Hegel himself an anti-historicist conceptualisation of history. As we saw in Chapter 1, the scissional interpretation of Hegel in this work effectively cuts off any teleological understanding of history as the incremental unfolding of World Spirit. By refusing to domesticate the negative within an emergent totality or absolute, Badiou shows us a Hegel attuned to the force of history destabilising any given present. To the extent that this 'force of history' is quite distinct from the bourgeois concept of history propping up the status quo, it is appropriate for us to designate it with a different term. To 'History' then, capitalised to reflect its Statist, bourgeois function, we can initially oppose 'historicity' with its greater proximity to change. By implicitly pitting Hegel's *Logic* against his *Philosophy of History*, *Le noyau rationnel de la dialectique hégélienne* contributes to the ongoing antagonism between Marxist and bourgeois historians, where this distinction between History and historicity has been at stake for some time.

Caricaturing the protagonists somewhat, we can say that for the bourgeois historian—whose ideology of neutral scholarship includes the notion that his discipline must distance itself from its own time and national context—History is nonetheless essentially the story of how 'we' arrived at the pinnacle that is the present. For the Marxist historian, however, history is always a synonym for historicity as the force of change, and only secondarily the story of the irruption of this force in the past. Far from upholding the ideal of neutral scholarship, the Marxist historian exposes the latter as bourgeois ideology, and openly links his non-neutral bias to the ongoing class struggle itself. Ultimately, however, the Marxist historian will claim that this is not a bias at all, insofar as it favours the only universal class, the proletariat. Rather conveniently, History is always on his side. Nonetheless, if Marxist history pertains to the present, it is to the extent that it tells the story of how that present can (and necessarily will) be changed.

However, as Badiou himself becomes more and more aware, this kind of historical materialism ultimately subordinates historicity to History. As we will see later, Jacques Rancière (1994; 2005) has similarly shown the ways in which, preoccupied with the fundamentally philosophical category of the 'masses', the Marxist historian has blinded himself to the somewhat different category of the poor. Indeed, if Marx's own analysis of the class struggle plays itself out in "the conjunction of the *not yet* and the *one more time*" (Rancière: 1994, 31)—i.e., between the always peremptory insurrection that fails to manifest the properly proletarian revolution, and the repeated victory of the bourgeoisie that is the form of this failure—it is because the communist future is supposedly guaranteed by a historicism that simply promises to reward a different class. But, returning to Badiou, the scissional Hegel developed in *Le noyau rationnel de la dialectique hégèlienne* is intended to deprive even the Marxist historian of any category of historical 'totality' or futural absolute, and thus of the covertly bourgeois notion of world-historical becoming. Together, these totalising categories make of the necessity of change inscribed in dialectical materialism an objective law, rather than a subjective procedure. Scission, then, cuts historicity away from History, and yet as long as he adheres to the classist definition of the proletariat, the former remains covertly borne by and reliant on the latter. Badiou's aim is ultimately to break this reliance.

But if there is no World History, no encompassing History of histories (no 'set of all sets' as later Badiou will put it), how can the dispersal of individual revolts into an ahistorical multiplicity be prevented? Subtracted from the false reassurances of the structural dialectic, the term 'historicity' still seems to encompass only the ever-present potential for change, not the inclusion of actualised change in, or its effects upon, History in its properly diachronic sense. It is in response to this problem that Badiou develops, at the apogee of his Maoism in *Theory of the Subject*, the concept of 'periodization'. This is what connects the generic emphasis of the communist invariant to its historical advent in a particular time and place, even as it prevents the particularity of that time and place concealing its timeless universality. Periodization could be said to be the distinctive operational mode of the proletarian historical project. To define it rather rapidly at first, we can say that periodization enacts a recursive 'diagonal' between two revolts that has the effect of 'completing' one period, and simultaneously opening up a new one. The key example in *Theory of the Subject* is the October Revolution's 'periodization' of the Paris Commune, figuratively crystallised by Lenin's famous dance in the snow outside the Kremlin.

October 1917 'periodizes' the Commune to the extent that it completes its rationality, rendering fully legible the problem posed to revolutionary history by its bloody disappearance, a rendering achieved in and through the practical solution offered by Lenin's invention of the centralised revolutionary party. Periodization therefore inscribes an arcing diagonal between two incidents of revolt that cuts across linear, bourgeois History. This is why, for Marxism, "history does not exist (it would be a figure of the whole). Only historical periods or historicizations [...] exist" (*TS*, p.92). Indeed, although Badiou does not bring this out sufficiently, it is clear that an important part of this process is the way in which the fold introduced into bourgeois History by periodization obscures a link in the causal chain that had hitherto consigned the first revolt to the category of failure.

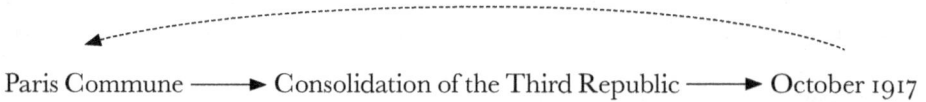

Paris Commune ——→ Consolidation of the Third Republic ——→ October 1917

By, as it were, leapfrogging *la semaine sanglante* and the consolidation of the Third Republic (which very nearly reconstituted the monarchy), October 1917 withdraws the Commune from the bourgeois narrative in which it illustrated the irrationality of working class mobilisation and the triumphant restoration of bourgeois 'law and order'. In fact, the third element in the linear sequence moving from left to right at the bottom is already a major challenge to bourgeois historiography insofar as, while it honours sequential time (October coming *after* the Commune), it pays no heed to national, cultural space. How does Moscow link backwards in time across forty six years to, of all places, Paris? Despite the bourgeois historian's claims to neutral scholarship, he is almost invariably an amenuensis to the dictates of nation and national identity. Only the internationalism of Marxism has no difficulty in seeing the universal plight of the worker as practically identical in France and in Russia—not concretely in the empirical terms of levels of industrialisation, urbanisation, unonisation etc., but in logical terms, in a common relation of resistance to exploitation.

Astute readers will already have noticed that, as throughout *Theory of the Subject*, Badiou is clearly drawing on Lacan here. In particular, he is drawing on the retrospective constitution of the real that Lacan, in turn, finds in Freud's notion of *nachträglichkeit* or 'belatedness' in the early theory of traumatic memory.[1] Just as Freud argues that an 'initial' trauma only enters consciousness through a symbolic connection to a 'second' memory, so Lacan argues that the master-signifier is only constituted retrospectively by means of a second signifier:

---

1. The structure of *nachträglichkeit* was developed in the pre-psychoanalytic *Project for a Scientific Psychology* which emerged from Freud's correspondence with Wilhelm Fliess in 1895 but remained unpublished until 1950. However, *Studies in Hysteria*, co-written with Josef Breuer, was published in 1895 and linked *nachträglichkeit* to repressed memories initially thought to relate to infantile sexual abuse.

$$S^1 \longrightarrow S^2$$

The bottom line in this schema is fundamentally imaginary in that the arrow moving from left to right, which indicates the intuitive sequence running from S_1 to S_2, or 'first trauma, then its recollection through a memory (a signifier)', is actually subsequent, not antecedent, to the curving arrow above. Despite being experienced as 'first', S_1 only comes into existence through a recursive effect of the signifier. This has enormous clinical ramifications for Lacan, since it indicates that the trauma of loss embodied by castration (S_1) might well be narrated at the level of an analysand's ego (complaints of the type 'I used to have everything, but he took it away from me' should be situated on this level), yet this apparently foundational loss is in fact inaugurated by the signifier itself rather than being 'factually' recorded by it. Certainly by Seminar XX, it becomes clear that for Lacan the real is not a pre-linguistic fullness foreclosed to the speaking being thanks to entry into the symbolic. On the contrary, the real is an effect of the logic of the signifier through and through.

This same model of the retrospective constitution of the real by means of the intervention of a 'second' signifier will come to dominate Badiou's account of the event, evident in concepts that we have already encountered such as 'evental recurrence', 'evental naming' and, as we shall see later, 'evental resurrection'. It is certainly with Lacan in mind that Badiou asks, enigmatically, "In what sense do we say that the Paris Commune is real? Certainly not in that it has taken place, which is merely the index of its reality" (*TS*, p.230). Bourgeois history gives a place to what has taken place, locating it on the left-to-right line of imaginary causality. Having 'taken place' can therefore only mean being put 'in order', and thus the domestication of force in a narrative of 'reality'. To become real by contrast, the Commune must puncture a hole in this reality. Badiou's argument is that the Commune was able to do so thanks entirely to the 'second', *Nachträglich* signifier of October 1917, whereupon it finally became real rather than imaginary.

But beyond this retrospective constitution of the real via a belated signifier, and beyond Lacan's supposed entanglements in the 'structural dialectic', Badiou is interested in positing periodization as a kind of hinge articulating *two* historical periods. If the stress in periodization was only on the way in which 'past' revolts are completed by new ones, we would be saddled with a redemptive history of overarching synthesis, confronting us, once again, with the idealist side of Hegel. On this partial account, periodization would in fact mark only the end of a sequence, and thus a closed circle (symbol par excellence of the 'structural dialectic'). Badiou, however, has no interest in redeeming the failures of the past, but only in marshalling them in a new present. Periodization, therefore, must simultaneously mark not only the closure of an old sequence but also the opening of a new one, indeed the very distinction between these must be folded back upon itself. With this in mind, the periodization of the Paris Commune by October 1917 can be schematically represented thus:

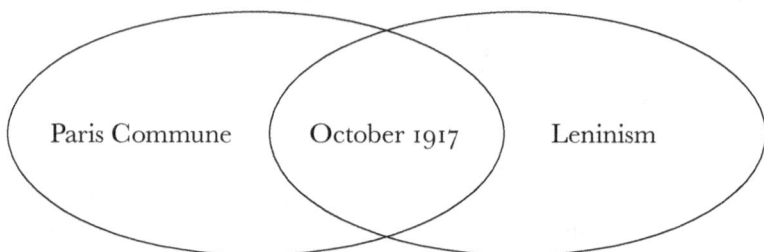

Paris Commune   October 1917   Leninism

For the first oval on the left, October 1917 'completes' the Paris Commune by making the apparent failure of its vanishing reappear as the precondition for its successful resolution (rather as Christ had to die on the cross for our sins to be redeemed): the chaos of insurrection is given consistency by the supplement of a disciplined, centralised party, or again, subjectivation enters into the subject-process. But for the second oval on the right, October 1917 is the novelty that initiates an entirely new phase in the history of Marxism known as Leninism. From the point of view of the first oval, it is the Paris Commune that is novel, whereas for the second, the Commune becomes "that *edge of the old* whose practical perception, by purifying force, partakes in the engendering of [October's] novelty" (*TS*, p.47).[2] What Badiou calls this "*discrepant double scission*"—which misleadingly appears in our diagram as an overlap, whereas it is not the same 'October 1917' that is at stake—is so crucial that it "grounds any historical periodization" (48). Vector of scissional historicity then, October 1917 itself is split into two. If it 'completes' the Commune it is nonetheless not causally deducible from it in its contribution to the situation in 1917, since if it were, it would not provide the basis for the strong novelty of the Leninist sequence. "For the materialist", explains Badiou, "there is no beginning unless it is marked by a novelty that is undeducible from the periodizing closure" (*TS*, p.48). Oliver Feltham puts this succinctly: "Periodization ensures that the process produces something different from what it starts with, and consequently that one dialectical process distinguishes itself from another" (Feltham: 2008, 43).

However, if in *Theory of the Subject* the concept of periodization seems like a militant redescription of Marxism's continuing basis in historical materialism, by *Peut-on penser la politique* (1985) the term periodization may be largely absent, but one can discern its melancholy echo in a reckoning with the historical death of Marxism-Leninism itself. *Peut-on penser la politique* is an extremely important transitional text in Badiou's development. In the space of only 120 or so pages, we witness his (nuanced, somehow faithful) turn away from Marxism, and towards the concept of the event, including the outlines of its set-theoretical support. And yet the very structure of the book repeats the 'double scission' we have just seen as characteristic of periodization. It is in two parts, the first concerned with 'destruction', the second with 'recomposition', and it is clear from the introduction—entitled, revealingly, 'liminaire'—that Badiou situates the work, and its context, at the

2. It would be easy to add an extra layer of complexity here by pointing out that the new calendar developed during the French Revolution but abolished by Napoléon in 1806 was briefly revived during the Paris Commune, thereby suggesting the recursive, discontinuous temporality of periodization.

intersection of *both* the destruction and the recomposition of Marxism. Just as the referent 'October 1917' has two sides in the diagram above, with one edge bordering on the past, the other opening out onto a new future, so Badiou seems to see, or more accurately, to force, a similar split in the emergent referent 'historical death of Marxism'.

From the vantage point of the edge facing destruction, things look pretty bleak for Marxism-Leninism for a number of reasons. Badiou notes that its tendency towards economism has come to coincide disastrously with the free-market logic of late capital and the supposed 'subjectivity' of competition. Its academic distortion into a sociology of the working classes has allowed its co-optation into the communitarian politics of the social contract, whereby sovereignty is tasked with including everyone via the mechanism of representation, 'even the poorest'. Furthermore, Marxism's divisive universalism has been displaced by a consensual model of democracy and so-called human rights. But most damagingly of all, "Marxism has been destroyed by its own history" (*PP*, p.14). If "Marxism, and it alone, presented itself as a revolutionary political doctrine which is, if not historically confirmed (something of another business), at least historically active" (*PP*, p.26), then it has paid the price for this historical suture by becoming historically *inactive* thanks to the accumulated 'baggage' of the show trails, the gulags, the Khmer Rouge and so on. In the first three quarters of the 20th century, Marxism may have built up a certain historical credit, but by the early 1980s it has exceeded its overdraft and is teetering on bankruptcy.

Badiou argues that three principal historical referents nourished the Marxism of old. Firstly, a statist reference which, thanks to both the Russian and Chinese (and should we not add Cuban?) Revolutions, sustained a "victorious reference" (*PP*, p.27) conducive to mobilising Marxist subjectivity around the world. Secondly, Marxist wars of national liberation such as those in China and Vietnam similarly inspired radicals everywhere. And thirdly, Marxism was further supported by the clear manifestations of a vigorous international worker's movement in which trade unions organised general strikes that posed major challenges to bourgeois States, and often extracted significant compromises from them. Combined with the cycle of economic crises intrinsic to capital, these referents managed to carve out a theoretical, political and subjective space in which Marxism could, and did, appear as a viable historical alternative.

However, it is precisely these referents—the existing Marxist State, the victorious Marxist army of national liberation, and the proud, Marx-informed international worker's movement—that had become irrevocably compromised by the early 1980s. Aleksandr Solzhenitsyn had exposed the full horrors of Stalin's gulags, thereby casting a dark shadow over the 'victorious referent' of October 1917 and the USSR. The very existence of a specifically 'Western' Marxism indicated a relative disdain for the Soviet signifier. Likewise, victorious national liberation movements had soon descended into oppressive militarism, paranoia, and in the case of Deng Xiaoping's China, into Mao's dreaded 'Capitalist road'. The worker's movement, moreover, had been sundered from its seemingly umbilical connection to Communism by the very success of the *Solidarity* movement in Poland, directed against the Soviet State. That a successful mass worker's social movement should not only not have Marxism as its primary reference point, but be pitted against a State bureaucracy calling itself Marxist (which even attempted to destroy the movement in the name of Marxism), was a catastrophic blow to Communism's traditional alliance with the labour movement from which it has never recovered.

And yet, Badiou still remains wedded enough to the dialectic at this time to see in the very wreckage of this abject situation for Marxism-Leninism the opportunity for its revitalisation: its death also borders on a new life. Indeed, recomposition is so dialectically imbricated with destruction that Badiou boldly claims the properly Marxist position in such a context is to *assist* in the destruction of Marxism! Hence the jarring note of defiance in his admission that "Marxism is historically defeated" (*PP*, p.48). What Badiou means is that the version of Marxism that tethered itself entirely to History as the terrain of its unfolding proof should, indeed, be allowed to sink into the oblivion to which the contrary movement of History is in the process of consigning it. To this extent, Badiou finds himself in surprising partial agreement with the historicizing tactic of *nouveaux philosophes* such as André Glucksman, whom he had vehemently attacked on just these grounds in *De l'idéologie* (*DI*, pp.52-56).

However, the crucial distinction is that, according to Baidou, this destruction of Marxism under the weight of its own historical baggage is the precondition for its recomposition as a *concept*, one uncoupled from the paralysing ballast of the weight of History. After all, Badiou points out, Marx himself founded what would become Marxism in the absence of Statist or victorious referents, and was able to do so thanks not to History, but to the contemporaneous historicity of the worker's movement ('there is politics' rather than 'there has been politics'). Following its much needed recomposition, Marxism will be conditioned by the contingency of *historicity* rather than falsely reassured by a putative dialectical necessity running like a red thread throughout History. Peter Hallward rightly describes this transitional phase as the search for an exit from History: "in Badiou's subsequent work he would strive to rise to the challenge posed by this destruction [of Marxism's historical ambitions], a challenge that effectively compelled the invention of a way out of the confines of history as such" (Hallward: 2003, 41). In *Peut-on-penser la politique?* therefore, Badiou continues to hold onto the term Marxism, but he is already insisting that the Marxism to come will no longer seek validation in an historical realm exterior to itself. Instead, it will immanently generate its own protocol of 'proof' through the anti-historicist affirmation it conducts in, and against, the historicised present.

THE BREAK WITH HISTORY

By *Being and Event*, the destruction of historically determined Marxism, and of the allure of the term itself (if not its logic), is arguably complete and all of Badiou's effort will go into conceptually clarifying the event's clean break with History. It is also here that philosophy becomes an increasingly vital resource, precisely in its traditional role as the rational suspension of historically accumulated *doxa*. I would argue that, although it appears to de-throne the primacy of politics, the turn in *Be-*

ing and Event to philosophy, and the corollary distribution of truth across four Platonic domains instead of a single Marxist one, is ultimately the same political strategy of subtracting truth from historical determination advocated in *Peut-on penser la politique?*.

But *Being and Event* pushes this project further by underscoring the incompatibility of the event with any form of knowledge whatsoever (whereas during Badiou's Maoist phase, revolt was always an immanent form of revolutionary knowledge). This incompatibility applies particularly to the pretensions to conceptual mastery at the convergence of the disciplines of Sociology and History. With *Being and Event*, there is now absolutely no way of *predicting* the emergence of an event through an historically informed sociology of the present. Every predictive formula is constrained to draw on those aspects of the encyclopaedia of the situation that construct probabilities. But these probabilities are built upon the selective accumulation of precedents—in other words, upon History as an explanatory resource—so that any attempt at prediction ultimately draws a hermeneutic circle that excludes historicity. *Being and Event* makes it clear that, qua excrescent, the evental multiple is unknowable because im-probable, indeed im-possible, from the point of view of knowledge. Even the existence of the 'evental site' does little to soften this radical unpredictability. Although such sites are 'in' the situation, and although they have certain ontological characteristics that make them minimally knowable, we have already seen that they are necessary but by no means sufficient conditions for events. Evental sites guarantee nothing except an open structural possibility that cannot be coerced into a dialectical probability, even by resistant individuals.

But *Being and Event* goes much further than prohibiting the predictability of events for an historically informed sociology. It also makes clear that the event cannot be grasped even retrospectively by a sociologically informed History of the kind favoured by both Marxist and revisionist historians, as we saw in Chapter 2. *Théorie de la contradiction* and *De l'idéologie* had already indicated that bourgeois historiography specialises in reducing the event to the pre-existing situation. But this insight is now given set-theoretical support through the founding distinction between 'inclusion' and 'belonging'. It is now much clearer that History tries to reduce all phenomena to inclusion because it is allied to the liberal, representational modelling of the situation as a one-to-one correspondence between everything that is counted, and the count of the count. History is thus one of the key functions of the State. By contrast, the notion of belonging as a distinct ontological category simply does not 'compute' for State History. Granted, the retrospective invention of a causal explanation for the emergence of an event remains an inevitable aspect of the State's response: we saw as much with our consideration of counter-nomination in the last chapter. But the exceptional nature of the void-multiple now ensures that such a historicizing gesture is doomed to miss what remains enigmatic about the event. It is this constitutive remainder that makes what I will go on to call 'evental historiography' possible at all. As Chapter 2 already demonstrated, reducing the French Revolution to the sequence designated 'Thermidor' does not capture what the term 'Revolution' continues to crystallise, any more than *la semaine sanglant* absolutely erases what was novel about the Paris Commune.

Yet if the Statist understanding of History is dealt a double blow in *Being and Event*, historicity is pushed much further to the foreground, and in two ways. Firstly, the book's very title indicates a distinction between ontological sets (the realm of being) and non-ontological sets which Badiou chooses to call 'historical' (the realm of events) (*BE*, Meditations 12 and 16). Natural sets are rather boring insofar as they are hermetically closed, normalising all their elements in a way that leaves no room for change. Historical sets, by contrast, are subject to sudden upheavals because they contain at least one multiple that is included without belonging. This abnormal, excrescent multiple is precisely the 'evental site' that prevents the closure of the set, thereby opening it out onto at least the structural possibility of an event. Badiou admits that in describing such open sets, he chose the far from innocent term 'historical' "in opposition to the intrinsic stability of natural situations" (*BE*, p.177). This link between 'historical' and instability here indicates that Badiou's reference is really to what we have been calling historicity. This is why he continues to insist, as in his explicitly Maoist period, that "We can think the *historicity* of certain multiples, but we cannot think *a* History" (*BE*, p.176).

The other way in which historicity is foregrounded in *Being and Event* is the introduction of the concept of 'conditioning', and the way in which the book itself is conditioned by the event of post-Cantorian set-theory. As was already evident when we considered the concept at the beginning of Chapter 2, conditioning cleaves together a *subjective* rather than objective historical determination on the one hand (it depends upon a subject's decision to subordinate themselves to the hypothesis of an event), and on the other, the force of history as change active in the present (this subordination allows philosophy, for example, to think the truths of its time). Conditioning effectively transfers the proletarian 'historical project' described in *De l'idéologie* onto the terrain of philosophy. Unlike the proletariat as the pinnacle of historical materialist progress, philosophy is characterised by its rational separation from all historical determination, thereby raising historicity to a transformative discipline of thought untrammelled by any privileged connection to a particular class.[3]

And yet it is this foregrounding of historicity that leads to a problematic ossification in *Being and Event* with regard to the event-History relation. Historicity is placed exclusively on the side of the subject and utterly divorced from History as in *any way* determinant. It is an essentially 'structuralist' concept to the extent that the evental site, an attribute of the structure of a set, is the prerequisite for a set's historical status. History in the explanatory, 'bourgeois' sense is deemed irrevocably Statist and conservative, reduced to a mere encyclopaedic reflex: there are no resources there for the subject to draw upon. Historical sets may open up the possibility of evental transformation, but historical *knowledge*, seemingly always merely

---

3. As Peter Osborne has pointed out, this appeal to philosophy as somehow transcendent to or at least partially separated from historical determination is a very un-Marxist position. Badiou is the one who most explicitly—indeed, massively—reinvests the field of Theory with the idea of philosophy. This time, though, (Badiou's Althusserian heritage notwithstanding) it is philosophy *without* Marxism—that is, without Marx's critique of philosophy—indeed, seemingly without any version of the critique of the self-sufficiency of philosophy (Osborne: 2007, 20)

symbolic, grasps nothing of the intimation of the real hidden within the void, either before its illumination by an event, or subsequently. Historicity, on the other hand, comes across as so stark and punctual that it becomes essentially atemporal.

Despite this, it is noteworthy that, not the event per se, but the truth-procedure is absolutely dependent on what could be called a minimal historical logic. As we have seen, forcing imposes on the situation the recognition that the generic extension *always already belonged to it*. This is the logical power that belonging can exercise over inclusion. Paradoxically then, radical novelty can only exist with the support of this implicative past intrinsic to the retroaction of forced belonging. However, Badiou is very careful not to conflate this formal necessity for the logic of a minimal past with the event's absorption into History, which, conversely, would amount to the victory of inclusion over belonging.

In general, in *Being and Event* it seems that an event cannot be historicised without succumbing entirely to historicism. For many, it is the absolutism of this divorce between historicity and History that leaves Badiou open to accusations of politically useless, even dangerous abstraction.

> By refusing to venture into the dense thickets of real history, into the social and historical determination of events, Badiou's notion of the political tips over into a wholly imaginary dimension: this is politics made tantamount to an act of levitation. As a result, history and the event become miraculous (Bensaïd in Hallward, 2004: p.98)

HISTORY AND 'WORLDING'

Bensaïd perhaps phrases this problem too much in the language of an unreconstructed historical materialism, but the issue of the relation between the historicity of the event and History is a crucial one. I would argue that we have to wait for *Logics of Worlds* for a partial solution, though one that is basically a return to periodization.

History *should* be a key theme in *Logics of Worlds*. The explicit move from being-qua-being to being-there, from the mathematical formalisation of the generic set to the appearance of objects in worlds, cannot help but confront the issue of temporalisation. Surely, at least in the worlds in which humans appear and thus the worlds in which politics can occasionally burst forth, being-there is always already linked to a having-been-there? As we will see, this is inherent in the very function of worlds insofar as they are conservative by definition: the objects that worlds 'envelope' only exist or appear thanks to a sort of sedimented temporal density. Without even delving into the technicalities of Badiou's argument about the logical operations of worlds—or what I am calling 'worlding', in order to invoke a transitive process necessarily taking place in a temporal dimension[4]—it makes immediate

---

4. Badiou would no doubt balk at the Heideggerian resonances of 'worlding', and Heidegger is, surprisingly, even less of a reference point in *Logics of Worlds* than in *Being and Event*. However, insofar as it invokes the ontologico-existential concept of Being-in-the-World and thus a primordial throwness with an inevitable temporal dimension, I welcome these resonances, since the primordial giveness of worlds underpins my subsequent argument regarding the necessity of an appearance of a past in a world.

intuitive sense that one of the best ways to conserve the status quo is to appeal to the past. The notion of 'tradition' in particular has always served to justify congealed values and practices in the present (although an opposite use can be made of it, as I shall argue at the end of this chapter). What makes Badiou's analysis of worlds so valuable, however, is the way in which it clarifies the form that this conservative function of tradition continues to take long after modernity's supposed obliteration of tradition, and postmodernity's declaration of the end of History. It is eminently possible to speak coherently of today's *tradition of the ever new*.

In fact, I would argue that *Logics of Worlds* does not emphasise the role of History in the process of worlding enough. Whereas historicity is very evident in Book I, Book V and the conclusion, the coincidence between the logic of History-as-historicism and the logic of worlds is not made sufficiently clear in the Books comprising 'the Greater Logic' (II-IV). Nonetheless, it is there that it becomes evident that worlds are worlds insofar as they present infinity as finitude, generic multiplicity as differential identity, and eternity as forever time-bound. It is because there is no stable and established 'being of the whole' (*LW*, p.571) that worlds must be transitive processes of world*ing*. Since, ontologically, there is no minimum or maximum, but only a radical multiplicity that goes all the way down (and all the way up), a world is needed if a multiple is to be seized by a logic and impelled to exist in objective form. On to the limitless, generic inconsistency so carefully established in *Being and Event*, a world imposes minimums and maximums, 'floors' and 'ceilings', but also, I would insist, beginnings and ends, in order to en-globe a symbolic terrain and maintain it over time.

Of the three key functions of the transcendental index of a world—'minimum', 'conjunction' and 'envelope'—it is arguably the latter that, though essentially topological, already includes the outlines of what will later take the form of a temporal containment of change. The envelope ensures that a subset is contained by an initial set by establishing that there is an element that is 'smaller' than the latter but 'bigger' than the former (see Books II and III). In other words, by interposing itself between a subset and a set, an envelope can impose on a new and complex grouping of objects the assertion 'this is of *this* world'. It keeps the sub-set 'sub' in relation to the initial set. In still other words, the envelope polices the maximal element that marks the upper limit of a world, and must do so precisely because worlds are infinite and inconsistent. Is this not the logical correlate of an historical incorporation that insists 'this subset has emerged from the past of this world'? After all, the dictum of democratic materialism is clearly strengthened by being endowed with this kind of cloying historical weight: 'there *have only ever been* bodies and languages'.

And yet Badiou is no better in *Logics of Worlds* at accounting for the institution of completely new worlds than he was at explaining the genesis of situations in *Being and Event*.[5] This is arguably one of the profound limitations of the set-theoretical basis of Badiou's philosophy, insofar as the very power of a set derives from its purely

---

5. Feltham observes that "set theory, as a condition of philosophy, does not allow Badiou to transcribe philosophical and political concepts into its language" so that his turn towards it "comes at a considerable expense" (Feltham: 2008, 95). Chapter 3 of Gillespie: 2008 interrogates the difficulties of the related transcription of worldly being into the axiomatic formalism of sets.

axiomatic generation. Sets have no history 'of their own' in terms of their constitution (although they may have a kind of secondary meta-history as problems treated by certain mathematicians in certain times and places). This potential weakness
in the transition from atemporal abstraction to the temporalised concrete becomes
more visible when it is itself transposed into the problematic of worlds and appearance. For worlds cannot help but have a history, insofar as they are historicizing
mechanisms par excellence. Exactly because they are only a logic, a set of transcendental functions whose purpose is to bind infinity into narrative time, worlds
both cannot countenance absolute commencement (every novelty must be enveloped within them) and cannot *not* tell the imaginary story of their own origins
(History as the imposition of narrative consistency upon the flux of change).

This becomes much clearer when one juxtaposes the Greater Logic with
Book V on the forms of change, for it is there that Badiou says outright that
"the appearing of a being in a world is the same thing as its modifications in
that world" (*LW*, p.358) and "the object absorbs, as elements of the multiplicity
that it is, the modifications which include it within the time of the world" (359).
Modification may be the weakest form of change, having nothing to do with the
emergence of singularity, but it is also that which, at the most basic level, a world
must have some way of modulating in order to remain a world at all. So close
is modification to worlding itself that Badiou explicitly erases the distinction between time and space when defining it:

> [a modification is] simply a temporal cut among objective successions, that is, a
> set of transcendental indexings which are constitutive of a temporalized object.
> In what concerns the differential evaluation of their intensities, *temporal differenc-
> es have no unique features that would set them apart from spatial differences* (*LW*, p.589—
> my emphasis).

Let us translate Badiou's complex point into a simple example. Take the 'world'
of a political party and the object 'leader' in that world. To maintain the world of
this party, it must remain the same party following the 'modification' of its leadership. The introduction of a 'temporal cut' with a leadership change does nothing
dramatic to the intensity of the appearance of the object 'leader' in this world. An-
alysing the logic of this object would not be altered by considering it either as the
outcome of a recent leadership election (time) or as a role designated by the party's constitution (space, in the sense that the constitution distributes the relations
between roles and functions within the party). Conversely, if an individual leader
is widely seen to *be* the party, his or her departure or defection would put an end
to that party as a specific logic of appearance. No world could risk overinvesting in
the being of one of its elements in this way without endangering the formal continuity of its logical operations. Worlds impose their transcendental index precisely
because change at the level of modification happens all the time. This 'all the time',
however, must be constantly inscribed into 'the time of the world' to prevent the
world from unravelling into the infinity from which it is covertly hewn. Indeed, as
we have argued from the outset, the real enemy of the politics of radical novelty is
not apparent stagnancy (almost a rare privilege today), but perpetual modification,
especially when it is presented as truly significant change—a point we shall come back to.

But beyond the capacity to modify the constant low-level flux of weak change, worlds must also have the power to meet more significant change with 'facts'. I would suggest that facts are, to the temporal dimension invoked by historicity, what the envelope is to the logical dimension invoked by History: "A fact is a real change such that the site comes to be assigned an interiority of existence that is strictly inferior to the maximum" (586). As this definition suggests, both the envelope and the fact are concerned with policing the maximum, and thus with expanding the parameters of a world to en-globe even unpredictable phenomena. The all-important difference between the two, however, is the intervention of an evental site. Whereas the envelope is a basic function of a world's transcendental, and relates to History as the narrative of diachronic inclusion in that world, a fact is generated as an emergency response to the irruption of historicity. What is at stake in the envelope is the scope or reach of the world, what it can logically contain. What is at stake in a fact is much more serious: no less than the possible existence of the inexistent *in that world as it is*. If successful, a fact can prevent a site from achieving a maximal existence that would profoundly challenge the existing world by, as it were, bursting its envelope. Reduced to a fact, the site is nullified by being redescribed within the existing resources of History. Since the site *is* disruptively novel, we can be sure that History itself will have to be reconfigured in some way to accommodate the site's emergence, but this will only involve a rearrangement of pre-existing elements. In short, History ensures that nothing significant happens.

The theme of the 'end of History' has been central to both philosophical postmodernism and the related triumph of neoliberalism, as its infamous articulation by Francis Fukuyama demonstrates. Both are connected to the emergence of a vast logic of inclusive appearance termed 'globalisation'. In this term we can already hear a technology of worlding, for globalisation specialises in enveloping the flux of change (often generated by its own imposition onto, and dissolution of, previously discrete 'worlds') by reducing all phenomena to the immovable 'fact' of capital. What need for History in the face of this omnipresent fact? Marx demonstrates that the key trait separating the capitalist mode of production from those that preceded it (primitive, feudal) is its capacity to absorb class antagonism, seen as the very motor of History, within the apparent reciprocity of the contract. Whereas the antagonism between resistant slaves and their owners, or between serfs and their landlords, was massively visible and contained only through an equally visible dissymmetry in violent power, the antagonism between the worker and the bourgeois factory owner is both conjured away and actively maintained by the contract of 'free' wage labour. It is the 'justice' of the daily wage that hides the injustice of the extraction of surplus value during an invisible part of the working day. In this way, capitalism *includes* class antagonism within the system of abstract exchange established by money by turning the kernel of this antagonism, labour, into a commodity like any other. In so doing, it institutes a universal equivalence that is profoundly useful to worldly modulation in its empty formalism. Even the upheavals caused by capital's destruction of traditional social bonds and modes of existence can be phrased as 'progress', and turned to profit.[6] A sort of super-State (in Badiou's sense

6. This is basically Naomi Klein's thesis in *The Shock Doctrine* (Klein: 2007).

of 'state'), globalization aspires to manufacture what he calls an 'atonic world', that is, one whose "transcendental is devoid of points" (*LW*, p.420). If a point is the testing ground of a subject, against which it disciplines its body and produces an organ capable of cleaving to truth, then in a world without such points "there's no truth, nothing but objects, nothing but bodies and languages" (*ibid.*)—the wet dream of democratic materialism! Atonic worlds, then, are predicated on the declaration of the end of History-as-historicity insofar as they perfect History-as-historicism. Despite appearances, this is exactly what 'the end of history' means.[7]

However, Badiou shrewdly notes that this historicist theme of the end of History coincides with a "fetishization of the past as a separable culture" (*LW*, p.509), with, that is, a whole cultural industry of memorialization and museumization that finds its reflection, in academia, in the explosion of 'memory studies'. If historicity has been relegated to the dustbin of History, so that all we can expect from the present (and indeed the future) is the soporific sameness of atonicity, then the past becomes nothing more than a cultural monument to this transcendence of historicity. This is what Badiou is getting at with his most astonishing attack on historicism in *Logics of Worlds* (which nonetheless recalls the insistence, in *Peut-on penser la politique?*, that the most Marxist position is to allow History to destroy Marxism): "Democratic materialism has a passion for history; it is truly the only authentic historical materialism" (509). That such a statement could come from the pen of the author of *De l'idéologie* is testament to the break with History enacted in *Being and Event*.

The more subtle argument that emerges from Badiou's analysis in *Logics of Worlds*, however, is the notion that atonic worlds often maintain their atonicity by presenting themselves as 'tensed worlds' in which, conversely, every single degree of the transcendental corresponds to a point, a choice (*LW*, p.422). That is to say, the ideology of, as it were, pointless post-Historical existence given philosophical weight by the likes of Fukuyama and Sloterdijk, is often supported at a more banal level by the appearance of everyday existence as a kind of multiple choice exam, a dizzying array of supposedly consequential decisions (should I be a doctor or a lawyer, should I rent or get a mortgage, should I buy Prada or Dolce & Gabana?). It is not difficult to discern why choice should have become the mantra of consumer logic, not only on the high street but now in relation to education, healthcare and political representation. The mantra of choice conceals the absence of *true* choices, of points, behind the simulacrum of their omnipresence throughout an apparently tensed environment.

It is worth keeping in mind that this ambivalent logic is already apparent in Badiou's description of the past in democratic materialism as a 'fetish'. The technical Lacanian defninition of the fetish (see SVIII) emphasises the notion of a substitute object that sustains the disavowal of the maternal phallus, i.e., the imaginary

---

7. Peter Sloterdijk is the contemporary heir of Francis Fukuyama's post-ideological end of history thesis, insofar as he both rails against the antiquated zealotry of 'left fascists' in the academy who continue to cling to a politics of resentment, and advocates an essentially biopolitical vision of liberalism in which the excesses of partisan affect are regulated into something more 'civilized'. See his *God's Zeal: The Battle of the Three Monotheisms* (Cambridge: Polity, 2009).

possibility of a non-lacking Other, and thus the disavowal of the reality of castration. At bottom, castration is the devastating experience that one *cannot* chose to
have everything, which also entails the fact that each choice is also a loss rather
than, as in the consumer dream, a pure gain. But in so doing, the fetishist sets up
an erotic relation to a displaced object that, in its repetitive dialectic of in-satisfac-
tion, is very amenable to capitalist commodification, as Marx's own pre-Freudian
reference to the 'commodity fetish' in *Capital* underlines. The transformation of
the past into a fetish, then, serves the same dual function of disavowing[8] the existence of strong change (as traumatic for an atonic world as castration is for the individual) on the one hand, and of establishing a substitute object with which one
can enjoy a libidinally invested relation on the other. In this way, the spectacle of
the petrified past can be as pleasurable for the inert denizens of atonic worlds as is
the fetish object for the pervert:

> [T]he past is charged with the task of endowing these instants with a fictive ho-
> rizon, with a cultural density. This also explains why the fetishism of history
> is accompanied by an unrelenting discourse on novelty, perpetual change and
> the imperative of modernization [...] There are monuments to visit and devas-
> tated instants to inhabit. Everything changes at every instant, which is why one
> is left to contemplate the majestic historical horizon of what does not change
> (LW, 509-510)

EVENTAL RESURRECTION

This critique of the fetishization of History is balanced by Badiou's continuing
commitment to historicity in *Logics of Worlds*. More importantly, he now actively
links historicity to History by re-invoking something like the mechanism of periodization found in *Theory of the Subject*, but abandoned in *Being and Event*: in *Logics
of Worlds*, periodization becomes 'resurrection'. It is this concept that opens up the
possibility of an evental historiography that does not simply oppose History, still
less break with it in a complete sense, but rather plunders it for subjective resources.

The resurrection of an event refers to the extraction, from beneath the bar of
occultation imposed by a previous obscure subject, of the truth concealed within a
'defeated' sequence in the past. Crucially, however, this is enabled by the new present produced by a *contemporary* event, so that, as with periodization, we are dealing with a transhistorical diagonal between two or more points. The strictly ontological concerns of *Being and Event* militated against this kind of resonance between
events, primarily because the event was barred from leaving any kind of ontological trace other than the subjects whose fidelity to it alone gave it consistency. By
Logics of Worlds, the resonance of the past in the present is made possible by a rem-
nant of the former sequence that manages to outlive its historical defeat in the form
of an 'evental trace'. These evental traces are usually egalitarian declarations which,
though brutally silenced when first uttered, are nonetheless still legible in the very

---

8. In Book I of *Logics of Worlds*, Badiou already refers to the full body imposed by the obscure
subject on the production of a new present as "an atemporal fetish", but also argues that "the
goal of the obscure subject is to make this fetish a contemporary of the present that demands to
be occulted" (LW, p.60).

History that tells of this silencing. Badiou gives an extended example that is worth outlining, not least because, once again, it is self-evidently a sequence of conflict.

Although the slave rebellion led by Spartacus in 73 BC ended in defeat and the crucifixion of an estimated 6,000 slaves along the Appian Way, it left an evental trace in its wake, namely, the egalitarian assertion that 'slaves can decide to be free'. Despite the counter-evidence of its failure during the Spartacus sequence, the evental trace itself has echoed loudly down the subsequent centuries. For instance, in extending the implications of the French Revolution to a colony such as Saint-Domingue (present-day Haiti) through his own slave rebellion, slave-turned-military-genius Toussaint-Louverture earned the epithet 'black Spartacus'. Similarly, when German communists such as Rosa Luxembourg and Karl Liebknecht called themselves 'Spartakistes' in the early Twentieth Century, they resurrected the truth of the original rebellion in ancient Rome by redeploying it within a different world, now as the communist aspiration for liberation and a free future state: a 'red Spartacus'.

But as proof that this resurrection is not merely semantic or semiotic, Badiou points out that the Spartacus event also continues to provoke its reactive subjects. Thus, the Hungarian-born British novelist Arthur Koestler, who specialised in anti-communist literature, published a novel entitled *The Gladiators* in 1939. In it, Spartacus' slave army 'repeats' the mistakes of Stalinism, and before that of the Jacobins, by allowing their virtuous utopian vision of a free society, the 'Sun City', to lapse into an oppressive system based on terror. One can see a kind of inversion of periodization/resurrection in Koestler's ploy, insofar as he links a past failure to a present one, exposing as their common denominator the intrinsic terror of the Idea. Subsequently, however, Stanley Kubrick responded to Koestler's denial of the egalitarian essence of the Spartacus sequence with his own epic filmic account (in fact based not on Koestler's novel, but Howard Fast's), entitled simply *Spartacus* (1960). Although Badiou does not refer to it in *Logics of Worlds*, the famous scene in Kubrick's film in which Kirk Douglas' admission that 'I am Spartacus' is repeated man for man by practically his whole (defeated) army, is an exemplary demonstration of the militantly unified character of faithful subject bodies. It also reminds us of the example of the political party invoked above, in which the exclusive reliance on the body and person of a leader is incompatible with the formalism of worlding.

It is crucial to note that this conception of evental resurrection rests upon a productive rather than a destructive model of power. Worldly power never succeeds in simply obliterating what challenges it, as if the event could be wiped out once and for all. Rather, the power of worlding is, as we have seen, a kind of reaction-formation in response to events and thus, despite itself, the negative affirmation of their occurrence. From this point of view, the romantic revolutionary humanism that celebrates revolt as the spontaneous *cri de coeur* of a people driven to overthrow the forces that oppress them needs standing on its head: it is not because there is power that people revolt, it is because people revolt that there is (reactive) power. It follows that there is always a pathway of repression criss-crossing the texture of historical discourse that, in the manner of the Freudian dreamwork, can be undone by tracing that pathway back to the fragments of an occulted truth. In this way, the Historical can be shown to be hysterical, exposing a lacking Other rather than indulging the imago of a complete Other, a closed set.

Of course, the basic idea that official historical discourse can be read against the grain has long been the presupposition behind 'bottom up' approaches to working class, feminist and other 'minority' histories. This is graphically demonstrated in the 'symptomatic readings' of the Subaltern Studies group who 'resurrect' from within the gaps, silences and omissions of India's colonial historiography those faceless masses on the margins, yet also in the pores, of power's discourse (Guha: 1999). These were, indeed, necessary omissions in the worlding of the nation of India but Badiou's evental resurrection does not draw on this miraculous, Lazarus-like logic of redemptive, counter-hegemonic historiography whereby bodies buried in the (text of the) past are somehow brought to life. As Gayatri Spivak has famously pointed out, despite her own participation in it, this project was problematically framed as one of Marxist History (Spivak: 1988). For Badiou, the only living, active body is a subject-body in the present. What evental resurrection brings to this body is a historical resonance and intelligibility that gives it form and gravitas in its world.

One must be very careful here, however. For this image of the past resonating powerfully in the present threatens to lead one up the metaphysical garden path towards something like the vitalist mysticism of Bergsonian duration, in which the past is the very active becoming of time and not at all the melancholic trace of a lost present or presence. At least for the Bergson of *Matter and Memory*, Spartacus could be said to be an aspect of a transcendent continuum of virtual time that is not partially remembered but fully actualised in the various presents Badiou enumerates. Badiou has long been opposed to such vitalism, including its Deleuzian inflection.[9] Here, with regard to evental recurrence, as with periodization, he insists that the evental trace does not allow us to somehow knit together diverse segements of time into a single, living, and ultimately atemporal virtual totality. Rather, worlds are discrete, discontinuous and self-contained (even if objects, especially human ones, can appear in multiple worlds). There is no metaphysical contact between the subject-bodies of the slave army of ancient Rome and those of Toussaint-Louverture in the late Eighteenth Century. Evental resurrection always presupposes a contemporary world, a second event, a new body and the production of a new present.

The kind of historiography of historicity implied by resurrection is clarified in the conclusion to *Logics of Worlds*. Here, the engagement with appearing pushes Badiou towards shifting what was the axiomatic pre-giveness of the set in *Being and Event* towards a new dimension of duration enabled by the evental trace. This pushes the event away from being conceived as a break with the past, and towards the 'incorporation' of a resurrected past in the present:

> Through the incorporation of the world's past to the present opened up by the trace, it is possible to learn that prior to what happened and is no longer, the ontological support of this intense existence was an inexistent of the world (*LW*, p.507)

9. For Badiou's position with regard to Deleuze, see *D* as well as chapter 4 of *BoE* and 381-387 of *LW*.

This is very close to the implicative past of forcing but what is forceful is no longer the generic extension that cannot *not* be included, but rather the historicity written into worlding's reliance on History. Hence the injunction: "Interrogate the flashes, probe into their past without glory" (*ibid.*). The past *with* glory is the History written by the winners of the battle for control over the worlding of the world. Historicity, by contrast, enables "a new birth beyond all the facts and markers of time", commencing not a reductive but a "creative time" (*LW*, p. 508). Still adhering to the structure of periodization, Badiou asserts that the new present produced by a strong singularity is a "creation that both constitutes and absorbs a new type of past" (*LW*, p.509). It constitutes a new past by *re*-writing it, absorbing existing referents into the inauguration of a novelty (just as the Paris Commune existed as a referent before October 1917, but was transformed by its absorption into the Bolshevik sequence). In this sense, the subject does not simply refute worldly historicism by opposing to it an ahistorical singularity, if indeed such a thing could ever exist in a world. Instead, it sets about "restoring the past as the amplitude of the present" (*ibid.*).

By turning up the volume on what was only whispered apologetically between the lines of official history, "one reconstitutes a different past, a history of achievements, breakthroughs, which is by no means a cultural monumentality but a legible succession of fragments of eternity" (*ibid.*). Once again, this eternity is not the metaphysical one of a Bergsonian duration persisting beneath, or above, particular historical moments, but one produced *in* those moments and bequeathed to the future by them: "truths are eternal because they have been created and not because they have been there forever" (*LW*, p.512). Equally, and echoing Badiou's old Maoist theory of revolt, this eternality appears differently 'each time': "That it belongs to the essence of a truth to be eternal does not dispense it in the least from having to appear in a world and to be inexistent prior to this appearance" (*ibid.*). Moreover, it does not dispense the subject from the task of *making* this eternality appear, necessarily through a sort of anti-historicist evental historiography, "a historicity of exception" that "has no other criterion than to establish, between disparate worlds, the evidence of an eternity" (*LW*, p.513).

At the very end of *Logics of Worlds*, it becomes apparent that if Badiou is not pessimistic in the face of the apparent atonicity of the globalized world, it is because he maintains that there is a specifically human capacity to exist or appear in multiple worlds, thereby multiplying the possibility of participating in the infinity each one conceals. This is the positive flipside of the fact that worlding is an ultimately empty formal operation (although the atomic logic does demonstrate that it has a recursive effect on being itself). Unchained to the fixity of being, one can appear multiply, even if, to paraphrase Marx, this cannot be in a manner of our own choosing. This is what Badiou means when he suggestively remarks "The infinite of worlds is what saves us from every finite dis-grace" (*LW*, p.514). 'Finite dis-grace' here would refer to submission to the imperative of democratic materialism to 'live without Ideas', without participation in truth, which for Badiou is not to live at all but to plod, zombified, toward a living death: 'dis-grace', specifically, would refer to the denial or occultation of the event. But the genitive in Badiou's reference to 'the infinity *of* worlds' should be read in both ways. In the objective sense of this genitive, it is the sheer uncontainable plurality of worlds and the human capacity to appear differently in them that offers a way out of atonicity. But in the subjective sense of the same genitive, it is the disruptive multiplicity within every single word that makes it historical in the sense of being endowed with historicity.

EVENTAL HISTORIOGRAPHY

I would now like to adopt a rather programmatic mode in order to extract from Badiou's own philosophical practice, and particularly the notion of 'resurrection', an embedded 'evental historiography' already present in his work. Despite its resemblance to an oxymoron, the term evental historiography attempts to circumscribe an affirmative *use* of history that acknowledges history as ineradicably implicated in both the worlding and the unworlding of a world, breaking, therefore. Evental historiography then, aims to break with the event as a total break with history. Adopting this programmatic mode then, I will initially confine myself to six points—the first three negative, the last three positive—which together can serve as a definition of 'evental historiography'. I will then outline four general methodological steps which any such evental historiography would have to take. This methodology is a logical consequence of the definition of evental historiography, but it is also derived from a distillation of Badiou's own approach to various historical referents characterised by conflict.

Firstly then, evental historiography cannot be a free-floating interpretative activity that merely provides 'militant' perspectives on the texts of History. Evental historiography is not a hermeneutic practice that simply filters History in order to separate out putative events from their reactionary erasure. On the contrary, evental historiography presupposes the ultimately unnarratable historicity of its own conditions of possibility. That is, it presupposes an event. This event, therefore, does not wait to be unleashed from the confines of 'reactionary' historical discourse by means of a practice of radical re-reading. This would be to imagine evental historiography pulling itself up by its own bootstraps (drawing its own novelty from the novelty it reads into History). Evental historiography is not a history *of* events, a rational and transparent account of the origins and consequences of extraordinary happenings. Rather, it is a mode of (re)writing History which presupposes the aleatory supplement of an irruption of historicity, to which it is faithful, and by which it is thoroughly conditioned *in the present of its production*. This is very different from the paradoxes into which historicist truth claims lapse, despite the fact that they also emphasise the present in which historical truth is produced. Whereas the historicist claim that 'all reality or truth is historical' draws its ringing certainty from the exclusion of this very statement from the supposedly universal condition it describes (in other words, the historical conditions of emergence that made it possible for such a claim to pass as true), by complete contrast, evental historiography conditions itself not on certainty but on ignorance, on an unknowable multiple rather than a 'fact'.

Secondly, evental historiography does not contest or dispute dominant or, for that matter, emergent interpretations of historical incidents. It does not present a better, fuller, more rigorous or more accurate account of 'what really happened and why'. These are the discursive rules of the encyclopaedic historiography to which it is opposed. Because it does not claim to do history better than conventional historians, evental historiography must not get involved in either reformist or revisionist quibbles about this or that referent of history. We saw in Chapter 2 Badiou's careful efforts to set-aside both 'revisionist' and indeed 'progressive' histories of the French Revolution, the Paris Commune, the Bolshevik Revolution and so on, in order to be able to begin his own evental distillations of them. Furthermore, this setting-aside clarifies the fact that evental historiography must eschew every liberal model of communication of the Rorty/Habermas variety, particularly their faith in the truth-constituting power of *discussion, debate, and dispute*. As we have seen, conflict must be maintained in its material, scissional dimension rather than being displaced onto the binarism of discourse. Such a 'talking shop' epistemology invariably absorbs the event into the encyclopaedia, subordinating its militant truth to a banal version of contested *veridicité*, a mere 'gentleman's disagreement' over referents. Such disagreements hardly constitute an attack on official historiography: they are its very legitimating modus operandi.

For this reason, and thirdly, evental historiography must subtract itself from every vestige of causal explanation. Causality theorises links of mutual influence between assumed entities and/or states of affairs, rendering normative—because marked by a retrospectively constructed necessity—the outcome of a supposedly objective causal chain. Essentially, our current reality happened, and will continue to happen, because of this unbreakable chain of causation. Yet the linear causality of Newtonian physics cannot be transplanted into the specifically human realms of love, politics, science and art. Moreover, insofar as causality describes an arc of necessity terminating in a present that it justifies, it is intrinsically *interested and particular*. On this terrain only, evental historiography, in its opposition to official history, coincides with that broadly Foucaultian version of historicism that reintroduces the dimension of power: the genealogical transformation of 'causality' into a narrative justification produced by the winners of the battle to write History.

Fourthly, and more positively now, evental historiography distils from the 'facts' of historical discourse evental statements which a wider militant truth-procedure deploys to force a *contemporary* truth. As we saw with regard to 'periodization' and the notion of 'Communist invariants', it creates a diagonal between two points of rupture, enabling past and present to resonate, as in an echo-chamber (although the relevant 'resonant frequency' is always that of the so-called present). In this sense, the ultimate result of an evental historiographical enquiry is not a lengthy, quasi-forensic narrative which, through the re-interpretation of old sources and perhaps the discovery of new ones, reconfigures 'our understanding' of History. Rather, its ultimate result is a ringing declaration of universal, *and therefore timeless*, import: 'all men are created equal', 'workers of the world unite', 'E = MC_2', 'there is no such thing as a sexual relation', 'slaves can be decide to be free', and so on.

Fifthly then, and perhaps counter-intuitively, the power of evental historiography comes from the subtraction of such egalitarian statements from the historical specificity of their 'original' conditions of enunciation. It is politically vital that concepts like 'Man' in the emancipatory discourse of the 'rights of man' evade reduction to the *sans culottes*, or even to black slaves and women of the revolutionary period of the late eighteenth century. If Enlightenment universalism has been rightly subjected to critique from a postmodernist direction (for the totalitarian destiny of its rationality) and from a postcolonial direction (for the imposition of its covertly Eurocentric world-view onto non-European peoples), this is arguably because it has not been universal enough. In fact, Thomas Paine's 'Man' of universal rights must be drained of all particularities, including not only those of sex and gender, but the specific inequalities of the *ancien régime* to which it was (historically) a response. Only then might the French (but not only French) Revolution persist in, through, and beyond the perpetual Thermidor of evental reaction that is the default setting of all 'worlds'.

Sixthly and finally, evental historiography does not make truth-claims in the usual sense. Far from producing 'facts' deemed true (insofar as they correspond in a relation of adequation to a pre-existing veridical schema), evental historiography produces statements that *demand* change on the basis of the implications of a generic truth that cannot be verified. All statements of truth in Badiou's sense have singular effects without providing rhetorical descriptions or rational justifications. However, the specifically historical form of truth's articulation in evental historiography—its scandalous citation from the text of accepted, official history—gives it a vicarious encyclopaedic presence that smuggles evental consequences into the very heart of a world. Militant fidelity to a truth necessarily appears in any world as irrational and extremist (terroristic, even). Yet adding a historical dimension to militant praxis enables a deconstruction of the world's justificatory self-description in and through its own terms.

Given these six interrelated traits, how would one proceed, methodologically, in undertaking such an evental historiography? The four minimal methodological steps indispensable to an evental mode of historiography are as follows:

1. Identification of an 'historical referent'
2. Distillation of an 'evental sequence'
3. Extrapolation of an 'evental statement'
4. Contemporary incorporation of the 'evental statement'

First Step: One would have to identify a basic discursive unit already at work in official history: what I will call an *historical referent*. Because evental historiography searches out occulted or denied events, and because events radically challenge their worlds, the most pertinent referents inevitably 'represent' major conflicts. Examples might include referents such as 'the English Civil War', 'the Counter-Reformation', 'the Intifada', and so on. Narratives of conflict are the traces of the state's attempts to police evental sites and subdue evental implications. The same applies to the sub-divisions of monolithic (that is, nation-state based) History, so that 'Impressionism' might function as a referent within art history, 'the twelve-tone system' for the history of western music, 'Darwinism' for natural history, and so on. Regardless of their disciplinary location, however, all historical referents will consist, minimally, in: a chronologically organised configuration of incidents, protagonists and putative causes and consequences, this ensemble being contained in a broad narrative of conflict. Official history necessarily includes accounts of conflict of this kind in order to construct its triumphal self-justification, in order to play out in cultural, collective, social memory the story of this *on-going* victory—what Foucault has called 'history in praise of Rome' (Foucault: 2003). If we take the nation as one type of 'world', this is clear in the role of narratives of conflict in nation-building, as is particularly clear in the case of the Truth and Reconciliation Commission in post-Apartheid South Africa.

This is not at all incompatible with the demonstrable fact that the internal elements of an historical referent—names, dates, motivations, triggers etc.—is a site of debate and dispute. On the contrary, the primary characteristic of a historical referent is its status as a stable 'container' for such dispute. Thus, while historians obviously argue about the complex causes of the French Revolution, for example, they share a founding presupposition around the general parameters of the referent itself (the fluid ensemble including the Estates General, the storming of the Bastille, Robespierre and St. Juste, the first Paris Commune, and so on). It is this sharing that enables disputes around the ordering and emphases of these elements. In other words, the referent functions as an 'envelope' and, if challenged by a novelty, also as the wellspring of 'facts'. The term *historical referent* therefore pertains neither to an established discursive 'object', nor even to the process of incessant dispute which partially triangulates such an 'object'. Rather, the term 'historical referent' pertains to the *enveloping principle* under whose heading these hermeneutic clashes can take place without threatening to transgress disciplinary boundaries. Historical referents are like Lacan's *points des captions* which pin, provisionally, the slippery fabric of the (historico)symbolic text.

Second Step: From this complex and always overdetermined historical referent, an *evental sequence* must be distilled. If a referent regulates the contents of a unit of historical discourse in order to contain, or discipline, the referential dispute constitutive of (liberal, democratic) history, an evental sequence cuts a diagonal through the field thereby constituted. A segment of the statist chronological count is cut out, like a patch from a quilt. An evental sequence can therefore be considered a 'smaller' sub-unit of the larger terrain enclosed by the historical referent, except that, as a diagonal, it arranges its material in such a way as to elevate it above the referential dispute. As we have already said, the result of the 'interpretation' of this sequence is not a fact, but a singular demand. As the term 'sequence' suggests, however, its form is classically chronologico-causal: a chain of interrelated incidents with a beginning, a middle, and an end, animated by some kind of internal logic, all marked by the minimal historical positivism of an assumption of past facticity. It is crucial that the evental sequence occupy an indispensable place within the historical referent as a whole, i.e., that in its absence, the referent itself would cease to be. Far from being concerned with incidents that happened in the wings of History's epic theatre, evental historiography draws on the most familiar aspects of History's official script, but edits it in a subversive manner (in this sense again, evental historiography is quite different from a 'symptomatic reading' or a 'bottom-up' approach).

Clearly, the 'editing' decision that determines the start and finish of such an evental sequence is not a rule-governed activity. Rather, it is a subjective intervention which cleaves into the text of official history by means of a choice that is 'illegal' from the point of view of that history, particularly in terms of the abruptness of its excision. The sequence is cut out, apparently violently, from a broader chain that is assumed to construct a causality which is therefore suspended. However, unlike the mathematico-ontological 'axiom of choice', it is not the case that the evental sequence that results from this *historiographic* axiom of choice is indiscernible (*BE*, p.499). On the contrary, history must recognise the sequence as one of its multiples, for it is cut from the same cloth. The evental sequence actually concentrates the radical element which official history is forced to include in order to constitute itself in reaction to it. What matters above all, then, is not the empirical *outcome or result* of an overall historical referent (what it led to and what lessons have been learnt from it: history as pedagogy), but the infinite implications of the evental sequence that resonate well beyond the discrete segment of chronological time enveloped by that referent. To take an obvious example, the truth of the French Revolution lies not in the 18th Brumaire of Napoleon Bonaparte, but in the *Declaration of the Rights of Man and of the Citizen*. Likewise, the truth of the Chinese Cultural Revolution lies not in Mao's eventual reassertion of state power (even less in Deng Xiaoping's subsequent 'economic reforms'), but in the experiment in direct mass democracy between 1966 and 1967. These sequences are fundamental to their respective referents, and yet, by affirming them in separation from their putative empirical consequences (often calamitous), they begin to radiate a truth incompatible with official causality. From this point of view, and as I tried to show in Chapter 2, even a history of failure carries the inerradicable promise of victories to come.

Third Step: From these sequences, an *evental statement* must be extrapolated. Such a statement is the final product, but not the final aim or goal, of evental historiographical enquiry. While the evental sequence is an apparently truncated segment of historical time, the evental statement crystallises, in a clear and simple assertion, the kernel of logic borne out, and carried along, by that sequence. This logic is essentially atemporal, even though it finds (encyclopaedic) support for its intervention into the world in its parasitic relation to historicized temporality. The refinement of the implications of an event into an evental statement separates the truth it carries from the time-bound contingency of the occurrence by means of which it first irrupted into the world: it is the result of a subtraction and a simplification. It is tempting to think of the evental statement as, linguistically speaking, a kind of performative insofar as it attempts to *do something by means of a saying*, i.e., to force a change by means of its enunciative circulation. Yet it is certainly not a constative reducible to protocols of proof or correspondence. Rather, it is a declarative so exorbitant that it defies the very speech community whose shared normative framework normally supports performative modalities of discourse. Perhaps most importantly, and unlike the context-bound efficacy of the performative, the evental statement carries a transformative potential well beyond the social, historical, political, cultural confines of its origin.

It matters little whether the evental statement can plausibly be ascribed to a specific actor caught within the lens of the historical referent itself, or whether it is an explicitly retrospective summation of the logic condensed within a sequence, formulated off-stage by the evental historian herself. This is a vital difference between truth-procedures per se, and evental historiography as a specific mode within a truth-procedure. As discussed in Chapter 3, Badiou is generally at pains to point out that the name of an event is supernumerary and drawn from the edge of the void. However, in the pseudo-hermeneutic subversions of evental historiography, the evental statement *is* highly readable, but primarily as the undecomposable rationality animating the evental sequence. As long as the statement has the stark, summary power of a slogan, it is a matter of relative indifference as to who coined it, or when, or why. To put this in Lacanian terms again, the evental statement aspires to have the integral, anti-Symbolic transmissibility of the *matheme*: evental historiography aims to be a science of the real of historicity rather than a science of reality.

Fourth Step: In fact, this fourth step precedes the first (such is the recursive structure of evental truth), for it relates to the deployment of this new evental statement in a *contemporary* sequence of fidelity to an event which is necessarily presupposed by evental historiography. The circulation of the evental statement in a present conflict constitutes the cutting edge of praxis without which the former has absolutely no meaning or value. For example, merely citing the historical referent 'Spartacus', establishing the evental sequence that encompassed the unprecedented political organisation of ex-slaves into freedom fighters, and then distilling from that sequence the resonant evental statement 'slaves can decide to be free', does not of itself constitute an *evental* historiography. The first through to the third steps alone are insufficient. They remain too much on the hermeneutic level. Merely attempting to extricate 'Spartacus' from the broader reactionary historical referent of 'the Servile Wars' threatens to actually shore up the pejoratively 'historical'—i.e., firmly past, academic, abstract—nature of the 'Spartacus' event. Properly speaking, the resurrection of the Spartacus event only becomes active if a connection is made between its infinite truth and contemporary modalities of unfreedom and resistant political organisation. This fourth step, which is really the first, is not a merely semantic connection, however. It is the full blown *incorporation* of the evental statement into a contemporary subject-body for which it functions as an unvarying guide in its encounter with points. These four operations—identification, distillation, extrapolation and incorporation—are the supports of an evental historiography that obtains historicity from History.

RANCIÈRE'S *THE NAMES OF HISTORY*

An important supplement to this notion of evental historiography can be found in Jacques Rancière's exceptional but rarely studied book, *The Names of History: On the Poetics of Knowledge* (Rancière: 1994). This supplement is needed for a number of reasons.

Firstly, Badiou's anti-historicism has caused him to remain extremely circumspect about historical discourse in general, so much so that we have just been

forced to render explicit what remains entirely implicit in his approach to historical sequences of conflict. Secondly then, the four-step methodology we have distilled from that approach in fact barely deserves the name 'historiography'. This
term is usually understood to refer to the history of history writing, i.e., to the mu-
tations in the literary conceits, scientific aspirations, archival methodologies, periods of analysis and privileged objects of study that occur in the discipline of history
over time. Evental historiography is doggedly indifferent to these issues. Its value
lies rather in the support it gives to the militant, who is decidedly *not* a historian.
History functions for the militant only as the *logical* point of entry of the infinity of
a truth into the finitude of a necessarily historicised world.

But is this stark opposition between evental historicity and historical discourse
really helpful to the militant, given that we have shown how crucial the historicis-
ing function is to worlding? Might historical *knowledge*, not simply a world's logical
reliance on the appearance of a past, contain important subjective resources? If so,
we would have to qualify our claim that the result of evental historiography only
takes the form of an evental statement incorporated into a new present. We would
have to entertain the idea that it could result in something compatible with historical discourse itself, appearing as such in its world. The residual structuralism
of Badiou's set-theoretical framework in fact makes this difficult to conceive: in a
very undialectical way, it constrains History, if taken solely as a conservative statist function, to being, like the state itself, fundamentally ahistorical and unchanging. But by taking the term 'historiography' seriously, we can entertain the notion
that History need not always be statist to the same degree, or in the same way, in
all times and places, and also that the style of its writing might be connected to its
proximity to, or distance from, the state.

This is what Rancière offers us in *The Names of History*, where he examines the
discursive logics of what we might provocatively term an 'event' within historiography: namely, the 'new history' developed by the *Annales* School that emerged in
France in the 1930s. At first sight, the approach refined by this group—including,
among others, Marc Bloch, Lucien Febvre, Fernand Braudel and, more recently,
Roger Chartier—seems totally incompatible with evental historiography. For the
Annales historians saw themselves as breaking precisely with the traditional focus
on cataclysmic events. They abjured elite politics, diplomacy and the 'Great Man'
theory of history with its obsessive focus on kings and battles and Machiavellian
court intrigues. They distanced themselves, too, from the sweeping narrative style
of dynastic monarchical histories, overly enamoured of the epic registers of Pliny
and Tacitus. Instead, the *Annales* historians emphasised a distinctively modern, scientific drive for uncovering truths which they viewed not as points of revelatory rupture, but as slow-burning, subterranean, often inhuman forces stretching
over almost geological timescales: they were the first advocates of *la longue durée*,
sometimes spanning millennia. In their search for these slow-burning truths, they
appealed to other sciences: geography, demographics, statistics in general, economics, political science and above all sociology. Though critical of Marxist class
analyses, their work was marked by the desire to recover the anonymous influence of the masses rumbling away beneath or behind spectacular events, often

favouring the rural regions over the capital cities for this reason. It was thus democratic as well as scientific in its aspirations.

What Rancière's analysis of the *Annales* School brings out, however, is not so much the success of what it consciously aimed at (ultimately the sociologization of history over and against its politicization), but rather the contradictions that it unconsciously encompassed. For these contradictions triangulate what is truly specific about modern historical discourse, namely, the following tripartite contract:

> The first is a scientific contract, which necessitates the discovery of the latent order beneath the manifest order [...] The second is a narrative contract, which commands the inscription of the structures of this hidden space [...] in the readable forms of a story with a beginning and an end, with characters and events. And the third is a political contract, which ties what is invisible in science and what is readable in narration to the contradictory constraints of the age of the masses (Rancière: 1994, p.9)

The emphasis on any one of these to the exclusion of the others leads to the suicidal self-destruction of historiography. Too much science, and the past becomes a mere prop for an objectivity about which, in the end, there is nothing much to write. Too much narrative, and the past becomes a monolithic and unchanging mythological chronicle. Too much politics, and the past becomes the rhetorical topos of a certainty that can persuade all sorts of excesses (as Demosthenes used the glory of past Athenian battles to rouse citizens of the Greek city-state into further wars).

Each of these biases unsettles the fundamental gap between word and thing that, according to Rancière, is the true wellspring of both history and historicity. The particular attitude taken to this relation between word and thing defines divergent practices of history writing. Thus, Marxist historians involved in the 'science' of ideology-critique tend to see all words as veils drawn over the truth of social contradictions. For example, behind the grand *political* discourse surrounding the French Revolution was a minor *social* shift in favour of the bourgeoisie (Alfred Cobban's argument in *The Social Interpretation of The French Revolution*). This kind of history prioritises things, by getting rid of deceptive words. Mythological, or we could even say 'postmodern', historians tend to see things as inhabiting a noumenal realm quite inaccessible to words. Their writings thus become pure linguistic constructions with aesthetic value, but no obligation to reveal buried causalities or the marginalised masses. This kind of history prioritises words at the expense of the truth of things. Political historians, armed but also burdened by an 'agenda', tend to lapse into believing that they can suture the gap between words and things by recovering the latter through the former—as when, for example, 'bottom up' historians hope to restore a voice to the silenced victims of official history's exclusions. But this is to misunderstand politics, basing it on inclusion in a collective consensus—here regarding the past—rather than, for Rancière as for Badiou, on the mobilisation of dissensus (Rancière: 2010). This kind of history cancels out the difference between words and things altogether, ultimately condemning itself to silence.

By contrast, Rancière enjoins historical discourse to *maintain* the irreducible gap between words and things from which it draws its own existence and mission.

Hence his reference to the role of the 'historical unconscious' (Rancière: 1994, 61-75), in which 'unconscious' should be understood in the Lacanian sense that builds on the Saussurean bar between signifier and signified, words and 'things'. Lacan's reference to speech as the 'locus of the Other' means that the signifiers we are forced to employ precede and exceed us, but also that we are constitutively barred from ever occupying this locus ourselves. That the place from which we speak never quite coincides with the Other is precisely why we *have* to speak with others through the mediation of the Other at all. Rancière makes the same point about historical discourse, in which this constitutive gap between words and things is elongated across time. The place *from* which the historian speaks or writes cannot be that *of* which she speaks or writes. After all, if things and words coincided, if there were no split between events and their record, history as a discipline would not exist. There would only be archives and our uncontroversial, immediate access to them. It is because there *is* a split or gap between words and things that there is both historicity (recall that the disjunction between representation and presentation is what makes sets 'historical' for Badiou as well), and the discourse of history which testifies to this gap—without eliminating it.

Just as the neurotic subject *is* a relation to castration and thus an orientation around a lack, so history is a relation to death, to what is not granted life by the partial documents of the past. In the kind of historiography Rancière admires then, this relation becomes a paradoxical cleaving together of both an ethico-political commitment to the *recovery* of the dead (the unheard voices of the anonymous poor, for example) and an equal commitment to the *maintenance* of death, insofar as it is the very condition of historicity. As Rancière puts it, "The redemption of absence is needed for history to be separated from novelistic treachery. But a *contract* with absence, the inclusion of death, is needed for it to be separated from the old tradition of chronicling" (Rancière: 1994, p.64). Novelistic treachery gives up on truth by subordinating history entirely to literature, whereas chronicling overconfidently assumes that it captures the truth of the past in its net of words, as if it could attain the literal by tightening the weave of its text. For 'novelistic treachery', death is everywhere since the word can never bring life to things anyway, whereas for the tradition of 'chronicling', death does not really exist because all of life is gathered up in the word as a comprehensive narrative of everything that has been. What Rancière seeks, and finds, in the *Annales* approach, is a third way, one that recovers the dead without cancelling out the death upon which history thrives. We have already encountered this logic of the maintenance of the emptiness of the cause in our discussion of *objet a* in the last chapter. Here, it is specifically applied to what could be called historical desire.

Rancière finds the exemplary exponent of this mode of historiography not in the *Annales* School itself, but in the figure whom Lucien Febvre, at least, was happy to call its founding father: the idiosyncratic French historian, Jules Michelet. It is Michelet, claims Rancière, who invents a solution to the impasses of the 'royal-empiricist' paradigm, i.e., the common relation to word and thing in both elite histories of sovereignty (royal), and 'scientific' histories that claim to ventriloquize the masses (empiricist). Michelet does so by opposing to it what Rancière calls the 'republican-romantic' paradigm (Rancière: 1994, p.42). This paradigm is republican insofar as it is directly conditioned by the French Revolution itself, carrying the principles of egalitarianism into the heart of historical discourse. It was Michelet who first insisted that history must include the people, not just their leaders and institutions. Before his example then, it is easier to see that Rancière is responding not so much to an event within historiography (something Badiou, of course, would refute) but to a fidelity to the French Revolution that takes *historiographic form*. That is, if the revolutionary calendar responded to the need to invent a "creative time" (*LW*, p.508), Michelet was among those who tried to respond, in the wake of that temporality, with a new history that would keep it going.

This paradigm is also Romantic, however, in the sense that it sings at moments rather syrupy odes to the honesty of the French peasantry, the fecundity of the French land, the beauty of the spirit of fraternity and freedom that flowered among the French people, and so on and so forth. This tone of sentimentality and its ideological coupling to the national framework in fact make Michelet an ambivalent figure to be held up as the founder of the *Annales* School, which, by stark contrast, emphasised the sobriety of statistics and transnational framing devices, such as the Mediterranean Sea for Braudel. Nonetheless, Rancière is adamant that modern historical discourse must emulate Michelet's republican-romantic paradigm "as long as it wishes to remain a history and not a comparative sociology or an annex of economic or political science" (Rancière: 1994, p.42). For Rancière then, very much in line with Badiou's interpretation, the Romantic ode to the nation in Michelet is in fact a mode of fidelity to the appearance of a militant collectivity: 'France' is the name of the subject that emerges from the French Revolution.

Consistent with his assertions about the connections between aesthetics and politics elsewhere, specifically with those concerning the democratic credentials of the 'aesthetic regime' (Rancière: 2006), Rancière argues here that Michelet's importance resides in significant part in his invention of a *style* of history writing. Far from being a mere decorative innovation, this style is a revolutionary redistribution of the historical logic determining the word's relation to the thing. Thus, if other accounts of the past had struggled to simultaneously redeem and maintain death, Michelet invents "the narrative that is not one and [...] thereby suits the event that doesn't have the character of an event" (Rancière: 1994, p.43). Despite their divergence on the issue of the politics of aesthetics, does Rancière's formulation here not immediately make us think of Badiou's sensitivity to the inexistence of the event and its incompatibility with knowledge? Could Michelet's narrative 'that is not a narrative', of an event 'that is not an event' correspond to Badiou's forcing, but within historical discourse? The narrative form that Michelet invents still deals with proper names and the incidents connected to them, as all historiography must, but it breaks up the diegesis of seamless presentation by inserting the historian into the scenes he recounts, thereby closing the gap between the event and its document, and between the putative past and the living present. As Hayden White puts it in his preface to *The Names of History*, "Michelet goes into the archive not in order to *read* the documents as the dead indices of events now past, but in order to immerse himself in those documents *as* fragments of the past still living in the present" (xvi). Again, doesn't this reminds us of Badiouian resurrection?

In his *History of the French Revolution*, Michelet will sustain the balancing act of redeeming and maintaining death by avoiding the representational trap of 'giving a voice' to the voiceless, of turning the historical stage over to *les peuples* and mock-humbly receding to the back of the stalls. On the contrary, says Rancière, Michelet *shows* the people's silence: "He invents the art of making the poor speak by keeping them silent, of making them speak as silent people […] the historian keeps them silent by making them *visible*" (Rancière: 1994, pp.5-46). Whenever he reports a speech from this period, Michelet does not convey its content, like a journalist reporting on the facts of the past. Instead he emulates the subjective power that speech had in the moment of its original enunciation. In this way, its status as what Badiou would call a 'subject language' is productively doubled by the prosopopeia of the historian. Michelet therefore also closes the gap between speaker and content, name and word, and even—contra Derrida—between word and *voice*. History invariably deals with proper names, but the challenge is to enable these names to speak, to produce words that resonate. Merely reporting words at one remove deprives them of voice, killing them, but by taking the non-place of the silent and echoing their voice, word and voice are made synonymous. This also has the effect of effacing the distinction, posited by Emile Benveniste, between narrative and discourse, where narrative is the presentation of scientifically established proofs, and discourse is the art of persuasion. Michelet does present material gleaned from archives but uses it to move the reader to feel the passion that originally animated the scenes thereby re-staged. This would be dubiously Bergsonian, except that it is only achieved by approaching the documents of the past like a text of the unconscious, with the historian occupying not the place of the other, as if it were possible to speak in their place and on their behalf, but the locus of the Other, the gap or lack that allows those documents to speak otherwise.

According to Rancière, this logic even operates at the syntactical level of Michelet's prose in the form of a calculated oscillation of tenses. Whereas conventional history generally prefers the distanced neutrality of the third person past tense, Michelet switches strategically between the preterit and the present tense in order to both present archival perspectives, and affectively induce in the reader the subjective significance of the archived scenes. In contemporary cinematographic terms, we could say that conventional history prefers the equivalent of the uninterrupted establishing shot, with the camera panning from a distance to allow for maximum information; whereas Michelet's lyrical approach adopts the equivalent of attributive shots, where the point of view of the camera becomes a subject among the others it records, jostled by the hurly burly of its subject. But this analogy falls down when, at his most intense moments, Michelet purges his expression of any and every "temporal mark in order to absolutize, in a nominal phrase, the meaning of the event ("No conventional symbol! All nature, all mind, all truth!")" (Rancière: 1994, p.49). The timelessness of this nominal phrase surely has deep connections to the invariance of Badiou's egalitarian eventual statement. Rancière clarifies its opposition to worldly temporalization: the nominal phrase is the neutralization of the *appearance of the past*. This appearance is the historian's cross to bear, what motivates his desperate recourse to the "contemporary soci-ologist". The appearance of the past takes on what is said of nontruth: uncertain-ty, death, inessentiality. The nominal phrase effaces this nontruth. It is a narra-tion without a past and an affirmation without a subject (Rancière: 1994, p.49)

With the exception of the last claim—since Badiou would certainly insist on the presence of a subject—does this passage not strike us as a nuanced account of the *incorporation* of historicity into History, beyond the simple antagonism between the two? Could this not move us beyond the merely logical necessity, in a world, for the appearance of a past upon which evental historiography seemed to rely, and towards an immanent disturbance of History, after which the transcendental of a world could never be the same?

THE IDEA OF HISTORY VERSUS THE HISTORY OF IDEAS

I have been arguing throughout this chapter that a creative relation to History through an evental mode of historiography can and indeed must function as a di-mension of the subjective truth-procedure. In many ways then, we have circled back to the positive concept of 'nostalgia' we discovered in Badiou's encounter with Beckett at the end of the last chapter. Just as nostalgia emerged there as a re-ordering of personal memories with a view to holding open the possibility of possi-bility even in the face of both death and the absence of an event, so the anti-histor-icist historiography we have carved out in this chapter disrupts History's worlding function with a view to insisting on the 'fact', precisely, that *there have been truths*, even if it is difficult to discern their circulation in the present. Against the back-drop of the apparent atonicity of globalisation, this constitutes an end to the 'end of History' and the beginning of History's transformation into a source of 'cour-age', again in the Beckettian sense, such that contemporary existence can be made less point-less.

I would now like to underline the importance of the 'Idea' in Badiou's recent thought in providing a space for this courageous relation to a nostalgically rec-ollected past that opens onto a transformative futurity. In the *Second Manifesto for Philosophy* and in *The Communist Hypothesis*, as well as the connection made with Life at the conclusion of *Logics of Worlds*, a concept of the Idea is developed that not only further articulates history and the event, but also implies a durability to the Idea that potentially provides the resistant individual with a militant resource even in the absence of the event. As I will go on to suggest, this indicates that History, sufficiently reworked, may provide what seems to be rigorously excluded in *Being and Event*: a radical because historically informed political imaginary, in something like Castoriadis' sense.

It is evident in *The Second Manifesto* that the 'Idea' is Badiou's response to the ne-cessity for a timeless truth to appear in a temporalised world. But it becomes more evident in *The Communist Hypothesis* that this appearance must also be in a *histori-cised* world. The latter text is closest to the concerns of *Logics of Worlds*, and particu-larly to the logic of 'our' globalised, neoliberal world, in which the term 'commu-nism' is a vital element of its historicist worlding, insofar as the dominant narrative has it that the death of communism was also the end of History and the birth, we could say, of atonicity. Moreover, Badiou's theory of the Idea directly addresses our on-going concern with the emergence of the subject from the constraints of the individual: "The Idea", he says explicitly in *The Second Manifesto*, "is the *mediation* between the individual and the subject of a truth" (*SM*, p.119—my emphasis), referring also to "this theory of the Idea as the exposition of a simple individual in its becoming-Subject" (*SM*, p.125).

Badiou's major reference point for the Idea in *The Second Manifesto* is, predictably, Plato. However, this is very much a materialist Plato rather than the standard metaphysical and idealist Plato whose realm of the 'Forms' is seen to be 'abstract' and 'extra-worldly'. That these same accusations are levelled at Badiou is indeed a result, in part, of his avowed Platonism. Yet the quite specific nature of Badiou's Platonism is already a riposte to these critiques: as he puts it rather defensively, "I am a sophisticated Platonist, not a vulgar Platonist" (*SM*, p.35). According to the vulgar Platonist, the Idea is the absolute, eternal and universal essence of things but also radically separate from them, occupying a quite distinct, immutable and incorruptible realm. This is idealist to the extent that this separate realm of the Ideal Forms governs the non-ideal realm of things, not the other way around. Badiou's sophisticated Platonism, by contrast, emphasises not only the abstraction of mathematical truths which are indeed eternal and more real than reality,[10] but also, and crucially, the inexistence of such truths outside their material inscription in the realm of matter. If Badiou's Platonism is 'of the multiple', it is because it is both against the transcendent One of a single unified Being, and constitutively entangled in the infinite multiplicity of things.

For this reason, by *The Second Manifesto* Badiou's notion of the Platonic Idea comes to emphasise the crucial notion of *participation*, referring broadly to the necessary passage of truth through worldly forms. It is this that prevents the idealist separation of the Idea from the realm of matter, insisting instead on their dialectical co-implication. Badiou discerns this primacy of participation even in the Idea that, in *The Republic*, Plato places at the pinnacle of the hierarchy of Ideas, that of the Good. This Good is not, as the vulgar Platonists would have it, a conceptual horizon regulating the political life of the ideal city-state, run, top-down, by a philosopher-king whose wisdom grants him privileged access to it. As Badiou had already argued in *The Century*, such an Idea would lend itself to the tyrannical reduction of the gap between this relentlessly abstract Good and the perceived deviations from it by the 'unruly' population. On the contrary says Badiou, the Platonic Good is manifested in the immanent, collective experience of the inhabitants of this city-state not *of* the truth—where the genitive indicates a direct encounter with something nonetheless external—but *in* the truth. This all-important

10. In the first *Manifesto for Philosophy* Badiou makes it clear that the 'Platonic gesture' consists in drawing on the abstraction of Platonic truth in order to 1) counter sophism, 2) separate truth from its historical conditioning, and 3) invoke the logic of the matheme as the mode of writing proper to truth. In the-then current context, this Platonic gesture was needed to critique 1) the dominance of the linguistic turn, 2) the Nietzschean historicization of truth in postmodernism and 3) the poetic 'suture' in neo-Heideggerian philosophies that correspondingly devalue mathematics.

'in' indicates both the individual's immersion in the subject and the necessary inscription of the Good in the world, outside of which it has no essence or existence
whatsoever.

The materialist principle of participation, then, is what thwarts the Idea of
the Good being separated, metaphysically, from the realm of things. It ensures
that the Idea itself is never presentable in its proper fullness, since it *is* presenta-
tion-in-truth in a determinate world, and therefore conditioned by the logic of
appearance of that world. If "there is no Idea of the Idea" (SM, 121), it is because
each Idea appears according to a world's specific logic and cannot be abstracted
into a single, overarching Archimedian point. Thus, although the Idea enables
the appearance of a truth, it does not follow that the truth *is* an Idea—we have
already seen how this misunderstanding can lead to speculative leftism. The in-
eradicable worldliness of the Idea also explains why the wisdom of the philosopher-king is better conceived as *phronesis* or practical prudence, a kind of reactive steering through the choppy and uncertain waters of change, rather than as
Sophia or cognitive mastery of the laws of the world as it is and presumed permanently to be (the application of a sociologically informed political science for
example). "The Idea", claims Badiou, "is nothing other than that through which
the individual marks in himself the action of thought as immanence to the true"
(SM, 123). He calls the *ongoing* fidelity that operationalises the Idea 'ideation', the
result of which is a "true life" (SM, 124).

Not that this true life is an easy life. Badiou illustrates this through the example of Georg Cantor. On the one hand, Cantor was almost unwillingly compelled
to pursue to the limit the transfinite logic he had himself had elaborated. He was
swept up in a "heroic determination" (SM, 128) that allowed the truth of transfinite numbers to appear in the world of mathematics. However, this same participation in the Idea of the infinite was simultaneously the source of severe torments
for Cantor, not as a thinker, but as an individual. The recurrent bouts of depression from which he suffered were at least partially triggered by the derision and
incomprehension of his peers, behaving as they did like reactive subjects keen to
deny that he had introduced a significant novelty into their discipline at all. The
'ideation', then, of the Cantor-event necessarily includes the very real suffering of
Cantor the individual in his *subjection* to the Idea in which he participated.

However, this rather melancholy note is off-set by the essay 'The Idea of
Communism' which closes the collection entitled *L'Hypothèse communiste* (*HC*,
pp.181-205). There the Idea not only mediates between the individual and the subject, but it very clearly facilitates an inscription into History. Confirming the assertion which has guided this chapter then, Badiou writes, contra *Being and Event*, that
"there is in effect an historical dimension of a truth" (*HC*, p.183); that "an Idea is
the subjectivation of a relation between the singularity of a truth-procedure and a
representation of History" (*HC*, p.185); and very specifically that "the Communist
Idea is that which constitutes the becoming-political-subject of the individual as
well as being at the same time its projection into History" (*HC*, p.187).

Much of this essay relies on a Lacanian vocabulary by means of which the
Idea is aligned with the real, History with the symbolic (as a narrative chain of

signifiers), and ideology with the imaginary. As with later Lacan and the clinic of the Borromean knot, the issue becomes the complex interweaving of these three registers rather than their strict distinction. What the Idea manages then, according to Badiou, is the synthesis of this corresponding triplet: politics (the real), history (the symbolic) and ideology (the imaginary). Each of these is required, but an emphasis on any one to the exclusion of the others spells disaster for truth. In other words, the Idea projects a real into the symbolic of a world, enabling the former to *participate* in the latter; yet ideation, as the ongoing subjectivation of this Idea, "can only be imaginary, for the capital reason that no real is symbolizable as such" (*HC*, p.188)—as Lacan repeatedly insisted in his references to 'little bits of the real' and the notion that the real is without law. It follows that ideology, far from being a distorting veil *concealing* the real as in the orthodox Marxist tradition, is indispensable in maintaining an orientation *towards* the real precisely because it cannot be presented but must transform representation. Ideology is not false consciousness, but ideo-logy, a logic of appearance of Ideas. And as Badiou had argued as far back as *De l'idéologie*, the resistant ideologies of the exploited necessarily draw on the dominant ideology, but also contribute to an historical project with a real at its core. Thus, writing some thirty four years after *De l'idéologie*, it is still the case that the "Communist Idea is the imaginary operation by which an individual subjectivation projects a fragment of the political real in the symbolic narration of a History" (*HC*, p.189).

The Idea of Communism specifically has a special status in this historical inscription of the truth of politics. As we saw in Chapter 2, there is of course a historicist narrative of Communism which reduces it primarily to the Soviet State, and attempts to conjoin the collapse of the latter to the destruction of the former. Prior to this, the Idea of Communism supported the adjective 'communist', which denoted membership of a party as well as solidarity with workers and the exploited around the world. Today, however, Badiou is adamant that the name of Communism cannot function as an adjective. To say of a politics that it *is* 'Communist' is to lapse into the excessive "passion for the real" from which the historical attempts to realise it did indeed suffer. With its roots in a certain reading of Hegel, this adjectival Communism relates to History as if it were the full unfolding of the real of politics. It was against this danger that Badiou had asserted, in *Theory of the Subject*, that "History doesn't exist" (*TS*, p.92). In 'The Idea of Communism', however, Badiou admits that this assertion now needs qualification. Though there is still no real of History per se, the real can only present itself in some sort of synthesis with History. It is the Idea that, provided it is subtracted from any predicative usage, can facilitate this synthesis: "We must save the Idea, but also free the real from every immediate coalescence with it" (*CH*, p.190).

It is in this way that Badiou can both retain his critique of historicism and acknowledge the role of History in a truth-procedure. He continues to insist that "History is the history of the State" (*HC, p*.193), acknowledging his debt to Sylvain Lazarus in this regard. History produces historical 'facts' that, as we saw, incorporate change into the existing world. But he now recognises that a crucial dimension of the truth-procedure is that "an Idea presents the truth as if it was a fact. Or again: that the Idea presents certain facts as symbols of the real of truth" (*ibid.*). Far from enacting a clean break with History, as seemed to the case in *Being and Event*, the event now "supposes the deployment of a palette of historical facts apt for symbolization" (*HC*, p.194). This does not make the event reducible to those facts, any more than, as we saw earlier, the novel sequence called 'Leninism' was reducible to the Paris Commune. And Communism is one of the worldly facts apt to symbolize the unsymbolisable real, since there has been Communism, it is part of our history—even in the form of the narrative of its decline which supports the triumphalism of neoliberal globalisation.

Badiou is nonetheless acutely aware of the dangers of linking evental truth to Statist History in this way:

> Since it is about an (imaginary) ideological relation between a truth-procedure and historical facts, why hesitate to push this relation to its limit, why not say that it is about a relation between event and State? (*HC*, p.195)

Needless to say, this line of thinking threatens the entire edifice established by *Being and Event*, in which the notion of the generic enables both a radical opposition between the event and the State, and the immanence of the evental multiple to the State's situational dominion. The potency of the Idea of Communism, however, lies precisely in the relation it forces to a paradoxical State, namely, the one that oversees the withering away of the State. Communism thus challenges the State with "the historical figure of an 'other State'" (*HC*, p.195). The very agent of exploitation and exclusion then, is turned by the Idea of Communism into the symbol of the political real. Crucially, there is an anticipatory dimension to this that supports a pre-evental radical political imaginary: "In order to anticipate [...] the creation of new possibles, we must have an Idea [...] An Idea is always the affirmation that a new truth is historically possible" (*HC*, p.201).

So how are we to view the relationship between history and conflict in Badiou's work now? Firstly, it is clear, and has been since Chapter 1, that no dialectical teleology exists to guarantee conflict as the painful but necessary birth pangs of emancipation. It follows that each conflict has very specific stakes which, in the absence of any cunning of historical reason, can be forced by subject that breaks with historical determination if not with history *tout court*. Secondly, there seems to be a double articulation in the worlding of worlds, such that the transcendental index implies a power of historicization on the one hand, while on the other, as Rancière argues in *The Names of History*, this very historicization simultaneously testifies to the gap between word and thing that threatens the transcendental power of envelopment. Thus, if history is for the most part a statist discourse that explicitly presents itself as a site of discursive conflict, as if the past were the product of a democratic consensus emerging from free debate, its real purpose could be described as a kind of cosmetic agonism that nullifies a deeper-seated antagonism. Part of escaping this nullification, therefore, is what I am calling 'evental historiography', which acknowledges that every novelty must be phrased *through* the past, with the support of an Idea, so as to reorder it and open the way to a new future.

part II: the jamaican situation

6

The Morant Bay Revolt: Event or Exception?

We are now going to turn our critical gaze toward the past, significantly a contested, 'non-European', colonial and postcolonial past: that of pre- and post-Emancipation Jamaica. We will therefore be putting the evental historiography elaborated in the last chapter to work in this one, as a way of testing the philosophy of conflict we have extrapolated from Badiou's wider oeuvre so far.

The choice of Jamaica for this 'putting to work' emerges from various factors. One—the most insignificant—is autobiographical: Jamaica happens to be my birthplace and the backdrop to my formative years. Secondly however, Jamaican history offers an extremely rich panorama of resistance, revolts, insurrections, uprisings and riots that together constitute an opportunity for establishing a differential typology of conflicts. This can only be helpful to our overall goal of parsing out distinctions between events, potential events, 'structural resistance' and, indeed, simulated events. Thirdly, Jamaica's history of conflicts is also self-evidently a history of transformations in modes of sovereignty, a topic which, as we saw in Chapter 3, is key to understanding the play between nomination and counter-nomination, and, as noted in the preceding chapter, transformation and modulation. As such, I hope to be able to sketch a model of British imperial sovereignty as an evolving technology of inclusion that has, perforce, responded to the disruptive belonging exposed by the evental elements of anti-colonial resistance. Fourthly then, shifting our focus to Jamaican conflicts enables us to ask some rather novel and counter-intuitive questions regarding Badiou's possible compatibility with, on the face of it, utterly incompatible modes of analysis, such as postcolonial theory, cultural studies and their shared emphasis on a cultural politics. In many ways, my inspiration for this attempt to look at Badiou askance from a Jamaican perspective comes from Susan Buck-Morss' reframing of Hegel by way of the Haitian Revolution (Buck-Morss: 2009). While postcolonial critics of this book lauded the decentring of Eurocentric accounts of modernity, they were less comfortable with her adherence to a universal notion of emancipatory history. Yet precisely through the Caribbean displacement, Buck-Morss demonstrates the ways in which the *situated* nature of universal logics of transformation can rebound upon the ineradicably

unequal and therefore interested origins of even egalitarian discourse. For my purposes, the specifically Jamaican displacement I am undertaking emphasises three
dimensions that the Badiouian framework largely occludes or under-emphasises:
resistance, statist reform, and culture. Although there will not be room here to explore all the complex ramifications of this partial rapprochement, I would nonetheless hope that, carefully handled, it could bring Badiou closer to a pre-evental
praxis of resistance, and cultural studies back to its radical roots.

In this chapter then, my main focus will be on one particular Jamaica conflict,
the Morant Bay Revolt of 1865, but in order to situate its importance and distinguish its evental dimensions from the exceptional ones imputed to it, I will first be
locating Morant Bay in relation to its prehistory in the venerable tradition of resistance in Jamaica, during slavery and after, and the role of that resistance in the
metropolitan movement for the abolition of the slave trade and then full emancipation. The overall aim of my analysis is to interrogate the dialectical interconnections between resistance, reaction and reform, and the basis this dialectic can lay
for genuine rupture.

SLAVE RESISTANCE IN JAMAICA

Slavery, and resistance to it, began the moment Europe had contact with Jamaica when Columbus washed up on what is now called Discovery Bay on the 4th of
May, 1494. He immediately set about brutally quelling the resistance of the indigenous Taino peoples in order to claim the island for Spain. Within 25 years, almost
the entire Taino population (several hundred thousand) had been exterminated
by a combination of forced labour, under-nourishment, and disease. Confronted
by the resulting vacuum of exploitable labour, it was the Spanish rather than the
English who first began importing African slaves to the island, albeit in relatively limited numbers. Despite possessing it for 300 years, the Spanish Empire invested little in Jamaica, viewing it largely as a launching pad for their more glamorous
adventures in Central and South America. Yet those very first Africans brought
to Jamaica by the Spanish immediately began what would become a tradition of
dogged resistance: within twenty or so years of the first arrivals, small communities of escaped slaves had already been established and defended in the dense jungle interior.

It was the entrepreneurial English, however, who spotted the potential value of Jamaica. Oliver Cromwell sent a fleet of 38 ships in May 1655 and its combined force of 8,000 men was easily enough to persuade the Spanish to surrender
their poorly defended possession. Jamaica was officially ceded to the English with
the Treaty of Madrid in 1670, but they had already been settling the island for
some time with the help of buccaneer pirates, making of Port Royal a notoriously rowdy capital (until 1692, when a massive earthquake caused it to sink into the
Caribbean Sea). As the Spanish fled to mainland America and Cuba, the slaves
they abandoned further swelled the ranks of the jungle-based escapees. Thus began the community of Maroons (from the Spanish for runaway, *cimarròn*), which
would play such an ambiguous role in Jamaica's future struggles against slavery, as
we shall see.

It was also the entrepreneurial English who established a system of large, slave-dependent plantations producing crops already introduced by the Spanish: bananas, tobacco, cocoa, but above all sugar. The arduous Middle Passage, the humid climate, the backbreaking work, the brutal treatment and consequent high mortality rates, all coupled with the rapid expansion and intensification of this plantation economy to create an insatiable demand for fresh supplies of slaves. Thanks to the British habit of meticulous book-keeping ('British', rather than 'English', following the Act of Union in 1706), we can be fairly sure of numbers: between 1655 and 1807, 747,506 mainly West African slaves from present-day Ghana and Nigeria were absorbed and often extinguished by the voracious Jamaican plantation system (Sherlock and Bennett: 1998, p.93). A census in 1778 already showed blacks outnumbering whites by eleven to one (Mason: 2000, p.17). By the mid-1700s, Jamaica's position at the apex of the profitable Atlantic 'triangle'—textiles sold on the Britain-to-Africa leg; slaves on the Africa-to-Jamaica leg; and then sugar and rum on the Jamaica-to-Britain leg—had turned the island into the jewel in Britain's Caribbean crown. However, the sweet success of Jamaican sugar relied on a precarious and inhumane system in which a tiny white colonial minority exercised necessarily oppressive control over a recalcitrant and volatile black majority.

As a result of this savage 'plantocracy', hardly a single year of the Eighteenth Century passed in Jamaica without a serious uprising, riot or plot. The Maroons in particular proved to be a persistent thorn in the side of the British. During what Jamaican historians refer to as the 'First Maroon War' (1655-1731), the British, like the Spanish before them, proved unequal to the Maroon's guerrilla tactics, survival skills and intimate knowledge of the jungle interior, and were thus forced to offer a peace treaty in 1739.[1] This treaty deployed a tactic of pacifying inclusion that colonial sovereignty would have frequent recourse to throughout its efforts to nullify conflict in Jamaica, as we shall see. In some respects, it represented an astonishing victory won through the sheer bloody-minded defiance of African rebels in the face of European colonial might. It not only granted the Maroons complete freedom, but also extended full autonomy to their communities in the cockpit country and on the slopes of the Blue Mountains, giving them 5,000 acres of land and the right to sell their produce to neighbouring market towns. To this day, this treaty enables Maroons to live in isolated communities such as Accompong and Trelawny where a distinct and very African culture is maintained at a genuine remove from surrounding Jamaican culture. Legally, too, it is a remarkable document. Peace treaties generally presupposed two or more sovereign states on the nascent model of European nations, whereas, in a paradoxically Hobbesian manner, this treaty effectively *instituted* the sovereignty of the Maroons in and through its signing, making them something approximate to a nation within a nation. In other respects, however, far from being an unqualified example of the value of armed resistance, the 1739 treaty was a pernicious strategy of colonial containment. The conferral of Maroon 'sovereignty' was conditional on service to the British army in times of rebellion, as well as on returning, rather than harbouring,

---

1. In fact there were two treaties, one for the Trelawny Maroons on the eastern side of the island, another for the Leeward Maroons on the West.

future escaped slaves.[2] This is the other way in which the treaty was a thoroughly Hobbesian 'contract': it bolstered both the legitimacy and the concrete capacity of colonial sovereign power in 'exceptional' circumstances, although the very need for the treaty showed that violent resistance to slavery in Jamaica, far from being exceptional, was almost banal. The seventh of the treaty's fifteen points also specified that in circumstances of invasion by a foreign force, the Maroons would join the colonial army in repelling it. In even more classically Hobbesian terms, the twelfth clause reserved the sovereign right to administer the death penalty within the Maroon community for the colonial Governor. The Maroon chiefs of this period—Cudjoe, Quao, and the powerful female leader Nanny—ought to be icons of heroic African resistance to Jamaican slavery. Unfortunately, this treaty ensured that their autonomy was gained at the expense of complicity with the slave-system, specifically its urgent need to control serious conflicts.

Arguably betrayed by the Maroons then, the slaves left on the sugar estates were forced to find their own forms of resistance. They did so in innumerable ways and on several levels, from the covert, the cunning and the everyday, to the spectacular, the violent and the insurrectionary. Everyday resistance ranged from deliberate idleness (what Victorian colonisers referred to as 'malingering') to feigned sickness, from the development of a pidgin language impenetrable to 'massa' to outright sabotage of machinery—including the machinery of biological reproduction: many slave women chose abortion in order to prevent another child being born into bondage. At this level, as we will see in more detail in the next chapter, *cultural* forms played a crucial part in both maintaining and masking resistance to slavery, whether through the preservation of African and neo-African stories, songs and dances (such as the selfish cunning of the spider 'Anancy', and the 'Jonkonnu' dance), or through the elaboration of syncretic interpretations of Christianity that distilled from it its emancipatory message (such as Native Baptism, Pocomania and Kumina). Germane to our interest in the relationship between individuals, resistant individuals and Badiouian subjects is the clear dialectic in Jamaica between this everyday, tactical and very often cultural form of resistance on the one hand, and the much rarer outbursts of insurrectionary violence on the other. While we must heed our own caveat—that 'big' and spectacular conflicts are not ipso facto 'events' (in fact, key to my analysis will be the claim that abolition was *not* an event)—I nonetheless hope to show that it was indeed the shift from everyday underhand resistance to outright antagonism that ultimately ensured the demise of slavery.

Along similar lines, Richard Burton (1997) has drawn on Michel de Certeau's distinction between 'opposition' and 'resistance' (de Certeau: 1980) in order to map Jamaican conflicts of the slave era. Clearly related to his better known distinction

---

2. Sherlock and Bennett cite the following from the treaty: "Captain Cudjoe and his successors would use their best endeavours to take, kill, suppress or destroy [...] all rebels wheresoever they be throughout the island" and "if any negroes shall hereafter run away from their masters or owners and fall into Captain Cudjoe's hands they shall immediately be sent back to the chief magistrate of the next Parish where they were taken; and those that bring them in are to be satisfied for their trouble" (Sherlock and Bennett: 1998, 141).

between 'tactics' and 'strategies' developed in *The Practice of Everyday Life* (1988), 'resistance' for de Certeau involves the strategic mobilisation of a utopian alternative external to the dominant regime, whereas 'opposition' resembles tactical subversion in that it has no space of its own outside the power it undermines from within. Opposition presupposes what it opposes, tailoring its tactics to the contours of the existing terrain. Resistance, by contrast, challenges the given head-on with an alternative it affirms without concession. Putting this binary to work in the Jamaican context, Burton follows the Caribbean historian Michael Craton (whose work we will discuss below) in discerning a general shift from African resistance to creolized opposition, which coincides with the demographic shift from a majority of African-born to a majority of Jamaican-born slaves with the end of the slave trade in 1807. Generally then, Burton observes a transition from the mobilisation of an African, often specifically Coromantee[3] resistance before around 1800, towards a complex internal-yet-oppositional negotiation with the plantation regime and the wider colonial system after 1800.

According to this schema then, the most 'resistant' slave revolt, after the first Maroon War, would be 'Tacky's rebellion' of 1760. Tacky, another Cormorantee slave who is alleged to have been a chief in his homeland, used African-derived rituals to initiate a revolt in the parish of St. Mary in May of that year, a revolt that spread almost to the entire island and lasted through June and July. In keeping with Burton's use of the term 'resistance', Tacky's followers explicitly intended to overthrow British colonial power and install an African kingdom in Jamaica. To that end they took over several plantations and killed their white owners. However, the rebellion was betrayed to the white authorities by a slave who had escaped from one of the commandeered plantations. A planter militia was quickly organised and, crucially, assisted by the Maroons. Indeed, it was a Maroon marksman that shot and killed Tacky himself, prompting many of his followers to commit suicide rather than be taken back into slavery. Four hundred black lives were lost in all, compared to a modest 60 white lives, but the ensuing disorder and unrest lasted well beyond the rebellion itself. A blueprint for resistance had been set.

If no comparably major revolt took place in Jamaica in the seventy years following Tacky's rebellion, Burton puts this down to the ambivalent effects of *creolization*, which is to say, the slow, multi-layered and uneven emergence of a distinctly Jamaican culture from the mixture of African and British cultures (see also Bathwaite: 1971). For our purposes, creolization can be understood as an informal version of the neutralisation-by-inclusion we just observed in the Maroon treaty. Both white colonisers and black colonised were assimilated into the disciplines, practices and interlocking values required by the peculiarities of the plantation system. Despite the agency they undoubtedly exercised in this process of creolization, it was thus *as* slaves that black men, women and children came to both oppose and conform to the regime in which they found themselves. *Resistant* energies

---

3. Coromantee (or 'Coromantin' or 'Coromanti') were the Akan speaking peoples, often of the Ashanti tribe, from the Gold Coast of Africa whose long history of inter-tribal warfare had inculcated in them a warrior culture. They were responsible for many of the slave rebellions in Jamaica.

then, Burton implies, were dissipated during the period between 1760 and the 1820s by the often 'cultural' pursuit of the tactical gains to be had *within* the interstices of the entrenched, violently hierarchical status quo. The complex and subtle theatre of subservience and dominance, allegiance and generosity, as well as defiance and authority, consciously and sometimes ironically enacted by both slave and master, was part and parcel of the hegemonic struggle for freedom within a rigidly repressive system. According to Burton, it was only when Sam Sharpe initiated the 'Christmas Uprising', also known by Jamaican historians as the 'Baptist War', in late 1831, that something resembling resistance once again emerged from what had become mere daily opposition (Burton: 1997, 48).

Although Burton does not stress this, it is significant for us that a dialectical interrelation, and not just a contrast, is discernible within this shift from African resistance, through creolized opposition, *and back to resistance*. The everyday creolized modes of opposition such as Jonkonnu, work songs and Obeah or Myalism[4] not only maintained African roots within a slave system that systematically erased African practices, but they often provided practical cover for facilitating the shift to full-blown resistance. In our terms, they pushed an individual towards being a *resistant* individual (this would be an 'oppositional individual' in Burton's de Certeauian terms), and perhaps even opened the way for the subject in Badiou's rather exalted sense. For example, the drumming that whites assumed to provide mere entertainment at all-night slave dances simultaneously functioned as a mode of communication between the plantations. Religious meetings, too, were often pretexts for establishing solidarity, stoking rebellious fervour, and hatching plots. This was certainly true in the case of Sam Sharpe, a charismatic black Baptist preacher who, outwardly evangelising around the plantations, was in fact organising a mass strike in the months leading up to December 1831. If Tacky essentially continued to be an African chief in Jamaica, Sharpe's 'external' appeal was not in fact to Africa, but to three 'external' discourses: firstly to a Christian God pitted against the ungodly planters; secondly to the metropolitan abolition movement of which he was certainly aware; and thirdly, to the notion of worker's rights emerging from the early labour movement in Britain. The key demand made by Sharpe's rebels was not an African kingdom in Jamaica, but emancipation and *wage-labour*. It is testament to their truly subaltern status that Sharpe's followers aspired to becoming proletarians! When this demand was not met, the strike escalated into violence. Although it lasted only ten bloody days, the Christmas Uprising of 1831-2 mobilised around 60,000 slaves, and engulfed almost the whole island. Fully 580 blacks were killed during and after the unrest, with only 14 white and three brown casualties (Sherlock and Bennett: 1998, p.221). And yet, as we shall see next, the importance of Sam Sharpe's Christmas Uprising lies primarily in the decisive push it gave to emancipation.

---

4. Jonkonnu is a dance which involves the ritual symbolic destruction of a representation of a 'great house' (the plantation owner's house) somewhat in the manner of a Mexican *piñata*; Obeah is a form of African spiritual practice related to Haitian Vodun (growing up in Jamaica, it was not the 'bogey man' with which I was threatened when misbehaving, but the 'Obeah man'); and Myalism might be considered the 'white magic' relative to Obeah's 'black magic' insofar as it focuses on shamanic and herbal healing.

ABOLITION AND EMANCIPATION

This long, honourable history of resistance on the part of black slaves (of which I have only given the roughest of sketches) was almost entirely whitewashed, however, during the self-congratulatory celebrations surrounding the bicentennial of the abolition of slavery in 2007, at least in mainstream British media. The hero of this account of abolition was, of course, neither Nanny nor Tacky but the white, evangelical Christian MP, William Wilberforce. It was Wilberforce who spearheaded the anti-slavery cause in the Houses of Parliament for twenty years until the Slave Trade Act was finally passed on the 25th of March 1807. This popular version of abolition foregrounds metropolitan moral superiority well ahead of black resistance in the colonies. It therefore fetishises the rational humanism of the parliamentary system, precisely to disavow the insurrectionary violence that also, nonetheless, played a crucial part. Within this historico-ideological trope, blacks appear primarily as the suffering victims of an unChristian regime of oppressive brutality, certainly not as political actors in their own right. Only by displaying their abject suffering do they move the hearts of white men powerful enough to change their lot. Alternatively, only by demonstrating their 'naturally' uppity dispositions do they justify the discipline needed to *impose* their lot. Crucially, this Wilberforce-centred account of abolition maintains the appearance of the autonomous executive power of the mother country, as if the spectacular collapse of slavery was simply a rationally deliberated decision that affected the colonies, but did not ultimately originate there. This, however, is to erase the fundamental connection we are exploring between conflict and change. Only such an erasure could support the pompous self-regard of British historian, W. E. H Lecky, who famously characterised abolition as "among the three or four perfectly virtuous pages comprised in the history of nations" (Lecky: 1897, p.153).

Reflecting on the complex historiography surrounding abolition can serve numerous overlapping purposes in this chapter. Firstly, it is perhaps the pre-eminent example of what I have already called a *simulacral event*, i.e., those upheavals that deploy the language of novelty and transformative subjectivity, perhaps even articulating these around a supposed void, but only in order to shore up the status quo. Similarly, it has been and continues to be in the interests of those who promulgate the self-satisfied account of the exclusively moral causality behind abolition to present it as a miraculous watershed that radically changed everything in the British Empire. In fact, it is clear from the very term 'abolition' that, at least by Badiou's criteria, important and welcome as it certainly was, it was not an event. As Badiou argued in relation to the apparent demise of Communism, "[e]verything dies— which also means that no death is an event" (*IT*, p.128). Like 1989 for Badiou, 1807 (abolition) and then 1833 (emancipation) can be seen as a warning that "not everything that changes is an event, and that surprise, speed, and disorder can be mere simulacra of the event, and not the promise of its truth" (*IT*, p.129).

However, precisely as a significant change that nonetheless falls well short of an event, I would argue that abolition and emancipation suggest a series of dialectical interconnections that complicate Badiou's favoured model of ruptural singularity. These linkages are between 1) slave resistance itself, which the Badiou of

Theory of Contradiction might designate as an inert 'reciprocal difference', 2) parliamentary reformism, which the Badiou of *Logics of Worlds* would designate as a mere 'modulation', and 3) the subsequent conditions for the possibility of an event inadvertently established by such Statist reformism (about which Badiou has seemingly nothing to say). For, as I will try to argue, the abolition of the slave trade and then emancipation may not have been an event itself. Yet they provided the necessary conditions for an upheaval that perhaps was—or, to invoke the more pertinent tense of the future anterior—*could still be forced to have been*. In a rather scandalous way, this threatens to invert Badiou's argument in the *Ethics* book that the evil of National Socialism *qua* simulacral event was made possible by the true event of October 1917. Here, I am exploring the possibility that the simulacral event of abolition and emancipation made possible the real *event* of the Morant Bay Revolt of 1865. It is my gamble that what one loses in terms of the punctual purity of the grace-like event as a result of this inversion, one nonetheless gains in terms of a more dialectical, active notion of the subject-individual relation, with resistance as a crucial mediating term. Philosophy's loss, then, may well be radical politic's gain.

In order to pick a pathway through the complex historiographic terrain on abolition, I would identify four main approaches.

Firstly, and as a direct attack on the model of 'heroic humanism' whose poster boy has always been William Wilberforce, there is the 'decline thesis' put forward in Eric Williams' highly influential *Capitalism and Slavery* (Williams: 1944). As its title implies, this was a broadly Marxist approach that located the primary causal factor for the end of slavery squarely on economic grounds. For Williams, abolition essentially arose out of a shift in the form of capitalism away from mercantilism and thus the protectionist model of trade encompassing the apexes of the Atlantic 'triangle', and towards industrialisation and the laissez-faire or free market model of liberal capitalism. In a sense then, the writing was on the wall for slavery not so much with the publication of Adam Smith's *Wealth of Nations* in 1776, in which he argued that slavery was anathema to both economic utility and social morality, as with the broader shifts of which that book was both effect and partial cause. Drawing on the careful economic history already provided by Lowell Ragatz,[5] Williams focussed his analysis on the Caribbean sugar trade in order to show that the profitability of Britain's colonies, particularly Jamaica, peaked in the first half of the 18th century but fell away dramatically in the second. The schema of his overall argument, then, could be presented in the image of a see-saw. Once the capital amassed through primitive accumulation and the super-exploitation of slavery was ploughed back into Britain to spark the Industrial Revolution,[6] this dynamic *rise* in the economic fortunes of the metropole led, at the other end of the colonial system, to a correspondingly dramatic decline. Suddenly, the colonies were worse than useless: they were an active drain. One could even use the jargon

---

5. Ragatz, Lowell, *The Fall of the Planter Class in the British Caribbean, 1763-1833*, London: Century, 1928.

6. Marx puts this pithily in the first volume of *Capital* as follows: "the veiled slavery of the wage-earners in Europe needed, for its pedestal, slavery pure and simple in the New World" (Marx: 1990, p. 925)

of contemporary economics and refer to the decline of the colonies as a 'double dip'. Not only had they become less profitable for the Empire as an exporter of British consumables, but their reduced buying power as a 'client economy' meant that they offered no export market for the newly mass produced goods flowing out of industrialised Britain either. Unlike today's banks, the colonies were not 'too big to fail'. Far from spurring the mother country to come up with a bailout package, the first and second dips of the see-sawing colonial economy were allowed to lapse into permanent spiralling deterioration at the margins—from which, arguably, the former colonies have never been able to recover.

True to his neo-Marxist framework, Williams views the explicit Christian humanism of the abolitionists as an ideological superstructure built upon their economic base as an emerging bourgeois class. In a chapter entitled, 'The 'Saints' and Slavery', he justifies those sardonic inverted commas with reference to the hypocrisy of key abolitionists whose saintliness indeed seemed suspiciously selective. In particular, he argues that while West Indian slavery had been the *cause célèbre* of the movement in the late 18th and very early 19th century, post-abolition, dubious distinctions were increasingly made regarding slavery in other parts of the world. Cotton picked by enslaved hands in the deep south of the U.S., for example, somehow had less blood on it than the 'white gold' coming from the Caribbean. Could this be because of the importance of the textile industry to British capitalism? Moreover, key abolitionists like James Cropper actively advocated Indian sugar as an ethical alternative to its blood-soaked Jamaican rival, despite the fact that it, too, was produced with slave labour (Cropper, Williams pointedly notes, was himself a major importer of East India sugar). Similarly, other abolitionists promoted Brazilian and Cuban sugar on the grounds of its importance to the British economy, despite the fact that the "barbarous removal of the Negroes from Africa continued for at least twenty five years after 1833, to the sugar plantations of Brazil and Cuba" (Williams: 1944, 192). Williams summarises his critique of these 'saints' in admirably aphoristic style: "Exeter Hall, the centre of British humanitarianism, yielded to the Manchester School, the spearhead of British free trade" (*ibid.*).

A second strand, however, in the historiography of British abolition offsets Williams' economism by emphasising the humanitarianism of these self-same 'saints'. This position is typified in the work of Seymour Drescher, particularly his seminal *Econocide: British Slavery in the Era of Abolition* (Drescher: 1977). Drescher acknowledges that the 'decline thesis' had attained the status of common sense by the 1970s. But using reliable data on the value of exports to and imports from the Caribbean in the period from 1770-1820—exactly the period of the snowballing success of the antislavery movement—Drescher shows that the percentage of the value of colonies such as Jamaica, relative to Britain's overseas trade as a whole, in fact rose sharply. Contra Williams then, Drescher claims that "[a]s late as 1821, the West Indies accounted for more of British overseas trade in both imports and exports than they had fifty years before" (19). Drescher finds little evidence of the decline in the Caribbean sugar trade until the very eve of emancipation (twenty six years after abolition). He therefore effectively inverts William's economic

determinism by arguing that "economic decline was contingent upon, not deter-
minative of, abolition" (Drescher: 1987, p.194). Nonetheless, the point of Drescher's
analysis is not to swing the pendulum in the other direction by ascribing exclusive
causal agency to the rhetoric of abolition alone, as if, rejecting crude materialism,
one must adopt an equally crude idealism. On the contrary, he aims to acknowledge complex social and political factors—Badiou might say 'subjective' factors—
irreducible to economic class interests. He takes abolition seriously as a movement
then, a political mobilisation of diverse peoples along religious as well as political,
ethical and economic lines. Ultimately however, the thrust of his argument is that
the combined force of these factors for change was sufficient for the British political elite to commit the titular 'econocide': that is, fiscal legislation enacted on moral grounds contrary to the profit motive, and amounting therefore to economic
suicide. The very title of his concluding chapter, 'Beyond Economic Interest', suggests that, characterised as a brake on the apparently implacable logic of the market, abolition offers an invaluable lesson to our corporatized present (in which the
term 'econocide' seems to have a diametrically opposed resonance: the disastrous
notion that the economic ills caused by neoliberalism can only be cured by admin-
istering *more* neoliberalism…).

From a Badiouian perspective, however, there is an obvious problem with
Drescher's position. It both elides the role of resistance in the colonies on the one
hand, and prioritises a sort of rationalist voluntarism on the part of the political agency of the mother country on the other: Drescher says explicitly "It was
the political leverage of the British metropolitan masses that gave them the decisive advantage over even the most heroic of Caribbean rebels" (Drescher: 1987,
207). Indeed, a third strand in the historiography of abolition can be identified in
a much stronger, even exclusive emphasis on the shifts—economic but also social,
sexual, religious, technological—within the British metropole, at the expense of
analyses of colony-metropole relations. David Brion Davis' *The Problem of Slavery
in the Age of Revolution: 1770-1823* (Davis: 1975) characterises the emergent humanitarianism of the anti-slavery movement not, *pace* Williams, as a mere ideological
smokescreen for bourgeois interests, but as a more complex synthesis of religion
and laissez-faire economics (somewhat in the manner of Max Weber's analysis of
the role of the Calvinist work ethic in the mass adoption of capitalist values). If
Davis sees abolitionist rhetoric as ideology then, it is in the tradition not of 'false
consciousness' but of Gramscian hegemony. Davis argues persuasively that hand-
wringing concern for the enslaved blacks in distant lands served the hegemonic
function of veiling the true antagonism bubbling away nearer to home. In other
words, the lofty preoccupation with slave labour diverted radical energy from the
more immediate concern of wage labour.[7]

_____

7. This tendency could be crystallized in Wilberforce's ardent support of the Corn Laws and of
the suppression of the British poor who rioted against them, even as he pushed for the emancipation of slaves in the colonies. Paradoxically, the Corn Laws, with their mercantilist protection-
ism, would be a key battleground for the ideologues of free trade. Like the abolitions, with whom
they overlapped in many ways, they were able to take the high moral ground (cheaper bread for
the poor thanks to competition from foreign imports) whilst laying the basis for wage labour as a
commodity that would 'naturally' find its correct price on an unfettered market.

Recent accounts of abolition such as Adam Hochschild's *Bury the Chains* (2005) follow Davis' lead in stressing the metropolitan interconnections between the emergence of a mass culture and the very possibility of a truly mass movement deploying techniques of what we would today recognise as marketing, promotion and public relations. Three key things separate British abolitionism from other European movements. One of its most powerful weapons, for example, was the popular petition. These were often started in the north of England (Manchester stands out), but soon circulated around the entire country. They rose exponentially in importance from "100 petitions and perhaps 60,000 to 75,000 signers in 1788, to over 5,000 petitions and almost 1,500,000 signers in 1833" (Drescher: 1987, 206). Secondly, the British abolition movement made canny use of the pervasive visual culture enabled by mass production. Two images stand out: the pendent designed by Josiah Wedgewood which showed the enchained body of a slave, on bended knee and with hands clasped imploringly before him, beneath the motto 'Am I not a Man and a Brother?'; and perhaps more famously, the schema of the slave ship *Brookes* showing its inhuman storage capacity for human cargo (292 bodies packed tightly together like sardines in a can). Both of these images found their way into many homes around the country, articulating the movement with everyday life. Thirdly, it is no exaggeration to say that the anti-slavery movement paved the way for today's model of ethical consumerism by pioneering abstention as a potent weapon against big business (Hochschild: 2005). Thomas Clarkson at the time estimated that approximately 300, 000 families were actively engaged in abstaining from Caribbean sugar on moral grounds. It is also worth noting that this engaged the involvement of women, then as now generally responsible for the shopping, who became very prominent activists in the movement as a whole.

Important as these aspects of metropolitan mobilisation undoubtedly are, however, they take little or no heed of connections with events in the colonies, such as those we have already related regarding Jamaica. Arguably then, it is to the fourth stand in the historiography of British abolition that one must turn in order to supplement the narrowness of the other three: Williams' economism, Drescher's voluntarism, and Bion and Hochschild's metrocentrism.[8] This fourth strand, then, pays due attention to the factor of resistance to slavery in the colonies, weaving it into the other three to produce a more complete picture of abolition and emancipation. Williams does make some suggestive gestures in this direction in the final chapter of *Capitalism and Slavery*, where he notes that it "would be a grave mistake [...] to treat the question as if it were merely a metropolitan struggle" (Williams: 1944, p.197). But the historian who has done the most to correct the mistake Williams highlights is probably Michael Craton. In a series of histories of the British Caribbean, Craton has re-focussed debate on the active and ongoing resistance of slaves, and its complex, catalyzing role in pushing the anti-slavery movement forward (Craton 1974, 1978, 1982).

It is fair to assume, as Williams also does, that news of an anti-slavery movement in Britain reached the ears of the slaves long before it enjoyed any legislative

8. A fifth strand could be identified, which focuses on the difficulties, post-Emancipation, of implementing both the end of the slave trade and manumission. The work of Marika Sherwood would be exemplary here (2007).

successes. Certainly in the case of both the Sam Sharpe and then Morant Bay Revolts, the rumour that the colonial authorities were concealing the fact that the King, and then the Queen, had *already* freed the slaves,[9] played a crucial role in inciting them to rise up in order claim that imagined right. The very existence of abolitionist discourse, then, emboldened the slaves to intensify their resistance. As Craton notes:

> Williams argues a direct connection between abolition in 1807 and an alleged revolt in British Guiana in 1808 [...], between the Registration dispute and the Barbadian revolt of 1816, between the Bathurst Amelioration Circular and the Demerara Revolt of 1823, and between the news of wide-ranging political reform in England between 1829 and 1831 and the Jamaica Christmas Rebellion of 1831-32 (Craton: 2004, p.261)

What Craton adds to Williams' account, however, is a clearer emphasis on the *recursive* effect of the interplay between reform, resistance and reaction. Where Williams tends to present slave uprisings as merely reactive on metropolitan developments, Craton demonstrates the extent to which they directly shaped the strategies of antislavery lobbyists in Britain, and added to the political and moral climate there in which ameliorative legislation could be pushed through. Ultimately— and despite the rhetoric of the time that purported to discern in the black race a natural propensity for servility—I would argue that it was in fact the ongoing, creative and indefatigable defiance of slaves that compelled the slave system to take such brutally repressive forms, thereby distancing it from the moral standards of the mother country. Craton's analysis brings out the 'feedback loop' between such slave resistance, repression by the colonial authorities, and the reforms being passed in Britain. Simplifying greatly, we could say that the direction of influence oscillated along two axes, from colony-to-metropole and from metropole-to-colony ('influence' here designating not a progressive impetus for incremental change, but a more complex zone of action and reaction).

Regarding the colony-to-metropole axis for example, the uprising of some 20,000 slaves in Barbados in 1816 led the naturally conservative Wilberforce to denounce violent resistance, to distance himself from emancipation as opposed to abolition, and to actively defend the rights and the security of the Barbadian planters. In this instance, violent resistance might well be described using early Badiou's recourse to Mao's non-antagonistic contradiction, in which, as we saw in Chapter 1, difference is *reciprocal* and therefore constitutive; or indeed, to his later 'diagram' of the commutative relations constitutive of the world of the Oka crisis in *Logics of Worlds* which we glossed in Chapter 4. Like the Mohawk protest in the Oka crisis, the Barbados uprising clearly caused the dominant terms or relations of the imperial situation to ossify and reassert themselves. This compelled Wilberforce and his followers to backtrack, precisely because theirs was a reformist agenda, and thus one articulated through, rather than against, those dominant terms: in Burton's de Certeauian vocabulary, it was 'oppositional' rather than 'resistant'. What we

---

9. This should remind us of Badiou's insistence on the *axiomatic* nature of freedom, not as something to be pursued in the future, but declared in the present as a fact to whose consequences we vow to remain faithful.

previously called the 'Hobbesian tourniquet' quickly tightens around this revolt insofar as there is no doubt about the legitimacy of its violent suppression, and the antislavery lobbyists join everyone else in recoiling in horror.

Regarding the metropole-to-colony axis, however, one could cite the 1823 uprising in Demerara in which 30,000 slaves rose up in response to the reluctance of the Guianese planters to implement the 'Bathurst Amelioration Circular' passed by the British House of Commons in July of that year.[10] Here, we can see the colonies trying to tighten the same Hobbesian tourniquet, whilst the mother country is beginning to loosen it. But perhaps the most significant pre-emancipation revolt on the metropole-to-colony axis *and back again*, was the aforementioned Christmas rebellion led by Sam Sharpe in Jamaica in late 1831. This was remarkable neither because of the numbers involved, nor its duration, nor its tactical successes—in all of these respects, it was more or less as short-lived and easily quashed as previous revolts. It was remarkable, instead, in the severity of the suppression it elicited from the Jamaican plantocracy, and the gap it thereby made visible between colonial and metropolitan jurisprudence as a raft of reforms were passed in the last years of the 1820s. Unlike previous irruptions of violence in the colonies that had always retarded the abolitionist cause, for Thomas Buxton (who had replaced the ailing Wilberforce by this time), the Jamaican Christmas rebellion was an absolute gift, one that undoubtedly sped up the process of emancipation. It allowed Buxton to argue that the colonial plantocracies, not the slaves, were irrational and uncivilized, that it was *their* brutality, not that of the slaves, that threatened the integrity of the Empire (he was helped in this by the fact that many planters had already responded to liberalising reforms by threatening secession). On the 7th of March 1832, Buxton declared to the House of Commons: "If the question respecting the West Indies was not speedily settled it would settle itself in an alarming way (i.e., by further rebellion) and the only way it could be settled was by extinction of slavery" (quoted in Sherlock and Bennett: 1998, p.223). Just over a year later, formally at least, slavery *was* extinct in the British Empire. We shall see this tension between colonial and imperial rule in more detail when we examine the Morant Bay Revolt. Suffice it to say here that the brutal violence with which the white plantocracy was compelled to meet the resistance of black slaves had a demonstrable recursive effect on the metropolitan attitude towards them. Once 'might' was no longer right, the colonies were deprived of the Hobbesian tourniquet as a tool of coercive statecraft.

This dialectic between colony and metropole and back again was nothing new, however. Its effects on European slavery generally had been visible since the French Revolution. There are clear if complex links between the principles of egalitarianism unleashed in 1789, and the slave revolution led by Toussaint-L'Ouverture in Saint-Domingue in 1791 (metropole-to-colony axis); and these links link again with those between L'Ouverture's tenacious military successes against the French, Spanish and British (and then the French again), and the emancipation decree that was finally passed by the French Republic, thanks mainly to the

---

10. This was a six point programme designed to mollify the more brutal aspects of the slave regime such as the flogging of female slaves.

radicalism of the Jacobins, in 1794 (colony-to-metropole axis).[11] They culminate in the *formal* breaking of the colonial link altogether with the establishment of an independent black republic of Saint Domingue in 1804.[12] Napoleon may have reinstated slavery in those parts of the French empire over which he still had control in 1802 (metropole-to-colony axis again), but when it was definitively abolished in June 1848, the decisive momentum came once more from a serious uprising in Martinique during the preceding month (colony-to-metropole axis again). The unanticipated and therefore 'excessive' linkages forged between white and black Jacobins in the Haitian revolution undoubtedly inspired both fear and paranoid overreaction amongst European slave-owners, and courage and fortitude amongst enslaved persons in the Caribbean, the Americas, and beyond. Yet it also conditioned the metropolitan antislavery movement from the outset, albeit as spectre of horror rather than as heroic example to be lauded. In this sense, the Haitian revolution could be described as the strong singularity against which 19th century colonial rule and imperial sovereignty were the compensatory (over)reactions, and for this reason Susan Buck-Morss has discerned in it the beginnings of the true universal history only promised by its French precursor (Buck-Morss: 2009).

Postcolonial historian Robert Young (2001) articulates the general shift I am mapping here as one between 'colonialism', defined as raw economic exploitation and territorial domination, to 'imperialism', defined as a relatively coherent ideological project with a legitimating narrative reliant upon some form of the *mission civilisatrice* initially developed by French imperialists as a contradictory outgrowth of revolutionary egalitarianism. The consequent "paradox of ethnocentric egalitarianism" (Young: 2001, p.32) that Young identifies at the core of French imperialism, whereby a common humanity is extended only by means of an aggressive 'saming' of non-French differences, is nonetheless also at work, I would argue, in the imperial phase of the British Empire which arguably begins in the middle of the 19th century. I want to assert with Young that in Europe in general, "imperialism itself was in part a defensive response to freedom movements" (p.28), but also that this response can best be characterised as a logic of reformist inclusion that attempted to subdue resistance.

FROM COLONIAL BELONGING TO IMPERIAL INCLUSION

Can we begin to make sense of this dialectic between resistance, reaction and reform in Badiouian terms? I believe we can, by characterising the shift from colonial to imperial forms of sovereignty in the mid 19th century as an issue of sets and subsets, of belonging and inclusion, and of elements and parts respectively.

11. Robert Young spells this direct relation out as follows: "The French colonial system of assimilation was originally derived, via the French Revolution, from an Enlightenment belief in a common liberty, equality and fraternity for humankind" (Young: 2001, 30).

12. Because imperialism is a cultural as well as politico-economic system, formal decolonization is never the clean break it is trumpeted as. French patterns of governance and education and thus modes of social, cultural and actual capital persisted well beyond the Haitian revolution, relying, as in Jamaica, on a brown creole class with metropolitan values, practices and pragmatic links. Haitian political history is dominated by a small number of wealthy elite families with their roots in this post-revolutionary creole class. See Hallward: 2007.

Was not the key issue at stake in abolition/emancipation already the way in which slaves were counted within the Empire and thus the form of inclusion to which they were subjected? And did the unifying ideology of imperialism not constitute a response to the dissolution of the slave-count?

Young reminds us that the terms 'Empire' and 'imperialism' are not synonyms, but to the extent that the British Empire became increasingly imperial as the 19th century wore on, I would argue that it also became more and more proximate to a 'state' or a 'world' in Badiou's technical senses. Precisely because the sun never set on its extensive territories, British imperial sovereignty attempted to ensure that the light of the ontological claim that 'there is Oneness' (*BE*, p.93) reached even the darkest of continents. To do so, like any state, it had to dis-count the void by counting the count. However, according to Badiou there are two dangers stemming from the necessary (in)existence of the void within any situation. On the one hand, the void threatens to expose the consistency produced by the initial count of presentation as pure inconsistency: the predicateless chaos of generic being-qua-being would then undo the ordered appearance of beings. On the other hand, the void threatens to expose the metastructuring One itself, produced by state re-presentation, as a purely operational and therefore entirely arbitrary result (p.98): worldly coherence would suddenly appear in all its violence and contingency, rather than in its putatively ontological or natural necessity. Both of these dangers constitute "the ruin of the One" (p.93).

For the British Empire, these two modes of potential ruination corresponded, respectively, to 1) the dispersal into 'non-British' multiplicities of all the diverse elements it attempted to gather as in some way 'British': British colonies through secession, decolonization and/or absorption by another 'set' such as the French or Spanish empires, and individual British colonisers through 'going native' or miscegenation etc.; and 2) to the violent and reactionary exercise of Imperial command even in the obvious absence of a legitimate claim to Oneness (as forced by Ghandi in British India for example). Like all set-theoretical states then, the British Empire attempted to counter "the errancy of the void" (p.95), and the axiomatic excess of inclusion over belonging resulting therefrom, by subjugating the supernumerary within an apparently totalising sovereign One. Its aim was to give a measure to the measureless gap between state and situation, between Empire and colonies.

Thus, the relation of the Caribbean plantocracies to the British Colonial Office could be characterised as subsets that were *initially* allowed to gather their own multiples in a discrete way during the colonial phase of British Empire, of which slavery was a key component. This applies especially to colonies such as Jamaica, which were not under Crown Colony rule, and therefore enjoyed executive autonomy: draconian legislation was often passed in the colonies that had long been repealed from the statute books in the mother country. However, thanks to the metastructuring function of the state, these colonial subsets were counted as basically autonomous parts only on condition that they, and the multiples they contained, remained *elements* of the overall set known as the British Empire conceived, during the colonial phase, in economic rather than ideological or cultural terms. This corresponds to Badiou's axiom of extension, which attempts to counter the axiom of excess by closing the gap between belonging and inclusion, 'normal-ising' and effectively de-historicizing the situation.

As Badiou's early theory of revolt suggests, however, animating the numerous Caribbean slave uprisings that we have already touched upon was a logic that pit-ted supernumerary excess against denumerable extension. Nonetheless, while cer-tain of these revolts potentially revealed enslaved Africans as singular multiples belonging to but not included in colonial sovereignty, the latter came to specialise in transforming such singularities into a 'term-part' (BE, 99), that is, in counting them within the reign of the One. We could represent this ideal relation between presented imperial belonging and represented inclusion in the colonies very sim-ply as follows:

Situation/Presentation:

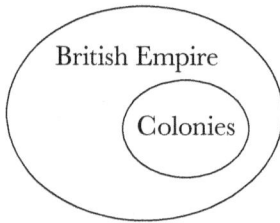

Colonies ∈ British Empire: the colonies belong to the British Empire as multiples that compose it, and are therefore among its presented elements. They count as one.

State of the Situation/Representation:

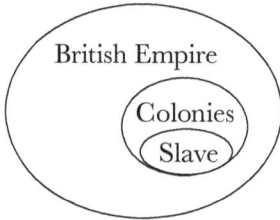

Slaves ⊂ British Empire: the slaves are included in the British Empire as parts of the subset of the colonies which, in turn, are elements of the Empire. The axiom of extension is satisfied insofar as the parts of the subset are also elements of the set. Slave-ones are counted as One.

Self-evidently, the mode of inclusion of slaves within the British Empire during its colonial phase was as *property*, more specifically as 'chattel'—a term, rather like Marx's 'variable capital', that refers to transferable personal property: slaves were to be placed on the same level as furniture or agricultural tools or livestock. For as long as the slave traders, planters and colonial administrators were encouraged to count slaves as equivalent units of mobile abstract value, there was no direct threat to the axiom of extension. Slaves were transitive to the British Empire insofar as the latter counted itself in nakedly economic terms. They were commodities that car-ried their own exchange value on the slave-market, but since their life expectan-cy was so short that selling on was rarely in itself profitable, much more important was their capacity to produce pure surplus value by dint of their unpaid labour.

That slaves *were* to be counted as property and nothing more was demonstrat-ed by the dreadful *Zong* insurance case of 1783. The *Zong* was a slave ship cap-tained by one Luke Collingwood who, faced with a serious outbreak of disease on board, reasoned that "if the slaves died a natural death, it would be the loss of the owners of the ship; but if they were thrown alive into the sea, it would be the loss of the underwriters" (cited in Craton, Walvin and Wright: 1976, p.48). One hundred and thirty three slaves were tossed overboard, and on economic if hardly ethical grounds, Collingwood's murderous logic proved cogent enough for the British judge to find in his favour. The insurers did indeed have to compensate the owners of the ship for their 'loss'. Though he expressed his unease about the case, the presiding judge had to recognise the logic of the count that sustained the distinction between slaves and free-persons. As long as slaves could be counted as chattel then, there was no clash between colonial and metropolitan regimes of counting. Both were concerned only with the ledgers balancing the Empire's books.

Paradoxically, however, it may well be that the chattel logic that ensured slaves—whether domestic helpers, overseers or field workers—were exhaustively counted in a single abstract way, simultaneously had the effect of turning them into what the Badiou of *Being and Event* would call an 'evental site', i.e., an abnormal, excrescent multiple none of whose own elements were presented as belonging to the overarching set. Abstract equivalence, as Marx recognised, both facilitates the disastrously dehumanising effects of capital *and* unleashes an intimation of the generic upon which proletarian politics must rest. *Mutatis mutandis*, the impoverished mode of counting that represented black labourers only as slaves in the colonies had to erase specific African differences of tribal region, linguistic inheritance, kinship structures, religious orientations and so on in order to transform them into tradable commodities. Marx's historical materialist analysis of the emergence of capitalism explicitly underlines this commonality between the chains encumbering slave and wage labourers, a commonality both captured and advocated in the declaration from the *Manifesto*, 'workers of the world unite!'.[13]

Despite its dream of a transitive relation between belonging and inclusion then, imperialism was also an attempted spatial displacement of this chain linking colonial and metropolitan modes of exploitation. Debate on both sides of the colony-metropole divide reflected this mania for spatialised difference. For example, several acts of colonial legislation demonstrate a deep concern with the status of slaves who, being chattel and thus *mobile* property, had travelled with their masters to the mother country. In Badiou's terms, this mobility suggested a transition from subset to set, and from included part to fundamental element. Anxiety centred particularly on those slaves that had converted to Christianity during their time in Britain, since that deprived the State of one of the predicates by which it distinguished between free and unfree elements (prior, that is, to the 'second

---

13. There is much more to say on Marx's changing position on slavery than can possibly be covered here. It is nonetheless worth noting that in texts such as *Poverty of Philosophy*, the *Gründrisse* and *Capital* he identifies three key points regarding slavery and its links with wage labour: firstly, that in general the historical tendency is that wage labour emerges from the dissolution of slavery and serfdom; but that secondly, slavery can exist anachronistically alongside wage labour, whereupon its brutality increases with the shift from production for use (commerce) to production for sale (industry); thirdly, that whereas the wage-relation presents the wage-labourer's surplus labour as if it were work for himself (when it is really temporary slavery for his employer's profit), the property-relation dominating slave-labour presents even that part of his labour which covers the cost of his own means of existence as work directly and exclusively for his master.

Empire' when Christian evangelism became a primary justification for imperialism). A 1764 act of the Bermuda legislature, to give just one example, specified that "Slaves being in England shall not be discharged from Slavery, without other proof of being manumitted there, and that Baptism of Slaves shall not exempt them from bondage" (cited in Craton, Walvin, Wright: 1976, 175).

Ultimately, however, it was a matter not of distinct administrative spaces but rather of the transcendental *logic* of appearance that organised the entire 'world' of the British Empire insofar as it aspired to be a single, unified, and stable set. Is not the essence of the word 'imperial' something like the establishment of a domain of command (*imperō*) in which order, in every sense, becomes performatively imperative? Thus, I would argue that as the more generic category of the 'citizen' emerged both philosophically and legally in Europe, and as ways of counting these new citizen-subjects within imperial sovereignty were extended to black bodies in the colonies (the better to include them in a pacifying manner), a clash of regimes of counting or logics of appearance was inevitable. As the diagrams above suggest, the colonial subset resembles the overarching set of the British Empire itself. A subset that behaves like a *state*, with pretensions to a meta- rather than a local structuring role, cannot be tolerated by a state if imperial command is to continue ordering the diverse elements it contains. As we have already seen, such state-like behaviour is precisely what makes the generic subset resulting from a truth-procedure so disconcerting to the state. It threatens the state not because it opposes it, but because it *resembles* it (even if, being based upon truth, it is a resemblance whose principle of ordering cannot be known by the state). It was to ensure that the colonies continued to belong within the domain of imperial command, therefore, that a new regime of inclusion was gradually imposed upon them with the shift away from the colonial count and towards a pseudo-egalitarian imperial One.

With this in mind, and drawing once again on Burton's de Certeauian binary between 'resistance' and 'opposition', we can distil the conflict-inclusion dialectic during the period of slavery in Jamaica into two phases, and two logics:

African Resistance (1655-1760):

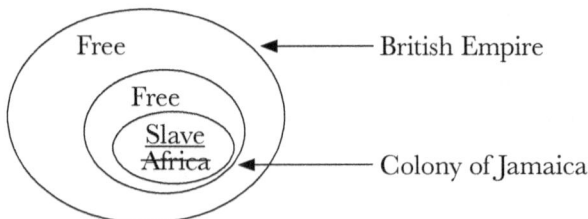

During this first phase, Jamaican sovereignty was predicated upon the establishment of the reciprocal binaries between free British elements and free Jamaican parts, and between free Jamaican elements and enslaved Jamaican parts. This reciprocal binary was, in turn, predicated upon the erasure of Africa as a political, cultural, spiritual, and racial alternative to plantocratic rule.

Employing the four categories of change elaborated by Badiou in *Logics of Worlds*, we could describe the first Maroon war (1655-1739) as both a 'weak singularity' and a 'fact'. It was a singularity insofar as a novel and distinct community *was* established which enjoyed, for a period, maximal appearance in relation to colonial power, but it was ultimately a weak singularity insofar as it failed to maintain this intensity of auto-appearance, and did not offer a truth by which to found infinite new beginnings. The Maroon War was also a fact, therefore, insofar as the treaty of 1739 placed this weak singularity firmly *within*, rather than against, the Jamaican situation. Just as a fact inscribes a novelty into worldly terms, so the treaty reduced the Maroon War to a supporting footnote in the narrative of Jamaican history. This strategy of inclusion was so effective that Maroon resistance ceased even to be oppositional, let alone resistant. This was because the Maroons, in Badiou's terms, became an 'excrescent' yet fixed multiple: they won sufficient 'representation' to be included after a fashion, but this was at the expense of any presentation, any being. Included without belonging, the Maroons were no longer sufficiently internal to the Jamaican situation to oppose it from within.

Despite the violence of Tacky's later rebellion of 1760 therefore, the previous inclusion/exclusion of the Maroons in this way effectively reduced African resistance to slave *opposition*, entrapping it within the very binary between free master and unfree slave from which the slave system drew its Hobbesian legitimacy. As Tacky and his followers attempted to remove Africa from its *sous-rature* status, they legitimised the colonial project of erasure, logically and also viscerally. Notwithstanding the numbers involved, the blood that was shed, and the duration of the intermittent unrest, by the logical criteria I am insisting on, Tacky's rebellion would barely even register as a 'fact', insofar as the Jamaican 'world' at this time was predicated on the conflictual relation between enslaved African and free white coloniser. Just as Badiou's analysis of the Oka incident suggested the 'universal exposure' of worldly relations rather than a challenge to them, so African resistance entangled itself in the Hobbesian tourniquet, which duly tightened. During this phase, the value of Badiou's warnings about allowing conflicts to be reduced to reciprocal differences can be fully appreciated.

Creolized Opposition (1760-1865):

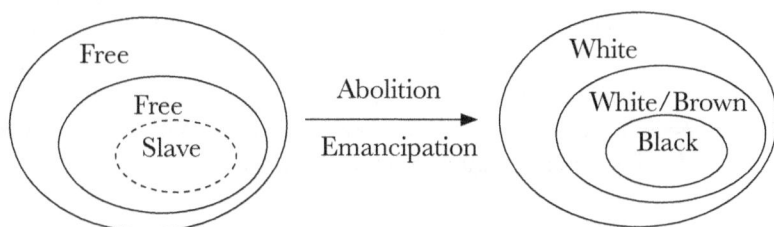

In this second phase, however, anti-slavery opposition takes on 'creolized' forms. The term 'creolization' here describes both absorption into the stark terms of slave society, and the ongoing hegemonic negotiations within and between those terms. A distinctly Jamaican plantation culture, affecting both colonisers and colonised, emerged from this process of ceaseless contestation within a shared terrain. Rather than attempting to rip up the perverse 'social contract' of slave society then, these creolized forms effectively aimed to subvert or displace its terms and conditions.

However, and this is crucial to our analysis, resistance re-emerged from this oppositional mode of anti-slavery activity, thanks to an appeal, in the Sam Sharpe rebellion of 1831, not to Africa at all, but to the liberalising reforms taking place in the imperialising British metropole, which were tending in precisely the opposite direction to the increasingly Hobbesian colonial rule developing in Jamaica. This appeal by slave rebels above the heads of the ruling Jamaican plantocracy is depicted above by the broken line extending beyond the Jamaican subset in the diagram on the left. The broken line around the subset of slaves indicates the way in which this tactic undermined the gathering of these elements according to the Jamaican slave count. However, as the evental site of the slave-subset dissolved due to the extension of inclusion (abolition in 1807 and then formal emancipation in 1833), it is important to note that it is also moved away from the 'edge of the void'. That is to say, the void's threat of exposing both "the in-existent or inconsistent multiple and the transparent operationality of the one" (*BE*, P.98) is nullified by this statist strategy.

Seen in this light, Emancipation is paradoxically one of the most dangerously disarming moments in the black struggle for concrete freedom in Jamaica. For, as we can see from the diagram on the right, post-emancipation, colonial sovereignty aggressively reinscribed its model of reciprocal binarism through newly *racialised* categories. Of course, a certain discursive deployment of race played its part even in the earliest colonial period, but I would agree with Young's analysis that "in Britain [...] the imperial phase was intrinsically linked to the development of a cultural ideology of race from the 1860s onwards" (Young: 2001, 32). In Foucault's terms (2006), this was a precisely Statist reappropriation of the discourse of race war originally deployed to progressive ends in the run up to the English civil war. Phrasing this point in our own terms, however, I would suggest that the discourse of race and racism had already taken on a particular counting function as it became a logic of the colonial subset of Jamaica. In the wake of the master/slave binary then, the white/black binary enabled the Jamaican state to distinguish between ex-slaves and the ruling elite by means of skin colour, and perpetuate its viciously hierarchical and repressive social arrangement. However, as another necessary concession to inclusion, this reinscription of adversarial binarism came at the price of a mediating buffer between the two opposing terms in the form of an emergent brown class. Inevitably perhaps, this class would constitute the future political elite overseeing the transition to a later mode of pacification-by-inclusion: independence. I will go on to characterise independence as a continuation of creolised opposition.

Creolized opposition, then, indicates a supple and complex dialectical appeal to metropolitan reformism that nonetheless relies on revolt and insurrection. Just as conflict in the colonies was the spark that enabled abolition and then emancipation to finally ignite in the metropole, so I would argue that sovereignty as a technology of inclusion had already developed in the metropole in response to the need to manage the conflicts intrinsic to industrialisation. As Marx notes, wage labour emerged in order to sublate the obvious antagonism between feudal land-owner and serf into the much more subtle relation of apparent reciprocity between capitalist and worker. This technology of hegemonic inclusion would then impose itself on the far-flung outposts of the British Empire, again in order to manage the conflicts that threatened its integrity.

If slavery ends with the (still colour-coded) citizen-subject, then, this was not solely due to economic determinism (Williams), or the upsurge of enlightened metropolitan morality (Drescher), or even to the violence of slave uprisings alone (Craton), but because British sovereignty was developing such that the notion of a 'British slave' became uncountable at exactly the same time that the 'British' set took on the qualities of an abstract, extended system of generic inclusion *in pragmatic response to anti-colonial violence*. If, as I will argue in a moment, the Morant Bay Revolt deserves to be considered an event, it is because it represents the point at which, to use Badiou's early Maoist terminology, a non-antagonistic contradiction takes on the qualitative intensity of an antagonistic contradiction.

BADIOU ON ROUSSEAU'S GENERAL WILL

Let us take a moment to step outside our discussion of Jamaican conflicts to consider meditation 32 in *Being and Event*, where Badiou presents Jean-Jacques Rousseau as a pivotal but ultimately *transitional* theorist of sovereignty. This seems pertinent at this juncture, given Rousseau's nourishment of the French Revolution and the connections I have just pointed out with the black slave revolution in Saint-Domingue and the wider effects on colonial sovereignty of the emergence of the citizen-subject. In this meditation, Badiou argues that Rousseau both points the way towards a Jacobin mode of sovereignty with his notion of the general will, but also fails to fully escape the Hobbesian paradigm dominating classical sovereignty which, as we shall see, continues to frame events at Morant Bay in 1865. Beyond this, however, this meditation will also serve to remind us of our criticism regarding Badiou's own tendency towards *absolute singularity*, and the limitations this places on a philosophy of conflict.

Rousseau, to give him his due firstly, does escape Hobbes in one very important respect. As is well known, Hobbes' contract theory is plagued by a causal problem that we have just seen in relation to the Maroon treaty of 1739—in essence, that the social contract presupposes the very Leviathan it claims to institute—but it negotiates this problem by grounding legitimacy in a primordial 'state of nature' preceding, and yet also necessitating in pseudo-Hegelian fashion, its contractual overcoming. This paradigm of sovereignty is therefore tied to a philosophical anthropology of Man as inherently brutal and selfish. Our schema of the first phase of African resistance in Jamaica suggested that precisely this vision of a substratum of brutishness in need of a violent master to oversee its domestication was grafted onto enslaved Africans and the need for colonial discipline. Although aspects of Rousseau have inspired anarchist assertions of a contrasting anthropology (inherent benevolence and spontaneous cooperation), which could in this context be said to connect provocatively with his contributions to the problematic image of the 'noble savage' so palpable in the 18th Century French colonial imaginary, the novelty of *Badiou's* Rousseau lies altogether elsewhere, namely, in the absolute separation between the legitimacy of sovereignty and any kind of necessity whatsoever:

> To suppose that the political convention results from the necessity of having to exit from a war of all against all, and thus to subordinate the event to the effects of force, is to submit its eventness to an extrinsic determination. On the contrary, what one must assume is the 'superfluous' character of the originary social pact (*BE*, p.345)

Superfluous here means singular. It means legitimacy is utterly immanent to the social contract itself and not dependent on some attribute preceding it or external to it, such as, again in the case of the Maroons, the threatened stability of the Jamaican slave system or the survival of the jungle-based community of escaped slaves. By suspending 'extrinsic factors' of this kind, the singularity of what will become Jacobin sovereignty during the French Revolution immediately tries to break the classical connection between security and legitimate violence that orients Hobbesian sovereignty as well as its contemporary Schmittian avatars. It is a break, precisely, with representation as inclusion.

For Rousseau, then, the social contract is a kind of axiom that generates political consequences that are their own justification. On Badiou's account therefore, the social contract is an event—something that, emerging from radical contingency rather than any form of necessity, has no causal explanation whatsoever. The declaration of this evental social contract is something like 'we are hereafter a people'. As we have seen, such events are very fragile. They need 'operators of fidelity' to sustain their implications into the 'hereafter' they attempt to inaugurate. It is one thing for a collective to declare that it constitutes the people, it is quite another to organise, decide, relate and basically live *as* the people. In Rousseau, this is precisely the function of the general will: it is the means by which the fragile collective is enabled to endure over time. But to do so—and this is what 'general' means here—the general will must be unconditionally inclusive, undivided, generic. The power of the term 'people' comes from its egalitarianism, it cannot be the index of a list of predicates (white, Christian, living within such-and-such borders, or indeed African, ex-slave and confined to such as such mountain settlements and so on) lest the general will become particular. If the 'general' part of the general will signifies generic belonging then, the 'will' part signifies two things: firstly, the will to participate in and maintain the generality of the collective, but secondly, will as the individual's willingness to abide by the sovereign dictates of the general will. Rousseauian sovereignty can therefore be defined in the following way: it is the constant binding of the general and the will in an indivisible, self-positing and self-legitimating singularity subtracted from all pre-existing forms of necessity.

Predictably, these are the aspects of Rousseau Badiou applauds. Critically, however, he points out that Rousseau ultimately ends up lapsing back into the Hobbesian paradigm of necessity. For when it comes to articulating the relation between law and this indivisible general will, Rousseau makes a distinction between what he calls 'sovereign law' and 'mere decrees'. Sovereign law, as the direct expression of the general will, occupies itself with the truth of the people in its generic emptiness (for example, the drawing up of a constitution in the name of an essentially abstract 'people'). Decrees, by contrast, deal in a procedural manner with individual cases and are thus of the order of knowledge rather than truth. If decrees arbitrate between competing particular interests, sovereign laws pertain to all because they emerge from and through them. But here Rousseau introduces a further distinction between 'important' and 'urgent' decisions. Important decisions are matters of State that can be administered democratically, which for Rousseau means procedurally, but 'urgent' decisions relate directly to the immediate survival of the people and so become a matter of sovereign general will. In other words, we are dealing now with the whole chequered history of the state of emergency. Because it deals only in particularistic decrees, law can become an impediment to the higher justice demanded by the general will. Thus, Rousseau reintroduces necessity by arguing in the *Social Contract* that "the more rapidly the business at hand has to be resolved, the narrower should be the prescribed difference in weighting opinions: *in deliberations which have to be concluded straight away, a majority of one should suffice*" (*ibid.*—my emphasis). A more succinct definition of the Schmittian sovereign than a 'majority of one' justified by a declared 'urgency' would be hard to imagine.

Badiou's critique of Rousseau then is that, while he was right in affirming the immanent singularity of what would become Jacobin sovereignty, he did not make it singular enough. Badiou's own well-known solution to this problem is to insist on the truly radical singularity of the event, as a total rupture with the given. Subjects faithful to the implications of such a rupture frequently claim to be 'the people'. Although this can congeal all-too quickly into 'the nation', for Badiou—and this is crucial for our insistence on conflict—such a claim is actually divisive rather than unifying. Going from the indefinite to the definite article, from *a* people to *the* people, is the collective political gesture par excellence. In this sense, and as we observed in Chapter 2, the true force of the French revolution is to be found not in the abstract assertions of the *Declaration of the Rights of Man and Citizen* of 1789, but in Abbé Sieyès' grounding of this abstraction in the insistence that the Third Estate (the working class, the rural peasants, but also elements of the bourgeoisie) was the *true* nation. There are two forms of universalism present here. One is abstract and formally inclusive (the *Declaration*). The other is divisive because it confronts the former with a singular multiple that belongs but cannot be included without changing the very definition of inclusion. While *a* people merely ask for inclusion in the abstract form of universalism, rather as the Jamaican Maroons effectively asked to be left alone to be Maroons, *the* people ask for nothing: instead, they assert their legitimacy in antagonistic opposition to a dominant narrative. This is why Ernesto Laclau refers to the 'internal frontier' imposed by democratic populism (Laclau: 2005). *The* people lose this divisive power the moment they interpret their own declaration through the representational fallacy, as if 'the people' named a substantive but fragile body in need of the protection of emergency measures. Despite the fact that Badiou speaks in *Logics of Worlds* of 'subject bodies', I hope I have made it clear that such bodies are ensembles of transformative actions and their material effects rather than bodies in any fleshy sense. This all-important distinction disentangles them from the problematic metaphor of the body-politic inherent to the Hobbesian as well as liberal models, which both assume the transitivity of belonging and inclusion. From Badiou's set-theoretical perspective, any politics based on a social bond that assumes the binding, into an overarching unity or corporeal (or imperial) One, of numerous self-identical elements is imaginary and conservative pure and simple.

The difficulty with Badiou's solution at this stage, however, and this has been pointed out by both Peter Hallward (2003), Nina Power (2006) and myself in the preceding chapters here, is that the stark singularity of the event itself shades into the Hobbesian tradition by being so absolutist as to have no relation to the world whatsoever. Otherwise put, does not the event resemble a little too closely the Schmittian exception itself, despite our attempt to separate them in Chapter 3? Hallward's recent description of a 'Communism of the will' goes a long way towards both highlighting and bridging the gap between Badiou's radical, ruptural singularity and the necessity of that singularity's emergence from, and engagement with, a particular terrain: as he puts it, if popular will bases itself upon something like Paolo Freire's aphorism that 'we make the way by walking it', this is "not to pretend that we invent the ground we traverse" (Hallward: 2009, p.17). This partial recuperation of the widely vilified category of voluntarism, then, acknowledges the practical constraints imposed by the implacable persistence of concrete context without lapsing into the politics of exceptional necessity. Let us now examine such a context.

THE MORANT BAY REVOLT: EVENT OR EXCEPTION?

Having outlined the dialectic between slavery and resistance, and between resistance and the reforms that led to abolition and eventually emancipation, but having also qualified abolition-emancipation as a *simulacral* rather than real event, we are now in a position to apply the evental historiography outlined in the previous chapter to the sequence of conflict which I believe has the potential to be forced to become a Jamaican event: the Morant Bay Revolt of 1865. We will follow three of the four methodological steps previously established (the fourth step will be undertaken in the next chapter): identification of an 'historical referent', distillation of an 'evental sequence', and extrapolation of an 'evental statement'.

Clarity obliges us here to state what 'happened' at Morant Bay in the autumn of 1865, even if the entire point of the subsequent analysis is to distil the evental dimension concealed within the form in which it is presented to us by conventional historical discourse. In essence, this revolt involved a violent protest, led by the black Baptist preacher Paul Bogle, against the injustices of the Jamaican justice system as manifested in the town of Morant Bay on the south-eastern coast of the island. This violence spread, but was eventually suppressed by the use of martial law, declared by the-then Governor, Edward John Eyre. An estimated 439 blacks were killed by soldiers in the process of restoring order, and a further 354 were arrested and executed on the basis of court martials, while 50 were shot without trial (Sherlock and Bennett: 1998, p.260). Among those executed by court martial were Bogle himself (who was captured by the Maroons honouring the 1739 treaty) but also the brown politician, George William Gordon. In an early instance of what we would today call 'strategic rendition', Gordon was taken from Kingston, where martial law did not apply, to Morant Bay where it did, so that he could be summarily tried and executed by court martial rather than a civil court. It was the legal uncertainty surrounding the execution/murder of an elected member of the Jamaican Assembly that sparked controversy in Britain, and a long debate about the jurisprudence of emergency in the metropole. This debate was of sufficient importance to lead to the formation of the Jamaica Committee which lobbied for Eyre's arrest and trial, to a Royal Commission into the disturbances, and, most significantly, to the retraction of the executive autonomy of the Jamaican Assembly through its demotion to a Crown Colony ruled from Westminster. Like the other Jamaican conflicts we have mapped then, the Morant Bay Revolt demonstrates imperial sovereignty as a technology of *inclusion*.

Identifying the Historical Referent

The historical referent usually referred to as the 'Morant Bay Revolt' therefore encompasses an ensemble of elements that can be broken down into its dates, protagonists, causes, and consequences (without, as yet, putting these elements into a chronological or causal order). While the concept of 'consequences' necessarily renders the end-point of a referent's date-series ambiguous, especially if we take Badiou's notion of the infinity of truths seriously, I would suggest that the core period of 'Morant Bay' nonetheless runs from the first outbreak of violence on the 8th of October 1865 to the conclusion of the Royal Commission in April 1866. The main protagonists active within this period include individuals—Paul Bogle, George William Gordon, Governor Eyre, Edward Cardwell—as well as institutional bodies—the Jamaican House of Assembly, the British Colonial Office, the British Parliament, the Jamaica Royal Commission and, less formally, the Jamaica Committee—and elements of 'civil society' such as church organisations, newspapers, scholars and various lobby groups. Needless to say, the interactions among these individuals, institutions and elements of civil society during this period are modelled within official history in terms of causes and consequences. Among the (retrospectively) cited causes of the outbreak of the violence that initiated the sequence are: poverty, acute racial tension, corruption in the judicial system, lack of political representation for poor blacks, a preceding drought, and also the radicalising effects of religious emancipatory discourse. While by their very nature the consequences that can be drawn from 'Morant Bay' are prey to ideological interpretations, we can nonetheless list among them: the dissolution of the Jamaican House of Assembly, the imposition of Crown Colony rule and, in England at least, a vigorous legal, political and philosophical debate about the status of martial law. This last in particular stretches beyond the specific period of the 'Morant Bay' referent, precisely because its implications echoed throughout the British Empire of the late nineteenth century.

In broad strokes, these are the minimal elements of the 'Morant Bay' referent. However, they are inseparable from their arrangement into a *named and therefore judged* unity. While 'Morant Bay' serves here to designate a spatially and temporally localisable site, the frequent characterisation of the incidents that unfolded there as a 'revolt' is already a statist reaction to what might have been/might yet be (this must be our operative assumption) an event. The word 'revolt' is a political and politicizing value-judgement that predetermines the topology of referential elements available for our exploration. The judgement 'revolt' is an integral part of the very series of incidents it abbreviates in at least two interrelated ways: firstly, it is discursively incorporated into the historiographical material that circulates it *qua* referent (it is part of its 'representation'), but secondly, it is temporally bound to its original 'truth' in the form of an on-going reaction. For the statist nomination 'revolt' continues to retrospectively justify the violence of the sovereign response to the disturbances that broke out at 'Morant Bay', even though this was the locus of its 'original' controversy. Particularly in the form of the debate about martial law that it sparked, but also in a displaced way in its historiographical framing, 'Morant Bay' fully exposed (and exposes) *sovereignty as a mechanism for the counter-nominating classification of conflicts.*

Was the bloodshed that occurred on October the 11th 1865 and after really best described as a revolt, suggesting a widespread rejection of all authority, particularly of the rule of law? Was it, perhaps, a riot, suggesting a spontaneous, ephemeral and disorganised expression of generalised social unrest? Or could it be referred to as an insurrection, implying a degree of organisation and planning and the goal of taking over the reigns of power (rather than simply rejecting its manifestations)? Could one even go so far as to describe it as an attempted revolution, indicating not only political organisation and the goal of assuming power, but also of imposing a radical change of the mode of governance? We will want to add 'event' to this list, but a glance at the rich historical literature on the 'Morant Bay' referent demonstrates the full gamut of these categorisations.

Philip Curtin (1955) characterises it as a demonstration that turned into a riot that then snowballed into a rebellion. Douglas Hall (1959) defines it as a riot similar to innumerable others in the wake of emancipation, significant only for the brutality of the suppression it met with. Likewise, Mavis Christine Campbell (1976) sees 'Morant Bay' "as 'nothing but a local riot' and in modern terms, as 'not unlike current "marches" or "sit-ins"'" (quoted in Heuman: 2000). Broadly anti-colonial positions tend to emphasise this local riot classification in order to critique the heavy-handedness of Eyre's response. Conversely, conservative commentators underline the fundamental threat to security the 'revolt' or 'uprising' represented in order to justify that response. Thus, William A. Green (1976) claims that the implications of 'Morant Bay' for Jamaican stability were dangerous enough to qualify it as an uprising, with the potential to spark into a full-scale, island-wide rebellion. Naturally, this argument based on a, today, all-too familiar security paradigm, was also typical of contemporaneous contributions to the debate on martial law: already evident in Eyre's own defensive correspondence with the Colonial Office, it was systematically expounded by W. F. Finlason in his deeply troubling *Treatise on Martial Law as Allowed by the Law of England in Time of Rebellion* published in 1866.

This politically motivated minimisation or maximisation of the threat posed by 'Morant Bay' becomes, however, rather complex in the context of openly 'radical' historiography of the period. Far from minimising its dangers in order to excoriate the excesses of the colonial authorities (an essentially 'liberal' tactic), this historiography amplifies the power of popular resistance. Abigail Bakan (1990) as well as Trevor Monroe and Don Robotham (1977), for example, prefer to situate 'Morant Bay' in the wider history of class conflict in Jamaica. Bakan uses a Gramscian framework in order to situate 'Morant Bay' (which she classifies as an 'uprising') as a critical moment in the hegemonic negotiation of power between metropole and colony, the latter forcing the former "to acknowledge that the peasantry was politically important" (1990: p.91). Monroe and Robotham, however, sound the most stridently 'revolutionary' tone: "The struggle [at Morant Bay] was a struggle for the ex-slaves, the masses, to seize the government and to take hold of the economy to make it into their own" (1977, p.25).[14] While this is a fairly naked case of retrofitting (there is scant historical evidence of anything like this degree of ideological cohesion or purposefulness), it does represent a version of a radical approach to historiography, of which, as we have suggested, eventual historiography may be considered a necessary refinement. Their claim comes in the context of an orthodox Marxist account of the 'struggles of the Jamaican people' which draws a deliberate dialectical line from 1865 right up to the author's (then) present, and the revival of anti-imperial, often pan-African, third worldist militancy in the 1970s. In Jamaica, as we will see in the next chapter, this took the form of a heady mixture of resurgent Garveyism, the cultural prominence of Rastafari and militant reggae, and the brand of 'popular democratic socialism' practiced by Michael Manley which, in its appeal to black Jamaicans, frequently deployed the trope of Africa. Clearly, the revolutionary classification of the 'Morant Bay' referent is here intended to resonate with then-contemporary, postcolonial radicalisms. However, I hope I have done enough in Chapters 2 and 5 to indicate the weaknesses of so-called radical historiography.

Other historians still, however—and this justifies our stress on the contiguous 'worlds' involved in imperial sovereignty—emphasise the consequences of the incident at Morant Bay not for Jamaica, but for Imperial Britain. Thus, Semmel (1962), Knox (1976), Hussain (2003) and particularly Kostal (2005) explore the legal, political and philosophical backwash flowing from the 'Governor Eyre Controversy' back to the metropole. In fact, this controversy is itself a sub-referent of 'Morant Bay' that nonetheless condenses the core problem of definition that appears to be a hermeneutic dispute, but which actually indexes, I would argue, the unrepresentable truth at the 'origin' of the event itself. Precisely as a kind of juridical but also moral and philosophical aporia, the 'Morant Bay' referent continues to carry a challenge to sovereignty's regulatory inclusion of conflict (and this is the source of its potential 'resurrection' in Badiou's sense). For any verdict on the legality or otherwise of Eyre's use of martial law in Jamaica clearly threatened a whole legitimating discourse supporting the sovereign use of the means of violence in the British colonies.

As a series of empirical incidents, 'Morant Bay' and its sub-set, 'the Governor Eyre controversy', dramatises the centrality of the sovereign classification of

---

14. A similarly orthodox Marxist interpretation is offered in Beckford and Witter: 1982.

conflicts in the nullification, through counter-nomination, of potential events. However, specifically as an historical referent, 'Morant Bay' demonstrates that this classificatory battle continues at a discursive level in the form of a range of diagnostic terms ('riot', 'rebellion', 'insurrection', 'revolution' etc.) that all serve to delimit a founding truth. In this sense, if sovereignty is to an important degree the power of counter-nomination over evental sites, then official history is one of its modes of on-going evental reaction. As we saw in the last chapter, sovereignty is not only a territorial but also a temporal and ultimately logical practice of incessant denial and occultation.

By way of a pertinent comparison, one could point to the similarly divided historiography of the armed uprisings against British colonial power in India between 1857 and 1858. Nationalistic Indian history draws on the rhetoric of the American revolution to refer to this period as the 'First War of Indian Independence', whereas standard British history still refers to it either as the 'Indian Mutiny' or the 'Indian Rebellion'. The role of historiography in nation-building, and specifically the narratology of conflict, becomes immediately apparent in this juxtaposition. This example is also worth mentioning insofar as the hyperbolic anxiety generated by the representation of the 'Indian Mutiny' in Britain played a crucial role in the response to Morant Bay, both in Jamaica and in the metropole. These connections suggest a certain internal resonance between the conflicts encompassed, but perhaps never truly contained, by Empire.

Distilling the Evental Sequence

At this point we become embroiled again in 'historical events' in the everyday sense: the cause-effect modelling of 'what happened and why' at Morant Bay. Necessarily then, we must adopt for a moment the habitual style of statist historical discourse which organises the elements of the historical referent we have just enumerated into a linear order. The more detailed chronology of 'what happened' at Morant Bay in 1865 is as follows:

A. On the 8th of October, 1865, in a court house in Morant Bay, one Lewis Miller was prosecuted for trespassing after going into a neighbour's pasture to recover his horse. When the verdict of guilty was reached, an angry crowd that had gathered outside the courthouse to protest previous injustices caused a major disturbance. This crowd was led by Paul Bogle, a Baptist deacon and political agitator who had been denouncing the appalling conditions for poor blacks in Jamaica from the pulpit of his church, and who had gathered a significant following, as well as support from one of the few coloured representatives in the Jamaican House of Assembly, George William Gordon. The magistrates in the court house issued 28 arrest warrants that day, including one for Bogle, but after scuffling broke out, Bogle escaped with most of his followers and returned to his home village of Stony Gut.

B. Three days later, Bogle and fully four hundred followers marched back into Morant Bay to resume their protest. They ransacked the police station before moving on to the court house. A volunteer militia had been organised to meet them there, and as they approached, a volley was fired into the crowd killing ten people. Nonetheless, they drove on into the court house, set fire to the school and adjoining buildings and released fifty-two prisoners from the jail house. Policemen, prison guards and legal clerks were hacked to pieces with machetes and beaten to death with clubs.

C. The rioting and killing continued into the following day, spreading out into the whole parish of St. Thomas-in-the-East. The day after that, the 13th, the governor of the island, Edward John Eyre, declared martial law, although he restricted it to the county of Surrey and excluded from within this zone the city of Kingston. Troops were immediately deployed and bloody fighting continued for ten days until a Maroon regiment captured Paul Bogle on the 23rd of October. Honouring the 1739 treaty, the Maroons handed him over to the authorities. The following day, Bogle was court-marshalled and hanged.

D. Prior to Bogle's execution, George William Gordon had been arrested on the 17th of October in Kingston, which was still under civil jurisdiction, and then transferred to Morant Bay where martial law operated. There he faced a court martial rather than a civil trial and, being found guilty of sedition and treason, was executed on the same day that Bogle was captured. The martial law by which Gordon was condemned to death stayed in effect until the 13th of November, by which time the 'rebellion' had been largely suppressed.

E. News of the 'rebellion' in Jamaica was met in Britain, initially, by relief that one of the Crown's most valuable possessions had been saved from near destruction. Yet as details of Governor Eyre's use of martial law emerged, particularly in relation to the execution of Gordon, murmurs of concern turned into a full-scale public outcry. Prodded into action by the Jamaica Committee (formed specifically in response to Morant Bay and boasting high-profile members such as the philosopher and economist, John Stuart Mill), the Colonial Office launched a Royal Commission into the disturbances. When this Commission concluded in April 1866, it found that the death penalty had been used too freely, that floggings had been unnecessarily vicious and sustained, and that the burning of over 1,000 homes of poor blacks was excessively cruel. Governor Eyre was dismissed but, much to the chagrin of the Jamaica Committee, he never faced trial for the murder of Gordon (although he was unsuccessfully tried for 'high crimes and misdemeanours').

F. The British Government's political response to Morant Bay was to dissolve the Jamaican House of Assembly, which had previously enjoyed independent executive power, and to impose on the island the ignominy of Crown Colony rule (rule directly from Westminster). The new Legislative Council that replaced it was composed overwhelmingly of metropolitan officials and lacked even the modicum of 'popular' representation the previous Assembly had had. That is, the sovereignty, both legal and administrative, of the mother country was reasserted through the inclusion of the Jamaican subset into the imperial set. As Sherlock and Bennett have put it,

"'Massa' was still there, but the crown was now in control" (1998, p.265).

G. As Kostal (2005) has exhaustively documented, the events at Morant Bay
    led to a lively, long-lasting and ultimately unresolved journalistic as well as
    scholarly debate in Britain as to the history, definition and morality of mar-
    tial law as a tool of metropolitan and imperial statecraft.

As already indicated, this narrative of the elements of the 'Morant Bay' referent are
shaped by and contained within an explanatory causal framework which includes
the following putative precursors (adapted from Robotham: 1981):

1. Immediately after emancipation in 1833, a form of feudalism arose in
    Jamaica under which ex-slaves were forced to live on land belonging to the
    very planters who had been their 'masters'. They were charged rents which
    they could only pay in kind in the form of their labour, and prevented by
    various legal mechanisms from acquiring enough land to be self-sufficient
    smallholders (see chapter 20 of Sherlock and Bennett: 1998). Thus, for all
    intents and purposes the concrete conditions of slavery continued after its
    merely formal abolition and even following the end of the apprenticeship
    system in 1838.

2. Numerous inflated taxes were imposed on the black population by the co-
    lonial Assembly to offset the losses incurred by the end of slavery. To give
    just one telling example, the tax on the cheap cotton worn by the poor in-
    creased by a staggering 1,150% between 1840 and the year of the distur-
    bances at Morant Bay.

3. The poor endured high unemployment and widespread underemployment
    because of the seasonal and irregular nature of work on the sugar estates.
    In the skewed client-economy of colonial Jamaica, these estates remained
    the primary employers on the island even though they had begun, after
    1854 in particular (when Britain removed the protective tariffs on sugar), to
    fall into such ruin that many were already being abandoned.

4. Even those who were employed saw massive decreases in wages caused by
    the price rises, on both local and imported goods, resulting from the dis-
    ruption in trade brought about by the American Civil War (1861-1865). The
    Civil War not only created a scarcity of goods on the island, dramatising its
    lack of self-sufficiency, but it also closed off a trade route that had already
    become vital following the end of protectionist privileges with Britain.

5. Poor blacks had almost no representation in the Jamaican House of
    Assembly which continued to be dominated by the white plantocracy long
    after emancipation, despite the gradual influx of a brown political class.
    This was in stark contrast to the racial composition of the island: census
    data from 1844 shows African-Jamaicans making up 78% of the popula-
    tion, whites only 4.2% (Sherlock and Bennett: 1998, p.192). The conse-
    quent racial tension on the island, alongside growing bitterness at the col-
    lapse of the plantation-system, contributed in no small part to the excess-
    es of Eyre's suppression.

6. The network of local courts which constituted the Jamaican justice system
    was also dominated by white or brown planter attorneys who openly used

law as a means of bolstering the minority's fragile grasp on power. For example, in the year of the disturbances at Morant Bay, in the Parish of St. Thomas-in-the-East where it took place, 24 of the 28 Justices of the Peace were proprietors, lessees, attorneys, or managers of sugar estates. Even as its economic base had begun to disintegrate then, the plantocracy maintained a vice-like grip on the Jamaican legal system and used it to maintain their dominance despite, or rather because of, their growing demographic as well as economic weakness.

7. The 'Great Revival' of religious belief, mainly Baptist, among poor Jamaican blacks between 1860 and 1866 "was the necessary and direct politico-ideological precursor of the Morant Bay Revolt" (Robotham: 1981, p.18), not least in providing a network for practical political organisation as well as an emancipatory discourse with which to galvanize the people. Paul Bogle, like Sam Sharpe before him, would emerge from and utilise this discursive space. [15]

While these contributing factors are indispensable in retrospectively explaining 'Morant Bay', for the eventing historiography in which we are engaged here, they represent a certain danger. For these relational, site- and time-specific factors threaten to constrain the eventual sequence, depending on which of their implied themes we chose to concentrate upon: poverty, racial tension, political disenfranchisement, an iniquitous judicial system, religious fervour, and so on. Privileging any one of these threatens to pave the way for a problem-solution narrative which pacifies the radicality of eventual truth by rendering it finite. For example, the (past) political disenfranchisement of poor Jamaican blacks can always be 'resolved' with reference to the extension of universal adult suffrage in 1944 and the granting of full independence in 1962, as if the former was not a fig-leaf for ongoing social inequalities distributed along racial lines, and as if the latter was not merely the inauguration of a new period of neo-colonial oppression (typified by Michael Manley's struggles with the IMF in the 1970s). Indeed, there are some grounds for positing a kind reactionary form of 'resurrection', with 1962 repeating the false freedom of 1833.

Precisely to avoid this sort of occultation of the truth of 'Morant Bay' by means of its causal domestication, I propose to follow Badiou's Maoist dictum that 'one divides into two' by positing a scissional eventual sequence that breaks the linearity of the referent's chronology into two elements: a truth-sequence, and a denial-sequence.

> Truth-sequence: October 8th—October 23rd, the 'subject-body' of Bogle's black peasant army, whose numbers grew as their fidelity to the truth of black exploitation was transmitted to other blacks, but which dissipated with Bogle's execution (A-C above).

> Denial-sequence: October 13th—April of 1866, the reactionary subjectivity of Governor Eyre and the use of martial law, the obscure subjectivity of imperial sovereignty (the imposition of Crown Colony rule). (D-G above).

---

15. For an analysis of the impact of missionaries on early slave rebellions, see Turner: 1998.

The truth sequence initiated and carried by the subject-body of Bogle's semi-organised black peasant army unleashed a law-breaking violence against the law-making violence of colonial sovereignty, ostensibly targeting its institutional manifestations in the court-house, the jail and the police station. The inclusive unity of this black subject-body arguably rendered visible a void of the Jamaican set or 'world' at this particular historical juncture, following emancipation as a form of compensatory inclusion within the British Empire. Increasingly understanding itself as predicated upon the spread of the rule of law, the civilizing mission, and even 'fair play', Empire could not countenance the intense appearance of this paradoxical Jamaican multiple which we shall name 'post-emancipation slavery'. It is precisely here that we are inverting Badiou's claim in *Ethics* that simulacral events are reliant upon real ones: for here, Morant Bay is dependent upon the simulacral event of emancipation. Albeit a modulation in the transcendental of the British Empire and its colonies, at the level precisely of the logic of appearance, the Morant Bay revolt would have been merely oppositional, perhaps even resistant, but certainly not evental, without the Emancipation Act of 1833. And yet simultaneously disentangling itself from the pacifying inclusion of emancipation, which in many ways robbed the ex-slaves of their locus of opposition, Bogle's subject-body exposed three interlinked continuities reaching back to the pre-emancipation slavery period. Firstly, the continuation of forced and therefore unfree labour by means of tax hikes, rent-in-kind, careful control of land entitlements and so on. Secondly, the colonial authority's continuing reliance on a (newly racialised) version of the old binary between free and slave. And thirdly, the continuing recourse, in Jamaica, to a Hobbesian model of sovereignty ultimately incompatible with metropolitan liberalisation: the revolt forced colonial power to show its reliance on the Hobbesian tourniquet, and its basis in the logic of the exception.

Thus, the denial-sequence incorporates two moments of reaction: the excesses committed under martial law as a violent denial (post-emancipation slaves *cannot* be free), and the imposition of Crown Colony rule as a more thoroughgoing occultation (there is no divisive difference here, since poor blacks are also Her Majesty's subjects). Here, however, we need to think of a colonial mode of sovereignty in transition. In Hardt and Negri's Deleuzian analysis of the emergence of today's Empire (Hardt & Negri: 2000), which, it should be noted, supposedly breaks with imperialism, European modernity is characterised by a constitutive tension between the unleashing of the emancipatory power of the 'multitude' on the one hand, and the reactionary, reterritorialising power of discipline on the other. In properly Deleuzian fashion, Hardt and Negri's fundamental point is that modernity is not some World Historical and therefore necessary passage from absolutism to ever more refined modes of popular sovereignty. Rather, modernity *is* the contradictory, oscillating product of this non-dialectical co-relation between immanence and transcendence, while sovereignty *is* the attempt to manage their interface to the benefit, ultimately, of the constituted power of discipline. We can agree with this analysis at a descriptive level, whilst adding, with Badiou, the crucial rupture of the event and thus a Rousseauian notion of sovereignty as neither immanent nor transcendental, but singular in the qualified sense we have tried to develop.

Nonetheless, the constitutive tension between transcendence and immanence identified by Hardt and Negri is clearly discernible in the 'Morant Bay' referent, in which it is spatialised by the colony/metropole relation. Martial law was already the residue of a transcendental model of sovereignty based on monarchical absolutism, long since overtaken, *in the metropole*, by a more 'liberal' immanent model of sovereignty partially acknowledging 'individual rights' (not least because of the increasingly bourgeois nature of civilian law, and therefore its protection of private property). Ironically, it was this very liberalising tendency in British law that had already created the political conditions in which the Emancipation of Slavery Act could be passed in 1833. Even though, aligning ourselves with Badiou, we cannot interpret this Act as anything but an example of statist reformism, as a modulation that presented itself as an event but certainly was not one, it nonetheless fundamentally changed the transcendental regime of appearance governing the British Empire. The universalising principles of British imperial law demanded that colonial difference did not contaminate it. As a case in point, "the Jamaica affair mainly concerned the moral and legal framework governing white Englishmen at home, not black subjects abroad [Morant Bay] exposed the tectonic stresses created by the nation's embrace of both the will to power and the rule of law" (Kostal: 2005, p.20).

For this reason, the crudity of the reactionary subjectivity inscribed in colonial martial law had to be conjured away in its turn by a strategy of imperial occultation (which we can now conceive as an inclusion which is simultaneously an erasure). In Jamaica in 1865, this involved an attempt, by British sovereign power, to once again include Jamaica more fully in order occlude the problematic belonging of 'post-emancipation black slavery', as if it was no longer allowed to be a sub-set with its own internal 'world' but a simple element of the overarching imperial set. In its constitutional and jurisprudential response to Morant Bay, then, we can see imperial sovereignty as a process of 'enveloping' in the sense developed in *Logics of Worlds*. The extension of Crown Colony rule was explicitly intended to occult the generic body of Bogle's followers within the sovereign body of Empire, to dis-count the threat of the void and stave off the ruination of the One.

Distilling the Evental Statement

Drawing on historical sources, whether official documents within the Colonial Office records or eyewitness testimonies brought to the attention of the Royal Commission, one can identify numerous 'diegetic' candidates for an evental statement crystallising the truth of the 'Morant Bay' sequence. Many, predictably, relate to the reality of the class-race nexus from which the violence clearly irrupted. The cry 'colour for colour!' was repeatedly heard, as well as an inversion of racist indiscrimination: 'we don't know one buckra [white person] from another, we will kill them all' (Heuman: 2000, p.7). Yet the complicated chromatism which still effects Jamaican society to this day, and which has long necessitated distinctions between black, brown and white that double as class indicators, meant that the demand 'colour for colour' was difficult in practice to enforce: those of suspect skin-hue and therefore allegiance were forced by Bogle's followers to swear an oath on the bible to 'cleave to the blacks'. Given the glaring mismatch between demography and power on the island, this racialisation of fidelity in Badiou's sense is hardly surprising.

Other statements, however, simply articulate the unconditional nature of evental fidelity. For example, in response to the desperate entreaties for 'Peace in Her Majesty's Name!' made by representatives of colonial law, Bogle's 'army' merely declared 'War not peace!' (Heuman: 2000, p.7). This exchange constitutes a direct confrontation between transcendant and immanent sovereignty, between discipline and 'people power', around the foundational right to the exercise of the means of violence. A letter sent to the Custos (or elected mayor) of the parish of St Mary at the time further demonstrates the stark divisiveness typical of faithful subjects:

> Our cutlass is now ready. Your swords we do not care about. Your firearms we don't care about. It must be life or death between us before we should live such a miserable life (qtd in Heuman: 2000, p.103).

The specificity of the experience of poor blacks coupled with a militant willingness to die for an improvement in their unhappy lot, initially seems to suggest an extreme form of identity politics (akin to the discourse of the early Black Panthers in the 1960s civil rights movement perhaps), and thus the exact opposite of the generic universalism characteristic of evental truths. However, I would argue that poor blacks operated in the Jamaican world of 1865 just as Marx argued the proletariat in general operates within capitalism: in *Contributions to the Critique of Hegel's Philosophy of Right*, Marx famously describes the proletariat as a class which has a universal character because its suffering is universal; it does not claim a particular redress, because the wrong done to it is not a particular wrong but wrong in general. This is not identity politics then. It is not *as* blacks in any essential sense, or *for* blacks in any communitarian sense, that Bogle's followers rebel, but as those who are dis-counted within their world *through* blackness as a differential mode of counting. Rather than the blackness filled by racist discourse with predicates such as 'inferior', 'backward', 'physical not cerebral' etc., this is the much more challenging because predicateless blackness of the void. In this sense, lacking sufficient land for independent subsistence as well as the political clout to change their situation, the suffering of poor Jamaican blacks arguably condemned the entire colonial system, articulating the exploitative truth at its rotten core even post-emancipation.

Here, nonetheless, we seem to confront a major tension between universal truths, and the locally situated, relational nature of truth-procedures, including the always local determination of multiples (see *LW*, p.122). How can Morant Bay articulate a universal truth when it is so clearly colour-coded? What is tremendously difficult, yet of paramount importance, is maintaining a term like 'race' as a descriptor of a purely formal, relational difference ordering the regime of appearance in the particular world of 19th century Jamaica. Overlaid, to be sure, by the discursive 'racisms' of which postcolonial theory has made us rightly aware, this relational understanding of race *has absolutely no ontological basis whatsoever*. Indeed, the whole rationale for the division of Badiou's monumental project in *Being and Event* into two separate volumes rests on the notion that the set-theoretical determination of the being of a given multiple provides absolutely no indication of its being-there in a world of appearances. As a discourse of appearance par excellence, race is clearly a transcendental rather than an ontological problematic: "We will call 'transcendental' the operative ensemble which permits the giving of a sense of 'more' or 'less' to identities and differences in a determined world" (*LW*, p.127). No discussion of Jamaica, past or present, could ignore the role of race in this specific sense in establishing the 'more' and 'less' characterising the distribution of actual and symbolic capital in Jamaican society. However, it is vital that the term 'transcendental' is understood as specific to a given world: Badiou's notion of the transcendental "is only about local dispositions, and not a universal theory of differences" (*LW*, pp.130-131), not least because "there is not a Universe, only worlds" (*LW*, p.150). If the familiar cultural studies/postcolonial theory critique of 'race' as merely discursive (with this 'merely' being always qualified by Edward Said's Foucaultian sense of discourse as a material force) is to be accepted, it follows that the specificity of its local deployment in a particular world must be acknowledged. Despite his antipathy for postcolonial intellectual trends, then, I would argue that Badiou's logic of appearance, precisely in its difference from his ontology, helps us to do exactly that.

However, where the ontological and transcendental orders do intersect is around the structural non-appearance of the void in a world. Here, we see how Badiou's ontology is inseparable from the kind of politics that can be extrapolated from his thought. His avowed Platonism turns on the argument put forward in the *Sophist* that carefully refutes the Parmenedian postulate of the being of non-being.[16] In the context of our example, to follow Parmenides and posit the being of non-being would indeed constitute an assertion of the essence of oppressed blackness upon which an identity politics might be built, somewhat in the manner of the *Négritude* movement led by Aimé Césaire and Léopold Senghor. By contrast, for Badiou, the relationality of appearance goes all the way down. Ontologically speaking, there is nothing that pre-exists a worldly configuration, 'no-thing' outside of relation, only relation itself as a constitutive operation. Thus, while there is the formal requirement of a zero degree of appearance in the ordering of any world, non-appearance does not index the *being of nothingness*, a kind of outside of representation that might be recouped. This is where Badiou's rather rigid emphasis on commutative relationality even in situations of conflict in *Logics of Worlds* comes into its own again. It enables us to perceive the race relation as both violently structuring and a matter of mere appearances, both concrete and without underlying essence. Moreover, non-appearance may expose a null degree of relation with the transcendental measure that organises that particular world (white privilege, for example), but *a null relation is still a relation*. This is another caveat against absolute singularity. The maximal 'intensity' which the existence of black exploitation suddenly embodied during the eventual sequence of Morant Bay remains a

---

16. In brief, Plato evades the trap set by Parmenides by defining the different not in relation to the same, but by means of the introduction of a third term, the Other. For a fuller account of this aspect of the *Sophist*, see the first chapter in Wright: 2006.

relational intensity, and not a Spinozan, vitalist, ontological one. Far from allowing itself to be captured by the dominant discursive construction of 'blackness', it is
only as the abject yet defining (relational) Other of colonial white supremacist discourse and material practice that 'blackness' here has revelatory and transformative power.

Difficult as this may be for many black Jamaicans, this can have nothing *directly* to do with a lost, metaphysical 'Africa', with the ancient civilizations of Ethiopia
or Egypt, or with the supposedly inherent qualities of African resistance to a tragic
history of oppression. As we will see in the next chapter, this does not prevent such
claims having an important role to play in maintaining resistant individuals. In order to achieve this difficult balancing act—evading the pacifying particularisations
of the site-specific determinants of the Morant Bay incident on the one hand, yet
remaining faithful to the particular logic of appearance of the Jamaican world on
the other—it is imperative that race is retained in our search for an evental statement, yet exclusively as an empty cipher for structural inequality.

In this sense, and returning to the evental sequence itself, it is clear that the primary target of the rage of Bogle's followers was *law as a support for a racist regime of
appearance*. Another potential evental statement, therefore, albeit arising from one
of the so-called Underhill meetings prior to the actual incidents at Morant Bay, [17]
is the call for 'an end to a law for the rich and a law for the poor' (Heuman, 2000:
p.53). For the reasons just outlined, this statement can legitimately be rendered as
'an end to a law for whites and a law for blacks'. It would be a mistake, however, to
transcribe this into 'Justice not Law!', even if this would seem to resonate powerfully with the militant declaration 'War not Peace!'. While Bogle's followers themselves were clearly motivated by something like a sense of natural justice over and
above procedural law, because martial law deploys *exactly the same logic of extra-legal legitimacy*, this statement threatens to reduce 'Morant Bay' to the very standoff
between competing sovereignties by which colonial power justified its lethal violence. That is, the statement 'Justice not law!' actually blurs the crucial distinction,
or scission, we have insisted upon between the truth-sequence and the reaction-se-
quence. After all, the notion of a supra-legal justice has its absolutist as well as its
Jacobin history. In neither case does it loosen the tourniquet of modern sovereignty in its dialectical reliance on conflict.

It would be far better to emphasise the immanent side of imperial sovereignty which extends non-discriminating, universal legal principles to everyone and
to extract from this a divisive singularity. [18] It would be preferable, therefore, to

---

17. Edward Underhill was the secretary of the Baptist Missionary Society in Britain. He had
toured Jamaica in 1859 and published his observations about its problems in 1862. However, it
was a letter that he wrote to the Secretary of State for the Colonies in January 1865, subsequently published in a Jamaican newspaper in March of the same year, that prompted a series of petitions and public meetings across the island at which the problems he had identified and the solutions he had suggested were debated. George William Gordon chaired several of these meetings.

18. An awareness of this ambivalence within modern sovereignty was actually evident in the
attitudes of many of Bogle's supporters to their sovereign representative, Queen Victoria:
They [...] maintained that the Queen had sent them clothes and money during the summer of
1865, only to have the goods diverted by the planters to the Indian indentured labourers. At var-

posit, as the evental statement articulating the truth of the Morant Bay referent, the unconditional demand: 'equality before the law!'. While this may sound like a weakly liberal rather than a strongly radical sentiment, in the specific world of mid-nineteenth century Jamaica—viciously stratified as it was by racial differences literally 'policed' by colonial law—it amounted to a veritable call for total social upheaval.

A DIAGRAM OF TWO JAMAICAS

We are now in a position to complete our diagram of the phases and logics of slave resistance and sovereign responses in Jamaica. We previously identified two phases. The first, from 1655 to 1760, was termed 'African Resistance' and included the first Maroon War and Tacky's Rebellion. It was based on the static antagonism of reciprocal difference between African and slave master. The second phase, from 1760 to 1865, was termed 'Creolized Opposition' and initially involved the hegemonic yet internal battle of competing interests between slaves and slave owners, but also encompassed the re-emergence of resistance through opposition in the form of the Sam Sharpe Rebellion of 1831-1832 which began to make tactical use of the appeal to metropolitan imperial sovereignty against its colonial counterpart. A violent call for inclusion, Sharpe's Rebellion culminated in the granting of emancipation in 1833.

With what we have just distilled from Morant Bay, however, we encounter a crucial splitting in the otherwise incremental arc of inclusion the previous two phases seem to describe. We can broadly agree, then, with Philip D. Curtin's thesis of the emergence of 'two Jamaica's' post-emancipation, one poor, black, and nourished by residually African practices and beliefs, the other white and brown and fundamentally metropolitan in outlook (Curtin: 1955). But here we can add to Curtin's thesis the logic of inclusion that dominated the latter, and the logic of singular difference that sustained the former. We will call the third phase 'Creolized Statism' and the fourth 'Jamaican Affirmation'. Both emerge from what I have tried to characterise as the event, rather than the exception, of the Morant Bay Revolt of 1865, the former as its occultation, the latter in fidelity to it.

Creolized Statism (1865-1962):

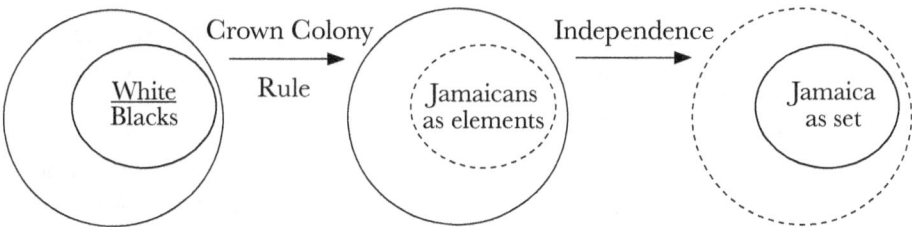

---

ious stages of the rebellion, Paul Bogle made it clear that he was not rebelling against the Queen. There was even a hope that the Queen would replace the current set of white authorities and send others with whom the rebels could negotiate (Heuman: 2000, p.36).

What seems like naïve subservience to an indoctrinated ideal here can actually be read as a sophisticated awareness, and deployment, of the emancipatory potential within the universalism of modern sovereignty.

From left to right then, the Morant Bay Revolt, like any truth procedure, divided its multiples into faithful and unfaithful elements responding positively and negatively to the evental imperative 'equality before the law'. Because of the divisive role of law in cleaving Jamaican society along racial lines, this division of faithful and unfaithful elements also largely followed racial lines. This dramatic exposure of the post-emancipation continuity with slavery led imperial sovereignty to prevent the Jamaican count continuing in a way that was now resolutely incompatible with the imperial count. Thus, Crown Colony rule was imposed, weakening the appearance of the Jamaican subset (hence the broken line in the middle circle of the diagram) in order to be able to include both blacks and whites as unitary Jamaican elements, rather than as antagonistic parts, of the British Empire.

Paradoxically however, already in this gesture of paternal inclusion the outlines of the logic of nationalism become discernible since it is necessarily as *Jamaicans* (not as slaves, not as masters, not as colonisers, not as colonised) that the inhabitants are indexed as being-there within the imperial world. Indeed, what I am calling 'creolized statism' would crystallize as bourgeois Jamaican nationalism in the aftermath of yet another conflict: the mass general strikes of 1938. The prominence of trade unions in this conflict, the mediating role of 'brown' union leaders such as Norman Washington Manley and Alexander Bustamante, and the fact that these two figures would go on to usher Jamaica towards both independence and a two-party political system based on the Westminster model, firmly places the 1938 strikes within the paradigm of 'creolized statism'. Bourgeois Jamaican nationalism was a creole phenomenon to the extent that it continued to negotiate compromises from *within* Empire rather than rejecting it outright. It was also statist insofar as it aspired to become a set in its own right. Creolized statism was successful by its own narrow terms: independence was granted on August 6th, 1962.[19]

The broken outer ring of the final circle on the right, therefore, represents the weakening of imperial sovereignty into the loosest form of inclusion, namely, the Commonwealth of Nations (even the qualifier 'British' was dropped as long ago as 1949, and it now includes two nations that are not even ex-British colonies—Rwanda and Mozambique). The various and progressively more effete modes of inclusion developed by the Empire—settler colony, crown colony, dominion, protectorate, mandate, dependency and now simply 'oversees territory'—were a series of responses to the supernumerary belonging forced onto the imperial count by the conflicts it faced. In a sense, it might not be wrong to claim that the British Empire modulated itself out of existence.

Crucially, however, despite its 'evental' appearances decolonization was little more than a transition to neo-colonialism in Kwame Nkruma's sense of nominal political independence from, but total economic dependence upon, the ex-colonial powers (see Nkrumah: 1965). One should go further. The culmination of creolised statism in independence inaugurated Jamaica into the contemporary technologies of pacifying inclusion that go by the name 'globalization', which continues to be deeply racially divided, and arguably neo-colonial or neo-imperial in

---

19. It is worth noting that independence was also granted first to the white settler colonies of Canada and then Australia and New Zealand—Ireland, of course, being the notable exception.

nature. Just as emancipation was a threat to the real struggles for black freedom in Jamaica, the same could be said for independence, after which black, white, brown and yellow were all said to be 'Jamaican' even as Jamaica struggled to assert its statist count in the newly globalised era. This is why it is crucial, I believe, to trace a quite different trajectory stemming from Morant Bay.

African-Jamaican Affirmation (1865–):

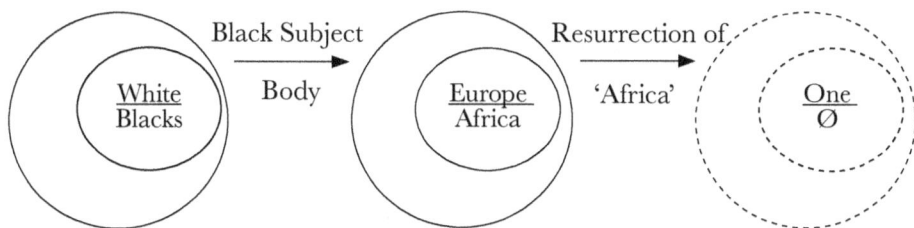

The cleaving of 'colour for colour' at Morant Bay inaugurated a black subject body distinct from individuals merely subjugated as black in the situation of post-emancipation exploitation. Far from allowing themselves to be incorporated into the British imperial set as loyal subjects, and without getting involved either in the white and brown creolised project of Jamaican nationalism and independence, this subject body effectively subtracted itself from the Jamaican situation by developing a divisive 'African' consciousness which was opposed to European imperialistic values, including nationalism.

However, the inverted commas here indicate that this Africa was *not* the same Africa as that to which the Maroons and Tacky had appealed back in the 18th century, through direct, lived experience and cultural proximity. Although much important work has been done to demonstrate the strong and vibrant African heritage in Jamaican culture, more important by far than the putative authenticity of origins often implied by this kind of work, is precisely the creolised nature of Jamaican culture, its hybrid sublation of the diverse strands it tries to weave together—African, British, but also Indian, Chinese, Jewish and increasingly American. Africa in Jamaica perhaps never was Africa per se (even first generation slaves rarely spoke the same language, or shared the same religious or spiritual beliefs). And a peculiarly Jamaican situation had emerged through creolization by the mid 19th century, by which time the vast majority of black Jamaicans were not African-born. Thus, unlike the binarism of the first phase of African resistance in Jamaica, which fell all-too easily into the trap of the Hobbesian tourniquet, the 'Africa' deployed in this fourth phase is what I would call, following Oliver Feltham (2008), a 'logic of incompletion' entirely specific to the Jamaican situation.

The final circle on the right hand side of our diagram indicates the generic trajectory of this logic of incompletion. Not only is the attempted set of sets that was the British Empire dissolved, but so also is the newly 'independent' Jamaican set, precisely because its postcolonial count continues to discount *this* Africa, the one that divides its national imaginary in two and refuses its mode of inclusion. Beneath the One of the new Jamaican State then, this black subject body incompletes the Jamaican situation in a way that pushes towards the generic *in its specifically Jamaican non-appearance.* It is simultaneously an affirmation and a subtraction, one that began to attain an intensity of appearance in the early 20th century, as we shall see in the next chapter.

7

Rastafarian Fidelities: Towards an Evental Culture

Ras Tafari is King of Kings and Lord of Lords. The black
people will no longer look to George the Fifth—Ras Tafari is
their king (Leonard Howell, 1932)

If the Morant Bay 'Revolt' of 1865 was an event, who are its faithful subjects and
what truth do they force onto the Jamaican situation? In this chapter I will make
the case for the Rastafari movement[1] as the contemporary heir of Paul Bogle's
black subject-body.

Examining this enigmatic movement as a political rather than intrinsically religious phenomenon (although this is a distinction we will have to question) returns
us to the themes explored in Chapter 4 where the singularity of the Badiouian subject was qualified, and where the issue of the relationship between resistance and
subjectivity proper was raised. Rastafari demonstrates both the residually 'worldly'
nature of subjects—it quite clearly emerges from the specifically Jamaican experience of exploitation and resistance—and the fine line between militant subtraction
and identity politics, between affirmation and assimilation. Turning to Rastafari
also leads us to confront something like a lived rather than scholarly version of the
evental historiography developed in Chapter 5. The Rasta belief-system is imbued
with a powerful and yet idiosyncratic historical consciousness. To the Rasta, the
present *is* the permanent resurrection of an occulted past: simultaneously the history of cultural dispossession, physical and spiritual dislocation and suffering associated with slavery; and the history of ancient African civilizations such as those of
Ethiopia and Egypt that preceded the European slave trade.

But focussing on the Rastafari movement also forces us beyond merely applying and extending what we have developed in previous chapters. It invites us
to underline the importance of something that within the Badiouian framework
remains an out-and-out oxymoron. I am referring to a specifically *cultural form of*

---

1. Many Rastas take offence to the term 'Rastafarianism'. I will not be using it here either,
since Rastafari's open, flexible, non-dogmatic nature makes its reduction to an 'ism' simply inaccurate. It is this combination of militancy and resistance to becoming an 'ism' that particularly interests me here.

politics. If we have spent previous chapters carving out the counter-intuitive concept of 'evental historiography', we must now risk outlining a similarly dubious notion: that of an 'evental culture'. It will be argued that an evental conception of culture contains a partial answer to Badiou's on-going question regarding the political organisation of fidelity addressed in Chapter 2. The example of Rastafari will enable us to develop this concept, but also underline its dangerous propensity for co-optation. Before undertaking this task however, it is important to begin by identifying those elements of the Badiouian approach that constitute serious obstacles to any notion of an evental culture.

THE OXYMORON OF CULTURAL POLITICS

With exquisite hauteur, Badiou has dismissed the very idea of cultural politics, associated primarily with Anglo-Saxon Cultural Studies, as "comical, purely comical" (Badiou: 1992, p.250). There are at least three reasons for this outright and arguably condescending dismissal.

Firstly and most problematically, Badiou implicitly prefixes the word 'culture' with the word 'mere' in order to indicate its interchangeability with the given, the quotidian, the banal. In his polemical deployments of the concept, particularly in the short book on St. Paul, what is offered is a deliberately *anthropological* version of culture as a ritualised way of life mired in dumb repetitiveness (a version of anthropology which has of course long been challenged from within anthropology itself). Culture is ordinary for Badiou then, not at all in Raymond Williams' democratising sense, but rather in its lifeless indifference to truth. Whereas Williams was diagnosing an historical moment of deep social change in which high culture was escaping the confines of the galleries and museums and being disseminated within a mass mediated and commodified public sphere, the 'ordinariness' of culture for Badiou is simply a pejorative condemning its inert fixity. Evental novelty *must* be fiercely acultural if culture is understood in this reductive way, as simply an honorific name for 'what is'.

Moreover, if Badiou addresses culture affirmatively at all, it is invariably under the exalted heading of art. But to be exalted, culture *qua* art must be rigorously separated from worldly notions of 'high culture' and the symbolic and cultural capital attaching to them. Badiou has explicitly complained that the "name 'culture' comes to obliterate that of 'art'" (*SP*, p.12). This is not at all the same problematisation of the high culture-low culture opposition at the root of Cultural Studies, based primarily in sociological observation of changes in mass consumption: Badiou's approach is the philosophical distillation of a concept from the ubiquitous dross of doxa. Thus, his acute readings of Mallarmé, Beckett, Celan, Pessoa, Brecht, Schoenberg and others all engage in a task of *subtractive purification* aiming to both honour the pure autonomy of art per se and prevent its co-optation by other discursive modes. This approach is particularly clear in his recent book on Wagner (Badiou: 2010). Wagner is of course a figure widely vilified as a precursor of the aestheticization of politics that Walter Benjamin believed could result only in fascism (Benjamin: 1993). Precisely as a moment when high culture takes on a mesmerising and emotive rather than rational mass appeal, the Wagnerian aesthetic, in its kitsch grandiosity, is said to foreshadow sinister mass political forms. Badiou's defence of Wagner then boils down to a careful separation from the link his name has been made to support—by Nietzsche, Heidegger and Lacoue-Labarthe among others—between high art and a bombastic 'blood and soil' mythology of the German people, which did indeed resonate darkly with the Nazis. Having conceptually severed this link, Badiou is then able to reveal the true *internal* logic of Wagner's operatic art, musically even more than theatrically: it becomes the aesthetic vehicle of a very un-'Wagnerian' (i.e., non-proto-fascist) message of hesitancy, openness and undecidability. This separation of high art from high culture, and culture from politics, may allow art to shine forth in its alleged autonomy, but it also inscribes a blindness to the role that cultural politics can and perhaps must play within truth-procedures.

Secondly therefore, and much more relevantly for Cultural Studies, the very conjunction of the two terms 'culture' and 'politics' can only be static and antinomic within Badiou's starkly binary framework. "Politics itself is acultural" (*C*, p.250) because it eschews tradition, identity and even history in favour of innovation and transformation. No doubt Badiou would argue that the kind of cultural politics associated with the critical race studies of Stuart Hall and Paul Gilroy, for example, and also with the counter-hegemonic democracy of Laclau and Mouffe, is inextricably linked to a Gramscian faith in the sphere of representation as a site of productive negotiation. As we have seen, Badiou refuses this extended sense of representation as subtending civil society precisely because it is still too 'parliamentary' for his tastes. Ultimately, the terms 'race', 'class', 'gender', 'sexuality', 'nationality', 'religion' and their various cognates remain State-based ways of counting the elements of a situation, and are consequently incompatible with a generic concept of humanity. To call 'politics' the piecemeal renegotiation of the semantics of these terms, Badiou would insist, is to evade the truly political task of fundamental change. His forthright rejection of the Cultural Studies approach is therefore directly connected to his rejection of the quasi-Levinasian ethics of alterity and 'multiculti' otherness endemic to some versions of poststructuralism, postcolonialism and postmodernism. This is an important and valuable intervention, and championing the notion of cultural politics threatens to undermine it, if, that is, cultural politics is not reconceptualised in the wake of the implications of this very intervention.

But these obstacles to thinking cultural politics within the Badiouian framework have their deepest origin in a specifically philosophical source. We know by now that Badiou follows Plato in insisting that there are only four truth-domains in which events can occur, and that they cannot overlap with one another. The loving encounter, for example, is only for the lovers concerned, not for sentimental artists who might feel moved to depict it (they are free to do so, but it will not touch on its intimate truth). In the first *Manifesto for Philosophy*, Badiou reserves the strong term 'disaster' for just this overlapping of truth-domains. Emulating Plato's purging of the Sophists and related expulsion of the poets, he tasks philosophy with disentangling itself from these disastrous 'sutures'. In particular, he bemoans the neo-Heideggerian Romanticism of deconstruction in its attempts to turn language into the site of an ontological revelation, as if the poets had snuck into the Republic via the backdoor, usurping the mathematicians whose true task ontology is. He warns also against the conflation of politics and science in dogmatic economism, whether Marxist or neoliberal, as well as cautioning, particularly in *The Century*, against the deadly results of merging aesthetic and political avant-gardes. In general then, the apparent overlapping of truths, such as art and politics, seems to send a shiver down Badiou's Platonic spine.

But it is around the question of culture, I would suggest, that Badiou could benefit from engaging precisely with developments in postcolonial anthropology, ethnography and Cultural Studies approaches to everyday life. These disciplines have helped to bring out not so much culture's dynamism (as I have shown, Badiou accepts that change on the level of modulation takes place constantly), but rather, the indispensable support culture provides to subjectivity even in his lofty sense. Far from being a mere mechanism of individuation, culture can sustain the ongoing appearance of the extra-ordinary. Granted, there are real dangers in this intersection between culture and the exceptional subject, and both Badiou and the example of Rastafari will help us to be cognisant of them. Clearly, cultural *recognition* must not be the concern of subjects per definition. The politics of identity understood as cultural or racial or ethnic specificity are entirely incompatible with a generic logic. Nor can the inherent flexibility and vitality of everyday culture often lauded within Cultural Studies be presented as a guarantee of significant change. The kind of interstitial agency Michel de Certeau, for example, discerns in creative yet also unconscious consumption, hardly amounts to a basis for profound social transformation (de Certeau: 1988).

However, the role cultural politics plays in the militant subjective cohesion of political movements, as well as in circulating the undecidable truths they carry through the development of novel modes of expression, is a demonstrably different understanding of the term, one much closer to Badiou's concerns. To take just one obvious example, can one really imagine the Zapatista movement without the specific 'way of life' developed by its militants in Chiapas, the fusion of anarchism, Marxism and indigenous Mayan cosmologies in its ideology, and the powerful rhetoric of Subcomondante Marcos in its communicative strategies with the rest of Mexico and indeed the world? Drawing on the central role of this kind of cultural politics in anti-colonial and anti-capitalist struggles in particular, Cultural Studies has perhaps been better at understanding this dimension of subjectivity than has Badiou's rather patrician, even aristocratic perspective on the issue. On the other hand, it might take a polemicist of Badiou's stature to pull today's Cultural Studies away from its current, lamentably statist preoccupation with multiculturalism, cultural policy and the creative industries, as if Stuart Hall's Gramscian intervention never took place.

In developing in this chapter the notion of an *evental* culture, these three interlinked obstacles—Badiou's reductively quotidian conceptualisation of culture, his separation between art and culture, and his general insistence on the disastrous consequences of the overlapping of truths—will have to be carefully negotiated if the potency of Badiou's intervention into today's modish theoretical paradigms is to be retained. And yet, in doing so, we are only taking our cue from Badiou's own suggestive comments:

> We need a theory of what I call the 'networking' or 'tying together' of truth-procedures. Eventually, I see no reason why this could not be called 'culture', provided that we completely reconstruct a formalized concept of culture (Riera: 2005, p.260)

Even in *Logics of Worlds* with its emphasis on relationality and appearance, Badiou does not seem to have responded in any sustained way to this acknowledged need for a theory of the 'tying together' of truths under the heading of a reconceptualised 'culture'. I would therefore like here to follow Bruno Bosteels' lead in pursuing that possibility:

> [T]his is perhaps how we might define a valid project for cultural studies, provided that we pass through a reflection on what constitutes an event: to study the interactions among the conditions of art, politics, and so on. (Riera 2005: p.260)

To that end, let us turn now to the example of Rastafari.

RASTA FIDELITY, BUT TO WHAT?

Most readers will already have an image of the Rasta: 'natty' dreadlocks; the 'spliff' of 'wisdom weed' or ganja; the symbol of the lion; the red, gold and green of the Ethiopian flag; and, of course, the music—from roots reggae through to dub and arguably on to elements of contemporary dancehall. Some may even have an awareness of the two interrelated beliefs that provide the theological nucleus of Rastafari: firstly, the supposed divinity of Emperor Haile Selassie I who was crowned king of Abyssinia (as it then was) in 1930, and secondly, the supposed status of Ethiopia (as it now is)[2] as the promised land to which one day the suffering black diaspora will be repatriated. But the ready-to-hand nature of this image of the Rasta already demonstrates that, outside the Jamaican context, the movement as a whole has been constructed as little more than either an eccentric religious cult, or a style-based youth movement akin to that of the Californian hippies (Dick Hebdige: 1991; 2000).

The 'whacky cult' caricature in fact stems from the island that spawned it. Arguably performing the counter-nominating functions of the state identified in Chapter 3, the Jamaican political elite has long belittled Rastafari as an extremist sect with criminal tendencies, and a corrupting influence on the young. Its early Kingston-based sociologists in the 1960s described it as a form of desperate escapism on the part of maladjusted youths from the ghettoes, not much different from turning to the bottle (Patterson: 1964; Lanternari: 1963). Within the specific sociology and psychology of religion, it has often been characterised as an irrational 'millenarian cult' (Simpson: 1970; Barrett: 1988). And within Christian theology, where it is studied seriously at all, it tends to be for its 'heretical' Biblical hermeneutics and its syncretic deployment of African belief systems (Bisnauth: 1989; Breiner: 1985; Chevannes: 1995; Erskine 1981). Such has been the encyclopaedia—in

---

2. The word 'Ethiopia' in Rasta discourse is often used as a metonymic reference to the whole African continent.

Badiou's sense—entry under 'R' for Rastafari. As a result, individual Rastas are still disproportionately subjected to police brutality, custodial sentences, and incarceration in mental institutions.

On the other hand, the political elite has also appropriated the movement's powerful symbolism when it suited them. This was notable during the general election of 1972, when the candidate for the People's National Party, Michael Manley, won a landslide victory by wielding a 'rod of correction' supposedly given to him by Haile Selassie himself, and by deploying Rasta themes to promise that 'Better must come' (see King: 2002).[3] It was also in the 1970s that Bob Marley shot to international stardom whilst preaching Rasta ideas. Thanks probably to Marley's fame, Rastas are today presented to the outside world as the smiling face of Jamaican tourism in various marketing materials, a bitter irony which I hope to underline in what follows. For if its semiotics have been appropriated for all sorts of dubious ends, I want to claim that Rastafari nonetheless continues to be a mode of militant fidelity to the black subject-body that emerged from Bogle's peasant army at Morant Bay. Far from an irrational millennial cult or a music-centred subculture, Rastafari is an extremely rich and sophisticated subjective response to slavery, colonialism, the class-race nexus in postcolonial Jamaica, and indeed the deeply racialised nature of today's economic, cultural and political globalisation. Rastafari therefore carries the baton of the mode of 'African-Jamaican affirmation' identified at the end of the previous chapter into the 21st century.

This is not to sing its praises uncritically. It is no doubt a complex mixture of progressive and reactionary elements. For example, the Rasta attitude to women or 'sistren' often mixes exaltation through references to Queen Amiga with outright patriarchal exclusion. Africa is frequently revered with uncritical devotion despite its problems with corruption and cronyism. Predictably, this extends to a wilful blindness regarding the more unpleasant aspects of Haile Selassie's own regime after his return to Ethiopia from exile in 1941 (for an exposé of the corruption of this regime, see Kapuściński: 2006). Rastafari's embryonic form in the 1930s and 1940s preached outright black superiority, dragging the movement into an antagonism of reciprocal differences that I have identified as unhelpful for real change. The rather buried anti-capitalist elements of the movement are often qualified by the inspiration it draws from Marcus Garvey, the influential Jamaican-born political activist who advocated entrepreneurialism as a path towards freedom, black pride, and self-sufficiency. Relatedly, I would argue that members of the Bobo Ashanti Mansion[4] have lapsed into the very monetary logic that drove slavery by demanding financial compensation for the suffering it caused (money with which they hope to fund mass repatriation), threby mistaking abstract equivalence for egalitarianism. And as I will go on to detail, many elements of Rastafari culture,

3. Supporting my later claim that reggae has served as the subject-language of the Rastafari subject-body, but also illustrating the dangers of the commodification of this language, this slogan 'Better Must Come' was also a reggae record by Delroy Wilson.

4. As will be explained below, Rastafari is not an organised religion but there are several orders or 'Mansions' with distinct interpretations of Rastafari principles, of which Bobo Ashanti is one.

from its ital cuisine to its 'trademark' dreadlocks, have surrendered themselves too readily to commodified appropriation in Jamaica and well beyond. Far from devaluing the example of the Rastafari movement, however, these weaknesses offer a useful cautionary tale regarding the shifting demarcation between what I am calling evental culture and decidedly non-evental culture, and between, in Badiou's terms, the efficacious and non-efficacious parts of subject-bodies.

But to what can Rastas be said to be faithful? Within Rastafari discourse itself, Paul Bogle would certainly be held up as an important figure, and Morant Bay as a crucial historical moment, but neither have the 'evental' status I am imputing to them. That honour would undoubtedly go to Haile Selassie's coronation in 1930. However, by Badiou's very rigorous criteria no multiple that is external to a situation or world can be considered an *evental* multiple, since it would fail the test of generic belonging. For this reason, a foreign invasion could never be an event. As we have been at pains to point out from the beginning, evental change cannot arise from the addition of what was not there previously, but only from a subtraction that renders visible what was invisibly present before. Contra the key tenet of Rastafari therefore, our Badiouian framework forces us to insist that Haile Selassie's coronation was not in fact an event for the Jamaican situation, simply because of its externality to it (although I would argue that this does not diminish its central importance). Far from challenging my interpretation of Rastafari as a subjective fidelity to the truly Jamaican event that was Morant Bay, this qualification of Selassie's coronation supports it. For as Badiou frequently reminds us, subjects are in no position to know the truth they carry. Rastafari discourse, then, may be faithful to Morant Bay without being explicitly conscious of it. As a language at least minimally readable within a particular social link, Rasta discourse, like any *langue-sujet*, must transmit its truth by means of the poetic torsion of signifiers already constitutive of that link. The coronation of Haile Selassie arguably represents not an event then, but the fortuitous alignment of diverse signifying chains, such that the novelty still nascent within the Morant Bay sequence could find a subject-language just 'worldly' enough to become forceful, yet 'other-worldly' enough to remain uncountable within the logic of the Jamaican state. Certainly, the Rastafari are the most trenchant and articulate witnesses to the continuing paradox of 'post-emancipation slavery' that Bogle first endowed with maximal intensity in 1865. They now force this truth onto post-independence Jamaica.

To understand how Selassie's coronation could echo with such spiritual and political force among Jamaica's 'sufferers' then, it must be placed in its historical context. As noted in the previous chapter, religion and resistance have been inseparable in Jamaica since at least the 1800s. The so-called 'Great Revival' of 1860–61 was pivotal in laying the groundwork, both ideological and practical, for the Morant Bay Revolt (see Turner: 1998). Sam Sharpe, too, was a Baptist preacher, and his particular style of firebrand oratory clearly had an electrifying effect that helped to spark the 1831 Christmas Rebellion. And long before both of these figures, slave resistance on the plantations had centred on African rites and rituals, combining music, mythology and magic into a volatile composite culture.

Rastafari ostensibly draws on this long and deep tradition of religiously inspired resistance to oppression and violence in Jamaica.

Yet for all its 'Jamaicanness', Rastafari was only able to emerge in the form it did from a very international political conjuncture taking shape well beyond Jamaica's shores in the 1930s. We are therefore dealing with the extra-Jamaican appeal developed during the phase of 'creolized opposition' (1760-1865) identified in the last chapter, with the crucial difference that the Rastafarian appeal was directed not at the liberalising metropole, but at Africa. In fact, a largely American-based pan-Africanist movement demanding 'Africa for Africans' was already well established by the late 18th century. The origins of the Pan-Africanist movement probably coincide with European slavery itself, with the process of suspending regional, cultural and ethnic differences that divided the slaves in order to establish a common solidarity. But by the late 18th century, a specifically political form of pan-Africanism was taking hold in the U.S., Britain and Africa itself. Moreover, thanks to the adoption and adaption of Christianity in the black diaspora during the imperial phase of European colonialism, the aims of pan-Africanism were increasingly articulated via an asserted Ethiopianism rooted in Biblical references to ancient Ethiopia. But if pan-Africanism began by advocating political unity in the African continent, thanks to the growing importance of the diaspora in its evolution, the philosophy of Afrocentrism increasingly took on the more cultural and/or spiritual connotation of the subjective unity of all peoples of African origin.

Marcus Garvey, whom many Rastafarians regard as a prophet, was a key player in the pan-Africanist movement in the Caribbean, Britain and particularly the U.S. in the early part of the 20th century. His Universal Negro Improvement Association was easily the largest pan-African organisation, at one time boasting "996 branches in 43 countries and over five million members" (Campbell: 2001, p.53). Garvey's status as a prophet for Rastafarians rests on his incendiary advice, proffered on the night before he left the island that he himself came to despise, to "look to Africa for the crowning of a Black King. He shall be the Redeemer". To poor black Jamaicans who continued to hold onto the image of return that had sustained their ancestors during the days of slavery, redemption already meant repatriation. Garvey's prophecy was (like all prophecies, retrospectively) confirmed with the coronation of Ras (meaning 'duke' or 'prince') Tafari Makonnen as Emperor of Abyssinia in 1930, who then took on the royal name of Haile Selassie, and would himself advocate African unity as a defence against European imperialism.

Abyssinia already held a central symbolic role in the pan-Africanist movement, not only because of the Biblical references already mentioned, but also because of its historical resistance to European domination. During the fierce scramble for Africa in 1896, invading Italian forces had been repelled and defeated at Adowa by Africans fighting under a Christian king. In 1935, Mussolini's fascist forces attempted to avenge that historical humiliation by once again invading Abyssinia, this time forcing Emperor Selassie into exile. For what Paul Gilroy has famously called the 'Black Atlantic' (Gilroy: 1993), Selassie's resistance to fascism became a resonant signifier of black defiance, nationalism and also yearning for an African homeland. In the desperate conditions in Jamaica in the 1930s, whose skewed client-economy had been badly battered by the Great Depression, this yearning would acquire messianic intensity.

Indeed, by the time Mussolini's fascist troops rumbled into Addis Abbaba, Selassie's divinity had already been claimed in Jamaica. As early as 1932, one Leonard Percival Howell—who had read Garvey and Marx and been briefly part of the Harlem Renaissance (see Lee: 2003)—began preaching Selassie's divinity to gatherings of over 800 poor Jamaican blacks at a time. His words form the epithet to this chapter, and are worth repeating for their crystallization of what I shall call the Rasta *logic of incompletion*: "Ras Tafari is King of Kings and Lord of Lords. The black people will no longer look to George the Fifth—Ras Tafari is *their* king" (quoted in Lee: 2003, p.64). For spreading such ideas, Howell was charged with sedition and sentenced to two years hard labour, primarily for recommending the non-payment of taxes and, of course, for doubting British sovereignty. Upon release, he established *Pinnacle*, the first Rastafarian commune in the remote hills of Sligoville which at its height boasted upwards of 5,000 members. Such was its perceived threat to the Jamaican State that *Pinnacle* was twice raided by police and then forcibly disbanded in 1954. Howell himself was eventually committed to a mental asylum in Kingston following assertions of his personal divinity, yet his dangerous talk of a King, and indeed a god, other than those offered by the British had already taken root among Jamaica's most oppressed black groups, who now looked to Africa, not England, for redemption. The international political consciousness of early Rastafari was evident in their reference to themselves as 'Nya men', in open solidarity with the anti-colonial movement in Uganda, *Nyabinghi*, a name that many Rastafarians now give to their meetings or 'grounations' and also to the form of drumming at those meetings. The image of African resistance to European aggression is even said to be behind the adoption of dreadlocks. According to Horace Campbell, they first appeared among Rastafarians in the early 1950s in direct response to photographs in the Jamaican press of Jomo Kenyatta's Freedom Fighters who were resisting British colonialism in Kenya.[5]

AFRICA AS A LOGIC OF JAMAICAN INCOMPLETION

Self-evidently, the history, culture and politics of the African continent is a key reference in Rasta discourse. However, I want to stress less the empirical 'reality' of present or indeed past Africa and more the 'logic of incompletion' the *signifier* of Africa serves in the Jamaican situation. As previously mentioned, I take this term 'logic of incompletion' from Oliver Feltham (2008), who uses it to insist both on the immanence of evental rupture and the de-totalising effect of this rupture on the statist attempt to establish a closed or complete set. Thus, far from presenting an *external* alternative, as during the phase we have identified as 'African Resistance' (1655-1760), the signifier 'Africa' in Rasta discourse from the 1930s onwards operates as a lever internal to the Jamaican situation yet capable of opening it out from within, of, that is, in-completing its claim to unity.

---

5. Barry Chevannes (1995) in fact dates their emergence earlier, around 1949, and ascribes causality not to the Mau Mau but to a particularly militant and influential Rastafarian group that called themselves the Youth Black Faith.

The oscillation between the naively referential meaning of Africa on the one hand and its deployment in a logic of incompletion on the other plays itself out most clearly in the changing fortunes of the concept of repatriation within Rasta discourse. For the first generations of slaves, the promise of a physical return to Africa was no doubt a very concrete aspiration. But with the end of the slave trade this direct link to Africa weakened in proportion to the emergence among Jamaican-born slaves and their owners of a creolized but specifically Jamaican culture (see Brathwaite: 1971), and it was arguably in this context that the notion of a 'return to Africa' took on more spiritual than concrete, more subjective than objective, resonance. This same trajectory is discernible in microcosm within the later Rastafari movement, in which, after an early literal reading, 'Africa' increasingly comes to stand for freedom paradoxically *in* Jamaica, rather than for a geographical alternative *to* Jamaica. This is a different logic than either 'resistance' or 'opposition' in Burton's de Certeauian sense to which we alluded in the previous chapter. Resistance presupposes an exterior alternative. Opposition involves a provisional acceptance of the terms interior to, and constitutive of, the situation as it is. The logic of incompletion, by contrast, finds a median path between resistance and opposition by singularising an existing term of the situation in such a way as to block the Statist count and its supposedly inclusive One. Only incompletion mobilises Badiou's dialectic of the void and generic extension.

More entangled in the politics of identity, early Rastafari was more closely linked with the kind of resistance displayed by Tacky's Rebellion and the Maroon War, and thus a literal understanding of Africa as referent, and repatriation as relocation. Marcus Garvey famously took measures to realise physical repatriation with his Black Star Line project.[6] Similarly, Rastas in the 1940s and 1950s who drew on Garvey's example took repatriation very literally, actively preparing for what they believed would be an imminent bodily departure from the oppressive constraints of Jamaican society and culture. This was given both validation and impetus in 1948 when Haile Selassie himself set aside approximately 500 acres of Ethiopian land specifically for returnees from the global black diaspora. In response to this, one early Kingston-based Rasta, Claudius Henry, was able to sell hundreds of 'tickets' for passage on to the Ethiopian ships that, he claimed, would come to Kingston's harbour on October 5th, 1959 (Barrett: 1988, p.94). They would reverse the Middle Passage by returning African-Jamaicans to the land bequeathed by Selassie. But like Garvey's Black Star Liner, the promise symbolised by these ships was never fulfilled. Moreover, when Haile Selassie himself visited Jamaica in 1966 (to scenes of wild jubilation amidst the Rasta communities), he reportedly recommended that the Rastafari should attempt to sort out Jamaica's problems before rushing 'back to Africa'. It was Selassie himself then who was responsible for switching the focus from geographical to spiritual repatriation. Nonetheless, following the Emperor's visit and an official Jamaican delegation to Ethiopia with Rasta participation, a trickle of Rastas

6. The Black Star Line was a shipping company set up through the Universal Negro Improvement Association which operated between the West Indies and the US between 1919 and 1922, shipping goods but with the eventual aim of transporting paying passengers back to Africa.

did in fact begin to take up Selassie's invitation, establishing a community called Shashamane in central Ethiopia. However, at its largest this community struggled to reach 2,000 members, and these have now dwindled to several hundred only, thanks partly to the Marxist coup that ousted Selassie in 1974 and thanks also to understandable ambivalence to the settlement from local Ethiopians. In practical terms then, physical repatriation to Africa has proved difficult, and perhaps ultimately beside the point (needless to say, most Rastas would not agree with this claim).

It is important to point out, too, that the Rastafari movement expanded exponentially *after* Haile Selassie's death (see Cashmore: 1983; Barrett: 1988 and Clarke: 1994). This indicates that just as the signifier 'Africa' is a poetic torsion carrying subject-effects rather than an objective index with only 'worldly' consequences, so Selassie's name does not refer—and arguably never has in any simple sense—to the embodied individual who bore it. Echoing the 'anthropology of the name' proposed by Sylvain Lazarus that we examined in Chapter 3, the prime function of Selassie's name, from the earliest appearance of Rastafari to its diverse contemporary manifestations, is as a catalyst by means of which a shared consciousness and militancy can be generated. As we saw, for Lazarus only an unnameable name can nominate the singularity internal to a political sequence, keeping its multiplicity open. Lazarus opposes this to the fixed or absolute name imposed by the state (what we have termed 'counter-nomination'), which would reduce such singular thought to modes of intellection exterior to it. Much is at stake, then, in determining whether 'Haile Selassie' is a statist or an exceptional name in Lazarus' sense. Clearly, it is in the interests of the opponents of Rastafari to reduce it to the former, keeping it 'proper' as it were. In this way, the death 'proper' to the biographical individual indexed by that name can of course be used to pour contempt on the Rasta tenet of his divinity. And yet, in its mystical resonance for adherents, it is clear that the name 'Haile Selassie' is stubbornly 'improper' in order to evade such encyclopaedic nomination. No sociology, discourse analysis, narrative pragmatics or even theology can triangulate its singular effects.

This is evidenced in the transformation of the Roman numeral attached to Selassie's regnal name into the habitual form of Rasta self-reference, 'I an I'. Within Rasta philosophy, this phrase indicates the divine unity between individual Rastas and the highest truth already within them as well as in every human being. In our preferred Badiouian register however, it is perhaps more productive to see this doubling of the personal pronoun (which significantly in Rasta discourse can double as a collective pronoun, designating all Rastas) as a confirmation of the model of subjectivity we stressed in Chapter 4. The first 'I' is individual, of the world, a locus of experience, whereas the second 'I' indexes a subject divorced from and set against the world, and thus the bearer of a truth. But note the all-important conjunctive between these two positions, operating in the same way as the 'and' of *Being and Event,* as the generic forcing of the latter onto the former. Leonard Howell's direct displacement of the English King with the Ethiopian king was from the outset a challenge to the sovereign statist count. In the Rasta logic of 'I an I', we can see the mark of the subjectivization of this deployment of one imperial count against another: if Selassie's name is made to pose an ultra-One to the Statist One, it is only capable of doing so through the individual's incorporation into the subject-body of this African void at the heart of the Jamaican situation.

To illustrate the distinction between the logic of incompletion deployed by 'African-Affirmation' and the logic of inclusion deployed by 'creolized statism', one should oppose the militant unity of the Rasta's 'I an I' to the statist dictum through which post-independence Jamaica has attempted to encompass the diversity—and the divisions—it contains: I am referring to the national slogan 'Out of Many, One People' (which I vividly recall adorning textbooks during my own school days in Kingston). The key ontological problematic of somehow representing inconsistent multiplicity as consistent unity is captured in this slogan, which clearly draws inspiration from the American adoption of '*e pluribus unum*' as a national motto during the Revolution (it appeared on the national seal from 1776 and on coins not long after independence).[7] This was a very self-conscious decision in preparation for Jamaican independence which, it was hoped, would be as revolutionary as the founding moments of the American nation. Interestingly, what this slogan replaced on the Jamaican coat of arms in 1962 was the rather different legend '*INDVS VTERQVE SERVIET VNT*', meaning 'two indians will serve united' or 'as one'. This referred explicitly to the subjugation of both Taino and Arawak indians to violent colonial rule at the origins of Jamaica's emergence as part of the 'new' world in the European imaginary. Moreover, although this motto may have changed with independence, the figures represented on the coat of arms remain a Taino woman and an Arawak man. To this day then, the national emblem of Jamaica depicts a long-dead indigenous peoples rather than anyone of African origin, despite the fact that they make up approximately 92% of the population. The apparent inclusivity of 'Out of Many, One People' therefore carries a graphic echo of the discounting of *a* people at the origins of the colonial count.

Of course, people of African origin are in fact counted in a demographic, bureaucratic sense by the Jamaican state (and active as professional politicians within the state), but, to repeat, the signifier 'Africa' in Rastafari must not be reduced to the continent, either in the present, or in the official past, lest its power of incompletion become nullified. Africa is, rather, an Idea in Badiou's sense, as "the affirmation that a new truth is historically possible" (*HC*, p.201). In defiance of the putative inclusivity of 'Out of Many, One People', the Rasta logic of 'I an I' opposes to this (post)colonial One the ultra-One of a *divisive* 'Africa' that is excrescent and uncountable for the Jamaican state. The legend above the entrance to Leonard Howell's Rasta commune, *Pinnacle*, read 'One God, One Aim, One Destiny'. We should read each 'one' here as an affirmative subtraction from even a creolized statist count.[8] This divisive 'Africa', and the alternative sovereignty in-

---

7. Problematic as this slogan is, it is arguably less so than the one that replaced it after an act of Congress in 1956: 'In God We Trust'.

8. In a song entitled 'People's Court Part 1', in which caricatures of Michael Manley and Edward Seaga are put on trial for misleading the poor black people of Jamaica, the Rastafarian dub poet Mutabaruka places a different slant on the national motto:

De only ting you have bin trutful about is your ting about 'out of many one people' [...]

voked by Haile Selassie I, incompletes the Jamaican situation, and prevents the excrescence of the Rasta from being 'enveloped' within the world as it is. This is why
many Rastas refer to themselves, proudly rather than merely melancholically, as
'strangers in a strange land'.

EVENTAL HISTORICAL CONSCIOUSNESS

In Chapter 5 we noted that, insofar as they are engaged in a transitive process of
world*ing*, logics of appearance necessarily involve an historical dimension: to be-
there, a world has to present itself as *having been* there. While this diachronic dimension both helps the transcendental index to modulate change and to 'envelope' novel combinations of multiples, we also argued that it is one of the planes on
which subjects can introduce novelty into the world. A vital aspect of the generic
extension carried by a subject is the implication that the generic multiple was always already there, rather than being a belated addition from the outside. It was
on this basis that we elaborated our concept of an evental historiography, by means
of which the past occultation of truths could be reversed, and resurrected in a new
present. The Idea of the possibility of change, held open even in apparently atonic worlds by signifiers such as 'Communism', can in this way shelter the transformative work of the subject.

All of this applies with uncanny accuracy to the Rastafari movement, which is
characterized by a deep and militant historical consciousness. One would be hard
put to find more avid or informed scholars of African but particularly Ethiopian
history, albeit one seen through the lens of a wilfully idiosyncratic interpretation of
the Bible. For Rastas however, the King James version of the Bible in particular is
a partial and biased translation that the white man has used to obscure an explo-
sive divine truth, namely, that Ethiopians, and by extension Rastas, are the true
Israelites. Many Rastas claim that there is in fact another half of the Bible where
this is spelt out in no uncertain terms, which is why the white man destroyed or
hid it away. Nonetheless, the 'truth' of the existence of black Israelites can be read
between the lines of the received version of the Bible if subjected to rigorous critical scrutiny. Just as Badiou argues that the reactive subject always leaves a trace
of his denial, so Rastas claim that even the King James Bible is littered with para-
praxes that reveal what has been repressed. Many Rastas even make the effort to
learn the official language of church and state in Ethiopia, Amharic, in order to
be able to read the version of the Bible Haile Selassie himself had translated into
this language. They also study closely the Ethiopian national epic known as the
Kebra Nagast which endows the imperial dynasty, of which Selassie himself was the
culmination, with a divine legitimacy allegedly stretching back to King Solomon.
This attempt to recover an 'African' Bible is explicitly framed as a counter to the
European version which did so much to legitimize colonialism during the imperial
phase. It would not be wrong, I think, to describe this as a form of what we have
called 'evental historiography'.

Only one people a clean de street, one people a eat out a garbage heap, one people to cut
sugarcane, one people inna sun an rain, one people a toil, and is a one people a collec de
kile [meaning money]

Extravagantly paranoid though this Rastafarian approach to biblical interpretation might seem, I would suggest that it serves a crucial *subjective* purpose in establishing what Paul Ricoeur has called a 'hermeneutics of suspicion', precisely in
a Jamaican culture whose every social strata is powerfully structured around biblical themes and values. European hermeneutics of course had its origins in the
study of biblical texts, but what is remarkable about the Rastafari movement is
that it has resolutely avoided the establishment of a professional hierarchy of interpreters. No single Rasta is entitled, let alone 'ordained', to interpret the truths
of the Bible on behalf of less learned 'bredren'. Recalling Badiou's Maoist theory of knowledge, Rasta knowledge is a matter not of expertise, but of *conviction*.
When asked if they believe Haile Selassie was God incarnate, most Rastas will re-
ply by saying 'I and I do not believe, I and I *know*'. Belief suggests the superseding
of doubt but also the possibility of refutation by 'facts', whereas Rasta 'confidence
in confidence' refuses protocols of proof external to its own vision: this was one of
the reasons that the death of Selassie only hardened adherent's faith. The truth
held up within Rastafari is simultaneously a very personal one, and yet *because of
that* universal. Amongst the poorest urban but particularly rural black Jamaicans,
this attitude of subjective conviction over and above technical knowledge has allowed completely illiterate subaltern peasants to read the truth of Rastafari into
their worlds and their lives without relying on a written text or a 'preacher' with
supposed expertise. Indeed, this notion that the truth is already in one's 'heart' is
predicated on the corollary notion that history, such as the black exodus that was
slavery, *lives* in the present beneath the redactions of the official account of the
past. This process of close but also creative reading of the Bible among Rastas
is one of the key modalities of its form of subjectivity. When faced with what the
Badiou of *Logics of Worlds* calls a 'point' (so a moment of decision vital to the con-
tinuance of a subject-body), the Rasta will turn to the Old Testament to organise a faithful response. Again, in a world such as Jamaica in which reference to
the Bible is an effective appeal to authority, presenting Rastafari as a variant of
Christianity gives it worldly purchase, even as the historical consciousness it in-
spires radically undermines Eurocentric Christianity with all its ideological links
to colonial history.

At the core of Rastafari then, are two intertwined claims to historical descent.
Firstly, there is the claim made in the *Kebra Nagast*, and very loosely hinted at in the
Old Testament, that the Queen of Sheba's visit to King Solomon may have resulted in—stating it bluntly—a one night stand. The consequence of that exalted union, it is claimed, was Menelik I, the first King of an imperial dynasty that would
rule Ethiopia almost unbroken for approaching 3,000 years. Haile Selassie was the
225th ruler in this Solomonic line, and the last. The second related claim of descent then, as already mentioned, is that Jamaican Rastas are the true Israelites.
By the mid-nineteenth century, the adoption of Christianity amongst the black
diaspora had already involved a strong identification with the experience of ancient Jews, specifically their enforced exile from the Kingdom of Judah and captiv-
ity in Babylon. The Rastafari movement took this identification one step further,
by identifying themselves not with, but *as*, the lost tribes of Israel. The promised

land of Israel becomes 'Zion' but now displaced to Africa, while 'Babylon' becomes a name for everything that is corrupt, life-denying and oppressive about
modern capitalist society: hence the Rastafarian threat to 'bun down Babylon', an
image which combines the idea of a cleansing wrathful conflagration with an injunction to uncompromising critique. That both of these claims of descent are effectively appeals to a *bloodline* rather than to putative factual accuracy supports the
transformation of history from a State discourse produced at the nexus of knowledge and power (from which poor Jamaican blacks are fundamentally excluded),
into a *lived* and embodied historical disposition in the world. Our fourth qualification of evental historiography in Chapter 5 was that the evental statement distilled
from an historical sequence must be incorporated into the present. This is certainly the emphasis in Rastafari, in which there is little or no interest in pitting its idiosyncratic historical consciousness against state History, but only in the subjective
pride, solidarity and militancy to be gained from making an unwritten past come
alive in the present.

　　Doubtless it is this combination of wild figurative slippages and historical and
geographical parallaxes on the one hand, and dogged and exuberant conviction
on the other, that has contributed to the widespread view of Rastafari as a 'millenarian cult'. However, Alberto Toscano's genealogy of political uses of the term 'fanaticism' uncovers a complex but progressive history of millenarian social movements (Toscano: 2010). Within the Enlightenment critique of religious dogmatism,
fanaticism has been deployed as a codeword for stubborn irrationality, and yet, following the bloodshed of the French Revolution, fanaticism becomes, in Hegel's
phrase, a dangerous 'enthusiasm for the abstract', and thus also a critique of the
dangerous excesses of the parologisms of pure reason. However, within Marxist
historiographies that continue to cleave to the emancipatory power of the necessarily abstract form of egalitarianism, there is room for an appreciation of the value of fanaticism, and thus millennialism as one particular form of fanaticism (see
Hobsbawm: 1959 and Bloch: 1977). As Toscano puts it:

> Millenarian anachronism—the reference to a vanished edenic compact or the
> wish to break out of time altogether—is ineluctably enmeshed in the now of eco-
> nomic development and its attendant political transformations (whether in the
> context of European state-formation or of imperial-colonial conquests), leading
> to unstable amalgams of nostalgias for a mythical past, encounters with a vio-
> lently novel present, and aspirations for a redeemed future (Toscano: 2010, p.46).

Once we take seriously, as Toscano implies here, the notion that worlds in Badiou's sense are intrinsically historical, and that subjects, as vectors of *historicity*,
must produce a "creative time" (*LW*, p.508) which "both constitutes and absorbs
a new kind of past" (509), then I believe Rastafari appears as brilliantly adapted
to the transcendental index of the Jamaican world precisely in its calculated millenarianism. To live the Rasta way of life is to force a mythical African past to
impose itself on a post-colonial culture and society whose own history has been
built upon the foreclosure of that same past: Rastas are "responding to the imposition of a new temporality with temporal imaginaries of their own" (Toscano: 2010, pp.46-47). The historical consciousness at the core of Rastafari is, as

Badiou said of Beckett's understanding of nostalgia, "a voluntarism of remembrance" (*OB*, p.67).

One might be tempted to articulate this voluntarism of remembrance within the framework offered by Homi Bhabha in his seminal book, *Locations of Culture* (Bhabha: 1994). In the chapter on 'DissemiNation' there, Bhabha exposes a constitutive contradiction at the heart of the modern nation whereby two incompatible temporalities are held together. On the one hand, there is a 'pedagogical' time which endows 'the people' with a narrative density that supports the 'homogeneous empty time' of tradition. But on the other hand, there is also a disjunctive, performative instantiation of this tradition which opens up an enunciative space of repetition-with-difference, allowing 'the people' to become the site not of a timeless plenitude but of an ongoing contestation of their symbolic interpellation. It is this disjunctive termporality of enunciation that makes the modern nation 'hybrid' in Bhabha's specific sense, which is deliberately opposed to multicultural nationalisms of the 'melting pot' variety built upon a plurality of supposedly respected differences. On the contrary, for Bhabha, hybridity demonstrates the weakness of state power such that it must adapt its monolithic sameness to the differences it attempts to encompass, topologically but also temporally.

It might seem that the Rastafari movement practices the politics of cultural difference and historical revision advocated by Bhabha in order to 'disseminate' the Jamaican nation. However, I would argue that Bhabha's paradigm is problematically textualist and thus formalist in a way that poses difficult questions of agency. With Bhabha, the politics of cultural difference in this strong sense just happen.[9] It is structural to the imposition of power: his position is therefore ultimately analogous to Althusser's 'process without a subject' that we saw Badiou criticizing so fiercely in our opening chapter. What a Badiouian perspective on Rastafari adds, then, to Bhabha's useful splitting of the temporality of the modern nation, is an emphasis on the absolute requirement for a subject in excess of structure, one conditioned only by an event. In the terms we have been developing over the last two chapters, we could say that Bhabha's iterative politics of hybrid difference resembles too much a faith in 'creolization' rather than 'affirmation'.

If we are to elaborate an evental concept of cultural politics, this distinction between culture as a difference inherent to the aporias of power structures on the one hand, and culture as an aleatory excess that supports a subject subtracted from encyclopedic determination on the other, must be rigorously maintained. Culture in the latter sense is what gives duration to the impossible. The former presents culture as always already *necessary*.

CULTURAL POLITICS QUA *ORGANISATION POLITIQUE*

If Rastafari is a lived praxis of evental historiography, it is also a subject-body in the sense elaborated by Badiou in *Logics of Worlds*. As such, it is an ongoing resolution of the contradiction between durable organisation and destructive novelty with which, in Chapter 2, we showed Badiou to be deeply concerned. As we stressed in Chapter 4 however, this subject-body is by no means a unified organ-

---

9. This is also Peter Hallward's critique in Hallward: 2001.

ic entity with clear 'epidermal' borders. On the contrary, it is a composite and flu-id assemblage that is not homogenous with the subject, even if it is its necessary worldly support. The subject-body has 'efficacious' but also 'inefficacious' parts, which is to say multiples that side with truth when confronted by a given point, and multiples that do not. To remain 'efficacious', Badiou insists that such incorporated truths must develop 'organs' which constitute "the immanent synthesis of the regional efficacy of bodies" (*LW*, p.470). Much of this can be transposed onto what I am calling the Rastafari subject-body.

Readers will recall that a fundamental axiom of Badiou's engagement with the paradox of a durable novelty in the activism of the *Organisation politique* was politics conducted 'at a distance from the state'. Thanks to their experience of both violent oppression and misrepresentation by the Jamaican state, Rasta's too have internalised a profound distrust of parliamentary politics. Bob Marley famously referred on his album *Rastaman Vibration* to elected politicians as 'crazy bald-heads', and as we shall see below, Rasta reggae lyrics frequently denounce the false promises made during election campaigns. There is even a neologism Rastas use to designate the inherent deceitfulness of representational democracy: 'politricks'. This term captures the poly-morphous duplicity of power-hungry politicians whose empty promises to tackle poverty and crime merely facilitate their own personal advancement. It is a warning to the poor black masses not to succumb to the siren song of alternate routes to redemption that lead only to more suffering.

The neologism 'politricks' finds its place within the remarkable semantic elasticity of the overarching critical term in Rasta discourse, 'Babylon'. As already noted, this term distils everything that is oppressive and deceptive about modern consumer society, and the forms of authority that impose its values and police its transgressions. Without doubt, professional politicians are seen by Rastas as 'whores of Babylon', i.e., as working only for the perpetuation of corruption and inequality. So contaminated is the word 'politics' for the majority of Rastas that they firmly resist its application to their creed. While some oppose this political interpretation by emphasising Rastafari's religious dimension, others cleave to a third position: Rastafari is not a religion at all they insist, but simply a 'way of life'. Indeed, an important aspect of Rastafari is its trenchant critique of imported institutionalised religion which imposes a 'pie in the sky' vision of a white God and recompense for the ills of this world in a heavenly hereafter. Foregrounding instead its distinct 'way of life', which I want to specify as its evental culture, ahead of either its religious or 'political' (in the everyday sense) dimensions, helps to maintain Rastafari's in-difference with regard to the re-presentational count of the State. In this sense, Rastafari's cultural politics of everyday life prevent its recuperation as merely an exotic extension of the black civil rights movement, with the State as its primary interlocutor.

Nonetheless, and exemplifying Badiou's insistence that subject-bodies also incorporate inefficacious regions, the movement has not always successfully resisted the pull of parliamentary politics. Ras Sam Brown for example—a Rastafarian poet, painter and activist—was the first Rasta to undertake an election campaign on an explicitly Rastafarian platform in 1961. His election statement in twenty one points demonstrates many of the contradictions of the movement, particularly as it lapses into conflating inclusion with affirmation. Brown's statement contains a perceptive analysis of the colour coding of the Jamaican class system: "To white supremacy has been added Brown-man supremacy" and "The existence of underprivileged man in Jamaica is a product of white and brown man supremacy" (Barrett: 1988, 149). But a deliberate distance is taken with regard to the mode of black identity politics which only demands greater inclusion in that same colour-coded system of social segregation: "if a man be Black as night, his colour is in our estimation of no avail if he is an oppressor and destroyer of his people" (*ibid.*, 150). To this he opposes an appeal to, in Badiouian terms, the generic: "God did not say 'come let us make underprivileged man, middle-class man, and rich man'. He said 'come let us make man'" (*ibid.*, 149). Africa as a logic of incompletion is clearly at work here, to the extent that all twenty one points are addressed to the 'Black people of Jamaica', and yet the final clause illustrates the confusion of inclusion and affirmation when it exhorts these same people to "set up a righteous Government, under the slogan *Repatriation* and *Power*" (*ibid.*, 150). The paradox of a Rastafarian Jamaican State with repatriation to Africa as its pre-eminent goal is not far removed from the paradox of the Leninist State that exists only in order to whither away, a sort of dictatorship of the Rastafari…

Leonard Barrett argues that the decade from 1961 to 1971 was a period of 'ambivalent routinization' for the Rastafari movement (see Barrett: 1988, 146-166). Although Sam Brown's electoral campaign hardly met with numerical success (he received less than a hundred votes), Barrett argues that it was taken up and to some extent implemented by Michael Manley. As noted above, Manley made elaborate symbolic appeals to both the Rastafarians and the popularity of reggae in his 1972 election campaign, earning himself a majority big enough to mandate his project of 'democratic socialism' (Manley: 1982). Following Ras Sam Brown's analysis, one could point out that this was made possible by the fact that Manley was a brown man from an elite family who made vague gestures in the direction of Rasta symbolism, rather than a 'Black as night' man, or the 'Blackheart man' to which Bunny Wailer's famous song of the same name refers, who positively espoused and lived the Rasta way of life. Moreover, Manley junior's leadership of the People's National Party coincided with growing participation in the Rastafari movement by middle-class intellectuals, with academics such as Walter Rodney providing an important intellectual bridge between Rasta philosophy and aspects of Marxism and socialism (Rodney: 1982). It was arguably this influence that encouraged Rastafarians to engage more directly and confrontationally with the State.

Today, there are many groups such as the House of Nyabinghi and the Rastafarian Centralisation Organisation, as well as others with primarily virtual existence on the internet, that continue in Ras Sam Brown's footsteps by advocating a Rastafari Theocracy, sometimes on a global scale. However, these organisations have arguably strayed a long way from the stubborn *distance politique* upheld by earlier Rastafari. A key practical question, which our analysis of Badiou's *Organisation politique* in Chapter 2 also explored, concerns the need to impose egalitarian prescriptions, often phrased in terms of a generically conceived country composed of its people, onto or against but not through the State. If *Organisation politique* arrived at the conclusion that "the place is not political", it was because it recognised that anti-State organisations must not tackle the State on its own terrain in Leninist fashion, but rather open up novel and unpredictable spaces beyond the cartography of topologising power. The places of true politics emerge from and simultaneously sustain militant prescriptions that challenge the State rather than passing through its recognised representational channels. For the most part, the Rastafari movement seems to have arrived at a similar prioritisation of prescription over place, and thus on a dispersed, diverse and inconstant, rather than a gathered, placed and unitary form of militancy.

For this reason, there are no churches or temples of Rastafari.[10] The first 'place' of Rasta politics is arguably the body itself, which many Rastas refer to as their own personal temple. The practice of 'ital livity'—with its emphasis on natural, organic foods, primarily vegetables and fruits, with prohibitions against many meats including pork as well as processed food in general [11]—arguably places Rastas at the early vanguard of the organic movement. This sort of Foucaultian self-fashioning of the black body can be seen as a mode of resistance to slavery's diametrically opposed exploitation of the black body, and also to the imposition of inferiority complexes inherent to colour-coded colonialism. Jamaica is still blighted by the shockingly widespread practice of 'bleaching', by means of which poor blacks attempt to lighten their skin colour at the risk of cancer. The second and probably most important 'place' of Rasta politics, where the collective subject sustains itself, is simply the tenement yard—indeed, Jamaica as a whole is often referred to as the 'yard', as when a returnee from abroad is described as being 'back a yard'. Still in the style of African villages, these spaces are communal centres rather than individually owned land, and Rastas use them for regular 'reasonings'. These are very informal ceremonies in which a 'chalice' of ganja is lit and passed round while elders lead critical discussions about issues of social justice as well as more esoteric matters of biblical interpretation. Ganja is thought to aid in reasoning insofar as everyday modes of thinking and perceiving the world are suspended by its sensory effects. Enhanced by ganja, reasoning is a way of continuously applying the Rastafarian outlook to the shifting values and demands of contemporary society. Without stretching the analogy too far, reasonings can thus be conceived in terms of the Maoist theory of dialectical knowledge in that both are conditioned by, and conditioning of, *praxis*. The largest gatherings of Rastafari come in the form of 'Grounations' or 'Binghi's which attract Rastas from around the island and beyond for several days of music, drumming, dancing, feasting, prayer and collective reasoning. Evidencing Barrett's 'ambivalent routinization', the Jamaican State has now recognised the right of Rasta's to assemble at these 'Binghi's, and even to smoke marijuana, otherwise illegal throughout the island. More permanent, and perhaps for this reason more dogmatic, 'places' for the Rasta way of life are the

---

10. This does not stop many Rastas from attending various church organisations, but particularly the Ethiopian Orthodox church.

11. These dietary requirements are based on the books of Leviticus and Deuteronomy in the Old Testament.

various rural communes that echo Howell's *Pinnacle*, some of which are run almost as rigidly as monasteries.

The only organisational forms within this amorphous movement are the 'Houses' or 'Mansions' which represent distinct interpretations of Rastafari philosophy and practice, but which are hardly top-down or doctrinaire. Membership of a particular 'House' does not exclude one from, or set one against, another, despite the significant differences in beliefs between them. Probably the most famous House, thanks to Bob Marley, is the Twelve Tribes of Israel, which has a more middle-class, and thus brown and even white membership, and is much closer to mainstream forms of Christianity. The House of Bobo Ashanti, by contrast, replaces the Christian trinity with Haile Selassie, Marcus Garvey, and its charismatic leader, Prince Edward Emannuel, who is viewed by its adherents as a living deity. Often referred to as 'Bobo dreads', Rastas of the Ashanti House are recognisable by their turban-like headgear and habit of carrying a sweeping brush, symbolic of their goal of cleaning up Jamaican society (an internationally famous Bobo dread is the dancehall artist, Sizzla). The House of Nyabinghi arguably occupies a middle ground, synthesising the Christian end of the spectrum occupied by the Twelve Tribes of Israel with the African end occupied by Bobo Ashanti. In any case, these Houses or Mansions are not tightly organised, sharply differentiated organisations that claim a monopoly on Rastafarian truth. They are loose and overlapping affiliations with little or no hierarchy.

EVENTAL CULTURE AS BRAIDING

In the absence of anything remotely resembling Lenin's 'iron party discipline' then, what holds this chaotic and in many ways very individualistic movement together? What prevents its dispersal into the regulated places of quotidian Jamaican life? I would argue that the answer to this question is, precisely, its *evental culture*. The music, song, poetry, painting, sculpture, symbolism and 'dread-talk' of Rastafari all maintain the cultural politics of a faithful subject-body without the need for a hierarchical leadership, strict membership criteria, or a 'party line'. Based on its example then, evental culture can be defined as follows: it is the ongoing, open and immanent creation of an alternative way of life that sustains the militant subjectivity required to force a truth on the dominant way of life.

Let us elaborate this definition further. An evental culture has two intertwined but ultimately separate dimensions. Firstly, at what might be called an anthropological level, it generates the cultural 'glue' needed for a community oriented around a truth to cohere and consist. This is vitally important, precisely because the world offers no criteria for gathering these disparate multiples in this peculiar way. At this anthropological level, evental culture resembles a collective project of *autopoesis* by means of which a subjective disposition opposed to the world can nonetheless survive within that world. Secondly, at what might be called an aesthetic level, evental cultures articulate novel modes of expression by means of which the unknowable truths subjects carry can nonetheless be forced onto their situations. This is also vitally important, since we know that truth cannot be spoken in the language of the world as it is. At this aesthetic level, evental cultures elaborate forms of writing, broadly conceived, that enable the formalisation of the consequences of radical novelty, whether it is a new egalitarian discourse, a new narrative of a life lived on the basis of the loving encounter, a new art work that shifts the coordinates defining art, or a new mathematical language in which to formulate unprecedented problems.

However, it is extremely important that we adhere to Badiou's own terminology of the 'tying together' of truth-procedures in such cultures, or perhaps more accurately, their *braiding*. Lacan's use of Borromean topology in *SXXII* and *SXXIII* demonstrates the possibility of interlinking structures that provide consistency without actually knotting the linked elements: the Borromean knot itself is technically no such thing, insofar as a single cut releases all three rings. In *SXXIII*, Lacan relates his enthusiasm when the topologists Soury and Thomé turned up on his doorstep with a solution to the problem he had been loosing sleep over for weeks: whether or not there exists a configuration of four triple knots linked together in a Borromean fashion (see *SXXIII*, pp.46-47). The colour-coded representation of this topological solution that appears in Jacques-Alain Miller's official edition of the seminar resembles a fairly simple braid, and like a braid, its shape is maintained without the two strings being linked at either end. It is the friction of their intertwined non-coincidence, as it were, that produces a stable form: at either end, the strings are an open set. This is already an important gesture towards a certain solution to the problem of the organisation of novelty. I refer to this topology of the braid because it helps us to conceive the cleaving together of distinct elements rather than their fusion. As it did for Lacan, this topology emphasises the constitutive gap of the real, or what in Badiou's ontological vocabulary would be called the void. To situate evental culture too rapidly at the *intersection* of an anthropological and an aesthetic understanding of culture, without this crucial notion of the gap or void to separate them, would be to invoke the very conflation of political and artistic avant-gardes that Badiou laments in *The Century*. The tradition of philosophical anthropology—in German thought particularly with Herder, Fichte and Schelling, but also influential, via Heidegger, on French phenomenology—in which man in some sense creates his world, lends itself to dangerously ambitious socio-political projects of the New Man. Moreover, this philosophical anthropology is predicated on a Kantian notion of culture as *Bildung*, as an act of rational self-creation that enables man to transcend his own origins in nature: culture as *kultura*, or cultivation in the old agricultural meaning, coincides with culture as aesthetic creation.[12]

Evental cultures, however, cannot base themselves on any notion of a plenitude of human nature, aesthetic heroism, technological determinism, or merely willed novelty. If at the level of 'anthropology' new collective subjects are created and given consistency, and if at the 'aesthetic' level new modes of expression are forged and disseminated, these dimensions must be braided together without

---

12. There are contemporary versions of this conflation of *bildung* and *kultura* but now inflected by an uncritical technophilia: I am referring to celebratory post- or trans-humanism in which technoculture is allegedly poised to enable man to transcend the ponderous rate of mere evolutionary change.

being tied into a single, continuous knot. Braiding provides a structure of consistency without indulging an imaginary of the totality. It prevents the ontologisation of the subject. Moreover, Lacan's most innovative use of Borromean topology in *SXXIII* coincides with an engagement with the question of creativity in the person and the writings of James Joyce. In this seminar, Lacan makes an important distinction between the symptom and what he now calls *le sinthome* (*SXXIII*, p.11). Whereas the symptom gives one a certain consistency in and with the symbolic Other (since a symptom is also a message directed towards the Other), *le sinthome* is an additional creative supplement that makes up for the failure of the knotting of the subject to its symbolic world. But again, there can be no sense of a reconciliation of symptom and *sinthome*, only of their braiding. At the level of his symptom, Joyce was able to give himself a certain, albeit grandiose subjective consistency by imagining himself capable of becoming the famous 'uncreated conscience of my race' announced at the end of *A Portrait of the Artist as a Young Man*, and of, as Lacan puts it, writing the book of himself. And yet the singularity of Joyce's *sinthome*—and thus its writing of the real as opposed to the imaginary consistency offered by his symptom—resides precisely in its unreadability in the eyes of the symbolic Other, armies of Joycean scholars notwithstanding. There is thus a disjunction between symptom and sinthome within the very knotting that enables them to consist at the imaginary level.

We should carry this topological lesson over to the braiding involved in evental cultures: they provide something like a symptomatic support for subjects at an anthropological level that affords a certain consistency vis-à-vis the Other (in other words, they do appear in the world), but they also facilitate the sinthomatic creation of creative modes of writing that resist assimilation *into* the Other (they baffle the world). Yet at the very same time, evental cultures must prevent both the ontologization of the collective subject as an ex nihilo creation, *and* the reduction of the *langue-sujet* it elaborates to a merely referential language of the state. Hence the importance of braiding these two levels rather than knotting them into One. But to define evental culture as the braiding of truths in this way is not simply to redescribe Badiou's notion of 'fidelity' under another heading, since 'culture' here necessarily embraces the mutually implicative interactions *between and among* at least two truth conditions. Contrary to his early warnings about 'disaster' then, 'evental culture' begins to describe the productive interaction between different but not incompatible fields of forcing in a lived militant assemblage, but one founded on the real of the void rather than on any imaginary essence. The three obstacles to thinking a Badiouian cultural politics identified earlier—his quotidian conceptualisation of culture, his separation between art and culture, and his insistence on the disastrous consequences of the overlapping of truths—are negotiated in this concept of evental culture as braiding, yet without lapsing into the prevailing culturalism of which Badiou is rightly critical.

To further complicate the stark distinction in Badiou's work between culture as a reductively anthropological notion of the repetitive rituals of banal, even animal existence on the one hand, and culture in the exalted sense of radical artistic creation on the other, I propose to inflict a deliberate violence on one of his own categories, that of 'configuration' as developed in *Inaesthetics*. "A configuration", he writes there:

> is not an art form, a genre, or an 'objective' period in the history of art, nor is it a 'technical' *dispositif*. Rather, it is an identifiable sequence, initiated by an event, comprising a virtually infinite complex of works, when speaking of which it makes sense to say that it produces—in a rigorous immanence to the art in question—a truth of *this art*, an art-truth (*HI*, p.13)

If we recall that *Logics of Worlds* allows for poems, paintings, and algebraic equations to function as subject-bodies just as effectively as 'actual' biological bodies, then forcing 'configuration' to con-figure, or bring together, the two figures of culture separated by Badiou—anthropological and artistic, with culture as *Bildung* as their convergence—into a single braided form seems less audacious. While the very title of *Inaesthetics* demonstrates Badiou's concern to subtract artistic truths from art history and the philosophical tradition of aesthetics, the difficult and underdeveloped notion of a 'work' there can be made to encompass the cultural dimension of political truths in its ambivalent shuttling between noun and adjective. By applying this re-worked concept of configuration specifically to the interrelations between Rastafari and the primary form of its creative *langue-sujet*—roots reggae—I am effectively deploying the first aspect of Badiou's definition ('a virtually infinite complex of works') in order to challenge the exclusivity of the second ('an art-truth'). In this way, we can begin to take up Badiou's own challenge and reconstruct evental 'culture' as the 'tying together' or braiding of truths.

RASTA REGGAE AS SUBJECT-LANGUAGE

Badiou's example of a musical event is usually Schoenberg's atonal system (see *LW*: pp.89-99), or more recently Wagner's ambient opera (see Badiou: 2011). Yet one could make similar claims for the aesthetic novelty of reggae's 'colonization in reverse'—to use Louise Bennett's[13] felicitous phrase—of the interstice upon which Western popular music had hitherto depended: rather as slaves utilised a deliberately languorous, 'malingering' bodily rhythm to upset the abstract time of forced labour, so reggae lopes and leaps in the in-between spaces of conventional musical time. The off-beat 'skank' or 'upstroke' characteristic of reggae's bouncy 'ridims' is quite distinct from the swinging tempos of Ska and Rocksteady, both of which had already departed from accepted Euro-American beats. Reggae is, then, a musical event in the 'virtually infinite complex of works' that it has unleashed not only in Jamaica but around the globe. Jawaian Reggae, Brazilian Samba-Reggae, Mexican Reggaeton and even British Lover's Rock are all multiples of the subject-body faithful to the Jamaican off-beat event, elements of its ongoing configuration.

However, reggae was also inextricably an event intertwined with what I have characterised as the political truth-procedure of Rastafari. What would one of these events be without its interactions with the other? Can we really imagine Rastafari without Bob Marley, or vice versa? Music is a vital part of Rasta ceremonies, with

---

13. See Louise Bennett, *Jamaica Labrish*, London: Sangster's Book Stores Jamaica, 1972.

slow, infectious drumming echoing what is referred to as the 'African heartbeat'. The golden period of Jamaican reggae music in the 1970s was simultaneously the period of so-called 'message music' when Rastafari began to reach a receptive international audience. Our term 'configuration' therefore describes the *mutual conditioning* of this event in the domain of politics (Morant Bay and its faithful black subject-body in the Rastafari movement) and another event in the domain of art (the emergence of reggae in the late 1960s). The explicit 'braiding' of these evental strands in Rasta Reggae, by which I mean reggae music with 'conscious' Rasta-inspired lyrics, constitutes what Badiou, in *Being and Event*, calls a *langue-sujet*: that is, an experimental mode of expression inimical to standard communication and yet both testifying to the enigma of an event and anticipating the future in which the truth it carries will have been forced. But as we have just insisted with evental cultures, Rasta-Reggae retains the disjunction which prevents the fusion of its two strands: neither is reducible to the other. Precisely with the global success of Reggae music, many Rastas became suspicious of its conflation with their faith. Similarly, many reggae musicians do not proclaim Rastafarian beliefs whilst producing 'classic' records of the genre.

The distinctive reggae sound arises from the clearest musical link back both to Africa, and to resistance during slavery (when it was used as a rebellious form of communication between the sugar estates): the drum. So-called *Nyabinghi* drumming, played on a three-piece drum set called the *akete* that provides the mesmeric backdrop to Rasta 'Binghis' and 'Grounations', emerged in the 1950s from the very same ghettoes of Western Kingston in which Rastafari began to flourish. Thanks to an influx of rural peasants as well as migrant workers returning from Cuba and Central America, Kingston was a genuine musical 'melting pot' at this time: Mento, Calypso, Jazz and Rhythm and Blues mixed exhilaratingly with residually African musical practices such as Burru. Burru was an African form of drumming which had survived the otherwise strict controls imposed by the Jamaican 'massa' for the same reason that slave owners in the deep South of America had allowed and even encouraged work songs. Although lyrically such songs often lamented the slave's plight (an emotional tone which would feed into later Blues), or even, in the form of 'spirituals', invoked Christian redemption from slavery, the extra productivity brought about by tying the repetitive movements of labouring bodies to percussive rhythms seemingly outweighed the subversiveness of such an expressive form. Burru continued to be practiced in Jamaica right up to the 1950s precisely because it had been the rhythmic accompaniment to machetes cutting sugarcane on the plantations. Reggae would give it an altogether more subversive post-independence afterlife. The Rasta-led resurrection of Burru suggests the complex connections mapped in the previous chapter between creolization and affirmation. Burru survived as part of the complex negotiations of creolization but went on to resonate much more disruptively with its incorporation into the Rastafari movement.

When Howell's *Pinnacle* was disbanded in 1954, many of its inhabitants took up residence in West Kingston amongst one of the few remaining concentrations of Burru practitioners. Recognising its African provenance, Rastafarians quickly embraced it and, indeed, absorbed the Burru people as a distinct social group (see

Campbell: 2001). Burru drumming was then mixed with elements of *Cumina* drumming to form the distinctive *Nyabinghi* 'riddims' of Rasta rituals. There is a clear link between Burru, Cumina, Rastafarian ceremonies, and reggae in the seminal figure of Count Ossie, née Oswald Williams. Ossie served a long apprenticeship with a Burru drummer, gaining a virtuoso grasp of its distinctive patterns which he then adapted and elaborated as he began playing with various Kingston bands, until he released a record in 1960 which many musicologists regard as the first ever Ska record, 'Oh Carolina' (later made internationally famous by Shaggy). Ossie subsequently established a reggae band called *The Mystic Revelation of Rastafari* which released the landmark triple LP *Grounation* in 1973.

Music was a powerful means of social critique for poor blacks in Jamaica long before the emergence of reggae. The infamous Jamaican sound system, with its huge speakers and booming bass (which so shocked and irritated Londoner's in the 1970s when Jamaican immigrants took them with them to the streets of Brixton and Toxteth) had been a feature of urban life in the poorer districts of Kingston since the early 1950s (see Stolzoff: 2000). The Jamaican sound system was born of poverty. Unable to afford the cost of hiring live bands (let alone of buying music systems of their own), the urban poor used these mobile musical sets as catalysts for carnivalesque street parties, in the full Bakhtinian sense. At first, these sound systems played imported American R&B records, but local demand for new tunes far outstripped the release cycles of the American labels. As DJs employed local musicians to produce one off, short-run singles called 'dubplates' in order to meet the street-level thirst for musical novelty, the idiosyncratic Jamaican music industry sprang up. This quickly led to new Jamaican sounds such as *Ska* (later beloved of British mods and then punks and recycled as 'two-tone'), which added to the R&B sound staccato guitar and piano riffs that accentuated the off-beat, and inspired a defiant 'rude bwoy' style and attitude. But by the time a recognisably reggae sound was emerging from Kingston studios in the late 1960s, the 'rudies' had begun to be replaced by the Rastafari as the dominant expression of black, working class resistance.

Many of reggae's earliest practitioners were already Rastafarians then, but it was really with *Bob Marley and The Wailers* that the new genre came to be stamped so strongly with the symbolism of the movement. This was apparent in the band's very album titles such as *African Herbsman*, *Natty Dread*, *Rasta Revolution*, *Rastaman Vibration* and the live album from the 1978 tour of the same humorous name, *Babylon by Bus*. Songs on these albums give eloquent voice to Rastafarian themes: the haunting vocals and simple guitar chords of Marley's famous 'Redemption Song', for example, articulate what we have called the evental historical consciousness of Rastafari with the call to 'emancipate yourselves from *mental* slavery', and thus with the political consciousness of present oppression. Other songs such as 'Exodus' conjoin this historico-political consciousness to the more messianic anticipation of a future repatriation to Africa.

A great deal of Cultural Studies scholarship exists that analyses the intersections between music subcultures and counter-cultural resistance, and reggae has been included in this approach. Scholars such as Carolyn Cooper (1993; 2004),

Donna Hope (2006) and Norman Stolzoff (2000) have continued to explore the critical power of Jamaican music since the shift from roots reggae to the very different ethos of dancehall. There is not space here to add to this body of work a detailed Badiouian supplement, but I can at least gesture in that direction.

Rasta reggae as a vehicle for evental historiography, for example, is perhaps nowhere more apparent than in the astonishing 1975 album, *Marcus Garvey*, by the artist Burning Spear. The song 'Slavery Days' on that album attempts to turn 300 year old history into lived, felt individual memory, and we should note the call-and-response structure so typical of work songs:

> And how they beat us (Do you remember the days of slav'ry?)
> And how they worked us (Do you remember the days of slav'ry?)
> And how they use us (Do you remember the days of slav'ry?)
> Till they refuse us (Do you remember the days of slav'ry?)

This album as a whole needs to be seen in the context of the post-independence project of the apparent re-Africanisation of Jamaican culture and history spearheaded by Michael Manley's People's National Party, when Rastas demonstrated an acute sense of the all-important distinction between inclusion and belonging. Africa was being absorbed at this time into a national narrative, thereby losing its divisive power of incompletion even as Rasta culture had done so much to rehabilitate it as a signifier of pride and defiance. In another song from the same album, 'Old Marcus Garvey', Burning Spear's plea is therefore for the Pan-Africanist Marcus Garvey to be counted alongside other candidates for 'national heroes', and thus, implicitly, for the 'incompletion' of the official moulding of a post-independence cultural identity.

> No one remember him, no one
> they been talking about Paul Bogle,
> They been talking about William Gordon
> They been talking about Norman Washington Manley,
> including Bustamante
> No-one remember old Marcus Garvey,
> No-one remember old Marcus Garvey

In both songs, the theme of memory recalls Badiou's formulation of a 'voluntarism of remembrance'. I would argue that the closing repeated lines, that 'Garvey is old yet young' crystallises the logic of evental resurrection. That this logic continues in more recent Rasta reggae is evidenced by Damian Marley, son of Bob Marley, whose collaboration with the American rapper 'Nas' resulted in a song entitled 'Dispear'. This title is already a reference to the artist 'Burning Spear and such and such before me', but through him, also to various signifiers of African anti-colonial resistance ('Shaka Zula, Bobo Shanti, Man a Mau Mau Warrior'). As such, it also embodies a dialectical argument regarding the connection between despair (which is homonymic with 'dispear' in a Jamaican accent) and militant defiance (as in 'dis spear' or 'this spear'). Thanks to his famous father, Damian Marley is able to piggyback, as it were, on his own father's Rasta resurrection. In the song 'Catch a Fire', Marley senior sings the chorus from his own famous eponymous song while Marley junior updates the same sentiments for new forms of exploitation: Bob complains that 'today deh say dat we are free, only to be jailed in poverty', and Damian laments the effects of gang violence so that 'we ambush we bredda, an gwaan like we never use to plan slave revolt'.

The example of Damian Marley, and his collaborations with American hip-hop artists, as well as his father's global iconic status, raises the issue of the forces behind the internationalisation of reggae well beyond Jamaica. Needless to say, there is an important economic answer to this question which pertains to the commodification of both culture and specifically cultures of apparent resistance, but for our purposes, since we are trying to focus on the logic of Rastafari, a more important answer centres on the question of the universal. As noted previously, Badiou's universal is a universal for a specific situation, but one that, thanks to its ontological connection to the generic substrate of pure multiplicity underlying every situation, also has a certain logical invariance across situations.

Thus, as well as the rather well-known story around Chris Blackwell and Island Records (see O'Brien Chang and Chen: 1998), I would suggest that a vital factor in the enormous international success of Bob Marley and his successors has been the seemingly universal critical purchase of the concept of Babylon, and the generic logic embedded within the apparent identity politics of Rastafari. Ernest Cashmore has tracked the growth of the Rastafari movement in the United Kingdom in the 1970s and early 1980s (1983), but a richer and more suggestive document of the cross-fertilizations between Jamaica and black Britain at this time would be the poetry and music of Linton Kwesi Johnson.

A TRAVELLING UNIVERSAL

Johnson was born in 1952 in Chapleton in Jamaica, but moved to London, England, before his 10th birthday. It was the experience of cultural dislocation and racism in the ghettoized Caribbean communities of Brixton, Peckham and Lewisham that radicalised the young Johnson, leading him to join the *Black Panthers* while still a schoolboy, and then to involvement with the *Race Today Collective* (whose journal was edited by Darcus Howe). Around the time that other British reggae bands were emerging, such as Birmingham-based *Steel Pulse* and London's *Matumbi* and *Aswad*, Johnson also hooked up with a band utilizing nyabinghi ridims called *Rasta Love*. Despite avoiding the public eye today, he still runs the reggae label *LKJ Records*. Although Johnson is not a Rasta, he acknowledges the importance of Rastafarian images and concepts in his music and poetry. More importantly for our purposes, his work redeploys the Rastafarian 'logic of incompletion' I have identified, but this repetition in a different locale produces an all-important iterative difference. Johnson's British context leads him to emphasise the critique of Babylon over and above the injunction to black historical consciousness. The Rastafarian theme of love and unity, too, is ciphered in Johnson's work through his commitment to international socialism, which endows it with an explicit egalitarian rhetoric.

Johnson's verse of the 1970s is the most militant and the closest to Rasta themes. The song 'Reggae Sounds' declares that "bass history is a moving/is a

hurting black story", arguably playing with the double-meaning of bass as musically resonating in the lowest rumbling registers but also as de-basement, de-human-
ization, denigration of basic rights. In the same song, fire and brimstone imagery mixes with the sense of impending riots: "flame-ridim of historical yearning/
flame-ridim of the time of turning, measuring the time for bombs and for burning". In other works such as "Come We Go Dung Deh", "All We Doin is Defendin"
and "Time Come" there is a Fanon-like emphasis on the necessity of a violent tip-
ping-point in the dialectical struggle for recognition amongst British blacks during
that period. Johnson has certainly studied Frantz Fanon's writings on colonial desire and the role of revolutionary violence, problems we will be broaching in the
next chapter. Perhaps as a result, history in Johnson's poems becomes a history of
pain that gathers inexorably into imminent violence, recalling a Kojèvian reading
of Hegel's master-slave dialectic on which Fanon also draws. Far from parroting
historical materialism, however, Johnson was responding to real and deep-seated
racial tensions in urban Britain. Throughout the seminal 1978 album *Dread Beat
an' Blood* there is a pervasive mood of simmering, barely suppressed frustration.
Sometimes the poet acts as a rabble-rouser advocating the lifting of the lid from
this social pressure cooker, as in the promise, in "All We Doin is Defendin", that
"wi will fite yu in di street wid we han/ we hav a plan/ soh lissen man/ get ready
fi tek some blows". And in "Time Come": "fruit soon ripe, fi tek wi bite, strength
soon come/ fi wi fling wi mite" and "wi goin smash di sky wid wi bad bad blood".
However, often at the very same time, the poet offers a warning to the wider community: "it soon come/ look out! look out! look out!", and, in the last couplet "it
too late now: I did warn you" ("Time Come"). This use of the phrase "soon come"
is the site of a politicising reinscription: typifying the supposed lassitude of the average indolent Jamaican, as putatively lazy as their slave forebears, "soon come"
here invokes the opposite, a visceral urgency coiled like a snake in the bodies of
angry British blacks, a coil which was in fact unleashed spectacularly during the
Brixton and Toxteth riots of 1981.

Arguably, however, Johnson's approach to history is focussed less on the ancient Ethiopian past and more on a social history of the present: it is thus an
evental historiography in the sense we have developed. He is at his best in these
poems of the 1970s when opening a poignant vignette onto the everyday realities of racist Britain. Poems like "Sonny's Lettah" and "Street 66" vividly document the brutality of white British police against the whole Caribbean community. In the former, a son writes home to his mother from Brixton prison, having
dared to resist police aggression, while the latter recounts the random house
raids that were typical for West Indian residents in London at the time. Just as
Rastas in Jamaica had long endured the unwarranted attentions of the JCF, so
black Britons in London, Liverpool, Birmingham and Manchester in the late
1970s were subjected to invidious stop-and-search policies, the notorious 'sus'
laws. The concept of 'Babylon' and its critique of State-based exclusion was able
to straddle this transatlantic experience, not because the universal it appealed
to was 'transcendental' in the Enlightenment sense, as if 'Babylonian downpression' was the same in both contexts, but because it conformed to Badiou's logic

of revolt in which there is something invariant even in unconnected irruptions of dissent and resistance.

In a way perhaps reminiscent of Sylvain Lazarus' anthropology of the name, Johnson punctuates this account of racism with iconic proper names that stand for the injustices Babylon commits even as it hypocritically lauds British justice. Take, for example, the song "It Dread Inna Inglan", dedicated in its very title to George Lindo, a Jamaican living in Bradford who was wrongfully convicted of armed robbery. Unlike the poem in its initial textual form, the song opens with the unmistakable sounds of a street protest: a crowd chants angrily and the poet's declaration comes, demagogue-style, through a megaphone. The song both documents an injustice and galvanizes a struggle for justice: as Fred D'Aguiar has argued, "Linton's work chants back to life the conscience of a society put to sleep by greed" (Johnson: 2004, p.xii). The cumulative repetition of proper names relating to moral outrages constitutes a leitmotif of Johnson's oeuvre. It can be understood as a form of litany, in both the religious sense of a repetitive prayer to which an audience shouts an unvarying response (like the chanting crowd in "It Dread Inna Inglan"), and in the semi-legal sense of enumerated complaints. In "Time Come" two similar figures are invoked in this way: Oluwale, a "Nigerian vagrant hounded to death by Leeds police officers" (Johnson: 2002, p.24), and Joshua Francis, a "Jamaican worker badly beaten by Brixton police officers in the early 1970s" (*ibid.*). The graphic song "Five Nights of Bleeding" is dedicated to Leroy Harris, identified in the footnote to the Penguin edition of Johnson's collected poetry as "A victim of internecine violence" (2002: p. 6). Perhaps most famously, "Reggae fi Peach" on the 1980 album *Bass Culture* laments the death of white New Zealander, Blair Peach, during an Anti-Nazi League demonstration in West London (this name recurs in the later poem, "Mekkin History").

As this last reference to a white New Zealander suggests, Johnson's approach to the role of race in Babylonian 'downpression' is more nuanced than the antagonistic chromatism of his days with the Black Panthers. This, I would suggest, is where the generic notion of love as a form of militant solidarity based precisely upon the suspension of differences enters into Johnson's work, though stripped of its ostensible Rasta symbolism. For example, as we just heard, "It Dread Inna Inglan" emphasises the common bonds between all non-white Britons opposed to racism:

> Maggi Tatcha on di go
> wid a racist show
> but she haffi go
> kaw,
> rite now,
> African
> Asian
> West Indian an Black British
> stan firm inna Inglan
> inna disya time yah

And again, in "Mekkin History", Indians and Pakistanis are praised for their resistance:

de Asians dem faam-up a human wall
gense di fashists an dem police shiel
an dem show dat di Asians gat plenty zeal.

Similarly, almost echoing Paul Gilroy's later Gramscian analysis of the class-race
nexus in *There Ain't No Black in the Union Jack* (Gilroy: 2002), Johnson's poem "Di
Black Pettybooshwa" recognises Babylonians with black skin:

true dem seh dem edicate dem a gwaan irate
true dem seh dem edicate dem a seek tap rate
dem seek a posishan af di backs of blacks
seek promoshan af di backs of blacks
dem a black petty-booshwah
dem full of flaw.

Perhaps acknowledging what John Tomlinson has called the "complex connectivi-
ty" of globalisation (Tomlinson: 1991), Johnson's poems of the early 1990s come increasingly to situate the dilemma of diasporic black communities in the context of
wider international politics. As we have already argued, globalisation has the effect of intensifying the question of the distinction between worlds as they become
subsumed, violently, under a single world. For example, the poem "New World
Hawdah" references Bosnia and Palestine as much as it does Rwanda. The 1991
album *Tings an' Times* attempts both to come to terms with the fall of Soviet Communism and retain the egalitarian impulse behind international socialism which,
I would argue, remains Johnson's version of Rasta 'love and unity' to this day. Witness the significant ordering of two consecutive songs on *Tings an' Times*: 'Mi Re-
valueshanary Fren' expresses dissatisfaction with the unreconstructed Marxist who
responds to the fall of the Soviet Union merely with parroted orthodoxies, whereas 'Di Good Life', against a lilting calypso beat, figures socialism in Biblical terms
as "a wise old shepherd/ im suvive tru flood/ tru drout/ tru blizad", and anticipates that those of the flock who have strayed from his protection will eventually
return. This song even eschews the juridical, rights-based version of justice in favour of the militant praxis of freedom: "freedam is nat noh ideology/ freedam
is a human necessity/ it cyaan depen pan noh wan somebaddy/ is up to each an
evry wan a wi".

Thus, Jamaican-born but Britain-raised-and-resident reggae poet, Linton
Kwesi Johnson, moulds the logic of incompletion of the Jamaican roots tradition
to the particularities of Thatcher's Britain. Historical consciousness becomes social
history of the present, the critique of Babylon targets claims of legal legitimacy in
the face of hypocrisy especially on the part of the police, and love is secularised as
a commitment to international socialism that nonetheless retains the centrality of a
generic humanity. Rather as Kwame Dawes has argued in his anthology of reggae
poetry *Wheel and Come Again* (Dawes: 1998), however, I would argue that there is a
coherent aesthetic—although I prefer the word 'logic'—which can be discerned
beneath these differences. Fred D'Aguiar recognises the continuity of this logic of
incompletion when he writes of Johnson: "he tests the civility of the nation by its
capacity to co-exist with the other: those who are in it but thought to be not of it"

(Johnson: 2002, p.xiii). Is this not a continuation of African-Jamaican affirmation in a post-colonial British context? And does not Johnson's invention of dub-poetry as a form of *langue-sujet* constitute the configuration of an evental form of cultural politics?

THE SPECTRE OF INCLUSION

I will close this chapter simply by highlighting the dangers in the concept of 'evental culture' that we have, if not elaborated, at least outlined. Clearly, Badiou's objection to the notion of cultural politics is motivated by both the necessity and the extreme fragility of the politics of radical novelty in his philosophy of conflict. Culture, narrowly conceived, represents the weight of the world and its tendency to crush true innovation. This problem is all the more acute in an apparently atonic world that has responded to the intermixture of cultures in the context of globalisation precisely by reifying, and in some cases 'museumising', cultures in order to include them more completely. A 'melting pot' model of culture has been promoted in order to parliamentarise difference. In this sense, cultural *recognition* for movements such as Rastafari is extremely damaging to their power of incompletion. But precisely for this reason, a distinctly *evental* notion of culture enables one to parse out the crucial distinctions that separate worldly individuals, even apparently resistant ones, from singular subjects; appropriation, even apparently 'progressive', from true affirmation.

The need for such parsing out is aptly demonstrated by the co-optation of perhaps the most iconic signifier of the Rasta way of life: dreadlocks. As already stated, these emerged in the 1950s out of sympathy with the defiance of the Mau Mau of Kenya. Their cultivation is in keeping with the ital philosophy that advocates the avoidance of unnatural chemical products (without relinquishing personal cleanliness), but perhaps their most important role has been as a visible marker of black pride in a racially stratified situation. So transgressive were dreadlocks of everyday codes of self-presentation in Jamaica that police oppression directly targeted them, with young Rastas often having to endure their forcible removal. The length and girth of dreads can indeed signify years of commitment to Rastafari and therefore add gravitas to Rasta elders. However, very few Rastas claim that dreads are either a sufficient or necessary condition of true Rastafarian faith: being nothing other than a militant inner conviction, this faith is irreducible to outer appearances. Indeed, the early adoption of dreads among Kingston's ghetto youths, many of whom participated in gang warfare, drug running and prostitution, allowed the negative associations attached to dreadlocks by the middle and upper classes to stick. Effectively, former rude boys began to sport dreads as a new signifier of social, racial and class defiance, but they utterly lacked the spiritual affinity with Rastafari that would have endowed them with a sense of an affirmative rather than simply antagonistic mode of subjectivity.[14]

This association between dreadlocks and criminality was further compounded when Jamaica's problems with politically funded gang violence were exported

---

14. Rastas often refer to non-Rastas with dreadlocks as 'wolves', as in 'wolves in sheep's clothing', to denote the danger they represent to the reputation of the Rastafari movement.

to the United States in the late 1970s and early 1980s. What Americans refer to as 'Yardies' became a serious issue in cities such as Florida and New York when Jamaican gangs attempted to control drug cartels, mostly dealing in crack cocaine (see Gunst: 2003). The image of gun-wielding dreadlocked Jamaican gangsters was soon endorsed in Hollywood movies such as Steven Segal's risible *Marked for Death* of 1991 (see Alymar: 1998). But perhaps even more damaging than the association of dreadlocks with criminality has been their commodification in the form of 'Sisterlocks TM' and also 'Napylocks TM'. This patented hairstyling process enables those who can afford it to adopt that 'rootsy' look around the office or to parties for as long as their whim dictates, after which the locks can be removed. The locks can be put in using the 'Nappy locks' tool, cleaned using 'Baby Dreadz' shampoo, and kept tight using 'Dreadz Wax'. All of the necessary equipment can be bought in a single set, revealingly called the 'Business in a Box'. 'Sisterlocks TM' and 'Napylocks TM' appeal particularly to African-American women who identify in a very loose way with their African heritage but always via the detour of fashion, by definition ephemeral: very often, it is a compensatory correction for years of hair straightening. Needless to say, neither have any subjective connection to Rastafari, despite the shrewd appeals to the 'spiritual' dimension of locks in their marketing materials.

A similar process of the commodification of Rasta culture can be discerned in the concept and practice of 'ital'. Interpretations of ital vary, with some Rastas maintaining strict vegetarianism and even veganism, while others are much less rigid. Nonetheless, the key concept of ital philosophy is a purity or naturalness of food production and consumption, one that enhances rather than reduced (v)itality. Yet the wealthier areas of uptown Kingston are now dotted with ital restaurants that tap into the overlap with global trends among tourists towards organic, fair trade and general ethical shopping. Menus offer ital dishes at prices most Rastas could not begin to afford. It is predominantly tourists, then, that can consume Jamaican 'authenticity' under large prints of Haile Selassie and off crockery in standard issue red, gold and green. In the supermarkets, too, there are brands that appeal to 'ital livity', but in so doing, I would suggest that they break with the politics of self-sufficiency out of which the philosophy of ital emerges. Post-Emancipation, one of the most important issues for 'free' blacks was that of land distribution: by drastically restricting the size and quality of the land which they could own, ex-slave's inability to become self-sufficient in the production of food and the maintenance of livestock enchained them to their former masters. Even today, tenement yards in the middle of Kingston's slums are tended as carefully as any allotment in Yorkshire, although it tends to be Yams and Okra that is grown rather than potatoes and peas. Introducing the mediation of capital by branding this 'ital livity' only places self-sufficiency at a further remove.

This branding of ital has now gone global, or at least, transatlantic, thanks to the successful entrepreneur, declared Rasta, and reggae musician, Levi Roots (née Keith Valentine Graham). Roots had been selling his 'Reggae Reggae' sauce, supposedly based on his Jamaican grandmother's secret jerk recipe, at the Notting Hill Carnival in the UK since the early 1990s but the product rose to prominence when Roots appeared on the TV show *Dragon's Den*, in which venture capitalists back (or don't) innovative ideas. Thanks partly to this exposure and a promotion campaign spearheaded by a reggae song, the Roots brand now provides a range of off-the-shelf Caribbean cuisine to every major supermarket chain in the UK. The brand's tagline, 'put some music in your food', suggests reggae not as a mode of *langue-sujet*, but as a marketing vehicle: reduced to a sauce that adds spice to life, 'Reggae Reggae' hardly continues the roots tradition to which its creator's pseudonym pays sideways homage. Once ital cuisine becomes just another section of the 'world foods' isle in the global multinational supermarket, one can no longer refer to evental culture.

Following this author's conversation with Jamaica's then-culture minister, Olivia 'Babsy' Grange, in 2010, I can confirm that the language of 'brand Jamaica', perhaps understandable beyond its shores, has infiltrated the discourse of the national political elite on the island itself. Grange has been a vigorous advocate on behalf of the reggae music industry and the cultural vitality of urban Jamaica since the 1980s, but her prime concern these days seems to be to claw back some of the money made by 'brand Jamaica' outside Jamaica. For example, she is concerned that in the now global reggae music industry, non-Jamaican artists such as the Jewish-American singer Matisyahu generate considerably more than their Jamaican counterparts (thanks partly to scandals surrounding dancehall music culture such as that sparked by the homophobic lyrics of Buju Banton's 1992 single, 'Boom Bye Bye'). Whilst this is an understandable response to the continuing legacy of the IMF loans Jamaica was forced to take by the oil crisis in 1974, and to the economic underdevelopment in which the country seems to be mired, it is nonetheless to submit cultural value to abstract equivalence, over and against its *worth*. As just one symptom of this commodification of Rasta-inspired Jamaican culture beyond the reach of average Jamaicans themselves, witness the Bob Marley Museum on Hope Road in Kingston. This uptown residence is a great deal more visible on the tourist radar than, say, Trench Town, the poorer roots of Marley's music and Rastafari faith. Moreover, at $20 (US), entry to the museum equates to almost a weekly wage for many low-skilled workers. Luckily, Marley has a quite different, vital presence on the streets of Jamaica where his lyrics and example still sustain a certain 'evental culture' to which no amount of dollars grant immediate access. Meanwhile, the affluent white female tourists who visit the Bob Marley Museum, and stay in the all-inclusive resorts on the North-Western coast of the island, are quite likely to encounter the so-called 'Rent-a-Rasta'. These are effectively male prostitutes who masquerade as Rastas in order to pander to exoticised and eroticised racial stereotypes. Mandatory dreadlocks notwithstanding then, this dimension of the tourist sex trade finds new and disturbing ways of both exploiting the black body and appropriating the symbolism of Rastafari for decidedly 'Babylonian' ends.

All of these examples demonstrate the crucial importance of distinguishing between worldly, commodified, ultimately conservative culture on the one hand, and singular, divisive and yet affirmative evental culture on the other. The primary measure for this distinction, I would suggest, is the ease of its appearance in the

world. If it is counted, even in a minoritarian way, sold, and held up as a commod-
ifiable form of what I have called 'rebel chic', then we can be sure that this culture
has become, as it were, too anthropological, too routinized, too banal to carry and
force a truth. If it cannot easily be subsumed under the heading of culture in the
usual sense, if unprecedented mobilizations of diverse and disconnected multiples
gather around it, and if it seems to have a meaning and a message for its adherents
that defies translation by its opponents, then we have grounds for hoping it is culture in an aesthetic sense understood through Rancière: that is, as a disturbance of
the dominant 'distribution of the sensible'. This also means that, just as its status as
'culture' must be an open question, so must its status as 'art' similarly remain ob-
durately enigmatic.

But this strange location between an anthropological and an aesthetic notion
of culture is, I believe, an important corrective to Badiou's notion of the event as
aggressively aculutral. Evental truth-procedures require a cultural dimension for
two interrelated reasons. Firstly, a novel culture is one form of subjective 'glue' that
can endow a subject with coherence in the absence of rigid, state-like organisational structures. Secondly, due to the fundamental incompatibility between truth and
encyclopaedic knowledge, novel cultural forms must be invented to articulate the
subject-body's *langue-sujet*. In the next and final chapter, we will explore the unavoidable role of violence in parsing out this crucial distinction between truth and
its simulacrum, change and mere reform, evental culture and museumised, commodified culture.

8

The Problem of Violence

I would like in this final chapter to ask a deliberately Leninist question of Badiou's philosophy of the event and its value for theorizing conflict, namely, *what is its relation to violence as a dimension of emancipatory politics*? The question of the role of violence in processes of change must be posed when considering the example of post-independence Jamaica, which has a chronic problem with urban violence, fuelled by the drug trade and a long tradition of politically supported gang rivalry. I will only return to the specific issues raised by violence in Jamaica at the end of this chapter, but it is in view of the problems that it poses that I will draw on Badiou's work to foreground violence generally as unavoidable in any politics of transformation. For as I argued in the introduction, what matters is not that Badiou's writings are 'new' in the marketing sense—fresh, exciting, the latest thing—but rather that they propose a politics *of* the new. And yet the inseparability of violence from such a politics has often been either tactfully glossed by sympathizers, or grossly exaggerated by opponents. My basic proposition in what follows then, will be that neither the reformist left-liberal dream of 'revolution without revolution' (i.e., real change without violence), nor the conservative dismissal of all revolution as destined for Terror (i.e., real change as dialectically implicated in Evil), enables the serious meditation on the political role of violence that we sorely need in today's conflict-riven, yet putatively 'atonal' world.

THE DIFFICULTY AND THE NECESSITY OF THE PROBLEM OF VIOLENCE

In the current climate, nothing could be more difficult to defend than a serious meditation on the political role of violence.[1] There are a number of reasons why this relation between politics and violence is almost unthinkable today, and we

---

1. I write as a member of a university which has recently facilitated not only the arrest, under the Terrorism Act, of an MA student whose dissertation led him to consult material produced by Al-Qaeda which is nonetheless openly circulating in the public realm (not least, on Amazon), but also the suspension of his supervisor for publishing a forensically detailed exposé of the university's handling of the case.

should enumerate some of them before insisting on the necessity of going beyond the limits they attempt to impose.

Firstly, the hegemony of liberal humanism and the doxa of human rights have succeeded in turning politics and violence into absolute antonyms. But the ethical obviousness of values of freedom, security and individual rights should be recognized as symptomatic not of transcendental givens, but of an ideology whose claims to universality often conceal very particular agendas. This is clear in the complicity between the discourse of human rights and that recent resurrection of the medieval doctrine of the *bellum iustum*, 'humanitarian intervention'. There is a distinct topology of auto-legitimation: the humanitarian space is here at home where we do not indulge in fanatical extremism, whereas violence is out there beyond our borders, where we are nonetheless duty-bound to intervene (violently) to put an end to violence by imposing human rights.[2] This was always the irrational kernel of the *bellum iustum*: war fought in the name of peace. Today's neo-liberal crusades seek to end violence in order to create the conditions in which politics 'proper' can blossom, namely, parliamentary democracy. But for all its repellant flaws, should we really accept the idea that Saddam Hussein's regime was not a *political* regime simply because of its use of violence? As Badiou argues, the related refusal to think Hitler's National Socialism as anything but an aberrant evil boils down to a refusal to think per se, leaving us willfully ignorant of the possibility of its return (what else are journalistic comparisons of Saddam Hussein, Slobodan Milosovic, and more recently Colonel Gaddafi with Hitler if not injunctions against serious analysis?). This preemptive strike against thinking violence prevents us seeing its centrality at the dark heart of liberal democracies as well.[3]

The corollary of the hegemony of liberal humanism is the undeniable decline of the radical discourses of the Left. Once upon a time, these not only refused this antonym between violence and politics, but actually fused them to the point of rendering them indistinguishable. From Robespierre's supposed conflation of Virtue and Terror to Lenin's advocacy of the State as an instrument of suppression, from Stalin's bureaucratic State-terror to Mao's chilling dictum that 'political power lies in the barrel of a gun', this fusion of politics and violence, creation and destruction, is now widely regarded as irredeemably condemned by the bloody history of its implementation. That the human cost of such utopian projects, communist or fascist, has been massive is incontrovertible. But let us pause for a moment with that phrase 'human cost'. It is well known that there has been an ethical hesitation around the appropriate measure for this human cost. On the one hand, it is obviously repugnant to place a numerical value on industrial-scale slaughter

---

2. And this is certainly a selective topology in which, for example, NATO and the UN can be mobilised to prevent genocide in the Balkans, but not in the heart of African darkness, where the proper names 'Rwanda' and now the 'Congo' index less countries, and more intensities of suffering and displacement that nonetheless fall short of being sufficiently 'human' to warrant full-scale intervention. At the time of writing, moreover, repressive State violence in Syria seems much more acceptable to the West than similar atrocities in Libya.

3. Appropriately for our Jamaican case-study, Losurdo's excellent counter-history of the rise of even classical liberalism foregrounds its origins in the exploitative violence of colonialism and slavery (2011).

(as if one hundred less would have been somehow more acceptable). But on the other, it nonetheless remains an essentially *quantitative* monstrosity. No wonder that the ethical discourse on the Final Solution so often circles around Kantian themes. Just as Kant describes a mathematical sublime at the limits of our perceptual horizon in the *Third Critique*, so the Hegelian 'bad infinity' of the deaths at Auschwitz induces a kind of cognitive jamming. To enumerate here would be to repeat the cold Fordist calculations behind the unspeakable crime itself. And yet such hesitation confirms the philosophical poverty of this notion of 'human cost' in remaining, precisely, numerical. Turning the refusal to count into *the* ethical gesture (Auschwitz as the limit of thought, the unrepresentable, the noumenal, the unnameable and so on) presupposes the absence of any alternative criterion for evaluation. At the origin of the category of the 'crime against humanity' is an uncircumscribable crime without limits which, in the eyes of procedural law at least, ought to be a contradiction in terms.

Yet there is an alternative, albeit a very obscure one today: that of valuing 'human costs' in terms of the cause to which they are a form of payment. Now, in the case of Auschwitz and everything it stands for, the true horror comes from the fact that death is imposed in the service of someone else's cause, with Jews being sacrificed to the Aryan ideal, but does it follow that *all* causes are intrinsically fascistic? Is it really the case that there is nothing worth dying rather than killing for (which is, after all, much the easier option)? Are we, in short, condemned to live without values transcending individualistic interests? The critique of representation coming from figures like Emmanuel Levinas and Jean-François Lyotard, which discerns an incipient totalitarianism in any and every project or grand narrative, is complicit—unwillingly I should add—with the postmodern quietism of our times. There is a direct link between the discursive disjunction of politics and violence and the infamous end of history thesis of Francis Fukuyama (1992). Neoliberal triumphalism asserts a mastery over the violence of contradiction, a domestication of the dialectic that makes emancipatory political projects pointless. With the subjectless politics of free market capitalism replacing the old ideological clashes, we are supposedly left blissed-out in the global shopping mall. In this context, the tinkling muzak of that mall deafens us to any suggestion of a possible connection between politics and violence. For example, who can really hear Jean-Paul Sartre today, when, in his preface to Frantz Fanon's *Wretched of the Earth*, he argues that "irrepressible violence is neither sound and fury, nor the resurrection of savage instincts, nor even the effect of resentment: it is man re-creating himself" (Fanon: 2001, p.18)? This truly sounds like a voice from the grave. On the other hand, there are those who, minus the secular humanism of 'man', hear Sartre's message loud and clear: radical Islamic fundamentalists. Does the seemingly endless supply of willing suicide bombers suggest that Ideas worth dying for live on only in jihadist fanaticism? Perhaps this is the biggest danger for a Left nostalgic for grand causes. Without thinking through the relation between violence and politics, some might be stupid enough to look askance at the terrorist atrocities of radical Islam and see in them the most militant resistance to global capitalism rather than, as I would argue, its symptomatic affirmation.

In fact, this debate has its roots in one of the most significant intellectual clashes of the previous century, one which has been made to resonate anew in the wake of 9/11: I am referring to the vicious disagreement in the 1950s on the issue of the legitimacy of political violence between Albert Camus and Jean-Paul Sartre. The Sartre of that preface to *Wretched of the Earth* and of 'The Communists and Peace' (rather than the Sartre of the *Critique of Dialectical Reason*) famously advocated terrorism as the only possible recourse for the oppressed. The violence to which Sartre applied his phenomenological acuity, however, was primarily the systemic, everyday violence of life as hierarchically structured under both capitalism and colonialism. As a result, he was for much of the 1950s a staunch supporter of both the Soviet model, and of the terroristic tactics of the *Front Libération Nationale*. By contrast, Camus, particularly in *The Rebel*, came to draw on an anti-Jacobin tradition that criticised the violence intrinsic to bottom-up revolutions (Camus: 1971). Echoing Hegel's critique of the French Revolution, he claimed that the absoluteness of the Idea animating Terror is in essence a frantic, and fanatical, denial of the meaningless absurdity of life. Although a man of the Left then, Camus became a vehement opponent of Communism on the Soviet model and, for related reasons, an equally vocal critic of the methods of the *FLN* in his native Algeria, whose independence from France he refused to support. If Sartre situated violence at the systemic level of an unjust social formation and its daily perpetuation, Camus situated it in the extremism of revolutionary movements hellbent on change.

Little surprise then that the binary that Sartre and Camus have been made to represent, between pro- and anti-terrorism respectively, has been redeployed post 9/11. Paul Berman, to take just one example, appeals to Camus to justify his rallying call against jihadist Islamic fundamentalism in *Liberalism and Terror* (2003). But this redeployment has been made possible by a wider resurgence of Manichean binarism. Sartre and Camus were shaped by the stark choice offered by the Cold War. Their conflict represented alignment on either side of the wall as it were. But similarly, Bush's rhetoric of 'with us or against us' following 9/11 has transposed the same Cold War discourse into the 21st century, even as the War on Terror is of a completely different nature. And just as this binarism proved deadly for the postwar Left, fatally dividing it around the Soviet blueprint of Marxism, so what remains of the contemporary Left today (arguably very little indeed) finds itself riven by a similarly limited conception of violence. As both Aronson (2004) and Santoni (2003) have argued therefore, it is not the closed antagonism between Sartre and Camus and the supposed choice between one or the other, but the *unresolved* nature of their disagreement that represents the richest critical resource for challenging our current conjuncture. I would add that the fact that both thinkers were responding to colonial and anti-colonial violence in the bloody example of Algeria is not inconsequential for the globalised (neo-colonial?) present. Fanon learned from Sartre, and Sartre from Fanon. We can still learn from both.

Thankfully, there are eccentric voices that continue to contribute to the debate opened up by Sartre and Camus, such as that of Slavoj Žižek, whose *In Defense of Lost Causes* includes the plea to 'give the dictatorship of the proletariat a chance'

(Žižek: 2008a, p.412). Žižek reminds us that Lenin's formulation was always about opposing a true, radical democracy to the corrupt bourgeois version. Indeed, in a work entirely devoted to the problem of violence (2008b), Žižek offers a useful distinction between three modalities of contemporary violence that draws primarily on the Sartrean legacy. Most superficially but most visibly, there are the riots, coups and international incidents that constitute what he calls 'subjective violence'. This epiphenomenal level is arguably the locus of analysis for Camus, whose instinct—notwithstanding his defense of the spirit of rebellion—was to recoil from it. At a deeper level, Žižek argues that there is a 'symbolic violence' built into language such that the very terms available to us constrain our capacity to testify to violence. The very language of the law, for example, can inflict violence both on the terms of a testimony and on the adequacy of a possible tribunal to hear it. And finally, at the deepest level, Žižek discerns an 'objective' or 'systemic violence' which is so thoroughly embedded in the political and economic institutions of everyday life that it is not merely invisible to us, but is paradoxically experienced as the guarantor of stability, security, continuity. Here, he segues with Sartre's analysis of the violence of the reproduction of an iniquitous 'practico-inert'. This excavation of forms of violence today, coupled with the piercing critiques of the aporias of liberal tolerance scattered throughout Žižek's work, certainly go a long way towards clearing the ground for taking the problem of violence seriously. But perhaps they do not escape fully enough the ideological binarism I have just identified as symptomatic of the post-9/11 displacement of Cold War discourse? Žižek, after all, is hardly immune to indulging a Sartre-like romanticization of revolutionary violence (he is often to be heard complaining that revolution without violence is as simulacral and unsatisfying as decaffeinated coffee).

Of all the contemporary theorists of radical subjectivity, I would argue that it is Badiou (former Sartrean of course) who has most consistently confronted the difficulty and necessity of violence. As Peter Hallward notes: "Badiou is one of very few contemporary thinkers prepared to accept the certainty of violence and the risk of disaster implicit in all genuine thought" (Hallward: 2003, p. 257). It is Badiou who has brought the mathematician's analytic rigor to the violence-politics relation in order to contest the false choice imposed on us today: either politics and violence are related as absolute antonyms (the liberal position), or they are related as synonyms (the fundamentalist position), or, apropos the War on Terror, the very 'choice' between these two modes of relation is suspended precisely through their conjunction (in Schmittian fashion, the liberal rule of law is conjoined to extra-legal violence). It is Badiou then who, like Sartre and like Fanon, begins with the very unpopular assertion that there *is* in fact a relation between politics and violence, but very quickly adds that this relation is one neither of *exteriority* (the liberal logic of security, violence on the outside of politics), nor *immanence* (the Jacobin logic of Terror, violence as homogenous with politics), nor, finally, *reciprocal synthesis* (the jurisprudence of exceptionalism analysed so perceptively by Giorgio Agamben (2005)). As I will argue in what follows, Badiou's work comes to articulate a new relation between politics and violence that, under the heading of 'destruction', both returns to and fundamentally re-orients his earlier Maoism.

FRENCH MAOISM AND MAY '68

It is illuminating to examine Badiou's position on violence, however, precisely because his *explicitly* Maoist phase, which as we saw in Chapter 1 culminated in 1982 with *Théorie du sujet* but ended in 1985 with *Peut-on penser la politique?*, revolved around a romantic attraction to creative violence, to the notion that destruction itself can be inherently liberating and productive. Like a moth to a candle flame, he singed himself against this problematic again and again throughout the 1970s in particular (not coincidentally, the decade which saw the integration of terrorism into what Guy Debord called the 'society of the spectacle' with bombings and assassinations by, amongst others, the IRA in the UK, ETA in Spain, the Red Brigades in Italy, and the RAF in Germany). In discussing Badiou's changing position on violence in this final chapter then, I am still addressing the shifting parameters of his Maoism explored in the first.

Badiou's commitment to Maoism began before the tumultuous events of May '68 in France, but it was forged in the heat of those remarkable weeks. I would therefore like to begin (again) with May '68 as the event to which his thought has remained unremittingly faithful, arguably, as we saw in Chapter 2, because it was such a spectacular failure. Beyond the merely chronological proximity with the Chinese Cultural Revolution, there are two main aspects of May '68 which Maoism was able not only to describe, but to intensify and catalyze in ways that neither Althusser's structuralist nor Sartre's existentialist Marxisms ever could: firstly, the unforeseeable novelty of the May events, and secondly, their incompatibility with the party as a model of political organisation.

The very idea that a protest by students at Nanterre could snowball out of the universities and into the factories, leading, in a matter of weeks, to a general strike that would bring France to the very brink of collapse would have seemed utterly fantastic to card-carrying Marxists as well as everybody else in the first few months of 1968. And yet this is what happened in May of that year. Marxist economic analyses of French society and its changing class-composition were seemingly bereft before *les événements*. But Mao had already challenged the dogmatism of Stalin's 'scientific Marxism' on this issue in the 1940s. In China, Mao had argued and then demonstrated in his long battle against the Kuomindang, that it was the rural peasants, not the urban proletariat, that could be galvanized into a revolutionary army—a position common to most 'third world Marxisms', including Fanon's. This was conceivable by Mao because he emphasised subjective will over objective social determination, thereby uncoupling agency from the 'final instance' of the economic—and, ultimately, Marxism from its foundations in historical materialism. Mao claimed that not objective but subjective determination, in the sense of disciplined revolutionary will, could wrench man from his banal constraints and turn him into a creative/destructive power. A corollary of this primacy of the will in Maoism was the primacy of practice over theory (see 'On Practice', pp.52-66 in Mao: 2007). Although he managed to write poetry even in the middle of the horrendous suffering of the Long March, there was in Mao something of the peasant's impatience with abstract intellectualism (see Chang and Halliday: 2006 and Short: 2004). Revolutionary theory for him was never an ossified schema into which reality must be made to fit. Rather, it was immanent to that praxis which forced reality in a communist direction.

For the French activists in 1968, Badiou among them, these aspects of Maoism seemed heaven-sent. They explained how this idiosyncratic insurrection could have come about at all. It was simply the student's and worker's autonomous will expressed with subjective determination. Maoism also justified the direct action which was the hallmark not only of student activism, but also of the workers, whose wildcat strikes openly challenged the trade unions: it was their revolutionary prax-is *en acte*. This was why Maoists and Situationists could be such creative collabo-rators during the May movement (see Viénet: 1992 and Knabb: 2006), or that as-pect of it that Badiou, as we have seen, specifies as the 'second May' (*HC*). Despite their differing relations to anarchism and the revolutionary role of art, Maoists and Situationists came together in foregrounding the punctual urgency of the present. Maoism also provided a rationale for setting this creative direct action against the clunky abstract frameworks offered by an older generation of Marxists. The Maoist theory of knowledge Badiou would later elaborate suggested that such theories had ceased to be truly dialectical, to be part of history. More simply, Mao openly sided with the young and many commentators on May '68, perhaps too many,[4] charac-terise it as a generational antagonism. As we saw in Chapter 1, the Chairman had told his own Red Guards, composed primarily of university students, that 'it is right to revolt against the reactionaries'. This was a message that would reverberate in Paris and throughout Badiou's later writings. And insofar as Mao had unleashed the Red Guards *against* the old cadres of the Chinese Communist Party itself, he had declared war on the Stalinist model of organisation. This echoed the irreverent disdain the students of May '68 showed for the *Parti Communiste Français* as well as for the trade unions, whose supposed monopoly on radicalism they simply refused to recognise. Disdain turned to fury when both organisations betrayed the work-ers at the barricades by recommending they accept the sops thrown to them by de Gaulle's tottering government, thereby fatally dissipating the movement's fervour.

By his own admission, these events were a 'road to Damascus' experience for Badiou. We saw the indelible mark they made on his theory of the subject in Chapter 1, but it was this very theory, especially as the subject came to be conditioned by the event, that pushed Badiou away from the notion of creative destruction, and to-wards a more nuanced, multilayered and technical understanding of the violence of change. In Chapter 4, we lamented the absence in Badiou's work of a phenomenol-ogy of the emergence of subjectivity from mundane individuation. Focussing on the violence inherent to that emergence perhaps begins to address this lack.

FIVE MOMENTS OF VIOLENCE

I would identify five moments of violence in the emergence of the subject from the individual, which I will term 'pre-figuration', 'de-individuation', 'subjectivization',

---

4. In her account of the reactionary historicization of May '68 spearheaded by the *nouveaux philosophes*, by means of which it has been reduced precisely to a 'folly of youth', Kristin Ross un-earths the importance of issues transcending the complaints of the young: Algeria, Vietnam, the General Strike and a militant anti-capitalism (Ross: 2002).

'singularisation', and 'counter-nomination'. However, before defining these terms, it is important to stress that one of my key claims is that the most fundamental violence of political novelty is the displacement of the Statist localisation of violence within a spectrum of legitimacy-illegitimacy. It follows that the mode of violence in each of these five moments is distinct rather than partaking of some metaphysical essence of violence common to all of them. Very simply, with each eventual sequence a new concept of violence must emerge concomitantly with the destruction of the old coordinates by which violence was defined and judged. I am here taking a little distance from Peter Hallward's assertion that Badiou's "separation of true subjects from merely objective 'individuals' allows him to consider violence as essentially external to any truth process" (Hallward: 2003, p.269). This is accurate for Badiou's stance in *Being and Event*, but as I will go on to argue, by *Logics of Worlds* violence in the form of 'destruction' becomes internal to the political truth process and arguably pushes him towards something resembling an ethics of violence. As in Sartre's and Fanon's analysis of colonial violence then, Badiou's approach demands that we *begin from the fact of existing systemic violence* in order to elaborate the consequences of this fact.[5] But there are distinct dimensions of violence in the process of rupturing from this systemic level, and in enduring in internal distance from it.

Pre-Figuration: I am taking this term from our interpretation of Badiou's reading of Beckett at the end of Chapter 4. We saw there that the apparently absurd, repetitive, circular and in many ways claustrophobic scenarios that litter Beckett's writings circumscribe not the hopelessness of the human condition, but a discipline of preparation for the event to come, precisely in the face of all evidence to the contrary. We also saw there that courage in Badiou's Beckett is not a passive prayer for some future redemption, but an active labour, in the present, on language and the symbolic order itself, such that it can be readied for the possibility of an event. Beckett's notion of nostalgia, too, was shown to be not a rose-tinted contemplation of a mythical past but a 'voluntarism of remembrance' that, again, opens the past onto the futurity of defiant hope.

All of these things could be applied to the Rastafari movement examined in the last chapter. As I argued, the messianic aspects of Rastafari are less about a utopian yearning for future admission to Zion, and more about a millenarianism that 'incompletes' the Jamaican situation in the present. Dread-talk, too, reworks Jamaican patois and Standard English to prepare the way for its particular truth to be heard and disseminated. To the extent that this undermines the colonial legacy inscribed in this inheritance of the 'Queen's English', dread-talk could be said

---

5. Liberal critics of Fanon's advocacy of revolutionary violence emanate from the (privileged) position of assuming a possible space of non-violence. Fanon's subtle admixture of psychoanalysis and Marxism, more connected to actual struggles than the Frankfurt School version of the same conjunction, demonstrates the individual and social production of the figure of 'the native' as a constitutive violence which is then dialectically turned back against the coloniser during anti-colonial resistance. Hence Fanon's acerbic dismissal of the Gandhian strategy of non-violence, as "an attempt to solve the colonial problem around a green baize table" (Fanon: 2001, p.48). I will be complicating this picture later on in this chapter by applying a Badiouian framework to Gandhi's *satyagraha*.

to be Rastafari's version of Beckettian courage. Finally, the radical reimagining of Africa's past in Rastafarian discourse constitutes a 'nostalgia' that attempts to reconfigure the temporal ordering of the present in post-independence Jamaica. Granted, I have characterised Rastafari as conditioned by the event of the Morant Bay revolt, but I want to stress the importance of *pre*-evental *pre*-figuration as the first indispensable mode of subjective violence.

Pre-figuration is a violence against the normative values and discourses that expunge from the world the possibility of possibility. It maintains the power of im-agination in the face of 'reality', ensuring that the idea that 'another world is pos-sible' is sustained when the perpetuation of the current world seems depressing-ly assured. To pre-figure an event, then, is to open a way for its hoped-for arrival. Yet in many ways pre-figuration is more difficult than post-evental fidelity because it is in the end a baseless optimism in the potential for change. Unlike the event, pre-figuration can point to no significant rupture or enigmatic multiple in order to support its transformative imaginary. Nonetheless, Beckett's famous 'you must go on, I can't go on, I'll go on' is the minimal violence needed to partially separate an individual from their worldly individuation, indicating a potential bridge between resistance and subjective affirmation.

De-Individuation: This refers to the Pauline experience of conversion from being a mere worldly individual (say, a Jew called Saul who persecutes Christians), even a courageous one engaged in pre-figuration, to a subject of truth (Paul, who converts others to Christianity by denying the worldly distinction between Greek and Jew). Such a conversion is downright traumatic, since it implies a complete break with pre-existing narratives of identity, meaning, value and legitimacy (*SP*, pp.16-30). De-individuation is the collapse of one's entire symbolic universe, a kind of voluntary psychosis. This second violence in becoming a militant therefore in-volves the absolute destruction of self-interest, or rather—since, as I have tried to stress, the subject *is* a part of its world—the reduction of interest to a single in-terest that coincides with a universal claim common to all. Violence here is es-sentially against the given structure of the social link as lived by the convert. De-individuation represents an intensification of pre-figuration insofar as an event allows the subject to occupy the space of possibility opened up by its preceding imaginative work.

In today's climate, de-individuation is specifically a violence against the ideo-logical predominance of individualism. Of course, individualism has its naked, all-too obvious side in conspicuous consumption and the mantra that 'greed is good'. However, individualism also increasingly accommodates the drive for 'equality' by transforming it into a *passive* form of assumed entitlement administered by institu-tions in the form of 'individual rights' (which Badiou has criticized as "droit sans principe"—SM: p.26). This transformation stifles any *active* politics of equality that would pursue the displacement of both individualism and its institutional as well as cultural and socio-symbolic supports (see Todd May: 2008).[6] This second violence

---

6. "The animating idea behind passive equality is that some form of equality is to be ensured by an institution for the sake of those whose equality is at stake. It is to be given, or at least pro-tected, rather than taken by the subjects of equality" (May: 2008, p.3).

of de-individuation therefore needs to oppose a politics of equality to the individualistic and legalistic paradigm of equity—note the slippage in this word from justice to property, indeed to the essence of capital itself. We will say more below about the kind of body presupposed by juridical individualism, and its incompatibility with Badiou's subject-body.

Subjectivization: This term, taken from *Theory of the Subject*, refers to the swallowing of what had been the egoic 'I' into the impersonal 'we' of a collective. Now, it is well known what kind of violence can be unleashed against individuals in the name of the Party, as the word 'purge' chillingly invokes for anyone familiar with Stalinism in the 1930s. However, this narrative is already external to the sequence it would represent, in that its measure for the violence of the collective remains the individual whose effacement is the collective's precondition. A collective cannot be a mere assemblage of individuals without fatally compromising its unity: to judge the former from the point of view of the latter would be to fail to think the logic of collectivity. Yet far from endorsing the Stalinist reification of the Party, as this renunciation of individualism might seem to imply, Badiou's Maoism provides him with, to put it simplistically, 'good' and 'bad' conceptions of collectivity with respectively 'good' and 'bad' forms of violence.

Thus, the dialectically necessary ossification of the collective 'group in fusion' into Fraternity-Terror that Sartre diagnosed apropos Stalinism in the *Critique of Dialectical Reason* would already be, for Badiou, the bad violence of the old, of what Sartre himself called the 'seriality' of the 'practico-inert' (Sartre: 2004). Such a party has ceased to be a subject precisely because its violence is essentially conservative, bound as it is to protecting its guiding 'project'. To this Badiou would oppose the 'good' violence of innovative praxis. During his early Maoist phase, it was the Maoist Party that could provide a constant space for the gathering and sheltering of such innovation, rather than being merely the accumulated will of effaced individuals. Such was the difference between Maoism and Stalinism on the issue of organisation. This third violence then is primarily the maintenance of disciplined *unity*. Because unity is not the same as identity, however, the category of the 'individual' and the notion of the destruction of its precious difference (legally protected in 'individual rights' and so on) is simply not an appropriate measure for the collective subject.

Having said that, this emphasis on the Maoist Party was a solution that failed to separate itself from the alluring image of 'creative destruction': the Party was something like a furnace, both containing and stoking the conflagration of the old in the flames of the new. We know that Badiou abandoned this solution, but not, as I will go on to show, the centrality of destruction. However, it is worth pointing out that our own analysis of the example of the Rastafari movement demonstrated a form of subjectivization much less enamoured of the image of collective unity. The Rasta logic of 'I an I', it was argued, both conjoins the individual and the subject and prevents the sublation of both into an ontologised collective.

Singularization: The violence of what I am calling singularization comes in the (split) collective subject's incessant work of maintaining its own separation vis-à-vis the situation it is overturning. An important part of this separation is the policing of the subject's own internal tendency toward complicity, reformism, and what Mao termed left and right 'deviation'. However, unlike either the violence of imposed unity or indeed the violence of de-individuation that precedes it, this fourth violence necessarily faces 'outward' in confronting the hegemonic power of the world it is challenging. It could therefore be described as a *counter*-violence pitted against the inertia of the everyday which closes around novelty like water. If subjectivization corresponds to what I called the anthropological dimension of evental cultures in the last chapter, singularization is connected to the aesthetic dimension and thus to the development of a *langue-sujet*. The violence of pre-figuration already involved the 'worsening' of quotidian language, but singularization involves the poetic creation of new terms to use as weapons against the dominant discourse. Although saturated today, 'revolution' has been during certain political sequences a singularised term vital in fending off the threat of reformism. More than that, such singularised terms become the subject-language thanks to which a truth can circulate. Since the subject is condition by its fidelity to that truth, singularization is an indispensable modality of violence for the subject's endurance.

After all, the pull of inertia exerts itself on multiple levels, from the micro-level at which other claims—be they marital, parental, or professional—threaten to drag the subject back into the realm of the individual, to the macro-level at which the collective subject is interpolated as a 'partner' in dialogue within a mechanism of representation. For example, the State offers to 'recognise' the demands of striking workers as legitimate so long as they are mediated by trade unions; or the demands of Rastafari so long as it is regulated as an 'official religion'. Although the collective subject is intensely visible in the world it challenges, it must not become *discernible* since this would constitute its domestication. Clearly, the demands of Rastafari are impossible for the Jamaican State to meet. This fourth form of violence then involves the refusal of all normative criteria for recognition or justice. For example, the legal granting of land to Australian aboriginals, while materially important, cannot be allowed to be presented as 'justice', since the legal concept of land granted along with the land itself is a violent injustice to the non-proprietorial concept of land within Aboriginal cosmologies.[7] But, beyond the negative refusal of official justice, singularization articulates a subject-language in which impossible demands can be made. In *Theory of the Subject*, singularisation is pushed to its absolute limit: the agent of creative destruction, still at this stage the proletariat, must destroy itself in turn if the new situation it brings forth is to be genuinely and persistently novel. This is why Badiou describes the proletariat as a 'vanishing' or 'evanescent' term. Its true historical calling is to disappear without a trace, to go up in flames along with everything else related to the capitalist mode of production. This is Badiou's gloss on Marx's vision of the withering away of the State. Again,

---

7. It is possible to discern the power of a similar refusal in the activism of the South African Kulumani Support Group: precisely because they do not recognise the 'justice' offered by the Truth and Reconciliation Commission, but *do* recognise the violence of the attempt to render this 'justice' definitive for the sake of nation-building in a still riven South Africa, Kulumani are attempting to sue several multi-national corporations that lent material assistance to the apartheid regime. This is a fascinating example of the refusal of Todd May's 'passive equality' in favour of an 'active equality' nonetheless sought via the law.

Badiou's later work moves beyond this destruction of destruction in order to think a logical or 'transcendental' destruction.

Counter-Nomination: Finally, it is imperative to point out that the transformative effects of the collective political subject are frequently experienced by non-militants as 'irrational', 'excessive', 'fanatical', 'terroristic'. Alberto Toscano has argued convincingly that the concept of 'fanaticism', beyond the Enlightenment critique of religious dogmatism, has a long history of reactionary use. It has been decisive in condemning the abstract universality and militant commitment of egalitarian politics (and Toscano shows how this pertained to the abolition movement, albeit the American rather than the British one we have focussed on—see chapter 1 of Toscano: 2010). Fanaticism has therefore served as a Statist counter-nomination, in the sense we developed in Chapter 3. The State's use of the word 'fanatic' and its homonyms simultaneously asserts the putative legitimacy and rationality of the State's own use of violence. The subject inevitably meets this violence of counter-nomination and its very visceral consequences. Just as Spartacus had to be crucified on the Appian Way for leading a slave revolt, so Jesus had to be subdued by Roman 'justice' for denying its imperial authority, and so also Toussaint L'Ouverture had to face wave upon wave of colonial military might for having the audacity to declare an independent Haitian republic. Indeed, by *Logics of Worlds*, where these examples are addressed, Badiou as we saw in Chapter 4 begins to refer to 'reactionary' and 'obscure' subjects that constitute themselves around the violent denial and effacement of a truth. This need not take the obvious form of the direct mobilisation of State violence—tanks rolling in, riot police with batons, tear gas and water canons—but certainly begins with the State's own pathologising diagnosis of the violent nature of faithful subjects and, for that matter, resistant individuals. Such and such a massive protest was *really* the result of a few extremists agitating the minds of the young and naïve.[8] Such and such a riot had nothing to do with large-scale socio-economic ghettoization but with a criminal underclass mostly composed of foreigners anyway. And so on. It is therefore clear today that the very term 'violence' is now *the* pre-eminent weapon in the armoury of reactionary counter-nomination, particularly in liberal democracies where a logic of security reigns. The very act of designating an incident, whether the establishment of a farmer's co-operative, a student sit-in, or vandalism by animal rights

---

8. During the student protests against the introduction of tuition fees in the UK in November 2010, the way in which the destruction of private property by an anarchist minority was used by the mainstream media to represent *all* the protestors as something akin to spoiled juvenile delinquents was a case in point. It also invites us to consider the ways in which counter-nomination may take on a predominantly imagistic quality in today's visually dominated media ecology. Leaving an empty police riot van in the middle of a crowd of protestors angry at being 'kettled' is of course very likely to produce the images of 'mindless vandalism' both the police, the government and the media (for the most part) want. In such a context, the very real violence committed against a protestor who required emergency brain surgery as a result of blows from a policeman's baton is reported, but enjoys a much lower visual profile and currency. Meanwhile, the systemic or macro-level violence of the introduction of tuition fees themselves, putting immense financial strains on many low income families and causing countless young people to give up on higher education altogether, remains practically invisible.

activists, as 'violent' is frequently the trigger for the full weight of the State being brought to bear.

I would suggest that propping up the logic of security here is violence measured by the State in at least three interlinked ways. Firstly, violence is conceived as being against the individual human body, explicitly protected by law, but also covertly constructed by it in a quintessentially Foucaultian manner. This physiologico-legal body is inherently vulnerable to physical, psychological and moral victimization. In a kind of self-authorizing feedback loop, it is this body's very propensity for sustaining bruises and wounds that *demands* the protection offered by the law. This first Statist measure of violence, the vulnerable physiologico-legal body, already includes violence against property which, from a Marxist perspective, would be the prime mover behind such an ideology: it is well-known that commercial law conceives of companies as bodies subject to damage. Secondly, this tropology of the sanctity of the vulnerable body is extrapolated to the wider social body. Any disruption to the normal, 'organic' functioning of this social body is also deemed to be a form of violence, even without physical traces on actual bodies. Thirdly, a link is made between domestic 'rights' that protect individuals, their property, and workaday normality on the one hand, and the defensive/aggressive foreign policy that protects the social body from *external* threats on the other. Ultimately, the overlap between these three modalities of the Statist discourse (and simultaneously practice) of violence constitute the knot tied between human rights and humanitarian intervention, in which the universality of the vulnerable body in need of protection justifies military incursions but quickly collapses into its inverse—bare life, *homo sacer*, the human pyramids at Abu Ghraib. In every way, this fragile, routinized and commodified body at the kernel of human rights discourse is the opposite of Badiou's subject-body.

It is therefore a desperate yet deliberate irony that what Badiou deems to be properly human, which is to say the capacity to leave one's finite interests behind and enter into the composition of an infinite truth, is invariably categorised today as 'violent' and, thereby, violently foreclosed. This fifth reactionary violence of counter-nomination therefore demonstrates a couple of things about what we have called, after Heidegger, the 'worlding of the world'. Firstly, it shows that 'worlding' necessarily incorporates a *structural* violence. It takes constant narrative and 'actual' violence simply to keep things as they are, because, at least for Badiou, what 'is' is secretly multiple all the way down. This is what Žižek, following Sartre, means by 'objective' or 'systemic violence'. But secondly, that thanks precisely to the antonymic separation between politics and violence which conjures this structural violence into the invisibility of omnipresence, the (liberal) Statist verdict 'violent' is itself one of the most effective means of policing the status quo, local and increasingly global.

Of paramount importance then is distinguishing progressive violence (if we dare such a formulation, and I think we must) from its Statist counter-nomination. Since the subject is nothing other than a praxis, it is clear that progressive violence must be in the form of a sustained disruptive act. However, and this is absolutely crucial, that act must completely distance itself from the Statist restriction of the horizon of violence to the vulnerable individual-social-political body. Instead, *it*

*must immanently invent its own novel determination of legitimate violence without lapsing into
the old romance with creative destruction.* This should immediately caution us against fet-
ishizing certain kinds of act—bombings, assassinations, the taking of hostages, military coups and so forth. These are violent in an obvious, I would even say stupid
sense: stupid because this obviousness indicates their a priori capture by the very
forces they target. History suggests that massive irruptions of social unrest are often little more than expressions of blind impotence which, in legitimising their own
repression, can actually exacerbate that impotence. This was precisely the point
made in Chapter 6 when we identified uprisings, such as those of the Maroon War
and Tacky's Rebellion, which utilised the logic of 'African Resistance' in Jamaica.
Also emerging from anti-colonial struggles, Fanon's rejection of the black cultural
politics of the *négritude* movement in *Black Skin, White Masks* is borne of an awareness of this trap (and of course, *Wretched of the Earth* has a whole chapter devoted to
'Spontaneity: Its Strengths and Weakness'). If Fanon claims that "[f]or the black
man there is only one destiny. And it is white" (Fanon: 1986, p.12), it is because 'the
black man' continues to be defined by the racialised category given to him by the
white man. To fight under the banner of the 'black man' alone is to inadvertently
consolidate the trope of 'uppity native' that has long legitimised the imposition of
white discipline. Badiou frequently borrows both Lenin's phrase, and its pejorative
tones, to describe the naïve valuation of spontaneous violence arising from a fully
'placed' or named multiple: 'juvenile Leftism'.

    In fact, as Žižek has also pointed out (Žižek: 2008b), in certain circumstanc-
es doing nothing can be a progressive form of violence in the sense I am trying
to develop. The General Strike in May '68 was undoubtedly the real challenge
to de Gaulle's government, not the student's pitched battles with the police in the
streets around the Sorbonne. Only when we assess a political sequence by its disruptive *consequences* can we coherently retain the term 'act' to describe doing nothing! Quite obviously, a general strike is only 'doing nothing' from the point of view
of a situation which defines action in the narrow terms of economic productivity.
By breaking the banal rhythms of workaday drudgery and transforming utilitarian
spaces, such as the factories themselves, into spaces of political participation and
creation, a general strike is certainly 'doing something'. In the same sense, a con-
scientious objector who abstains from military action is by no means being passive.
These are ideas with which the 'malingering' slaves of Jamaica's past would have
been intuitively familiar, and the later Rastafarian resistance to 'political' participation could be said to draw on the same sources.

DESTRUCTION

It is to distinguish progressive from Statist violence that Badiou resurrects in *Logics
of Worlds* a concept he had deployed freely during his Maoist phase but later abjured, namely, 'destruction'.

    While in *Theory of the Subject* destruction is dangerously close to what I have
termed 'creative violence', which is to say the iconoclastic belief that destruction
is directly and intrinsically progressive, by *Being and Event* Badiou openly criticizes
his former position:

I was, I must admit, a little misguided in *Théorie du sujet* concerning the theme of destruction. I still maintained, back then, the idea of an essential link between destruction and novelty. Empirically, novelty (for example, political novelty) is accompanied by destruction. But it must be clear that this accompaniment is not linked to intrinsic novelty; on the contrary, the latter is always a supplementation by a truth. *Destruction is the ancient effect of the new supplementation amidst the ancient* (*BE*, p.407)

Otherwise put, 'destruction' is the name given to absolute novelty as measured against the values of the old situation. If "destruction is a merely objective category" (Hallward: 2003, p.162) it follows that it "is not true, it is knowledgeable" (*BE*, p.408). This objective rather than truthful use of 'destruction' can be self-evidently conservative, as in diatribes against the 'destruction of property', of 'family values', of the 'racial purity' of the nation and so on. But it is no less enmeshed in the old situation when it becomes paradigmatic for putatively radical discourse. Aiming to seize and then destroy the State is ultimately a form of Statism, just as viewing anarchism as the wilful transgression of the law remains fully ensconced within the law—something acutely recognised by psychoanalysis. In essence, "Killing somebody is always a matter of the (ancient) state of things; it cannot be a prerequisite for novelty" (*ibid.*).

Badiou's position in *Being and Event* thus has the considerable benefit of moving us away from the easy romanticism of anti-State violence. The Leninist instrumentalization of destruction in the name of politics always faced the enormous empirical asymmetry between a rather idealised 'people power' and the brutal reality of State power, and thus subordinated itself to the extreme rarity of opportune moments, such as October 1917, when the gap between the two had been closed by the destablizing effects of WWI and the preceding bourgeois revolution. Maoism and also *Fidelismo*, in their emphasis on the asymmetric form of warfare that is guerrilla combat, tried to close this gap through the application of tactical violence itself (Jayatilleka: 2007). And yet in today's context, in which this asymmetry is both more pronounced and infinitely more complex—networked surveillance, biopolitics, the production of docile bodies subjected at the capillary level and so forth—maintaining this crude understanding of the destruction of the State as the *sine qua non* of radical politics would surely be a recipe for despair and paralysis.

Notwithstanding this benefit of Badiou's new position, however, the contrast between creation and destruction in *Being and Event* is so stark that, as Peter Hallward puts it, Badiou can "consider violence as essentially external to any truth process" (Hallward: 2003, p.269). *This* would be the most ethically worrisome gesture, and also the most politically self-defeating insofar as it actually repeats the liberal antinomy of politics and violence which is the basis of a reactionary deployment of the term 'violent'. Destruction is discarded in *Being and Event* not only because of a theoretical move from a politics of obliteration to one of subtraction (as I will elaborate in a moment), but also because the historic ascendancy of liberalism has transformed the term into an exclusively moral and moralizing category. Liberals would certainly be wrong in thinking that Badiou is motivated in his rejection of 'destruction' by any *acceptance* of their morality, but equally, in dropping it, he implicitly conceded to them at this time its hegemonically moralistic encryption.

To get out of this double-bind and recover the emancipatory force of destruction, Badiou arguably required exactly the kind of patient, balanced and paradoxically very Maoist 'self-criticism' which he undertook in *The Century*. For it is by meditating there both on the centrality of violence in the 20th century *and his own participation in its thought*, that he manages to steer a nuanced course between the pitfalls surrounding the politics-violence relation. On the one hand, he sounds like the ossified Maoist terrorist some still take him to be when he praises the Twentieth Century's heroic commitment to the real, contrasting it to today's complacent acceptance of reality (which in this Lacanian register is an imaginary construct). Yet on the other hand, he might sound moderately mainstream in critiquing the century's disastrous love affair with destruction: specifically, its vicious will to realise an indestructable real through the total destruction of semblance (for Lacan, on the contrary, the real cannot be actualised and any direct encounter with it would necessarily be traumatic). The concept 'purge' and its brutal practice is indeed key to Badiou's understanding of the excesses of the twentieth century, from Stalin and Hitler through to Mao and Pol-Pot. For 'purge' concentrates the century's deadly dalliance with the illusion that, by peeling away the onion-layers of semblance whose folds constitute reality, the unmediated real, utopia in all its plenitude, could somehow be attained. When the real only emerges through the purging of semblance, nothing is above suspicion, *particularly* the appearance of fidelity itself. Trotsky was dangerous not just because he opposed Stalin, but because he resembled him. Hence the paranoid involution of Stalinist state terror in the purges. Categorically for Badiou, this aesthetico-political appreciation of the awesome role of destruction in the creation of a New Man and a New Society was, and is, a terrible error and a complete dead-end.

Yet in his sanguine old age Badiou is certainly not falling into line with those *nouveaux philosophes* who, in turning their backs on their own former Maoism in many cases, have delighted in condemning the bloodshed of 'totalitarianism'—a term which Badiou rightly dislikes for its elision of the specificity of the Nazi and Stalinist sequences. His measure for the mistakes of the past is not the easy moral yardstick of the body-count.[9] Rather, he judges the century on the terms by which it thought itself, as an heroic, but also tragic, and certainly *real* drive for human transformation. Thus, when he is critical of what he calls 'terrorist nihilism'—that is, the absolute valorization of destruction as a direct pathway to the actualization of the real—it is because its ultimate destination must be the ruins of nothingness that inevitably follow an annihilation of reality. It is certainly *not* because of a critique of the 'passion for the real' itself. This is why Badiou also points out that

---

9. The body count is unethical on two counts, as it were: because it reduces the dead to equivalence, and also because it refuses the properly ethical (in Badiou's Lacanian sense) measure of unyielding fidelity to the Idea. It is also demonstrably ideological rather than objective. How many people know the number of deaths resulting from the collapse of the World Trade Centre compared to those that know the official total death toll resulting from the consequent war in Iraq?

'terrorist nihilism' "does not *consent* to the nothing; it is a creation, and in it one should recognise the lineaments of an active nihilism" (*C*, p.64). The phrase 'active nihilism' here tries to isolate the positive passion for the real that animates, but is not reducible to, the indulgence of destruction for its own sake which is the error of 'terrorist nihilism'. So Badiou's true target is not the various attempts to create the new by destroying the old, since this appetite for change he wholly endorses, but rather it is the "passive, or reactive, nihilism" of our *contemporary* ennui which is allergic to change, subjugated as it is to "a nihilism hostile to every action as well as every thought" (*ibid.*, p.65).

And it is here, in order to move away from the worldliness of nihilism, which makes even its active form always residually negative rather than productive, that Badiou sketches an alternative path:

> The other path that the century sketched out—the one that attempts to hold onto the passion for the real without falling for the paroxysmal charms of terror—is what I call the subtractive path: to exhibit as a real point, not the destruction of reality, but minimal difference. To purify reality, not in order to annihilate it at its surface, but to subtract it from its apparent unity so as to detect within it the miniscule difference, the vanishing term that constitutes it (*C*, p.65)

Subtraction differs fundamentally from destruction because it does not identify elements whose negation would emancipate the inhabitants of a world, such as the bourgeoisie or the State, nor does it get directly involved in 'worldly' antagonisms that are perfectly and indeed relentlessly discerned within that world, such as class struggle or the 'battle of the sexes'. On the contrary, subtraction withdraws from *all* worldly predicates in order to expose a minimal difference the exclusion of which enables all the other relational differences (including those of class and gender) that hierarchically structure a given world. Whereas the destination of terroristic destruction was nothingness, the destination of subtraction is the void, an ontologically distinct concept. As the logical negation of *something*, nothingness remains a relation, albeit of the most reduced kind, to that which has been negated, like ruins recalling a former architecture. The void, by contrast, is constitutively uncountable precisely because it is the inadmissible point of contact with the inconsistent multiplicity that is a world's hidden generic foundation. As Žižek points out, however, subtraction remains connected to violence, perhaps even of a more fundamental kind:

> Such a subtraction is extremely violent, even more violent than destruction/purification: it is a reduction to minimal difference, to a difference of part(s)/no-part, 1 and 0, groups and the proletariat. It is not only a subtraction of the subject *from* the hegemonic field, but a subtraction which violently *affects* this field itself, laying bare its true coordinates (Žižek: 2008b, p.411)

Thanks to Badiou's reckoning with the bloodshed of the 20th century and his own philosophical participation in the thought that shaped it in *The Century*, he conceptually contained the notion of destruction whose moralization legitimates the antonym between violence and politics. More importantly, he disentangled his own approach from that antonym with the concept of 'subtraction'. He was then in a position to return 'destruction' to the core of the subjective truth process as part of the larger task today, "to de-moralise philosophy" (*SM*, p.83).

By *Logics of Worlds* then, in which his focus is on beings rather than Being, and thus on how a truth appears in a world rather than on the 'classical' universe of set-theoretical ontology, he must undo the abrupt opposition between creation and destruction if he is to formulate a nuanced logic of change. As we have already seen, he now acknowledges a kind of sliding scale of intensities of change which considerably ameliorates the ruptural pathos of *Being and Event*: in ascending order of intensity, the stages on this scale are 'modifications', 'facts', 'weak singularities' and 'strong singularities' (*LW*, see section 1of Book V)

Respectively then, 'modifications' barely ripple the surface of appearance regulated by the 'transcendental' of a world since they are part and parcel of its becoming—a world *is* the transcendental incorporation of its modifications. The arrival of a new headmaster to a school might be thought of as such a 'modification'. The element 'headmaster' is as fixed as before, and its ordering relation to staff, students, local community and national educational structures etc. is also unchanged, so that the school is no less a school following this mere change of personnel. Indeed, what makes it a school is its capacity to endure across such modifications.

More substantial changes, while being ontologically significant in exposing a certain incompletion of a world, can nonetheless be *existentially* subdued at the level of appearance by being reduced to 'facts' which are still fully readable within the given transcendental regime. This is what I have termed 'counter-nomination'. To prevent serious race riots from indexing the excrescent multiple of poor black youths in housing projects who belong to the social situation but are not included in it, a 'cultural fact' might be constructed such that the outbreak of violence was really due to the baleful influence of incendiary hip-hop (a classic catachresis of cause and effect), or even a pseudo-anthropological 'fact' according to which the black race is genetically predisposed to outbursts of rage which are not political but natural, something like the random eruption cycles of volcanoes.

Finally 'singularities' can emerge that do actually challenge a transcendental regime of appearance, but they can do this in two ways. Either the challenge is relatively weak because the consequences of the emergence of this singularity are rendered ephemeral by being historically or narratologically contained. One might give May '68 itself as an example of a weak singularity in that it seems to have been successfully locked up in the vaults of history as an instance of youthful enthusiasm, appearing now primarily through a haze of nostalgia (though not in Badiou's Beckettian sense). Or the challenge of a singularity can be strong because its consequences are infinite and timeless, and these Badiou continues to call 'events'. While nothing is quite the same after even a weak singularity, so that Nicolas Sarkozy still felt compelled to *re*-draw the line under May '68 in the run up to his election victory in 2007, a strong singularity is an irreversible inauguration that continually authorizes ever-new beginnings. Thus, the truth unleashed by the French Revolution, that everyone is created equal, cannot be historically contained, and egalitarianism continues to irrupt among beings and to disrupt their worlds.

Now, one might have imagined that the introduction of shades or gradations of change could have pushed Badiou closer to the kind of reformism he has always despised, and perhaps further away still from any engagement with a positive notion of destruction. However, this is not the case at all. Using category theory rather than set-theory now, he argues that at the level of existence—which again is not that of being-qua-being but of beings in their relational appearance—every world must have a minimal degree of appearance (the 'miniscule difference' referenced above) upon which every other degree, right up to the maximum, builds itself as a relation of 'larger than' or 'more than'. He calls this structurally necessary minimal degree of appearance the 'in-existent' of a world: it does appear in the world, but only as 'null' for that world. The term is well chosen, for the in-existent is not homogeneous with non-existence or non-being, since the latter would fall below appearance altogether. As discussed in Chapter 2, the key example in *Logics of Worlds* of a strong singularity that traverses the gap between minimal and maximal appearance is the Paris Commune, specifically the simultaneous destruction of the notion of the worker's exclusion from political action and the maximal appearance of their politicisation. Although the Commune was bloody then, its value lies on the side of creation rather than simplistic destruction, on the side of its repeated 'completion', by Lenin in October 1917, or Mao in 1967.

This is crucial because it subtracts political truth from the spilling of blood altogether, so that 'progressive violence' not only should not be measured by body-counts, but it cannot be, without a weakening of its transformative power. At the theoretical level, Lenin's practical analysis of the Commune in *The State and Revolution*, reminiscent of a defeated general picking grimly over the mistakes of a lost battle, failed to get out of the model of war that invariably instrumentalises destruction. Lenin's aim was to learn from the mistakes of the Communards, in their failure to focus and maintain their destructive potential through 'iron discipline' and the Party structure, so as to ensure that in future battles the blood that would *have to be* spilt would be, pint for pint, more bourgeois than proletariat. And yet, although Badiou concurs that destruction was intrinsic to the Commune, it was not of Lenin's worldly type (where individuated elements are targeted and obliterated in order to turn social hierarchies upsidedown). The 1871 Commune destroyed not "the dominant group and its politicians; but [...] something more important: the political subordination of workers and the people. What was destroyed was of the order of subjective incapacity" (*P*, pp.287-288). In sum, never again could the capacity for political self-organisation among the working classes be truthfully denied after the event of the Commune.

In Badiou's own terms, this is a logical destruction rather than an empirical one, a seismic blow at the level of existence or appearance, but not an ontological annihilation at the level of being as such. The fact that this logical notion of destruction—as the necessary disappearance of an old existent with the surging forth of a new one—has no internally necessary connection to violence in the everyday Statist sense, is clear from the fact that the next example of destruction Badiou gives in *Logics of Worlds*, following that of the Commune, is love. Citing Rousseau's character Saint-Preux on the deranging power of what the French

rightly call *amour fou*, he points out that what is destroyed by the loving encounter is the Cartesian isolation that firmly separates two individuals as '*x* with *y* and
z properties', and '*a* with *b* and *c* properties'. Love, which is to say militant fidelity
to the uncertain consequences opened up by the loving encounter, creates a defi-
antly anti-worldly (ultra)One precisely by dividing the world into two (either our
fidelity to each other informs our every decision and the world must reinvent itself
around us, or it doesn't, and the One of our love dissipates back into mundane differences). If love can be a form of destruction, then we are much closer to meeting
Peter Hallward's piquant challenge to Badiou's earlier externalization of violence
from any truth process:

> It might be more consistent, and arguably more courageous, to insist that the
> break with our established order will come not through recourse to alterna-
> tive forms of violence, but with the organized, uncompromising imposition of
> a radical non-violence. Only a precisely axiomatic commitment to non-vio-
> lence offers any hope of a lasting break in the futile recycling of violence (Hall-
> ward: 2003, p.269)

VIOLENCE, ANTI-VIOLENCE, NON-VIOLENCE: GANDHI'S *SATYAGRAHA*

Because colonial and anti-colonial violence have been central to our analysis of the
Jamaican example, and as we have pointed out played a decisive role in the Sar-
tre-Camus debate on violence, I would now like to turn to the logic of another independence struggle: namely, that of India and the role in its national liberation
struggle played by Mahatma Gandhi.

Etienne Balibar has already asked 'Lenin and Gandhi: A Missed Encounter?'
(Balibar: 2004). Balibar points out that the two figures have of course been compared many times, but, rather like Sartre and Camus, always in the form of binary opposites that never meet: "violent revolution and non-violent revolution, socialist revolution and national or nationalist revolution, revolution grounded on a
scientific ideology, a theory of social relations, and revolution grounded on a religious ideology, or an ethic of religious inspiration" (*ibid.*, p.2). This binarism is a
condensed version of the historicization of the 20th century that continues to support the antonymic disjunction between politics and violence: Gandhi, the pacifist
good guy, can be placed under the heading of politics, but Lenin, the terrorist bad
guy, must be ostracised beyond the boundaries of what we now accept as politics.
I would like to demonstrate the extent to which Gandhi's strategy of supposedly
non-violent *satyagraha* was very precisely violent in the sense I have distilled from
Badiou's own rejection of the Leninist instrumentalisation of violence. However,
rather like the example of Rastafari in the previous chapter, Gandhi is perhaps as
useful to us in illustrating certain weaknesses as in exemplifying the political use
of (non)violence.

That the set of sequences from 1908 to 1947 which challenged, first, racist legislation against Indian immigrants in South Africa, and then, colonial exploitation
under British rule in India itself, can justifiably be considered a generic political
truth procedure in Badiou's sense, is clearest, I believe, in Gandhi's own prolific

writings on the strategy of *satyagraha*, the form of both organisation and collective subjectivity that animated them. We can start with the term itself.

Although he used it initially, Gandhi was deeply dissatisfied with the English phrase 'passive resistance' which named an adjacent, but hardly identical tradition of civil disobedience in the metropole, for example that deployed by First Wave feminists in the Suffragette movement. His experience as a lawyer in Johannesburg already showed that what was required was not passivity, but on the contrary, intense commitment and discipline (on this at least, Gandhi was a pure Leninist). Moreover, while Christianity had been central in many progressive European movements since the late Eighteenth Century, from the abolition of slavery to welfare initiatives for the moral problem of the poor and so forth, Gandhi recognised that Christianity in its contribution to the civilizing mission of imperialism had also imparted to 'passive resistance' the image of a "weapon of the weak" (Gandhi: 2008, p.317). This contrasted with his own rather more Hegelian vision, that *satyagraha's* determinate negation is immediately and immanently an affirmative strength. This, as we shall see, stemmed from his grasp not of Hegel per se but of the duality of imperial sovereignty.

The cognate English term 'non-violence' did not suit his needs either. Not only does such a term presuppose the option of a space outside violence, somewhat problematic in the broiling pressure-cooker that Indian society under the British was becoming in the first half of the 20th century, but it misses both the subjective and objective dimensions of *satyagraha*: on the subjective side, the strong connotation within 'non-violence' of dormant inaction elides the profound mental, moral and spiritual discipline required of the *stayagrahi*, and on the objective side, which is to say on the side of the situation itself, it crucially passes over the necessity of drawing a violent response from the State. In particular, 'non-violence' fails to describe the ideal outcome of a movement that has succeeded, by drawing the State to exercise its immense capacity for violence against 'its own', in achieving a moral victory, since the far-reaching consequences of that victory must necessarily be violent change.

In other words, Gandhi was acutely sensitive to the insufficiency of 'worldly' names for singular truth processes. He was so stumped by the absence of an appropriate name that he set a competition in the newspaper *Indian Opinion* to solicit the suggestions of others. The winning coinage—*satyagraha*—was quickly adopted by Gujarati speakers within the resistance movement and then others because it crystallized two quintessentially Badiouian elements: *Sat*, truth, *Agraha*: firmness (p.317), whose combination Gandhi usually translated as 'truth-force', 'love-force' and, more problematically, 'soul-force'.

Truth seems not to have any Platonic ideality for Gandhi, but rather to be another name for militant will: "Truth [...] has necessarily to be followed, and that at any cost" (p.323), making *satyagraha* "insistence on truth, and force derivable from such insistence" (p.324). Despite articulating it via an appeal to religion which I will problematise in a moment, I would argue that Gandhian truth can be read as a generic category. This is why, like Ché Guevara in a very different context, he comes to connect political truth to love:

> One of the axioms of religion is, there is no religion other than truth. Another is, religion is love. And as there can be only one religion, it follows that truth is love and love is truth. We shall find too, on further reflection, that conduct based on truth is impossible without love (Ghandi: 2008, p.324)[10]

Needless to say, Gandhi completely lacks Badiou's ontology of the multiple from which truth cannot ultimately be separated. Nonetheless, on the level of the equally necessary *subjectivization as well as singularization* of a truth, Gandhi intuitively recognises the militant resources latent within the concept of love, which Badiou has called "a minimal collectivity" (*SM*, p.113). It is love that enables the attainment of a "stage away from brute life" which, if practiced as an antidote to the hatred maintaining hierarchies of caste, class, gender and religion, can enable humanity as a whole to transcend "brute nature" itself (Gandhi: 2008 p.325). Drawing on a strong Hindu tradition, Gandhi's elaboration of the subjectivity of love is rather ascetic, requiring us to "observe perfect chastity, adopt poverty, follow truth, and cultivate fearlessness" (p.322). These are clearly tactics for loosening the bonds of the quotidian, thereby bolstering one's capacity to continue serving as a subject in Badiou's demanding sense. Chastity subtracts one from the institution of marriage, poverty from both actual and symbolic wealth, truth from the reigning doxa, and fearlessness from the psychology of subservience that domesticates one into obeying, not the content, but the mere form of law. Love is also the mode of fidelity that both de-individuates and collectivizes. The *ashrams* Gandhi established (he often referred to them as his most successful contribution) were clearly experiments in living a communal form of love, a communism of sorts. Gandhi also stressed the universalism of love as the source of its emancipatory power: *satyagraha* as love-force "is a force which, if it became universal, would revolutionize social ideals and do away with despotisms and the ever-growing militarism under which the nations of the West are groaning" (p.310). Thus, the "only force of universal application can, therefore, be that of *ahimsa* or love" (p.332). A militant *discourse* of love then can function as the singularisation of a truth, providing it with a term that circulates readably within the situation as it is.

And yet just as Badiou's universal must always emerge within *a* world rather than all worlds (thanks to the set-theoretical injunction against a set-of-all-sets, which is also its profound secularism), so Gandhi's *satyagraha* is embedded in the world of pre-independence, pre-Partition India. For it is readily apparent that *satyagraha* is not a tactic that could be deployed in crudely 'totalitarian' regimes where the rule of law is easily suspended in preference for the 'right of might'. Even as late as 1989, the Chinese Communist Party did not hesitate to send tanks in against pro-democracy protestors in Tiananmen Square, though the wider world was looking on. There have been much more recent examples in Iran, Libya and now Syria in which political leaders seem willing to butcher their own citizens in

---

10. Where this syllogism falls down, of course, is in the middle term, where it is asserted that there can be only one religion. Gandhi is here pushing towards the generic, and elsewhere he substitutes 'spirituality' for religion to this end, but contemporary India demonstrates that this declaration—there can be only one religion— is more suited to the hate-filled separatist zeal of religious fundamentalists than to the generic language of love.

order to hold back the tide of the so-called 'Arab Spring'. In such situations, sitting down in peaceful groups just makes it easier for the powers that be to run you over. This is why an absolute commitment to pacifism, in other words a denial of the necessity of violence, is incompatible with emancipatory politics. Civil disobedience on a massive scale, such as a general strike, can certainly throw a spanner into the functional workings of any State, but *satyagraha* has an intrinsically moral dimension which throws a parallel spanner into the machinery of State *legitimation*—in other words, into its logic of appearance. This is perhaps most effective in liberal democracies that worry about manufacturing, rather than imposing, consent for their rule, or in imperial formations that justify themselves through high-handed religious/philanthropic/humanitarian discourse, as was the case with the so-called 'Second Empire' of British colonialism. And yet, even though the West always seems in a hurry to designate popular uprisings in non-liberal contexts as 'pro-democracy'—even when, as in the 'Arab Spring', the true constellation of motivations is diverse and often contradictory—it may still be that globalisation is forcing the overlapping of 'worlds' in ways that make what we have been calling progressive violence more widely effective. In a manner reminiscent of Hardt and Negri then, Gandhi insists on the dual nature of sovereignty and something like a Lockean right of resistance:

No clapping is possible without two hands to do it, and no quarrel without two persons to make it. Similarly, no State is possible without two entities, the rulers and the ruled. You are our sovereign, our Government, only so long as we consider ourselves your subjects. When we are not subjects, you are not sovereign either (Gandhi: 2008, p.313).

In this sense, Gandhi's metropolitan legal training in London was just as pivotal as the self-education in world religions he undertook during the same period. Only by grasping the universal and ultimately egalitarian dimension of even colonial law (which we showed to be vital in Jamaican struggles for emancipation) could he pit this against law's obverse, the particularising, differentiating, and hierarchizing of a colonised world such as the Transvaal so as to militate *against* the equality of Indian immigrants. To the extent that the term 'non-violence' has any purchase at all on *satyagraha*, it can only be this: that the latter's power comes from its disciplined subtraction from any form of violence nameable as such by the State, as if the 'non' of 'non-violence' were really a French *non* to the ultimately Leninist violence which confronts head-on what Weber called 'the State's monopoly of the means of violence'. In other words, *satyagraha* is a 'non-violence' to the extent that it is a subtraction from what I have called the Hobbesian 'tourniquet' of sovereignty, whereby violent resistance feeds the legitimating mechanism of reactionary power. Gandhi is adamant that *satyagraha* "is the reverse of resistance by arms" (Gandhi: 2008, p.319). This is why the only kind of defeat, but it is for that very reason the most absolute, that can be suffered by a *satyagraha* movement is the ill-disciplined irruption of 'mob violence' from within the ranks of the activists themselves. This happened at Ahmedabad and Viramgamin in 1919 when Gandhi had to temporarily suspend civil disobedience for fear that the Hobbesian tourniquet would garrott the movement altogether. Clearly, such lapses into a Statist understanding of violence threaten to drown progressive violence in blood.

Perhaps because of his sensitivity to the importance of the naming of *satyagraha* and to the intrinsically anti-State nature of its politics, Gandhi also demonstrates an awareness of history's role in the worlding of a world without *satyagraha*, without truth or its force. Eurocentric history, as the history written by military victors in order to glorify and justify their bloody reigns, has a built-in blind-spot when it comes to the emergence of loving fidelities: "if it [history] means the doings of kings and emperors, there can be no evidence of soul-force or passive resistance in such history. You cannot expect silver ore in a tin mine" (Gandhi: 2008, p.318). It follows—and this is a lesson that the Rastafari have learned particularly thoroughly—that history is a reactive discourse which often writes out those attempts to write *in* Rancière's 'part of no part': "History", Gandhi argues, "is really a record of every interruption of the even working force of love or of the soul" (*ibid.*). Isn't love and history Gandhi's version of Badiou's ontology of the generic and knowledge respectively? Just as the occurrence of truth necessitates a knowledge that papers over the void the truth exposes, so rare irruptions of the collective enthusiasm we might call 'political love'[11] necessitate their historical erasure in the interests of narratives of 'national unity'. In Jamaica, this has been the purpose of creolised nationalism. Badiou reads such histories as the work of reactionary subjectivities, and Gandhi likewise asserts that "soul-force, being natural, is not noted in history" (p.319).

Perhaps, though, 'soul-force' can be resurrected? After all, many interpreters have seen the practice of non-violent civil disobedience in the American black civil rights movement of the 1960s[12] as such a continuation of the Gandhian sequence. Whether this is simplistic or not, what is crucial is that the temporal robustness suggested by the possibility of 'resurrection', and further supported by Badiou's recent emphasis on the transhistorical invariance of the 'communist hypothesis', indicate that the contingent outcomes of particular battles, especially when measured by the numerical logic of the body-count, can no longer be the standard of victory. Gandhi again:

> [I]n the usual kind of fighting, all the members of the losing side should be deemed to have been defeated, and in fact they do think that way. In *satyagraha*, the victory of a single member may be taken to mean the victory of all, but the defeat of the side as a whole does not spell defeat for the person who has not himself yielded (Gandhi: 2008, p.327)

---

11. Badiou himself is cautious about the conflation of love and politics. In *Éloge de l'Amour* he points out that while politics always involves the designation of an enemy, love does not involve rivals. Where it is said to, as in Proust, it is a variant of the sceptical take on love, which only ever sees it as an illusion (*EA*, p.54). He therefore advocates the separation of politics and love (p.62), but also confesses to a "secret resonance" (*EA*, p.64) between love and politics that is reflected both in his own fiction, and his personal experience post May '68, when his militant commitment to radical politics 'harmonised' with a loving commitment.

12. The same crude historiography which opposes a caricature of Lenin to one of Gandhi in order to firmly separate violence from politics is visible in some histories of the Black Civil Rights movement: a pantomime Malcolm X, as the reviled Leninist advocate of emancipatory violence, is contrasted with Martin Luther King, as the Christ-like martyr to the cause of pacifism.

Like the Paris Commune of 1871, and like the anthem 'we shall overcome' that motivated Martin Luther King's followers, this "admirable battle [...] admits of no defeat" and "can have only one result" (*ibid.*): victory for the forces of change.

In placing, as we should, Gandhi's militant optimism here against the backdrop of religiously fuelled sectarian violence internal to modern India but also to its relations with Pakistan and Kashmir, are we forced to deny Hallward's claim that only an "axiomatic commitment to non-violence offers any hope of a lasting break in the futile recycling of violence" (Hallward: 2003, p.269)? Not really, insofar as those behind the terrorist attacks in Mumbai in 2008, to take only the most spectacular example, were clearly not *satyagrahi*! They were 'terrorist nihilists' in Badiou's sense. And it is crucial to point out that independence, undeniably forced in substantial part by the mass mobilisations around the person of Gandhi, took a form that completely betrayed the Mahatma's generic vision of *purna swaraj*: an extraordinarily violent and arbitrary geographical partition along Hindu/Muslim lines which led to one of the biggest diasporic movements in human history. Nonetheless, it is equally important to point out that it was precisely the religious question that Gandhi was literally in no position to answer. Balibar identifies as the "internal aporia of the Gandhian model" (Balibar: 2004, p.14) the centrality of religious identification in the person of Gandhi himself as spiritual leader. Though this did endow him with an unparalleled power of collective mobilisation, it also rendered the subjective link uniting the atoms of this collective body prone to a kind of cult of saintly personality. Gandhi himself helped to entrench this when, at moments of political impasse, he attempted to embody the entire movement: "I have arrived at the conclusion that in the present circumstances only one, and that myself and no other, should for the time being bear the responsibility of civil resistance" (Gandhi: 2008, p.369). This is a gesture with ambivalent consequences. On the one hand, Gandhi's body acted as a totem uniting the group identity of the collective, but on the other, it rendered that collective vulnerable, not only in the prosaic sense which his assassination by a Hindu fundamentalist exposed, but in a more 'logical' sense. For the narcissistic/masochistic embodiment of India's entire politicized masses in the rather spindly figure of Gandhi himself amounted to a form of the *naming* of a political community: the Badiou of *Ethics*, at least, prohibits this kind of naming as destined for disaster.

Modern India might be said to bear this out. Notwithstanding his claim that world religions are but different pathways to the same single spiritual truth, it is difficult to deny that Gandhi's deployment of the semiotics of even a non-denominational 'spirituality' has ultimately left a bloody legacy. Indeed, his religiously inspired discourse of non-violence has paradoxically resulted in more violence in India than can be attributed to other intersections between religion and emancipatory politics, such as Thomas Müntzer's invocation of 'godly law' in catalyzing the Peasant's War of 1524-1525, the liberation theology movement in Latin America in which the Catholic church genuinely furthered the cause of the poor and, as we argued in the last chapter, the Rastafari movement in Jamaica where a syncretic Afro-Christian messianism became the vehicle of anti-colonial and post-colonial struggle.

But here, are we not encountering the unavoidable problems that arise from the fact that a universal is always constrained to appear within the particularities of a given world, including one that is theologically structured? Certainly, despite the admirable efforts of Indian Marxists like M. N. Roy[13], and exceptions such as the state of Kerala, secular communist internationalism has struggled to gain ground in India's devout culture perhaps because secularism is a European invention emerging from the Enlightenment tradition. Should we, then, acknowledge the strategic importance of particularities and admit that, in practical terms, Gandhi *had to* present himself as a spiritual leader recognisable to the majority such that they would follow him? In fact, this is the danger of qualifying in any way whatsoever, even under the weight of a very real pragmatic consideration, the singularity of a truth. Any particular link back to the previous world can serve as a bridge opening the way for the violence of the old which, as reactionary, paranoid and vengeful, is much worse than the violence of transformation. Indeed, one might even argue that lurking behind the apparently commonsensical suggestion that Gandhi *had* to present himself in a religious mode, there is a more unpalatable implication, namely, that not everyone has the capacity to renounce their world and become a subject. It was precisely this gesture of barring a people from the capacity for politics that the British imperialists used as a paternalistic legitimation for their on-going exploitation of India and other territories.

Ultimately, Balibar's "internal aporias of the Gandhian model" (Balibar: 2004, p.14) may already have been present in the latter's conceptualisation of *satyagraha* itself. To the extent that the suffering body, whether it be subjected to beatings, incarceration, hunger-strike or even execution, is the moral cornerstone but also the transformative lever of *satyagraha*—particularly with Gandhi's own body as the sacred avatar of the entire collective—he perhaps inadvertently drew on a Christian martyrology when he argued that "*satyagraha* means fighting oppression through voluntary suffering" (Gandhi: 2008, p.331). As I have already pointed out, this genealogically Christian vision also finds its way into Statist legal figurations of the body and thus legitimate-illegitimate violence. Although Gandhi managed to evade the Statist nomination of violence, in drawing on religious sources that the law also drew on, *he failed to invent a novel concept and practice of violence internal to the movement he unleashed.* Moreover, insofar as he offered up the individual fragile body in the form of a sacrifice to a higher cause, he did not escape the lapse back into a certain romanticism of creative destruction. Satyagraha demands that the State utilise the body-count in the particularising sense, rather than confronting it with the uncountable subject-body. In the end then, Gandhi remained too internal to the law. And his very British faith in the rule of law seems of particularly dubious appeal to us today, precisely as liberal democracies have started to more and more resemble the totalitarian states and fundamentalist ideologies from which they purport to be protecting us.

---

13. Roy, in his spats at the Second International with Stalin over the 'national question' (i.e., whether the global revolution had to begin in the most developed regions of Europe or the colonial peripheries) was rather hampered by the fact, which Stalin was extremely quick to point out, that India didn't even have its own Marxist party at that time. See Young: 2001.

As Jayatilleka (2007) has argued, the vast majority of theoretical work on the ethics of political violence is on the side of just war theory, and thus on the side of established States. It is therefore incompatible with the Marxist tradition and Badiou's inheritance from it. Moreover, just war theory is further tainted both by its religious origins in the thought of Saints Augustine, Ambrose and Aquinas, and by the resurrection of these origins in the current War on Terror with its Christian fundamentalist supporters. It is *this* pre-Enlightenment medieval tradition of religious fanaticism that was countered by the counter-fanaticism of egalitarianism and what Hegel called, critically, its 'enthusiasm for the abstract'. But the radical tradition cannot be shamed by Hegel's critique of the bloody excesses of Jacobinism into thinking that, simply because just war theory cannot offer it an ethics of violence of its own,[14] it must settle instead for a caricatured Gandhianism, in which unbending pacifism somehow transforms the world through sheer moral superiority.

I have tried to show that the 'non-violence' of *satyagraha* is in fact a progressive form of violence and that no politics of change can evade the problem and necessity of violence. Yet I have also indicated how the religious limitations that encumbered *satyagraha* from the outset caused Gandhi to draw up short before a recognition of this necessity of violence. Although subtracting himself from Statist violence, he did not sufficiently reflect upon transformative violence. Squarely within the Marxist heritage if not orthodoxy, radicals such as Jose Martí, Ché Guevara, Fidel Castro, Mao Tse-Tung, Frantz Fanon, Jean-Paul Sartre, Subcommandante Marcos of the Zapatistas, and even Michael Hardt and Antonio Negri as well as Badiou on the theoretical level, all eschew pacifism because of their common recognition of at least two interrelated forms of violence in any political sequence: firstly, a *defensive* violence which holds open those rare spaces of possibility in which, secondly, *progressive* violence destroys the 'logic of appearance' of a world which perpetuates inequality.

RASTAFARI AGAIN

Let me turn, in closing this final chapter, back to the example of Jamaica and the Rastafari movement. As already noted, Jamaica is no stranger to violence. The island has been vying with South Africa and Columbia for the dubious honour of per capita murder capital of the world for some years now, and at least one recent book is extremely sanguine about the prospects of improvement (see Thomson: 2009). The roots of the problem are deep and knotted, but it is widely accepted that the key factor in the emergence of the gang culture which accounts for the vast majority of these murders is the two main political parties, the Jamaica Labour Party (JLP) and the People's National Party (PNP). Both encouraged gangs to intimidate voters in their favour from the late 1950s onwards. To this day, zones of Kingston are divided up into JLP and PNP districts, with complex semiotic codes identifying allegiances in ways that are reminiscent of the Bloods

---

14. Jayatilleka's claim is that Castro invented a form of just war theory appropriate to guerrilla war, and that this Marxist ethics of the correct use of violence is precisely what has allowed the Cuban revolution to survive while others imploded under the effects of internecine violence.

and the Cripps in the US, and Catholics and Protestants in the Republic of Ireland and Northern Ireland (for example, Budweiser is a beer indicating PNP allegiance because of its red logo, whereas Heineken, with its green label, indicates
JLP support, and one would be ill-advised to order the wrong drink in the wrong
area). This divided, zonal existence in downtown Kingston has recently shifted
from party political allegiance to equally fanatical support of 'top rankin'' Dancehall DJs. The violence of their 'sound clashes', in which they attempt to 'murder' each other with the weapon of the microphone whilst audiences simulate
the sound of gunfire to express their approval, often spills over into less symbolic
forms amongst their followers.

Generations of Jamaicans have grown up in this divided society in which the
violence of 'shottas', or gangsters, is openly glorified, particularly by the youth,
as the only means of fighting one's way out of the ghetto. There is a peculiarly
Jamaican hyper-masculinity that encourages men to equate 'respect' with the gun,
and with the readiness to use it. This problem is exacerbated by the fact that the
police are widely seen to be equally casual with lethal violence, and sometimes difficult to distinguish from the gang members themselves. When in late the 1970s,
the gangs that had been armed by the respective parties proved impossible to control, the Jamaican police were forced to up the ante as well. As Laurie Gunst documents (2003), this led to an exodus of Jamaican gangsters to the US, where they
quickly monopolized the trade in crack cocaine in cities like New York and Miami.
A comprehensive Amnesty International report in 2001 documented the extent of
a culture of 'extra judicial killing' in the Jamaica Constabulary Force ranks, as well
as the extensive cover-ups that make it possible, with police officers almost never
being prosecuted (see Amnesty International: 2001). As a direct result of the lack
of trust in the police, there is a profusion of conflict resolution and violence prevention projects in Jamaica, particularly Kingston. Some of them are government
initiatives while others are grassroots movements often emerging out of church
communities.[15] As innovative as some of these projects are however, the seemingly
ingrained problem of violence in Jamaica displays a depressing resilience.

It is out of this riven and troubled context that the Rastafari have emerged,
and it has been precisely as the urban violence has worsened that they have honed
and disseminated a discourse of 'peace, love, and unity'. However, it would be a serious mistake to conflate this discourse with what might seem to be a Californian
equivalent in the Hippy movement (although that, too, had its potency as a component of the anti-war campaign opposed to Vietnam). Specifically, the Rastafari
appeal to love is a conscious and deliberate alternative to the state-sponsored culture of violence that continues to dominate aspects of Jamaican life today. Reggae
music has, once again, been crucial in the development and dissemination of this
Rastafarian message. There is not space here to perform a lyrical analysis of songs
by artists such as Big Youth, I Roy, Bunny Wailer and, of course, Bob Marley, but

---

15. To list just some of the projects of which I am aware: the Dispute Resolution Foundation,
the Violence Prevention Alliance, the Peace Management Initiative, the Jamaica Partners for
Peace, the Churches Violence Prevention Network, and the outreach activities of the Institute of
Criminal Justice and Security at the University of the West Indies, Mona Campus.

roots reggae demonstrates a curious blend of barbed social critique, in the form of verbal attacks on Babylon, and, at first glance, rather saccharine appeals to love and peace. Indeed, as Carolyn Cooper has noted (2004), the retrospective packaging of the Marley image has tended to obscure the more militant injunctions to 'bun down Babylon' behind a watered down pacifism more palatable to the tourist market.[16] And yet in the Jamaican context of division and particularly black-on-black violence, such appeals to love and peace were a counter to the old (post) colonial tactic of divide and rule, for what I have called the excrescent multiple of 'post-emancipation slavery' is certainly easier to manage when this fundamental antagonism is fractured and diffused across multiple manufactured enmities. Beyond lyrical content, moreover, a more ethnomusicological approach to roots reggae would foreground the spaces and modes of the circulation and consumption of reggae music. Though it has become associated with a particular style often contrasted to the roots tradition in its use of electronic drum machines, faster tempos, 'slackness' or hypersexuality, and 'bling' messages of conspicuous consumption, Norman Stolzoff (2000) points out that the dancehall itself long predates the genre that has taken its name since the 1980s. Arguably since the rise of the mobile sound system in 1950s, the dancehall has been the site of a complex set of social interactions cutting across colour distinctions between black, brown and eventually white, as well as related class distinctions between 'uptown' and 'downtown'.

The canonical moment that exemplifies reggae music's ability to transcend divisive differences comes with the 'One Love Peace Concert' of 22nd April 1978 (the date was chosen because it was the twelfth anniversary of Haile Selassie's visit to Jamaica). Explicitly presented as an antidote to the political violence that was rife on the island at that time, the week leading up to the concert was marked by an unprecedented ceasefire between the feuding gangs, for the most part impeccably observed. And during the actual concert, much to both men's evident chagrin, Bob Marley managed to persuade the leaders of the two political parties, Michael Manley and Edward Seaga, over whom so much blood was being shed, to come on stage during his own extended version of 'Jammin' and publicly join hands, which Marley then held aloft triumphantly. It is easy to get carried away with the romance of such images, and in truth the ceasefire was already crumbling as this iconic moment was literally staged, but I would argue that there is a deeper logic at work here that deserves attention.

In his own definition of love, Badiou argues that it stages the 'scene of the Two' (Badiou: 2000), but a particular kind of 'two'. The two of love is not the result of the addition of two ones. This would be the imaginary illusion in which the lover is able to say to his partner, to cite the last scene from the movie *Jeremy McGuire*, 'you complete me'. Nor, Badiou insists, is love the emergence of a Third that is able to fix the relation conjoining the two lovers. Love is neither summation nor fusion then, because the loving encounter inaugurates something novel. As he argues elsewhere (*EA*), fidelity to the loving encounter involves the joint construction of

16. One could argue that the short-lived 'Lover's Rock' movement in British reggae in the late 1970s also took this sweet tone in Marley's reggae and stripped it of its militancy, although it was primarily intended as music for couples to dance to.

a world based on difference (everything, including my own egoic self, is different from now on) rather than identity (I am my ego). This resonates interestingly with the Rastafarian discourse of love, which is in turn perhaps related to Gandhi's deployment of *ahimsa*. Far from a two that the state can count, for example the founding two of the two party Westminster system, Rasta love forces an immanent two which at least carries the promise of the cooperative construction of a different world. As with *satyagraha*, the Rasta concept of love could equally be said to be a mode of violence from the point of view of both the egoic individual and the state that would count him or her: it is a love that necessarily suspends self-interest and challenges the state to count the irrational collectivities that can result. It also dispenses with any romance of destruction.

However, I would argue that there are ways in which Rastafari represents alternatives to the internal aporia that we identified above with regard to Gandhi's strategy of *satyagraha*. We argued that Gandhi himself functioned too individualistically as a single totemic spiritual leader; that, related to this, he remained enmeshed in a sacrificial model of the body; that his appeal to a deliberately diffuse 'spirituality', while intended to pave the way for an inclusive, multi-faith India, actually opened to door to religious violence; and finally, that his conception of violence ultimately remained problematically juridical. The peculiarities of Rastafari allow it to sidestep these aporia (although it undoubtedly has others of its own). The Rasta concept of love is precisely not focused, in the form of adulation, on a single spiritual leader, but used as a generic logic with which to suspend divisive differences. The black body, as we noted in the last chapter, is a site of pride and 'ital' self-fashioning rather than an object to be offered up to persecution. Indeed, Rastafarian pride in blackness is explicitly opposed to the shame and degradation associated with 400 years of slavery, during which the black body was whipped and chained and, as in the *Zong* case mentioned in Chapter 6, literally sacrificed. Moreover, Rastafarian spirituality is not a diffuse and ultimately liberal gesture of universal inclusivity (all paths lead to the same God etc.), but rather, it is a crucial subjective support of its militant fidelity. The internal distance to the dominant religious framework, Christianity, and indeed the careful distance from the very notion of religion itself, which it has created through a strong counter-reading of Biblical history, is a much more rigorously immanent approach to the Jamaican situation than Gandhi's, by comparison, New Age permissiveness perhaps resulting from the multiple-faith context of India. In its combination of love, a pseudo-religious framework of belief, and a commitment to a certain transformative violence (though one subtracted from the romance of destruction as well as the model of bodily sacrifice), Rastafari is arguably a mode of fanaticism that concentrates "a refusal of compromise and a seemingly boundless drive for the universal" (Toscano: 2010, p. xii).

conclusion

Conclusion

A Polemology of Novelty

Since 9/11, it has been widely noted that Fukuyama's end of history thesis has been overtaken by 'events'—but, I would insist, *not* in Badiou's specific sense. If there was a moment following the fall of the Berlin Wall and the rise of American economic hegemony which enabled certain excitable *doxosophers*—Plato's term for "technicians of opinion who think themselves wise" (Bourdieu: 1998, p.7)—to imagine the dawn of an era of global peace, this naïvité was brutally exposed the moment those commercial planes slammed into the Twin Towers, and allegedly changed the world forever. With a jolt (so this argument goes), History began again like an enormous rusty mechanism creaking back into action, now in the form of nothing less than a renewed clash of civilizations. Previously suspended in the amber of the postmodern 1990s, the notion of 'stakes' suddenly re-emerged in the truly exalted and at the same time elusive form of 'Western values of freedom and democracy'. Even that soothsayer of the simulacrum and herald of the hyper-real, Jean Baudrillard, found himself arguing that the repressed real had returned (Baudrillard: 2003). Consequently, a whole new discourse arose around conflict to announce its resurgence and transformation: enemy combatants, strategic rendition, low intensity conflicts, security operations, peace enforcement, remote warfare, humanitarian intervention, and battles for 'hearts and minds'.

And yet this narrative of the re-commencement of History on 9/11 is clearly every bit as ideological as the preceding assertion of its cessation. The two are linked, recto and verso. Just because America enjoyed a bubble of prosperity in the 1990s (thanks largely to the illusory dot com boom and the development of the very financial instruments that led to the economic collapse in 2008), History—understood as struggle and conflict in which outcomes are uncertain—clearly did not stop for other parts of the globe. The supposed resurrection of iconoclastic violence was more of a homecoming then. But if History awoke from the dream of its own slumber on 9/11, that awakening has been framed by tropes with their own narrow yet unsleeping histories: the 'return' of conflict and change has specifically involved the resurrection of Cold War discourse in the new millennium. In particular, the slippage between the rabid, McCarthyite anti-Communism of the 20th century and the anti-Islamism of the 21st has—thanks to the common denominator of the pejorative 'political religion' (see chapter 6 of Toscano: 2010)—restored a crude binarism that serves the ideologues of both neoliberalism and fundamentalist Islam all too well. Capital, with all its vicious contradictions, was always destined to tear apart the image of History's calm repose, for it cannot abide the economic stagnation of peace, but it is simultaneously adept at masking and containing its *true* contradictions within fake binaries that cleave along inessential lines and channel revolutionary fervour into cul-de-sacs.

That conflict is of more instrumental value to neoliberal states than peace ever could be should come as no surprise. When Foucault, in his late lectures at the Collège de France, distinguished between classical liberalism and neoliberalism, his analysis was remarkably prescient. In contrast to the emphasis on laissez-faire in classical liberalism, he identified two key traits of neoliberal governance that have clearly been intensified post 9/11: a "culture of danger" (Foucault: 2008, p.67) legitimising the notion that 'society must be defended', and a corollary "permanent vigilance, activity and intervention" (p.132) on the part of militarised yet 'biopolitical' states. As the state does indeed get smaller in its *social* role as a guarantor of welfare for the most vulnerable, it simultaneously gets bigger in its policing role as a guarantor of the unhindered operation of the market. Is not David Cameron's 'Big Society' nothing but a clumsy veiling of this fact as it plays out in the UK?

In the terms Badiou develops in *Logics of Worlds*, we could say that neoliberalism is in the process of creating a globalised world that is simultaneously 'atonic' and 'tensed'. An atonic world is literally 'pointless', i.e., nothing significant happens such that a subject can emerge and be tested against choices that would determine its survival or demise. The atonic world is "so ramified and nuanced—or so quiescent and homogeneous—that no instance of the Two, and consequently no figure of decision, is capable of evaluating" (*LW*, p.420) what little change does take place. This is the world as micro-managed down to its last detail, where capillary power circulates like nanobots beneath our very pores. It is dominated by a managerial approach to life itself, with technologically augmented calculation supposedly eradicating the unpredictable, the complex, the uncertain. And yet, adjacent to and imbricated within this muffled atonic world—in which, to quote the band *Radiohead*, there 'are no alarms and no surprises'—there is also and at the same time the appearance of a 'tensed' world, one composed entirely of points and thus of decisions with maximal stakes at every turn. At the level of the police actions of the neoliberal state, nothing less than the 'West' itself is at stake in every single act of the interpretation of even the flimsiest bit of intelligence, in the daily administration of immigration, in the relentless surveillance of troublesome citizens, and in the military support given to 'pro-democracy' popular movements elsewhere. It is as if we are suspended between an atonic world in which nothing is at stake, and a tensed one in which everything is. History has both ended, and continues apace.

All the more reason, therefore, to attempt to distinguish between what we might call structural conflicts (those that simply oppose existing elements of a world), and anti-structural conflicts (those that are the sites of emergence of a genuinely disruptive novelty discontinuous with the world as it is). This book has been motivated by the belief that Badiou's oeuvre offers the most nuanced and developed resource for undertaking such a distinction. However, we have had to use the concept of conflict itself in order to re-read that oeuvre in such a way as to force its proximity to themes of conflict which a certain reading of the event places at a problematic distance. The concept of conflict has been useful in this sense in at least four ways. Firstly, in its invocation of an open sequence rather than (only) a punctual aporia, 'conflict' potentially envelops both pre- and post-evental temporalities and therefore invites the *articulation* between, rather than total separation of, situation and event, or world and singularity, that I would argue is the real core of Badiou's philosophy. Or perhaps should be. Secondly, in its suggestion of a transitive process whose outcome remains uncertain, 'conflict' underscores the utter contingency of the event's 'happening' from the point of view of the situation *and* the resultant centrality of militant commitment. Thirdly, 'conflict' provides a narrative space for the analysis of the oscillations between active and reactive subjectivities to which concrete truth-procedures necessarily give rise. Fourthly, 'conflict' reopens the question of the relationship between 'encyclopedic' History and the historicity of political sequences, including those that might be said to be, or might be *forced* to be, active in our own time. In this way, the ideology of atonicity might be exposed for what it is (the neutralising parliamentarisation of difference), while the ideology of the 'tensed' world of global terror can also be exposed for what it is (a Manichean veil cast over the true contradictions of late capital).

Re-situating the event in closer proximity to conflict in this way allows us to make some very broad generalizations about the distinction between structural and anti-structural conflicts. Structural conflicts involve protagonists that appear with a high intensity of existence in their worlds during the conflict sequence, and perhaps before. It is precisely on the basis of the strength of their existence that they engage in battle with their adversaries. For this reason, structural conflicts are characterized not by the articulation of anonymous principles, but by the pursuit of concrete interests enmeshed in the relations that make those protagonists exist so visibly. Because they are jostling for position in *this* world, protagonists in structural conflicts inevitably mirror the transcendental index, dealing always in predicates of identity and difference. It is the distribution of the 'more' and 'less' of identities and differences that both protagonists contest, not the logic structuring their hierarchical appearance. For this reason, representation is often an explicit goal of structural conflict, whether the granting of State sovereignty on identitarian grounds, as in ethnic or religious separatism, or the push for a 'greater say' within the existing institutions of political and economic power, as in the rise of extreme right wing parties pursuing (and, lamentably, gaining) electoral success. In one way or another then, structural conflicts revolve around the state. However, the state is no longer conceived as vertical, centralized and autonomous as was the case for modern theories of the state, but as what Foucault describes as "the mobile effect of multiple regimes of governmentalities" (Foucault: 2008, p. 77). Badiou's cultivated slippage between political state and set-theoretical state proves useful at this juncture, insofar as it emphasises a power of ordering, counting, and managing appearance, rather than particular institutional forms of that ordering, counting and appearing. Finally, because the existing state is the arena and often target of structural conflicts, the latter will be clearly and loudly nominated *as* conflicts by the state. Given that what I have previously called the 'Hobbesian tourniquet' places conflict and its management at the center of the legitimacy of Leviathan-like states, one can expect that the *discourse* of conflict is likely to be particularly bombastic in the case of structural conflicts where, paradoxically, nothing is at stake precisely because the state says everything is.

Anti-structural conflicts can be contrasted with structural conflicts on every count. They do not pit pre-existing protagonists against one another in a sort of staged gladiatorial contest because what Badiou terms the 'subject' only ever emerges with the event that conditions it. The state cannot fix the rationality of the link that brings together this—from its point of view—utterly random assemblage of individuals. Whereas protagonists in structural conflicts exist intensely in their worlds, the subject, *qua* subject, inexists for its world by breaching the laws of appearance. Anti-structural conflicts are not therefore a matter of contending identifiable interests vying for the lion's share of the world as it is. It follows that the state cannot respond by attempting to arbitrate between competing interests, because the subject is per definition dis-interested. For this reason, anti-structural conflicts are characterized by a partisan adherence to abstract principles, in the face of which no redistribution of social wealth or power or increased representation is sufficient. The effect of this unstinting deployment of abstraction is 'scissional' in early Badiou's sense, rather than merely divisive, in the manner of a Cold War cleavage of the world into opposing but pre-existing Manichean camps. Moreover, unlike the identitarian predicates fuelling the often bloody clashes inherent to structural conflict, participants in anti-structural conflicts cohere around a generic logic and are thus without qualification or condition as subjects. Finally, because anti-structural conflicts do not involve identifiable protagonists with clear interests, and because they make entirely abstract demands that eschew the vocabulary of representational politics, the state is invariably hard put to actually identify them *as* conflicts. While it may be able to recognize a massive disruption of normality and attempt to ascribe a quotidian causality to it (to counter-name it), ultimately, the state cannot find an adequate name for this disturbance. We can therefore reverse our formula above: with anti-structural conflicts, everything is at stake (for the state) precisely because the state says nothing is—beyond, that is, the restoration of 'law and order'.

Needless to say, this broad distinction in no way offers itself as a stable grid through which to pass various conflicts, be they past or present, in order to produce a robust taxonomy with which to orient our radicalism. While it does imply that, for example, the two state solution to the Israeli-Palestinian conflict, and particularly the ethno-religious basis of the claim for the sovereignty of each respective state, can only ever remain ensconced in the logic of structural conflict, this certainly does not prohibit the existence of anti-structural dimensions internal to an apparently binary conflict, such as progressive anti-Zionist Israeli Jews and Palestinian advocates of a single, secular state. My analysis of the statist nomination of conflicts has suggested that the application of such a binary taxonomy to putatively stable referents already participates in the narrative reduction of the novelty that maybe locked within a past conflict, one that may yet become an event (this was the rationale behind the 'evental historiography' applied to the Morant Bay Revolt of 1865).

It should be pointed out that, following recent shifts within dominant approaches to conflict resolution and post-conflict nation-building, the idea that binarism is ineffective is hardly news. There has been a general shift away from dimplomatic discussion between warring factions with a view to brokering conciliatory peace settlements (on the model, say, of the Good Friday Agreement), and even from the restorative justice of collective healing (on the model of the Truth and Reconciliation Commissions in South Africa and Chile), and towards the imposition of fiscal and governmental practices on the neoliberal blueprint which is now widely presumed to be a panacea for such old-fashioned 'ideological' differences and sectarian tensions. In this sense, the true symbol of Fukuyama-esque triumphalism was not so much the fall of the Berlin Wall, but rather the rise, in former East Germany, of the first McDonald's (just as more recently, the symbol of victory in Iraq is not less the toppling of Saddam's statue in Baghdad, and more the opening of the first Starbuck's). The fact that this process is now almost entirely facilitated by non-state actors such as private security firms, NGOs with dubious corporate connections, multinational construction companies and commercial banks, confirms both Foucault's definition of the neoliberal state as a composite of 'multiple regimes of governmentalities' and the broadly neo-imperial account of the deteritorrialised forms that previous modes of colonial plunder, domination and exploitation take in our globalsed world. Hardt and Negri's *Empire*, in short.

As Eric Finlay has pointed out (2010), this so-called 'liberal peace project' attempts to de-politicize conflict by interposing between the two or more factions the 'neutrality' of the market. Yet in so doing, Finlay claims, it also imposes a conciliatory framework that is in fact quite illiberal by liberalism's own standards. By orienting 'peace' around mechanisms that give adequate representation to both (or all) previously conflictual groups *and* foster market logics, the liberal peace project ends up giving primacy to communal group identities and often ethnicities, rather than to the free and effectively colourless and creedless individuals beloved of classical liberalism, as well of its more recent consumerist inscription. However, as Vivienne Jabri points out in her review of the book (Jabri: 2011, p.62), Finlay deems 'illiberal' precisely what Foucault argues is *constitutive* of *neo*liberalism: the imperative of a security apparatus with which to both protect and extend the primacy, not of communitarian identities, but of the market. If this is a contradiction then, it is an entirely structural one.

What Badiou allows us to perceive, however, is that the alternative to identitarian binarism held within a state framework and an old, vertical model of politics is *not* the smooth horizontal space of multiplicities of 'apolitical' non-state actors spreading and practicing market democracy on the other. This is where Badiou's ambiguity around the relation between politics and the state arguably becomes a strength, since it encompasses two important critiques: the One of the state is shown to be constitutively errant and without measure, and yet an uncritically conceived 'Deleuzian multiplicity' is also shown to be in perfect conformity with the ideology of neoliberal managerialism, and its extension to war and conflict management. The concept of the event allows a critique of both binarism and the dispersal of identities into mobile intensities of ephemeral affect. If binarism was helpful for the divide and rule governance of imperialism and has found a new but related value in Empire, we should bot be blind to the fact that dispersed, multiple and flexible subjectivities are also all-too amenable to neo-imperial late capital (see Boltanski and Chiapello: 2007). In a sense, Badiou follows Marx in giving us an alternative to the closed dialectic identified in the *Manifesto* between the destruction of the ossified old and the dynamism of capitalist innovation. By adding the 'twist' of the event, Badiou allows us to conceptualise radical novelty as rigorously distinct from its distorted mirror-image in the market rhetoric of entrepreneurial innovation, creativity, adaptability, spontaneity and so forth. Only with this distinction will it be possible to invent a new time at the end of times.

Brought into more consistent contact with the issue of conflict then, I would argue that Badiou's notion of the event represents a major contribution to, and reorientation of, traditional conflict theory, and specifically as a *philosophy*. For traditional conflict theory's roots in sociology, anthropology, comparative religion and international relations, from Max Weber to Max Gluckman, from Georg Simmel to Pierre Bourdieu, necessarily tend it towards the descriptive and thus to what we have identified as structural conflicts. Indeed, where it is not explicitly Marxist, the overwhelming emphasis in conflict theory and peace studies has been on the need for stability and social cohesion, and thus on conflict management and resolution rather than on conflict as a site of social and political transformation. But even where Marx is a fundamental reference point, and where therefore this descriptive sociological bias towards the pacific is off-set by a more dynamic vision of the dialectic, this can all-too easily tip over into an exorbitant faith in a teleological understanding of the dialectic that contains the seeds of a problematic quietism, as early Badiou in particular makes clear.

Badiou's *philosophy*, rather than sociology, of conflict, generates concepts that do not simply describe but actively crystallize the emancipatory dimensions of particular conflicts, and thereby participate directly in them. Given that anti-structural conflicts do not generally register with the state *as* conflicts, the philosophical elaboration of concepts that provide an articulation of the generic stakes of a particular disturbance or protest can be seen as an internal and necessary part of the truth procedure. Ultimately, this is Badiou's great value for a philosophy of conflict. He not only provides a rigorously formal distinction between those conflicts that sustain the status quo and those that inaugurate genuine transformation, but he also demonstrates how the thinking of the latter (thinking as active and practical rather than passively reflective and immaterial) is a necessary vector of radical novelty. Far from indulging speculative idealism, Badiou's early theory of dialectical knowledge illustrates how thought, refined against but also within practice, becomes an indispensable weapon in struggle. And thought is one of the most difficult tasks in a world that presents itself as both atonic (there is nothing new under the sun) and tensed (there is no time to think, only to act decisively). Badiou therefore offers us the framework needed to sustain what I would call a 'polemology of novelty', which is to say, a polemical critique of state-driven wars, intervention into the ideology of allegedly humanitarian conflicts and 'surgical strikes', and a an active participation in transformative novelty as it emerges from the sites of disruption and resistance that escape the current world's logics.

Bibliography

Agamben, Giorgio, *The State of Exception*, trans. Kevin Attell, London: The University of Chicago Press, 2005.

Althusser, Louis, *For Marx*, trans. Ben Brewster, London: Penguin Books, 1969.

Althusser, Louis, *Lenin and Philosophy, and Other Essays*, trans. Ben Brewster, New York: Monthly Review Press, 1971.

Althusser, Louis, *Philosophy of the Encounter: Later Writings, 1978-1987*, trans. G. M. Goshgarian, London: Verso, 2006.

Alymar, Keven, 'Towering Babble and Glimpses of Zion: Recent Depictions of Rastafari in Cinema', 284-310 in Murrell, Nathaniel et al, *Chanting Down Babylon: The Rastafari Reader*, Philadelphia: Temple University Press, 1998.

Amnesty International, *Killings and Violence by Police: How Many More Victims?*, AI Index, 2001.

Arendt, Hannah, *On Violence*, London: Harcourt Breace & Company, 1970.

Arendt, Hannah, *On Revolution*, London: Penguin Books, 1990.

Aronson, Ronald, *Camus & Sartre: The Story of a Friendship and the Quarrel that Ended It*, London: The University of Chicago Press, 2004.

Ashton, Paul, Bartlett, A. J. , Clemens, Justin (eds.), *The Praxis of Alain Badiou*, Melbourne: re.Press, 2006.

Badou, Alain, *Conditions*, Paris: Seuil, 1992.

Badiou, Alain, 'La Scène du Deux', pp. 177-190 in *De l'Amour*, Paris: Flammarion, 2000.

Badiou, Alain, *The Concept of Model: An Introduction to the Materialist Epistemology of Mathematics*, trans. Zachary Luke Fraser and Tzuchien Tho, Melbourne: re.Press, 2007.

Badiou, Alain, *Pocket Pantheon: Figures of Postwar Philosophy*, trans. David Macey, London: Verso, 2009.

Badiou, Alain, *Five Lessons on Wagner*, London: Verso, 2010.

Badiou, Alain and Žižek, Slavoj, *Philosophy in the Present*, trans. Peter Thomas and Alberto Toscano, Cambridge: Polity, 2009.

Badiou, Alain, Žižek, Slavoj (eds.), *L'idée du Communisme II*, Clamecy: Lignes, 2011.

Bakan, Abigail, *Ideology and Class Conflict in Jamaica: The Politics of Rebellion*, Montreal: McGill-Queen's University Press, 1990.

Bakunin, Michael, *On Anarchism*, trans. Sam Dolgoff, London: Black Rose Books, 2002.

Balibar, Étienne, 'Lénine et Gandhi: une rencontre manquée?', *Communication au Colloque Marx International IV*, 2004.

Barker, Jason, *Alain Badiou: A Critical Introduction*, London: Pluto Press, 2002.

Barrett, Leonard, *The Rastafarians: A Study in Messianic Cultism in Jamaica.* Puerto Rico: Institute of Caribbean Studies, University of Puerto Rico, 1969.

Barrett, Leonard, *The Rastafarians: The Dreadlocks of Jamaica*, Kingston: Heinemann & Sangster's Bookstores Ltd, 1977.

Barthes, Roland, *Mythologies*, trans. Annette Lavers, London: Vintage, 1993.

Baudrillard, Jean, 'Les suicidés du spectacle', *Libération*, July 16th, 2003.

Beckett, Samuel, *Samuel Beckett: The Grove Centenary Edition, Volume 2: Novels*, New York: Grove Press, 2006.

Beckett, Samuel, *Company, Ill Seen Ill Said, Worstword Ho, Stirring Still*, London: Faber and Faber Ltd, 2009.

Beckford, George, Witter, Michael, *Small Garden ... Bitter Weed: Struggle and Change in Jamaica*, London: Zed Press, 1982.

Barrett, Leondard, *The Rastafarians: Sounds of Cultural Dissonance*, Boston: Beacon Press, 1988.

Bennett, Louise, *Jamaica Labrish*, London: Sangster's Book Stores Ltd Jamaica, 1972.

Benjamin, Walter, 'The Work of Art in the Age of Mechanical Reproduction', pp. 211-244 in *Illuminations*, trans Harry Zohn, London: Fontana Press, 1992.

Bensaïd, Daniel, 'Alain Badiou and the Miracle of the Event', pp. 94-105 in Hallward, Peter (ed.), *Think Again: Alain Badiou and the Future of Philosophy*, London: Continuum, 2004.

Berman, Paul, *Terror and Liberalism*, London: Norton, 2003.

Bhabha, Homi, *Locations of Culture*, London: Routledge, 1994.

Bisnauth, Dale, *A History of Religions in the Caribbean*, Kingston: Kingston Publishing, 1989.

Bloch, Ernst, 'Non-synchronism and the Obligation to Its Dialectics', trans. M. Ritter, *New German Critique*, No. 11, 1977, pp.22-38.

Boal, Ian, Clark, T. J., Matthews, Joseph and Watts, Michael, *Afflicted Powers: Capital and Spectacle in a New Age of War*, London: Verso, 2006.

Boltanski, Luc, Chiappello, *The New Spirit of Capitalism*, trans. Gregory Elliot, London: Verso, 2007.

Bosteels, Bruno, 'Post-Maoism: Badiou and Politics', *Positions: East Asia Cultures Critique*, Vol. 13, No. 3, 2005, pp. 575-634.

Bourdieu, Pierre, *Acts of Resistance: Against the New Myths of Our Times*, trans. Richard Nice, Oxford: Polity Press, 1998.

Brathwaite, Edward Kamau, *The Development of Creole Society in Jamaica, 1770-1820*, Oxford: Clarendon Press, 1971.

Burnard, Trevor, *Mastery, Tyranny, & Desire: Thomas Thistlewood and His Slaves in the Anglo-Jamaican World*, London: The University of North Carolina Press, 2004.

Briener, Laurence, 'The English Bible in Jamaican Rastafari', *Journal of Religious Thought*, Vol. 42, No. 2, 1985, pp.30-43.

Campbell, Mavis Christine, *The Dynamics of Change in a Slave Society: A Socio-political History of the Free Coloureds of Jamaica, 1800-1865*, New Jersey: Fairleigh Dickinson University Press, 1976.

Campbell, Horace, *Rasta and Resistance: From Marcus Garvey to Walter Rodney*. New Jersey: African World Press, 2001.

Camus, Albert, *The Rebel*, trans. Anthony Bower, London: Penguin Books, 1971.

Carey, Brycchan and Kitson, Peter (eds.), *Slavery and the Cultures of Abolition: Essays Marking the Bicentennial of the British Abolition Act of 1807*, Cambridge: D. S. Brewer, 2007.

Cashmore, Ernest, *Rastaman: The Rastafarian Movement in England*, London: Unwin Paperbacks, 1983.

Certeau, Michel de, 'On the Oppositional Practices of Everyday Life', *Social Text*, Vol. 3, No. 3, 1980, pp.3-43.

Certeau, Michel de, *The Practice of Everyday Life*, trans. Steven Rendell, London: University of California Press, 1988.

Chang, Jung, Hallidary, Jon, *Mao: The Unknown Story*, London: Vintage, 2006.

Chartier, Roger, *The Cultural Origins of the French Revolution*, trans. Lydia G. Cochrane, London: Duke University Press, 1991.

Chevannes, Barry, *Rastafari: Roots and Ideology*, Kingston: The Press, 1995.

Clarke, Peter B., *Black Paradise: The Rastafarian Movement*, California: The Borgo Press, 1994.

Cobban, Alfred, 'Noncapitalist Wealth and the Origins of the French Revolution', *American Historical Review*, No. 72, 1967, pp. 469-496.

Cooper, Carolyn, *Noises in the Blood: Orality, Gender and the 'Vulgar' Body of Jamaican Popular Culture*, London: Macmillan Press Ltd, 1993.

Cooper, Carolyn, *Sound Clash: Jamaican Dancehall Culture at Large*, London: Palgrave Macmillan, 2004.

Craton, Michael, *Sinews of Empire: a Short History of British Slavery*, London: Temple Smith, 1974.

Craton, Michael, *Searching for the Invisible Man: Slaves and Plantation Life in Jamaica*, London: Harvard University Press, 1978.

Craton, Michael, *Testing the Chains: Resistance to Slavery in the British West Indies*, London: Cornell University Press, 1982.

Craton, Michael, Walvin, James and Wright, David (eds.), *Slavery, Abolition, and Emancipation: Black Slaves and the British Empire—A Thematic Documentary*, London: Longman, 1976.

Craton, Michael, 'What and Who to Whom and What: The Significance of Slave Resistance', pp.259-282 in Engerman, Stanley and Solow, Barbara (eds.), *British Capitalism and Caribbean Slavery: the Legacy of Eric Williams*, Cambridge: Cambridge University Press, 2004.

Critchley, Simon, *Infinitely Demanding: Ethics of Commitment, Politics of Resistance*, London: Verso, 2008.

Curtin, Phillip, *Two Jamaicas: The Role of Ideas in a Tropical Colony, 1830-1865*, Cambridge, Mass.: Harvard University Press, 1955.

Dark Star, *Beneath the Paving Stones: Situationists and the Beach, May 1968*, Edinburgh: AK Press, 2001.

Dawes, Kwame, *Wheel and Come Again: An Anthology of Reggae Poetry*, Leeds: Peepal Tree Ltd, 1998.

Deleuze, Gilles, Guattari, Félix, *Anti- Oedipus: Capitalism & Schizophrenia*, London: The Athalone Press, 2000.

Deleuze, Gilles, *Nietzsche and Philosophy*, London: Continuum, 2002.

Depoortere, Frederiek, *Badiou and Theology*, London: t & t Clark, 2009.

Derrida, Jacques, *Spectres of Marx: The State of the Debt, the Work of Mourning, & the New International*, trans. Peggy Kamuf, London: Routledge, 1994.

Derrida, Jacques, *Of Grammatology*, trans. Gayatri Chakravorty Spivak, London: John Hopkins University Press, 1997.

Douzinas, Costas, Žižek, Slavoj (eds.), *The Idea of Communism*, London: Verso, 2010.

Doyle, William, *Origins of the French Revolution*, Oxford: Oxford University Press, 1999.

Drescher, Seymore, *Econocide: British Slavery in the Era of Abolition*, London: University of Pittsburgh Press, 1977.

Drescher, Seymour, *Capitalism and Antislavery: British Mobilization in a Comparative Perspective*, Oxford: Oxford University Press, 1987.

Drescher, Seymore, 'Paradigms Tossed: Captialism and the Political Sources of Abolition', pp.191-208 in Engerman, Stanley and Solow, Barbara (eds.), *British Capitalism and Caribbean Slavery: the Legacy of Eric Williams*, Cambridge: Cambridge University Press, 2004.

Eaton, George E., *Alexander Bustamante and Modern Jamaica*, Kingston: LMH Publishing, 2000.

Edmonds, Ennis Barrington, *Rastafari: From Outcasts to Culture Bearers*. Oxford: Oxford University Press, 2003.

Engels, Friedrich, *Herr Eugen Dühring's Revolution in Science: Anti-Dühring*, trans. Emile Burns, London: Lawrence, 1935.

Engerman, Stanley and Solow, Barbara (eds.), *British Capitalism and Caribbean Slavery: the Legacy of Eric Williams*, Cambridge: Cambridge University Press, 2004.

Fanon, Frantz, *The Wretched of the Earth*, trans. Constance Farrington, London: Penguin, 2001.

Fanon, Frantz, *Black Skin, White Masks*, trans. Charles Lam Markmann, London: Pluto Press, 1986.

Feenberg, Andrew and Freedman, Jim, *When Poetry Ruled the Streets: The French Events of May 1968*, SUNY Press: New York, 2001.

Feldstein, Richard, Fink, Bruce, and Jaanus, Mairie (eds.), *Reading Seminars I and II: Lacan's Return to Freud*, SUNY: New York, 1996.

Feltham, Oliver, *Alain Badiou: Live Theory*, London: Continuum, 2008.

Finlay, Eric, *Governing Ethnic Conflict: Consociation, Identity, and the Price of Peace*, London: Routledge, 2010.

Fisher, Mark, *Capitalist Realism: Is There No Alternative?*, Winchester: Zero Books, 2009.

Ford, Simon, *The Situationist International: A User's Guide*, London: Black Dog Publishing, 2005.

Foucault, Michel, *The Order of Things: An Archaeology of the Human Sciences*, London: Routledge, 2000.

Foucault, Michel, *The Archaeology of Knowledge*, London: Routledge, 2003.

Foucault, Michel, *Society Must Be Defended: Lectures at the Collège de France, 1975-1976*, trans. David Macey, London: Penguin Books, 2003.

Foucault, Michel, *The Birth of Biopolitics: Lectures at the Collège de France, 1978-1979*, trans. Graham Burchell, Basingstoke: Palgrave Macmillan, 2010.

Fukuyama, Francis, *The End of History and the Last Man*, London: Penguin, 1992.

Gandhi, Mahatma, *The Essential Writings*, Oxford: Oxford University Press, 2008.

Gillespie, Sam, *The Mathematics of Novelty: Badiou's Minimalist Metaphysics*, Melbourne: re.Press, 2008.

Gilroy, Paul, *The Black Atlantic: Modernity and Double Consciousness*, London: Verso, 1993.

Gilroy, Paul, *There Ain't No Black in the Union Jack: The Cultural Politics of Race and Nation*, London: Routledge, 2002.

Gray, Obika, *Radicalism and Social Change in Jamaica, 1960-1972*, Knoxville: The University of Tennessee Press, 1991.

Green, William A., *British Slave Emancipation: The Sugar Colonies and the Great Experiment, 1830-1865*, Oxford: Clarendon Press, 1976.

Guha, Ranajit, *Elementary Aspects of Peasant Insurgency in Colonial India*, Durham: Duke University Press, 1999.

Gunst, Laurie, *Born Fi' Dead: A Journey Through the Yardie Underworld*, Edinburgh: Canongate Books Ltd, 2003.

Hall, Douglas, *Feree Jamaica, 1838-1865: An Economic History*, New Haven: Yale University Press, 1959.

Hallward, Peter, *Absolutely Postcolonial: Writing Between the Singular and the Specific*, Manchester: Manchester University Press, 2001.

Hallward, Peter, *Badiou: A Subject to Truth*, London: University of Minnesota Press, 2003.

Hallward, Peter (ed.), *Think Again: Alain Badiou and the Future of Philosophy*, London: Continuum, 2004.

Hallward, Peter, *Damning the Flood: Haiti, Aristide, and the Politics of Containment*, London: Verso, 2007.

Hallward, Peter, 'The Will of the People: Notes Towards a Dialectical Voluntarism', *Radical Philosophy*, No. 155, May/June 2009, pp.17-29.

Hambourg, Serge, *Protest in Paris 1968: Photographs by Serge Hambourg*, London: University Press of New England, 2006.

Harari, Roberto, *How James Joyce Made His Name: A Reading of the Final Lacan*, trans. Luke Thurston, New York: Other Press, 2002.

Harari, Roberto, *Lacan's Four Fundamental Concepts of Psychoanalysis: An Introduction*, New York: Other Press, 2004.

Hardt, Michael, Negri, Antonio, *Empire*, London: Harvard University Press, 2000.

Hebdige, Dick, *Subculture: The Meaning of Style*. London: Routledge, 1991.

Hebdige, Dick, *Cut n' Mix: Culture, Identity and Caribbean Music*. London: Routledge, 2000.

Hegel, G. W. F., *Lectures on the History of Philosophy*, trans. R.F. Brown, J.M. Stewart, and H.S. Harris, Oxford: Clarendon Press, 2006.

Heidegger, Martin, *On the Way to Language*, trans. Peter D. Hertz, New York: HarperSanFrancisco, 1982.

Heidegger, Martin, *Being and Time*, trans. John Macquarrie and Edward Robinson, Oxford: Blackwell Publishers Ltd, 1998.

Heuman, Gad, *'The Killing Time': The Morant Bay Rebellion in Jamaica*, Knoxville: The University of Tennessee Press, 2000.

Hobsbawm, Eric, *Primitive Rebels: Studies in Archaic Forms of Social Movement in the 19th and 20th Centuries*, New York: Norton, 1965.

Hope, Donna, *Inna di Dancehall: Popular Culture and the Politics of Identity in Jamaica*, Kingston: University of the West Indies Press, 2006.

Horne, Alistair, *The Terrible Year: The Paris Commune, 1871*, London: Phoenix, 2004.

Hussain, Nasser, *The Jurisprudence of Emergency: Colonialism and the Rule of Law*, Ann Arbor: University of Michigan Press, 2003.

Jabri, Vivienne, 'Global Foucault', *Radical Philosophy*, No. 168, July/August 2011, pp. 60-62.

James, C. L. R., *The Black Jacobins: Toussaint L'Ouverture and the San Domingo Revolution*, London: Penguin Books, 2001.

Jayatilleka, Dayan, *Fidel's Ethics of Violence: The Moral Dimension of the Political Thought of Fidel Castro*, London: Pluto Press, 2007.

Johnson, Linton Kwesi, *Mi Revalushuanry Fren: Selected Poems*, London: Penguin, 2002.

Johnston, Adrian, *Badiou, Žižek, and Political Transformations: The Cadence of Change*, Illinois: Northwestern University Press, 2009.

Kacem, Mehdi Belhaj, *L'affect*, Paris: Éditions Tristram, 2004

Kacem, Mehdi Belhaj, *Événement et repetition*, Paris: Éditions Tristram, 2004.

Kant, Immanuel, *The Critique of Judgement*, trans. Werner S. Pluhar, Cambridge: Hackett Publishing Company, 1987.

Kapuściński, Ryszard, *The Emperor: Downfall of an Autocrat*, London: Penguin Books, 2006.

King, Stephen A., *Reggae, Rastafari and the Rhetoric of Social Control*, Mississippi: University of Mississippi Press, 2002.

Klein, Naomi, *The Shock Doctrine: The Rise of Disaster Capitalism*, London: Penguin Books, 2008.

Knabb, Ken (ed.), *Situationist International Anthology*, Berkeley: Bureau of Public Secrets, 1995.

Knox, B. A., 'The British Government and the Governor Eyre Controversy', pp. 877-900 in *The Historical Journal*, No. 19, Vol. 4, 1976.

Kostal, Rande W., A Jurisprudence of Power: Victorian Empire and the Rule of Law, Oxford: Oxford University Press, 2005

Lacan, Jacques, *Écrits*, trans. Bruce Fink, London: W. W. Norton & Company, 2006.

Laclau, Ernesto, Mouffe, Chantal, *Hegemony and Socialist Strategy: Towards a Radical Democratic Politics*, London: Verso, 2001.

Laclau, Ernesto, *On Populist Reason*, London: Verso, 2005.

Lanternari, Vittorio, *The Religions of the Oppressed: A Study of Modern Messianic Cults*, trans. L. Sergio, New York: Mentor, 1965.

Lazarus, Sylvain, *Anthropologie du nom*, Paris: Éditions du Seuil, 1996.

Lecky, W. E. G., *A History of European Morals: From Augustus to Charlemagne*, 3rd ed., vol. 1, New York: D. Appleton, 1897.

Lee, Hélène, *The First Rasta: Leonard Howell and the Rise of Rastafarianism*, Chicago: Lawrence Hill, 2003.

Lefebvre, Georges, *The French Revolution*, trans. Elizabeth Moss Evanson, London: Routledge, 2002.

Lefebvre, Henri, *The Explosion: Marxism and the French Upheaval*, New York: Monthly Review Press, 1969.

Lenin, Vladimir, *The State and Revolution*, trans. Robert Service, London: Penguin, 1992.

Lipovetsky, Gilles, *L'ère du vide: essays sur l'indiviualisme contemporaine*, Paris: Gallimard, 1983.

Lissagaray, *History of the Paris Commune*, trans. Eleanor Marx, New Park Publications Ltd: London, 1976.

Liu, Alan, *The Laws of Cool: Knowledge Work and the Culture of Information*, Chicago: University of Chicago Press, 2004.

Losurdo, Domenico, *Liberalism: A Counter-History*, London: Verso, 2011.

Lukács, Georg, *History and Class Consciousness*, London; Merlin Press, 1990.

Manley, Michael, *Jamaica: Struggle in the Periphery*, London: Third World Media, 1982.

Mao, Tse-Tung, *On Practice and Contradiction*, London: Verso, 2007.

Marx, Karl, *The Paris Commune 1871*, trans. Christopher Hitchens, Sidgwick & Jackson: London, 1971.

Marx, *Capital: A Critique of Political Economy, Volume 1*, trans. Ben Fowkes, London: Penguin Books, 1990.

Marx, *Contributions to the Critique of Hegel's Philosophy of Right*, trans. by Annette Jolin and Joseph O'Malley, Cambridge: Cambridge University Press, 1970.

Mason, Peter, *Jamaica: A Guide to the People, Politics and Culture*, New York: Interlink Books, 2000.

May, Todd, *The Political Thought of Jacques Rancière: Creating Equality*, Edinburgh: Edinburgh University Press, 2008.

McFarlane, Adrian Anthony, 'The Epistemological Significance of 'I-an-I' as a Response to Quashie and Anancyism in Jamaican Culture', 107-124 in Murrell, Nathaniel et al, *Chanting Down Babylon: The Rastafari Reader*, Philadelphia: Temple University Press, 1998.

Meillassoux, Quentin, *After Finitude: An Essay on the Necessity of Contingency*, trans. Ray Brassier, London: Continuum, 2008.

Monroe, Trevor, Robothom, Don, *Struggles of the Jamaican People*, Kingston: Worker's Liberation League, 1977.

Morineau, Michel, *Les Faux-Semblants d'un demurrage économique: Agriculture et démographie en France au XVIIIe siècle*, Cahiers des Annales 30: Paris, 1970.

Mouffe, Chantale (ed.), *The Challenge of Carl Schmitt*, London: Verso, 1999.

Negri, Antonio, *Time for Revolution*, trans. Matteo Mandarini, London: Continuum, 2003.

Nkrumah, Kwame, *Neo-colonialism: The Last Stage of Imperialism*, London: Nelson, 1965.

Norris, Christopher, *Badiou's Being and Event: A Reader's Guide*, London: Continuum, 2009.

O'Brien Chang, Kevin, Chen, Wayne, *Reggae Roots: The Story of Jamaican Music*, Kingston: Ian Randle Publishers, 1998.

Paton, Diana, *No Bond But The Law: Punishment, Race and Gender in Jamaican State Formation, 1780-1870*, London: Duke University Press, 2004.

Patterson, Orlando, *The Children of Sisyphus*, Essex, Longman: 1995.

Pluth, Ed, *Badiou: A Philosophy of the New*, Cambridge: Polity, 2010.

Popper, Karl, *The Open Society and its Enemies*, London : Routledge, 2002.

Power, Nina, 'The Terror of Collectivity: Sartre's Theory of Political Groups', *Prelom*, No. 8, 2006, pp.93-103.

Power, Nina, 'Towards an Anthropology of Infinitude: Badiou and the Political Subject', pp.309-338 in Ashton, Paul, Bartlett, A. J. , Clemens, Justin (eds.), *The Praxis of Alain Badiou*, Melbourne: re.Press, 2006.

Quattrocchi, Angelo and Nairn, Tom, *The Beginning of the End: France, May 1968*, London: Verso, 1998.

Ragatz, Lowell, *The Fall of the Planter Class in the British Caribbean, 1763-1833*, London: Century, 1928.

Ramond, Charles, Ed., *Alain Badiou: Penser le multiple*, Paris: L'Harmattan, 2002.

Rancière, Jacques, *The Names of History: One the Poetics of Knowledge*, London: University of Minnesota Press, 1994.

Rancière, Jacques, *Disagreement: Politics and Philosophy*, London: University of Minnesota Press, 1998.

Rancière, Jacques, *The Philosopher and His Poor*, trans. John Drury, Corinne Oster and Andrew Parker, London: Duke University Press, 2004.

Rancière, Jacques, *The Politics of Aesthetics: The Distribution of the Sensible*, trans. Gabriel Rockhill, London: Continuum, 2006.

Rancière, Jacques, *Dissensus: On Politics and Aesthetics*, trans. Steve Corcoran, London: Continuum, 2010.

Riera, Gabriel, Ed., *Alain Badiou: Philosophy and its Conditions*, New York: SUNY Press, 2005.

Robothom, Don, *'The Notorious Riot': The Socio-Economic and Political Bases of Paul Bogle's Revolt*, Kingston: Institute of Social and Economic Research, 1981.

Rodney, Walter, *How Europe underdeveloped Africa*, Washington, D.C.: Howard University Press, 1982.

Ross, Kristin, *May '68 and its Afterlives*, London: University of Chicago Press, 2002.

Santoni, Ronald, *Sartre on Violence: Curiously Ambivalent*, Pennsylvania: Pennsylvania State University Press, 2003.

Sartre, Jean-Paul, *Anti-Semite and Jew: An Exploration of the Etiology of Hate*, trans George J. Becker, New York: Schocken Books, 1995.

Sartre, Jean-Paul, *Critique of Dialectical Reason, Volume Two*, trans Quintin Hoare, London: Verso, 2004.

Sartre, Jean-Paul, *Being and Nothingness: An Essay on Phenomenological Ontology*, trans.Hazel E. Barnes, London: Routledge, 2006.

Semmel, Bernard, *The Governor Eyre Controversy*, London: McKibbon & Kee, 1962.

Schmitt, Carl, *The Concept of the Political*, trans. George Schwab, London: The University of Chicago Press, 1996.

Schmitt, Carl, *Political Theology: Four Chapters on the Concept of Sovereignty*, trans George Schwab, London: The University of Chicago Press, 2005.

Sherlock, Philip, Bennett, Hazel, *The Story of the Jamaican People*, Kingston: Ian Randle Publishers, 1998.

Sherwood, Marika, *After Abolition: Britain and the Slave Trade since 1807*, London: I.B. Tauris, 2007.

Short, Philip, *Mao: A Life*, London: John Murray, 2004.

Simpson, George Eaton, *Black Religions in the New World*. New York: Columbia University Press, 1978.

Spivak, Gayatri Chakravorty, 'Can the Subaltern Speak', pp.271-313 in Nelson, C. and Grossberg, L. (eds.), *Marxism and the Interpretation of Culture*, Illinois: University of Illinois Press, 1988.

Starr, Peter, *Logics of Failed Revolt: French Theory After May '68*, Stanford, California: Stanford University Press, 1995.

Stavrakakis, Yanis, *Lacan and the Political*, London: Routledge, 1999.

Stolzoff, Norman C., *Wake the Town and Tell the People: Dancehall Culture in Jamaica*, London: Duke University Press, 2000.

Sutherland, D. G. M., *France 1789-1815: Revolution and Counter-Revolution*, London: Fontana Press, 1985.

Sutherland, D. M. G., *The French Revolution and Empire: The Quest for a Civic Order*, Oxford: Blackwell Publishing, 2003.

Taylor, George V., 'Types of Capitalism in Eighteenth Century France', *English Heritage Review*, pp.478-497, 1964.

Thomson, Ian, *The Dead Yard: Tales of Modern Jamaica*, London: Faber and Faber, 2009.

Tombs, Robert, *The Paris Commune 1871*, London: Longman, 1999.

Tomlinson, John, *Cultural Imperialism: A Critical Introduction* , London: Continuum, 1991.

Toscano, Alberto, *Fanaticism: On the Uses of an Idea*, London: Verso, 2010.

Turner, Mary, *Slaves and Missionaries: The Disintegration of Jamaican Slave Society, 1787-1834*, Kingston: The Press University of the West Indies, 1998.

Viénet, René, *Enragés and Situationists in the Occupation Movement, France, May '68*, London: Rebel Press, 1992.

Williams, Eric, *Capitalism and Slavery*, Richmond: The University of North Carolina Press, 1944.

Wright, Colin, *Philosophy, Rhetoric, Ideology: Towards a Sophistic Democracy*, Auckland: Magnolia Press, 2006.

Young, Robert, *Postcolonialism: An Historical Introduction*, Oxford: Blackwell Publishers, 2001.

Žižek, Slavoj, *The Ticklish Subject: The Absent Centre of Political Ontology*, London: Verso, 2000.

Žižek, Slavoj, *In Defense of Lost Causes*, London: Verso, 2008a.

Žižek, Slavoj, *Violence: Six Sideways Reflections*, London: Profile Books, 2008b.

www.ingramcontent.com/pod-product-compliance
Lightning Source LLC
Chambersburg PA
CBHW020821270326
41928CB00006B/402